CAMBRIDGE LIBRARY COLLEC

Books of enduring scholarly value

Art and Architecture

From the middle of the eighteenth century, with the growth of travel at home and abroad and the increase in leisure for the wealthier classes, the arts became the subject of more widespread appreciation and discussion. The rapid expansion of book and periodical publishing in this area both reflected and encouraged interest in art and art history among the wider reading public. This series throws light on the development of visual culture and aesthetics. It covers topics from the Grand Tour to the great exhibitions of the nineteenth century, and includes art criticism and biography.

Cambria Depicta

First published in 1816, this lively and informative narrative of a walking tour of North Wales was written by Edward Pugh (1763–1813) and richly illustrated with engravings of his own watercolour drawings of people and landscapes. (In this reissue, the drawings are reproduced in black and white, but the colour originals can be viewed at http://www.cambridge.org/9781108061483.) It was unique in the Romantic period as the work of a native Welsh speaker with an intimate knowledge of the people and culture of the region. Pugh travelled some 800 miles, criss-crossing Wales in every direction, collecting information about the industrial and agricultural condition of the country. He conversed with almost everyone he met, on the road and in the inns where he stayed. The book began as a guide to artists unwilling to risk departing from the main tourist routes where English was spoken. By the time it was published, however, its main aim was to vindicate the character of the Welsh people from the ill-informed accounts of English tourists.

Cambria Depicta

A Tour through North Wales,
Illustrated with Picturesque Views

Edward Pugh

Cambridge
University Press

CAMBRIDGE UNIVERSITY PRESS

Cambridge, New York, Melbourne, Madrid, Cape Town,
Singapore, São Paolo, Delhi, Mexico City

Published in the United States of America by Cambridge University Press, New York

www.cambridge.org
Information on this title: www.cambridge.org/9781108061483

This edition first published 1816
This digitally printed version 2013

ISBN 978-1-108-06148-3 Paperback

FRONTISPIECE

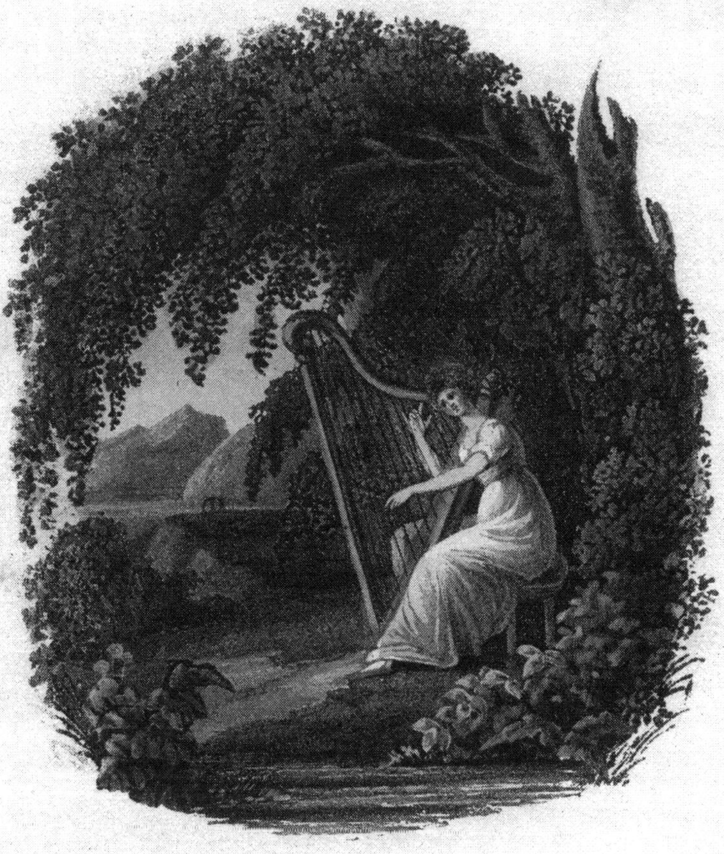

TO

CAMBRIA DEPICTA.

CAMBRIA DEPICTA:

A

Tour through North Wales,

ILLUSTRATED WITH

PICTURESQUE VIEWS.

By a Native Artist.

—And I perceive that it would have been an advantage, had I been able to have given a more copious account of them (the Welsh); but the requisite knowledge of a sufficient number of circumstances from which to deduce a NATIONAL CHARACTER, is not to be acquired without long residence, and much intercourse with the inhabitants.

PREFACE TO DR. AIKIN'S TOUR THROUGH NORTH WALES.

London:

PRINTED BY W. CLOWES, NORTHUMBERLAND-COURT;

FOR E. WILLIAMS, BOOKSELLER TO THE DUKE AND DUCHESS OF YORK,

No. 11, STRAND.

1816.

PREFACE.

A FEW years before the demise of that venerable patron of the arts, ALDERMAN BOYDELL, chance gave me the opportunity of an hour's conversation with him, at the Shakespeare Gallery. To that conversation the following work owes its origin. Mr. Boydell lamented that the landscape painters, whom he had employed in Wales, confined the efforts of their pencils to the neighbourhood of Snowdon: thus multiplying copies upon copies of the same sketches, and frustrating the worthy Alderman's intention of publishing a just series of Welsh views. This practice they defended on the ground of the difficulty in which a stranger, unacquainted with the language or the country, involved himself, the moment that he quitted the high roads, and plunged into the intricacies of the mountains. To obviate this inconvenience, Mr. Boydell suggested the expediency of publishing a small volume of direction by a native, whose local knowledge should qualify him for the task. At that time, circumstances induced me to decline an undertaking which, from its being calculated for the use of but a small number, was not likely to be sufficiently productive, in point of sale, even to pay the expense of the publication. In the spring of 1804, however, the idea of a combination of objects forced itself strongly upon my mind, and I soon resolved upon a plan, which promised to be serviceable, not only to the artist, but also to the general observer.

The following volume, I have the presumption to hope, will lead the painter to numberless objects, well worthy of his exertions, in representing them on his canvass; whether his genius incline him to the mountain's craggy side, the cwm's solemn profundity, the frightful brink of the cataract, and the rocky margin of the sea: or to the milder features of Nature, observable in the shadowy recesses of the grove, the cultivation of the expanded valley, and the tufted banks of the serpentine *afon**, he will here find frequent and tempting opportunities of indulging and exercising it.

To the antiquary, also, will be pointed out frequent occasions of contemplating the magnificent remains of ancient times. The relics of Druidical superstition the hasty but durable labours of the Romans, contrasted with the comparatively insignificant productions of later periods: nor are the massive military fortifications of the ancient Britons, or those structures of later date, the abbeys or monasteries of Catholic devotees, left unnoticed.

The mineralogist will, likewise, receive in the course of the work some assistance in his researches.

Nor, as I hope, will the general observer, whose object is Nature in all her varieties, be wholly disappointed by the perusal.

The many volumes published under the appellation of "Tours through North Wales" have invariably been found defective in their description of the people, their manners, and customs: nor is this deficiency surprising, when we recollect that these descriptions

* The Welsh name for river.

have generally been undertaken by complete strangers to those people, their manners, and customs; and who, therefore, could not possibly avoid numerous inaccuracies. The confined route which they prescribed to themselves, seldom quitting the repeatedly beaten tract, is another pregnant cause of their inadequacy.

I have included in this volume a topographical history of the North of the Principality, deriving my information from the most authentic sources, and relying frequently on that faithful writer the late T. Pennant, Esq. I have also been variously and materially assisted by many gentlemen of the country, whose names will be found gratefully recorded. Nor have I fastidiously refused occasionally to refer to the narratives of such of my countrymen, as appeared to me to be actuated by the spirit of intelligence and impartiality. These sheets also contain biographical notices of many celebrated persons mentioned in the annals of Ancient Britain.

In drawing the portraits of the different classes of the ancient Britons, unwilling to rely on my own knowledge of their character, and to avoid the imputation of being biassed in their favour, I have availed myself of the opinions of the best informed among them; and I may therefore venture the more confidently to assert that my delineation is correct.

In my choice of views, I have abandoned the common practice of giving portraits of towns, castles, *&c.*, which have been so often repeated that they now fill every portfolio.

The picturesque embellishments of the following volume, are all of them (as far as I know) new to the public, and they describe very striking contrasts in the features of the six counties. From this observation I must except St. Winefred's-well, published in Mr. Pennant's Tour, and the monument at Maes Garmon, etched many years ago by an artist in the country, both of which had sufficient interest with me to obtain admission into my work; but even of these I have varied the points of view. Upon the whole, if, from my knowledge of the ancient British language, *from my intimacy with* my native country and its inhabitants, their economy, customs, and character, and from the moderate talent as an artist, which I possess, I may be thought in some degree to have attained the end which I proposed to myself, I shall feel amply recompensed for the fatigue which I experienced for many months, in travelling as a pedestrian, between two and three thousand miles, over one of the roughest districts of Great Britain.

EDWARD PUGH.

Ruthin, May 10, 1813.

The Author of this Valuable Work is no more. He died at Ruthin in June, 1813. He was Ten Years in completing the Drawings for this Volume.

CONTENTS.

CHAPTER I.

CHAPTER II.

CHAPTER III.

CHAPTER IV.

CHAPTER V.

CHAPTER VI.

CHAPTER VII.

CHAPTER VIII.

CHAPTER IX.

CHAPTER X.

CHAPTER XI.

DIRECTIONS FOR PLACING THE PLATES.

A

Tour through North Wales,

&c. &c.

CHAPTER I.

Chester.—Liverpool.—Saltney.—Buckley-Mountain.—Carregcarn-March Arthur.—Loggerheads.—Wilson.—Vale of Clwyd.—Moel Famma.—Moel Enlly-Llanrhyadr Church.—Denbigh.—Henllan.—Bettws.—Coed Coch.—Teyrden.—Llanelian-Well.—Bryn Euryn.—Great Ormeshead.—Gloddaeth.—Maniac-Conway.—Peniarth.—Conovium.—Graig Wyllt.—Sorbus Aucuparia.—Rocking Stone.—Great Flood at Roe.—Bwlch y Ddeu-faen.—Hermit of Penmaenmawr.—De Breos.—Aber-Inn.—Lavan-Sands.—Osmund's-Air.—Beaumaris.—Feudal Oppression.—Joan's Coffin.—Lleiniog-Castle.—Llanvaes-Monastery.—Bishop's-Throne.—Arthur's Round Table.—Priestholm-Island.—Heligob-Glanog.—Penmon-Priory.—Jane Williams, a Dwarf.—Red-Wharf-Sands.—Penllech.—An Odd Meeting.

AS Chester, to which city I proceeded directly from the capital, stands immediately connected with North Wales, of which it forms one of the eastern avenues, it would be unpardonable in me to pass it over without that full and circumstantial description, to which it is on every account entitled.

Within and without the walls of this ancient city, the artist will find many objects to solicit and engage his attention; the streets, from the singularity and the great diversity of the houses (some referable to the age of Elizabeth, some of a still earlier origin, and some the productions of modern times), will present him with subjects, in a grotesque group, which he cannot any where else expect to find in such a striking combination. I have seen some of these subjects treated in a manner that does great credit to that able artist, Mr. John Varley.

Here strangers must be highly entertained. The elevation of the walls, which environ the city in a uniform quadrangular figure, offers, in the views on all sides, a most delicious feast to the eye. The eastern gate is the best and most gratifying entrance; for, whether you turn to the right or to the left, you are for a short space enclosed with houses, and it is only by degrees, that the beautiful prospects open upon the sight. Turning northwards, your first object is the cathedral, the venerable sides of which are rapidly mouldering to decay. It is a heavy mass, without elegance, and destitute of all those pleasing Gothic ornaments, which generally accompany our antique episcopal buildings. With the exception of the windows, the structure bears the semblance of the old Gothic architecture of the fifth century. From no near point will it arrest the attention of the artist; but from many situations without the walls, I have seen it, when half buried among trees and ruined cottages, or from the side of the water, assume an appearance sufficiently grand to challenge the pencil of an adept in art.

The next object on the right is the Chester canal, now united to the Ellesmere; which, having been an unfortunate speculation, remained unused and unproductive for many years; of late, however, the spirited exertions of a Mr. Fletcher, the worthy proprietor of the Chester Chronicle, has rendered it, in some degree, productive. On the side of this water was lately erected a very extensive shot-manufactory, by Messrs. Walker, Maltbee, and Co.; the tower of which, carried up to the great height of one hundred and fifty feet, is an object pleasing enough to the sight. The eye perceives, in the same direction, a fine, flat, well-wooded country, terminated by gently rising hills, adorned with gentlemen's seats. You now come to the Phœnix-tower, called also King Charles's tower, from the circumstance of Charles I. having, from the roof of this building, viewed the defeat of his army, upon Rawton-heath, under Sir Marmaduke Langdale, on the 24th of September, 1645, by the parliament forces, under the command of the more fortunate General, Pointz.

From this tower you proceed, in a right line, to the north gate, and pass in the way a perpendicular precipice of great depth, the terror of which is considerably increased by the canal which traverses its foot. The excavated rock, with the bridge thrown over it, has a good effect: and here the artist should descend, to view each side of it. Over this bridge is the north gate, an elegant arch, erected on the site of the old one.

The large trilateral brick building on the right is the Blue-coat school. On the left, after passing a few houses, are seen, close to the walls, a rope-walk and some good houses, receding a little from these parapets. On the right is the canal, descending, by locks, into the Ellesmere. Here is a good inn, built with a view to the accommodation of passengers, by the Ellesmere canal; which, at the distance of nine miles, unites with the Mersey*. From hence is seen a fine range of Welsh mountains,

* The passage-boats, drawn by two horses, are very handsome, spacious, and convenient; being covered and divided into three apartments; those for the passengers are fore and aft,

running north and south, which make a conspicuous figure in the landscape. Turning the angle here, you come to the Infirmary, a very handsome brick building, with a proper establishment, conducted upon a plan that brings down the blessings of Heaven upon the institution. Near it is the newly-raised City-jail. You now reach Stanley-place, at the furthest end of which is the great Irish-linen hall, enclosing a large area. The Water-gate, at which you next arrive, is a handsome arch, from whence you look down towards the harbour. On leaving it, the race-course, called the Rood-eye, comes full in view: a fine piece of pasture land, secured (about the year 1587) from the arbitrary encroachments of the tide, by an embankment on the south-west side. On this piece of land, in former times, the youths used to amuse themselves in the sports of wrestling, leaping, running, archery, mock-fights, and other manly exercises. After passing some handsome well-cultivated gardens, on the left, the old Castle appears, with its new companion, the County-jail. This latter building impresses the mind with the notion of impenetrable strength: but, when viewed in front, it presents another character, that of strength combined with elegance. The exterior is of the Doric order: in the centre is a handsome entrance, with a portico and columns, the shaft of each of which is made of a single

one called the best, the other the inferior; both calculated to make each party happy. In the centre of the vessel is a small kitchen, where are prepared dinners and breakfasts in good style, and at a very moderate charge. At the entrance into the Mersey, the passengers proceed in another boat, conducted by able and experienced sailors, ten miles along the broad bosom of the Mersey; they have at first but a partial view of Liverpool, but by degrees the stranger is delighted with the prospect. Merchant-ships and men-of-war at anchor, the noble docks filled with shipping, warehouses excelling those of the metropolis, the lofty spires and the swelling town, the hills behind overspread with fine houses, &c., give an idea of immense wealth and commerce, exceeded only by the British emporium itself.

stone, forming the portal of the court, in which the sessions are held. This hall is extremely elegant, of a semi-circular figure, and of the Ionic order. The auditory stand upon steps, a disposition which is thought to be peculiarly adapted to the purposes of seeing and hearing. The expense of this noble building is defrayed by the county, from the profits arising from the tonnage of vessels sailing on the river Weever. Though the building is not yet finished, it has already cost upwards of one hundred thousand pounds. The architect is Mr. Thomas Harrison.

You now proceed, and soon come to the bridge, coeval with some of the oldest buildings in the city. Adjoining the bridge are the city mills, lately rebuilt, the old ones having, a few years ago, been demolished by fire. At low water, the fall of the Dee here is rather a curiosity, and causes a loud stunning noise. You now ascend two flights of steps, from whence the Dee is seen stealing along the beautiful meadows. The distant country, and the uplifted and isolated castle of Beeston, towering above all other objects, form an interesting picture.

St. John's church is a good old building: its tower is extremely grand and lofty, not in any other way inferior to that of Wrexham, but deficient in Gothic ornament. After passing a few houses and gardens, you arrive at the east gate, from whence you set out, having traversed a distance of two miles.

When the stranger has thus walked round the city, he may amuse himself in the interior; where the rows will afford him entertainment, from the singularity of their structure. The churches, the castle, and jail, the shot-manufactory, and the shipping at the Crane, are all well worthy of his attention; at the latter place, ships take in their freight of cheese for London, *&c.* Every body knows, that of all cheeses made in England, the preference is justly given to those manufactured in Cheshire. It is somewhat remarkable, that the inhabitants were taught the art of making it by the Romans: but they have since improved upon their method, and people of *good taste* will readily allow that Cheshire still keeps the lead of all other cheese counties in Britain.

From hence there is a delightful walk of three miles, by the side of the Dee, on the embankment called the Cop; upon which the natives frequently take a salutary ramble, to meet the spring-tides. I once went, with some gentlemen, on the river in a small boat at low water; and at the distance of two miles we saw an amazing surge rolling on to meet us, which to me, who had never seen it before, appeared tremendous, as threatening to overwhelm us all in an instant. It rushed on us with such velocity, that had we been inclined to escape it, we could not have succeeded; and if my friends had not possessed some knowledge of naval tactics, we might have been swallowed up by it*. I am told, however, that it is by no means dangerous, if proper attention is paid to the boat. By keeping the boat's head right to the surge, we were lifted up on high, the elevation producing at the same time a most pleasing sensation. Now another sight was presented to us; a fleet of market-boats, that had been fairly outrun by the tide, bringing with them the luxuries of the table, in exchange for the one thing so universally needful, cash.

Another charming walk there is, for three miles, by the side of the Dee to Eaton-hall, the seat of Lord Grosvenor; a most superb mansion, now building under the direction of Mr. Porden, who furnished the design. It is of the light modern Gothic, and

* In the East Indies, the flood-tide sets in with great fury. The head of the tide is frequently ten or twelve yards in height. It is called a *Boar*, and sometimes forces vessels from the strongest anchorage.

evinces his lordship's good taste. It commands with one front the soft-flowing Dee, and some beautiful meadow grounds; whilst with the other it looks westward, over an agreeable prospect. A public road, to vary the walk, will bring you back; and you may find refreshment at, and, at the same time, be pleased with the rusticity of, the little public-house, called the Iron-bridge, situated nearly in the half way.

The commerce of Chester is not so great as it was before its neighbour, Liverpool, became so powerful a rival. It is chiefly confined to the Baltic, for timber, besides some little coasting-trade; but many vessels are built here, of from fifty to five hundred tons burden, and disposed of to the Liverpool merchants. The tanning and glove trades are carried on here to some extent. Chester is supposed to contain near twenty thousand inhabitants. It has two fairs in the year, one in July, and the other in October; each of which continues nearly three weeks. The goods sold are Irish linen, Welsh flannels, webs, yarn, coarse linen cloths, Manchester goods, Yorkshire cloths, Birmingham hardware, Coventry ribands, horses, and horned cattle, *&c.*

During the race week, Chester is the centre of fashion and gaiety. The races commence the first Monday in May, and are attended by the first people in the country, when the theatre royal is open for the week.

The higher ranks of the society, though in general not very opulent, are accomplished; the ladies are handsome, open, and unreserved in their conversation; the gentlemen free and communicative, and generally disposed to be friendly to the arts. The tradesmen are ready and active. The large towns that are in the immediate neighbourhood of Chester, prevent it from enjoying much commerce on the English side; and the inhabitants acknowledge the benefit they derive from their intercourse with Wales. The working part of the community are sober and industrious.

Chester has always been noted for its loyalty to the sovereign; nor is that loyalty in the least diminished. It has a fine regiment of well-disciplined defenders of their country, consisting of about fourteen hundred men. I saw them returning from three weeks' permanent duty at Ellesmere. Their appearance was truly martial; and, by their expertness in the manual and platoon exercise, it was evident that they must have been under excellent military tuition: they were commanded by Colonel Barnston.

This city, as is asserted by the historian Bradshaw*, was founded by "King *Leir*, a *Brittain* fine, and valiant," who called it Guerleer; a name somewhat like the proper one, still retained by the Welsh, Caer Lleon, the Camp, or City of the Legion, being the station of the twentieth legion, which came into Britain prior to the year 61, as this legion is ascertained, by Suetonius, to have been engaged in the defeat of Boadicea. The plan of the city is precisely the same as that of the Roman camps, which evinces it to have derived its origin from them. There are four principal streets, stretching towards the four cardinal points, and many smaller ones crossing them at right angles. The present walls stand upon the site of the Roman, and mark their limits; but not a vestige of them remains. The streets were sunk by excavations, many feet below the present surface of the ground, so that the kitchens are now as many feet above them.

On the departure of the Roman legions from Britain, in 448, this city fell under the government of the natives, who, however,

* Life of St. Werburg.

were soon obliged to give way to another, more barbarous, enemy, the Saxons.

In the year 607, Ethelfrid king of Northumbria, determining to add this tract of country to his dominions, was opposed by Brochmail Yscithrve, king of Powys, who, like the Britons under St. Germanus, at the Hallelujah victory, near Mold, relying on divine interposition, brought with him from Bangor twelve hundred of the religious of that convent, to pray for his success Ethelfrid perceiving these enthusiasts collected upon the hill, and understanding their business, instantly put them all to the sword. Brochmail, who was soon afterwards easily routed, escaped with not more than fifty men*. Ethelfrid having pillaged the city, left it to the former possessors, reserving to himself the territory; which he possessed, till it was wrested from him by the King of Mercia. The city, after this, seems to have been held by the Britons, and to have been considered by them as the capital of North Wales, till it passed under the dominion of Egbert, about the year 828. During a series of years, it appears subsequently to have undergone many changes, and to have experienced some calamities, in consequence of the incursions of the Saxons, Danes, &c.

William the Conqueror appointed Hugh Lupus the first (Norman) Earl of Chester, with the possession of the county; which was then erected into a county palatine, and indulged with a sovereign jurisdiction; the earls being allowed their distinct parliaments and their courts of law.

The sword, by which Lupus was invested with his dignity, is still kept as a relic in the British Museum, and has this inscription, *Hugo comes cestriæ.* By virtue of this sword, the Earl of Chester

* Saxon Chron. 25.

was created sword-bearer of England, and as such he was accustomed to officiate at the coronation of the kings.

From the conquest to the reign of Henry III., a period of one hundred and seventy-four years, this sort of government continued without interruption. Henry himself became the Earl of Chester, and this earldom has ever since remained in the royal family. The city then assumed a new form of government, by a mayor and sheriffs. Henry first granted it a charter, and his successors, the Edwards, augmented, in various ways, the privileges of the corporation. In consequence of some distresses which it experienced, about 1506, Henry VII. remitted eighty pounds of its annual rent, and granted it a fresh charter, by which the city was separated from the county; a privilege which Chester still enjoys.

Having taken leave of Chester, I began my tour on foot, and with no other companion than a very pretty little dog, presented to me by a very pretty young lady, whose injunctions respecting it I regarded with the most scrupulous observance.

Two miles from Chester, on my way to Ruthin, I entered the principality of Wales on a very extensive flat, called Saltney, many years ago a salt-marsh, but of late so well cultivated and improved, that it has now the appearance of a rich valley Passing Broughton-hall, on my left, I ascended a rising ground, called the Warren, lately a park for rabbits, and a waste, but recently enclosed for the better use of man. Descending on the other side, I came to what the Welsh justly call Milltir Fudyr, or the Dirty Mile; at the conclusion of which, I passed the extensive pottery and colliery on Buckley-mountain, belonging to Mr. Rigby, of Hawarden; and soon arrived at Mold, a description of which is reserved for another place. Leaving Mold on my

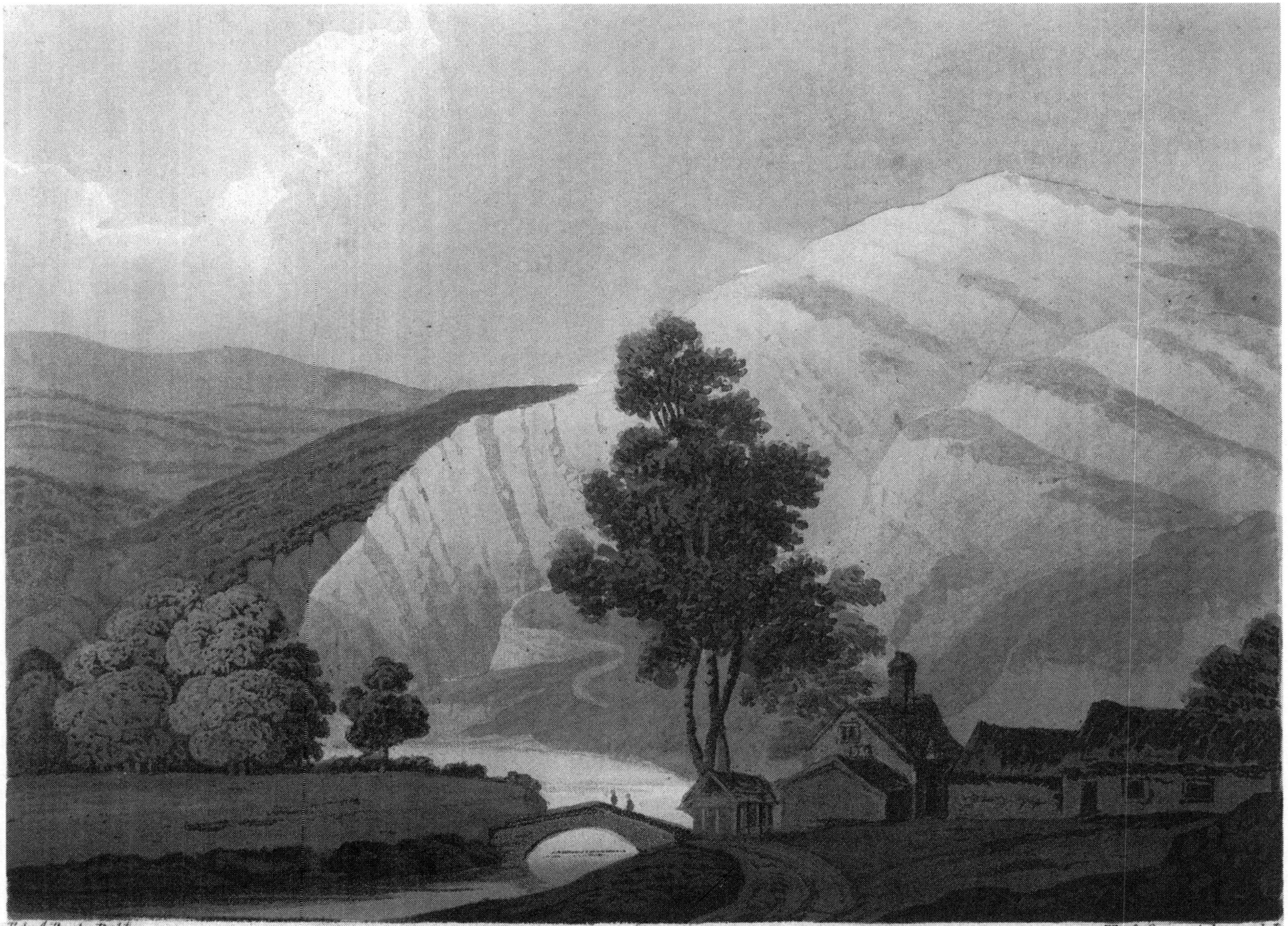

Edw.d Pugh Del.t   Tho.s Cartwright sculp.t

VIEW NEAR THE LOGGERHEADS.

Published 15 April 1813, by E. Williams Strand

right, I struck up the mountain, and passing on my left the residence of the Rev. Mr. Williams, called Fron, gained the summit, from which I had immediately in front those noble mountains so visible from Chester, called Moel Enlly, and Moel Famma, the latter inferior in height to few in Wales. This is a path frequently trodden by the artists. On the right of the road stands a rude-looking arch, underneath which is a stone, called Carregcarn-March Arthur, with a cavity in it very like the impression of a horse's hoof. This has given rise to a traditional story, that King Arthur, when hunting on the hills, took a leap from the summit of Moel Famma, and his horse alighting upon this stone, impressed it with his hoof. This arch was erected as a boundary between the parish of Mold in Flintshire, and the parish of Llanferres in Denbighshire, and commemorates, by an inscription almost totally effaced, a law-suit between the Grosvenor family and the lords of the manor of Mold; the first laying claim to it, as part of his mineral grant of the hundred of Yale, while the latter successfully contended that it belonged to the parish of Mold, and the decision of the Court of Exchequer, in 1763, was in favour of the lords.

Descending the hill, I came to the Loggerheads, a public-house on the road. Here is a sign over the door, painted by that incomparable artist, the late Mr. Wilson, R. A. The master of this public-house, a tenant of a cousin of Mr. Wilson (Mr. Jones), was importunate in his solicitations for a sign, and his cousin, at Clomender, seconding the petition, the artist very good-naturedly sat down, and amusing himself, as he said, to make the people laugh, painted the sign. At present, it only exhibits traits just sufficient to shew the great hand that produced it; but it is said that the reverse side has also a picture, which, covered as it is by the eves of the house, may probably be in high preservation. Mr. Wilson was the first who visited North Wales professionally as an artist: he unfolded its beauties, and, with his bewitching performances, enticed others to extend their visits to those inexhaustible resources of the arts. Mr. Wilson was a warm admirer of the scenery about this spot; and here the artist, induced to give up his time to examine its recesses, will be amply rewarded by the fine subjects which it will offer, from numerous points, for the exercise of his pencil, in rock, wood, water, and hills, in every variety of intermixture.

I walked on the heights above this river, whence the various landscapes looked delightfully, backed by noble mountains, whose tops touch the clouds. At the distance of two miles are the great lead mines, belonging to Mr. Wilkinson. Returning, by the bed of the river Alyn, a young mountaineer pointed out to me the fissures where this river disappears; and, in about a mile further, where it again oozes out of its dark passage. He very gravely asked me if I knew the cause of this. Upon my replying in the negative, he said, that when the Saxons and the Welsh were engaged in a dreadful conflict on its banks (alluding, probably, to the battle of Maes Garmon), the Almighty, to favour the Britons, had caused the water to run underground, so that the Saxons, being cut off from this necessary supply, soon became prisoners to his countrymen.

This legend is not generally believed, or, indeed, known, in this neighbourhood, and may probably have been kept alive solely by this young man's grandmother, who, fond of talking of what she heard in her youthful days, had, as he confessed, told him this. This river has been noticed by several old writers; amongst them, Drayton says,

> Then Alen makes approach (to Dee most inly deere,)
> Taking Cegidog in; who, earnest to be there,
> For haste, twice under earth his crystol head doth runne.

Returning to the Loggerheads, I met an old friend, who had come thus far to meet me, and after dinner, we walked together to Ruthin. Having gained the height of the Bwlch, we stayed a few minutes to gaze on the charming prospects before us; and though they had for years been familiar to us, yet we could still discover fresh assemblages of beauties in the noble Vale of Clwyd. I would advise strangers who go this way, when they are near the top of the road, to avoid looking towards the vale till they have gained the summit, and then, having first cast their eye on the black mountain-road, which they have just left, to face about, and the striking contrast cannot fail to produce the most agreeable effect. We quitted the hill at the moment when the sun was setting, and arrived at Ruthin; where I had the happiness once more to meet my aged and excellent mother. I stayed here a few days, while some things were preparing for my journey, and during this time ascended, with two friends, the lofty mountain of Moel Famma, just above the town. We deviated a little to the left of the road to Chester, and, passing over several fertile farms, came to a neat small farm-house, lately belonging to Judge Lloyd (but now to his son). It is but justice to the memory of this gentleman, to say, that it seemed a gratification to his mind to make his tenants happy; the small houses attached to his farms being neat and comfortable, the easy rents at which they were let, and the additional circumstance of his having adhered to the good old system, of "not adding farm to farm," speaks decidedly in favour of this opinion. After the experience of considerable inconvenience from the influence of the sun, slippery footing, and steep ascents, we reached the summit, and were fortunate enough to suffer no molestations from mists or clouds. A fine serene clear sky enabled us to enjoy a sight, eminently remarkable for its beauties. On the north-east were seen the shores of Cheshire and Lancashire, with the estuaries of the Dee and Mersey. Liverpool, though at the distance of twenty-eight miles, is a conspicuous object; and, when viewed through a good telescope, its buildings, docks, and shipping, are distinctly made out. The celebrated sea-bathing town of Parkgate is observable, in the same direction, on the edge of the Dee; and easterly stands Chester, and the county as far as Farndon. More contiguous to the eye, is the little town of Mold, with the noble laminated rocks, near the Loggerheads. To the southward is some fine mountain-scenery, with Moel Enlly; another high mountain, which Camden regards as the higher of the two. In this, however, he is certainly mistaken, Moel Famma being thirty feet higher than his competitor. On the summit of Moel Enlly is a British post, of immense strength, consisting of a rampart and trench, composed of earth and loose stones; the entrance to which was from the west. The position of this station was very favourable to the Britons, as they could easily discover the movements of their enemies, approaching the different passes in the neighbourhood, and make their attacks with advantage. This mountain has, upon its summit, a small spring, which is not a little singular: the whole is worthy the observation of the traveller. Close to this mountain is Bwlch Agricla, or Agricola's Pass, and, no doubt, it was the passage through which he went to Mona.

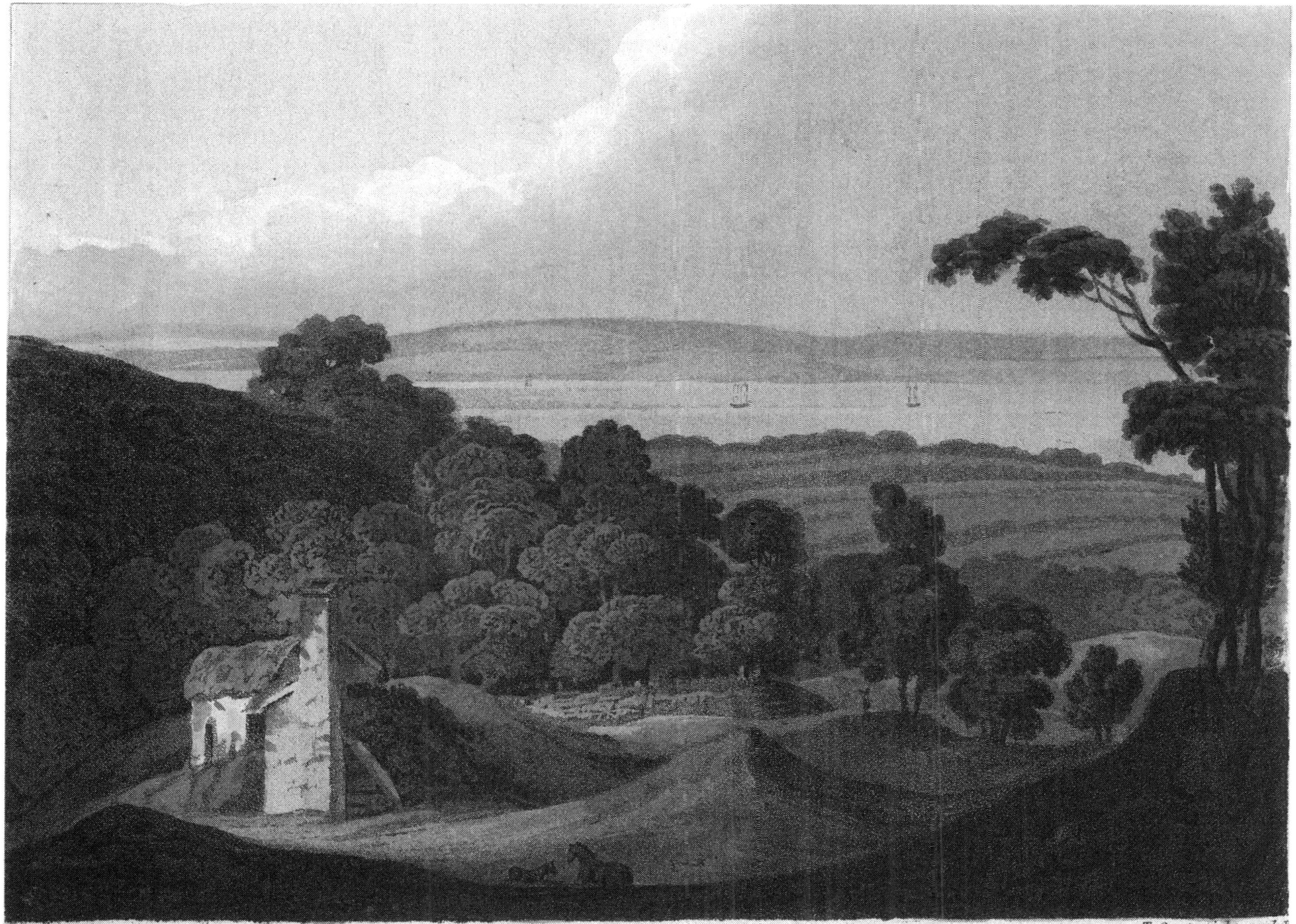

E. Pugh del.t T. Cartwright sculp.t

THE ESTUARIES OF THE DEE & MERSEY.

Published 15 March, 1814 by F. Williams Strand.

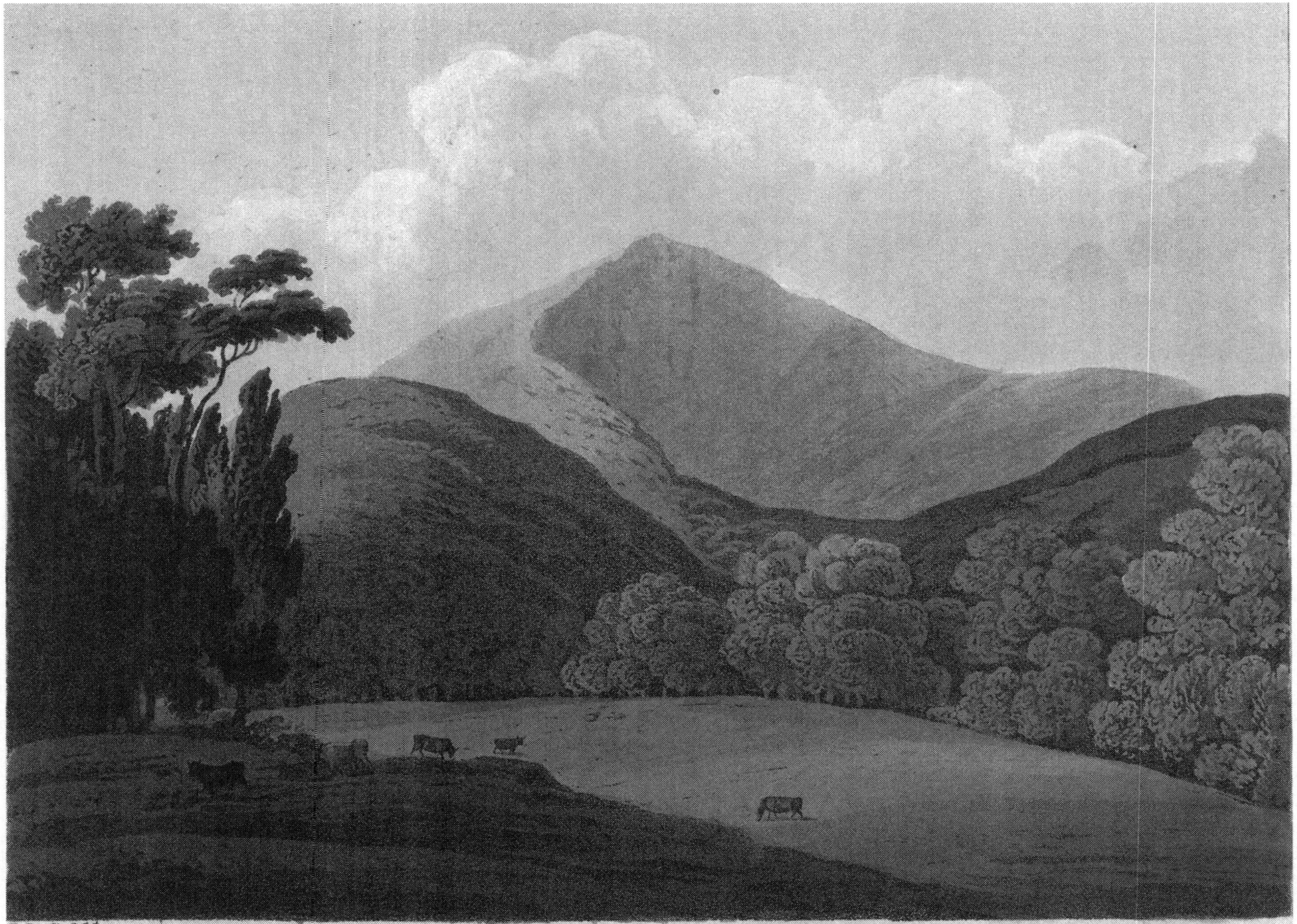

E. Pugh delᵗ T. Cartwright sculpᵗ

MOEL FAMMA.

Published 15 December 1813, by E. Williams Strand.

But, to return to Moel Famma. Beginning again in the north, we find, skirting the horizon, part of Scotland, Cumberland, Westmoreland; the Yorkshire, Derbyshire, and Staffordshire hills. In the south we behold the confines of the Vale of Clwyd, formed by some very picturesque hills, over which tower the Berwin mountains: and more to the right, those conical rocks, called the Arenig, and Cader Idris, in Merionethshire, display themselves; whilst still more to the right, we discover Moel Siabad, Snowdon, Carned Dafydd, Carned Llewelyn, and other subordinate mountains, lessening progressively as they approach to Bangor. The Vale of Clwyd, a beautiful expanse of country, lay beneath us, extending, from north to south, about twenty-five miles; and from east to west, about six. It is highly cultivated, even to the very tops of the hills that flank it, on the western side. The town of Ruthin was seated just below us. Denbigh, with its noble ruins, at the distance of nine miles, and St. Asaph, five miles further, together with a prodigious number of gentlemen's seats, farm-houses, and cottages, scattered about, and the small, but pretty meandering river Clwyd, with other tributary streams, falling gently into the Irish sea, render the scene altogether one of the greatest beauty in the world. Upon the apex of this mountain is now erecting a jubilee edifice, dedicated to his Majesty George III., who, on the 26th of October, 1810, had swayed the sceptre of Great Britain fifty years. The edifice is of a pyramidical form; at the angles are attached four small ones*.

When we were about quitting the mountain, I suddenly missed my dog. After calling and whistling for some time, one of my

* Mr. Harrison, architect.

companions perceived several boys running down the hill, who, a few minutes before, were seated about a hundred yards from us; and from so suspicious an appearance, we concluded that they had seduced, or carried it away. The thoughts of my obligation to the fair giver, urged me to its instant release. I rushed down the mountain with no inconsiderable speed, and soon came up with these supposed thieves: but, to my disappointment, the dog was not among them. I singled out the least of the lads, and brought him back with me a hundred yards up the hill, closely interrogating him by the way: but he declared his innocence, and that of his comrades, with looks so ingenuous, his hands uplifted, and the tear trickling down his cheek, I could not doubt him; so, shaking him by the hand, he returned to his friends, and I to mine.

I thought it might be possible that the dog had gone to sleep among the gorse, and, when we shifted our situation, that he might still remain there. When I reached my friends again, I found this supposition verified. Though myself somewhat mortified with my wild-goose chase of two miles, we returned to Ruthin entertained with the whimsicality of the accident.

Various are the modes of travelling through this country. They who are pent up in coaches, lose many of its beauties; and they who ride, fare but little better. The scenery indeed is more open to them: but in many parts, riding is rendered very difficult; and in others, where the visit is most strongly solicited, it is absolutely impracticable. We sometimes hear of tourists, who, for the sake of expedition, will hire, or purchase, horses for the whole of their journey, who meet with "hair-breadth 'scapes," which, as it might be thought, would deter others from following their example. Mr. Barber, in crossing the Loughan, South

Wales, by a sudden slip of his horse was separated from him, and both had to swim for their lives to the opposite shore: by which accident many valuable documents and drawings were utterly spoiled." To the pedestrian all is free—to him no difficulty or danger is presented, and he may make excursions with the greatest ease. Aware of the conveniency of this latter mode, I set out from Ruthin, thus equipped; a light knapsack on my back, containing only what was barely necessary, an umbrella in my right hand, and under my left arm a small portfölio suspended to my right shoulder by a broad piece of tape. I passed through the meadows, a charming walk of three miles, till I met the public road near Llanrhyadr: this is a pretty little village, and much improved since Mr. Wilding possessed the adjacent hall and estate. The church is spacious, its interior possessing nothing remarkable except the large and handsome east window*, with the subject of the genealogy of Christ; from Jesse, painted in a good style, and in good preservation; as also a beautiful little metaphorical figure to the memory of Watkin Edwards Wynne, Esq. of Llwyn, major-commandant of the Merionethshire militia, heir of the ancient house of Gwydir; erected by his widow, Anna Maria Wynne, of Llwesog-lodge, in this neighbourhood. Passing the alms-houses, and through a romantic well-wooded walk of 300 yards, to a pretty spring-water bath, dedicated to St. Dyfnog, I could not but lament the general neglect and decay of these repositories of health, which it is well known have been thoroughly efficacious even in the cure of the most obstinate chronic diseases. It might be a great conveniency to the afflicted, if this bath were repaired and made free. Proceeding by the

* Date on window 1°.ccccc.III.iii.

public road, I soon had a sight of the picturesque and exalted castle of Denbigh: the painter may gain some favourable points of view by deviating from the road, but I shall have occasion hereafter to bring him to situations of greater consequence. Setting out early next morning from Denbigh, I soon came to Henllan, a little straggling village which possesses but little to recommend it to the stranger. It has a neat new church built upon the site of the old one; the tower belonging to it stands at the distance of six or eight yards. Formerly, and in monkish times, it was said and believed, by the people, that in a great thaw the church, and the rock upon which it stood, slipped down and left the tower where it remains; but now, when strangers ask the reason of this singular sight, they stare, but (jocosely) refer to the same cause. I went through a dull and uninteresting country to Bettws; this is also a small village rather pleasantly situated, having a peep of the Irish sea, between two rocks, at a place called Llandulas, or Black and Blue. Whilst I was enjoying my cup of cwrw (ale), after a wholesome lunch of bacon and beans, there came in a man and a woman whose appearance drew some observations from the people about me, from which I learnt they were going to visit Llanelian-well. More of this in another place. I was highly entertained with the conversation of a jolly grey-headed old man, whose broad face betrayed no symptoms either of grief or famine. He dwelt with peculiar delight upon the subject of two matrimonial connexions which he had contracted: both wives were lovely, both were good, and, with him, both were happy; no uncommon augmentation of his family ever depressed his spirits, and though each of his wives had repeatedly presented him with twins, it only served to increase his natural fondness for them. He was going on upon this theme with great volubility of speech, when my watch warned me that it was time to be gone; I therefore left this merry old fellow with some reluctance. The country now began to wear a more agreeable aspect, till I was shut in between the hills in a small well-wooded valley, in which stands Coedloch, the old family mansion of John Wynne, Esq. After dinner this gentleman and his lady very politely conducted me to the brow of a noble rock, from whence we had a delightful sight of the adjacent country, with the sea, and a number of ships with their expanded sails hastening to their place of destination, Liverpool. Next morning, after viewing a spacious, handsome, stone house, erecting from a plan by Heckwell, I took my leave of Mr. and Mrs. Wynne, under whose roof I experienced the greatest degree of cordiality and friendship; I pursued my way through a very pleasant country, and touched at Tyrden, the residence of John Holland, Esq., whose polite invitation, together with the sylvan grounds, and beauties that surrounded me, very nearly proved fatal to the plan I had struck out. I shortly came to the village of Llanelian, a few hundred yards beyond which is the famous immolating well of the same name; I saw the door open, and close by a very large mastiff dog, looking more fiercely and terrible than a whiskered soldier on guard. I approached with some caution in full hopes of coming in upon the parties in the midst of their imprecations.—Cæsar was civil. Listening a moment at the door, I was mortified to find no one there. This well is circular, its diameter about two feet six inches, covered with a stone arch and sods; it is enclosed by a strong square wall, seven feet high, and situated in a close, by the road-side This well is a relic of Roman-catholic superstition. The well is emptied, after which begins the ceremony, some wishing for diseases upon their neighbour's cattle;

others, upon the family; and in various ways, all which is recorded in a book kept by the lady whose property the well is, and who has, upon this occasion, assumed the functions of officiating clergyman of the parish. This subject has frequently been canvassed at the quarter-sessions in this county *. I am informed that the late laudable efforts of Sir Watkin William Wynn, to abolish this infamous trick upon human ignorance, have proved abortive; the well being private property. The lady who keeps it, is supposed to have made, annually, a pretty round sum; but it certainly is on the decline. Is it not the indispensable duty of the clergy to preach it out of countenance and use? Whilst I was surveying the place, there came in a young woman with her apron full of leaves, and began to prepare the well, no doubt for the man and woman I saw at Bettws. I questioned her closely on the use of the leaves, the nature of the ceremony, *&c.*, and received the most vague, shifting, artful answers; not pleased with my interrogations, she hurried away. It was not likely, after this, that I should see the farce acted, so I took my departure. I soon joined the public road from Chester to Conway. My reader will perceive I have made but few observations upon the country through which I have already passed, as it is comparatively unimportant. I have repeatedly travelled the great or lower road from Denbigh to Conway, and wished to know which of the two roads was likely to yield the greatest gratification to the man of taste. By all means I would prefer the lower, which runs by the sea-side from Abergeley to the little Ormeshead, and avoid the old mountain-road which has nothing to recommend it. I turned to the right of the road

* Denbigh.

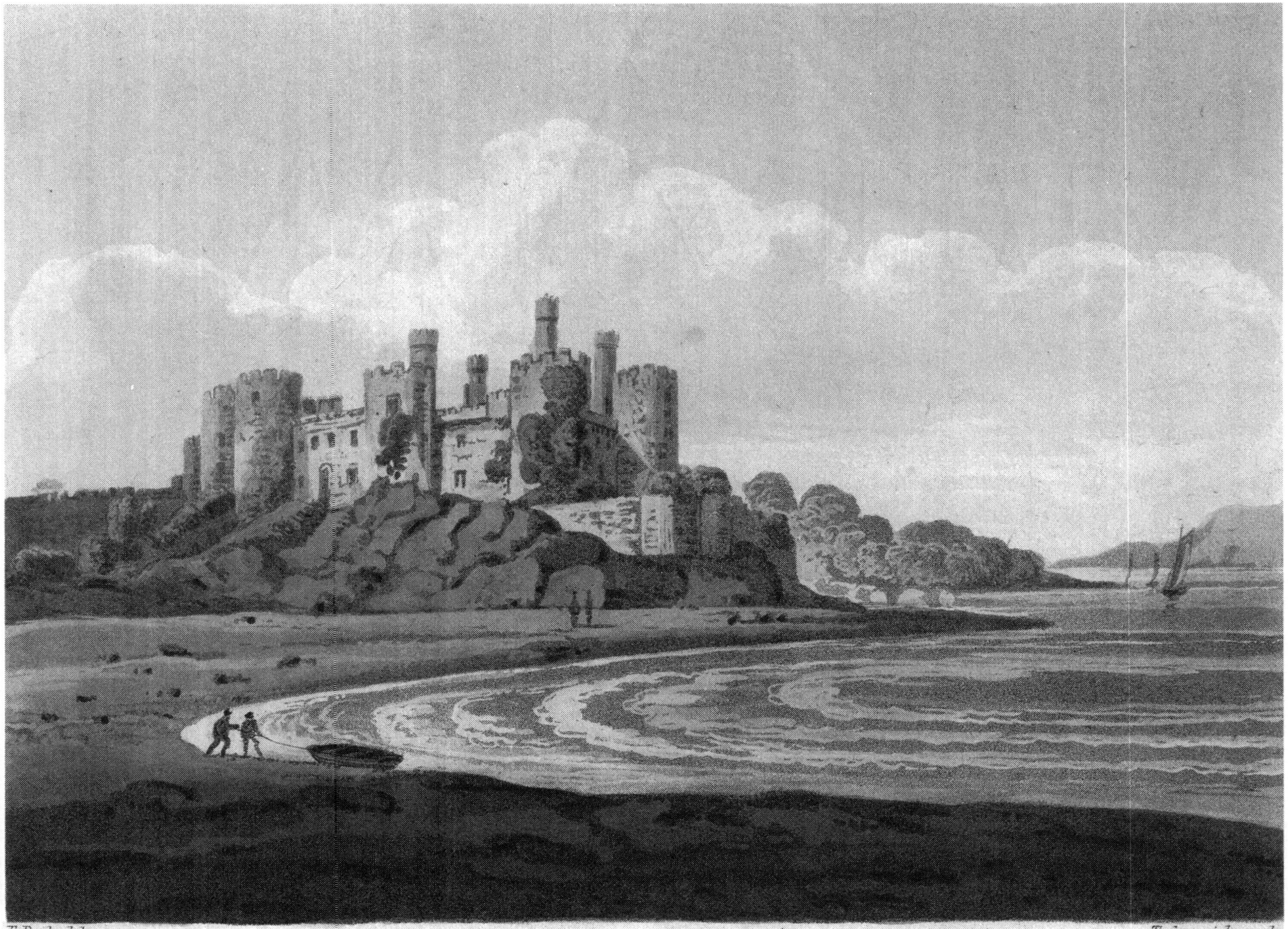

E. Pugh del. T. Cartwright sculp.

CONWAY CASTLE.

Published 25 January 1815, by E. Williams, Strand.

towards Llandrillo, a quarter of a mile, to see the ruins of one of Ednyfed Fychan's houses, called Bryn Euryn, inhabited by him in the 12th century. If we may judge by what remains of this building it must have been a considerable one, of a castellated form and appearance. Its situation is fine, commanding a view of the sea, the shores of Denbigh, Flint, and Lancashire, &c. It will from no point form a picture. Returning to the road, for the space of two miles towards Conway-ferry, the country is very beautiful and woody; the valley soon opens and discovers a scene so grand as to eclipse every object I had seen since the commencement of my journey Though I had frequently beheld Conway-castle with delight, I now saw it with increased pleasure, and with feelings more alive to its importance than ever. Its elevated and elegant turrets, raised upon the main edifice, starting out of the water; and the town couchant by its side, seconded by the noble and picturesque hills behind, with the additional circumstances of a broad river and the hanging-wood on the left, combine to make it one of the finest pictures in nature. If it is no wonder that the artists annually exhibit pictures of this castle at Somerset-place, yet it is a little remarkable they do not vary their points:—I have seen pictures repeatedly painted by different hands from the same spot, as if the space about the castle was so circumscribed or limited, that the artist could choose but two or three situations to sketch from. I would persuade them to try the following grounds, &c. The heights above the town for bird's-eye views; the ramparts, which are easily ascended; on the opposite shore; from the heights above Bodscallen; but Bryneisteddfa, and the beautiful grounds about it, belonging to J. Chambres Jones, Esq., command the most luxuriant prospects, and is the happiest situation in the neighbourhood. I left Conway-ferry after dinner, and went by the shore till I met the ruins of a religious house, facing Penmaenmawr, but time has so changed its form that the original shape cannot be traced From hence I went along the peninsula to the rocks of Great Ormeshead. I had heard much of them in the neighbourhood. It is very difficult to see them to perfection without a boat, a thing I could not procure on the spot, but am of opinion, with the help of one, which may be had at Conway, a sight of these cliffs would be a treat to the stranger. In returning, I visited Gloddaeth, an old mansion belonging to Sir Thomas Mostyn : its interior is dull, it is very irregular in its plan, and is of that heavy specimen of architecture so prevalent in the fifteenth and sixteenth centuries :—Its situation is charming, on the side of a woody eminence that overlooks a pretty little dale. Following a serpentine walk through the woods, I passed on my left Bodscallen, another old house belonging to Sir Thomas Mostyn, which I did not visit, and arrived very much fatigued at the Ferry-house. Early in the morning, when discharging my bill, I met with some impertinence from the female waiter here, such as I never experienced before, or since, in the principality : —Giving her, as is usual, a piece of silver, she impudently told me, "It was not half enough !" I crossed the water, and entering Conway, put up at the Harp-inn, where I met with civility and good treatment.

Quitting Conway I made through a handsome wood, opposite the castle, for Pennarth, a charming house, lately the residence of Sir George Beaumont, Bart., a gentleman whose pictures are held in high estimation among connoisseurs. It is now occupied by Lady Clarges, who has been so annoyed by the appearance of strangers on the grounds, that it has become difficult to procure a peep. From hence I entered the public road to Llanrwst.—It was this day so excessively sultry, that my movements were beyond measure slow; the sun, in his meridian glory, darting down his rays with so much force and heat, that I was every hundred yards compelled to seek shelter in the shade; a brook crossing the road afforded me a treat highly gratifying to my feelings: I sat upon a stone in the centre of it, and placed my feet in the stream, apprehending no danger, as I was aware that the heat of the sun would cause such evaporation as to leave my feet dry in ten minutes, which was the case. At this moment a chariot and a barouche drove by, and the ladies and gentlemen, by their smiles and their jokes, seemed to wish a participation in so great a luxury. I now came to Caer-hûn. Nothing can exceed this situation: the grounds are well wooded;—the late worthy Mr. Griffith possessed a mind not vitiated by the false taste, so prevalent in these days, of planting trees in square, round, and oval *clumps*, which at a small distance appear like so many spots; and destroy that picturesque effect which a negligent distribution, like that on these grounds, produces. The soft flowery Conway—the noble and majestic or prouder sublime cliff, Craig Siberi—the rich middle distance formed by a bold headland, loaded with wood and farm-houses, and the frowning rocks of Craig Wyllt receding towards Llanrwst, complete a scenery indescribable, except by the pen of Pope or Gray.

The Rev. Mr. Williams of Conway, being here upon a visit, very politely offered me his company to explore the wilds (as they are justly designated by the Welsh term) of Craig Wyllt. On ascending these rocks we met another Rev. Mr. Williams, whose comfortable house commands an extensive prospect of the vale of Conway; and after taking his advice of participating in a cold repast ere we mounted to this airy elevation, we accepted of his very obliging offer to assist us. After passing many fine bits of rock and wood, we arrived at a wooden bridge, called Pont y Cammau, or the Bridge of the Leaps; for, as soon as the passenger quits it, he has, ere he safely lands, to leap from one great stone to another; a performance of some difficulty. A long continuance of fine weather had rendered the scene less picturesque than if we had seen it with a torrent rushing down from the mountains above: in which case it must be wonderfully grand. The bed of the river is rough beyond description, the stones in great masses lying in the most varied and fantastic positions, and creating a succession of waterfalls; and the wood and rocks on each side, with a cottage suspended in mid air, finish this picturesque spot. We proceeded further to the cascade at Craig Wyllt, which, in a rainy season, must be very fine indeed. Independently of the fall, the whole is so disposed in parts, that the artist may, at the expense of half a day, carry away with him a number of sketches.

On these heights is seen the *sorbus aucuparia,* or mountain-ash, or the whitty. It is the last tree to be met with on going up our mountains. Of the beautiful red berries of this tree, the poor people, by infusing and fermenting them in water, make a drink which they call diod griafol.

> "And whitty glitters up the mountain's side
> The hardy whitty, that o'er Cambrian snows
> Beams its red glance, and in bleak winter glows."
>
> KNIGHT'S *Landscape.*

In times more superstitious, thank God! than the present, the

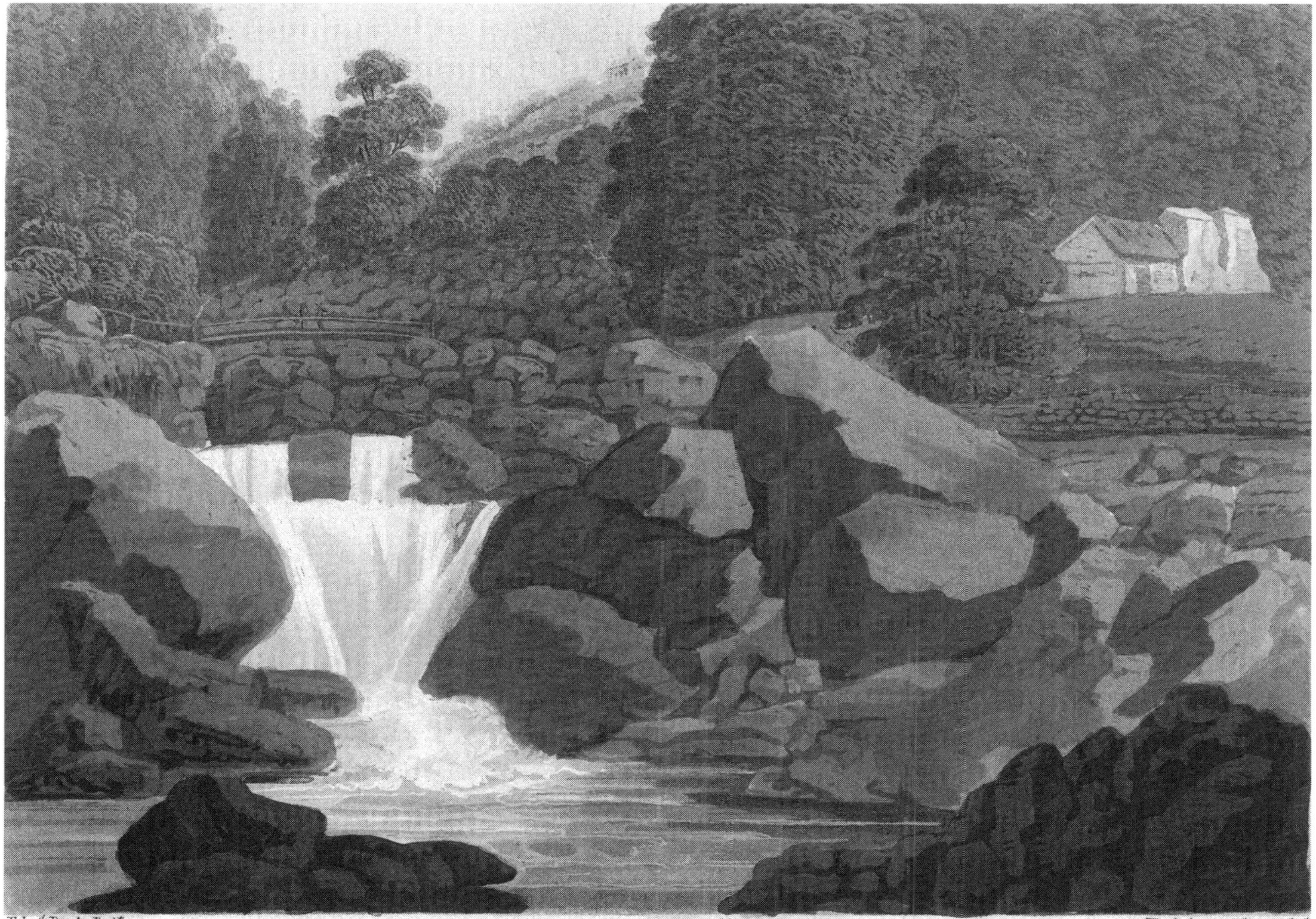

Edw.d Pugh Del.t Thos. Cartwright sculp.t

PONT-Y-CAMMAU.

Published 15 April 1813. by E. Williams, Strand.

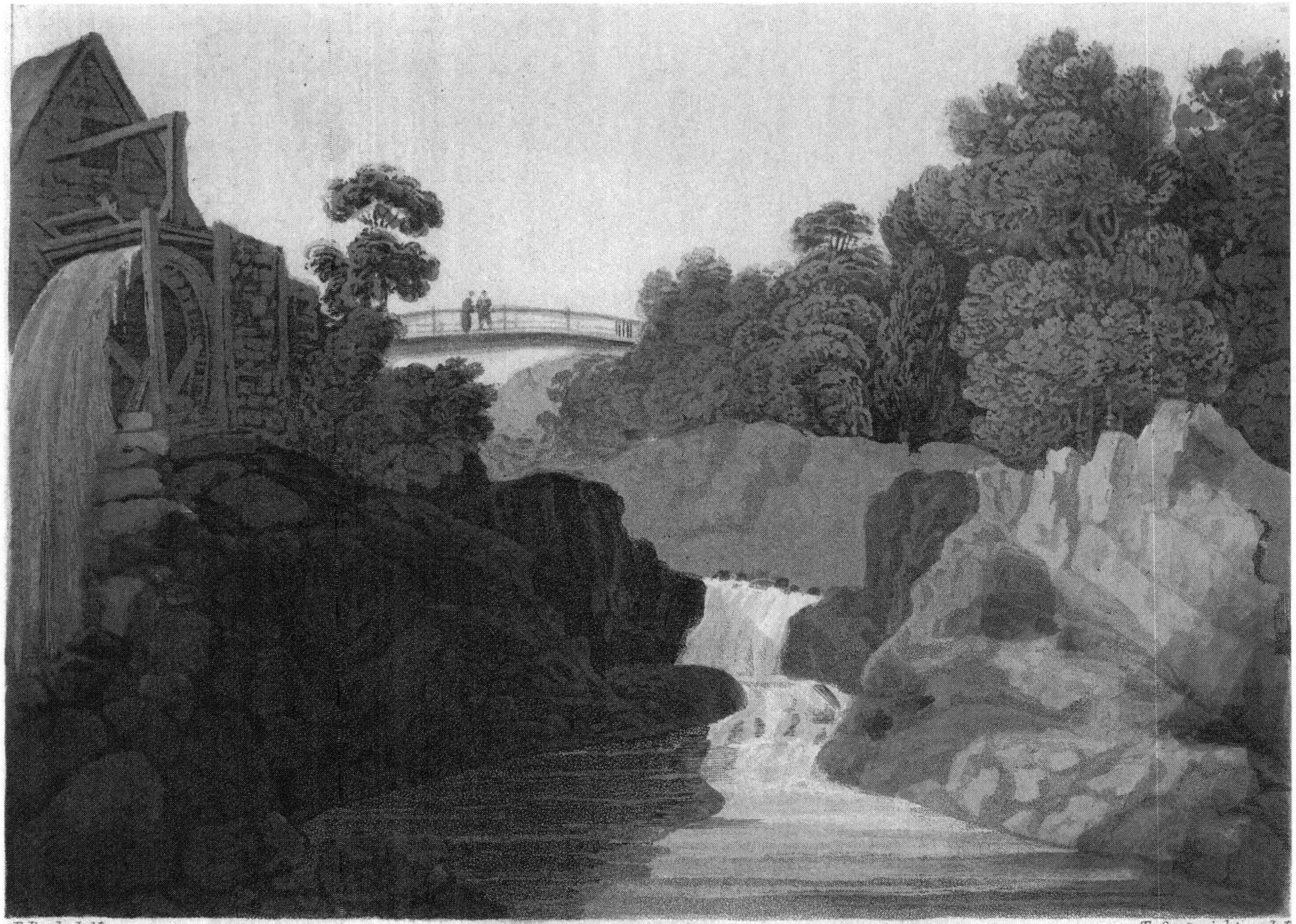

E. Pugh del.t T. Cartwright sculp.t

AN OVERSHOT MILL NEAR CAER HÛN.

Published 15 March 1814, by E. Williams Strand.

catholic priests had the art of converting the wood of this tree into money, by the following mode:—they wore amulets of it about the neck; and, forming crosses of it, they persuaded their followers that if they carried one always in their pocket, its virtue would be an infallible preservative against all sorts of fascinations: and so much was this believed, that crosses were as numerous as the people.

Returning by another path, we passed a great number of cottages, so singular in their appearance and situation, that my companions were no less gratified with the sight than myself. I perceived that they were in general built close up to the perpendicular side of a rock, with trees and shrubs about them; and that some of them pent between, and placed under, tremendously frightful hanging rocks; but so artfully contrived as to evade the sight till we came immediately upon them. These cottages are the produce of the laborious industry of the peasantry, who enjoy them free of all demands or molestation. The number of them creates such a labyrinth, that we were glad to have a guide to extricate us. In our descent, this guide climbed upon a huge logan, or rocking-stone, of probably a hundred tons weight, and, without any apparent difficulty, made it move in its socket. The gentlemen who were with me, though many years inhabitants of the neighbourhood, had never heard of this Druidical curiosity.

Taking leave of the Rev. Mr. Williams, we returned to Caer-hûn. At the request of Mrs. Griffith, I saw an overshot mill in the vicinity, turned by a stream that tumbles over a rude blue stone rock, which has been worn, by the eddying of the water, into very singular forms. It certainly is very romantic; and the mill on the left, uplifted upon a precipice, greatly adds to the effect. The sides of the rocks exhibit a variety of shapes, which give to the whole an interest which is of value to a drawing. It was a favourite spot with Sir George Beaumont.

From hence I proceeded, a little further, to Roe. This village discovers vestiges of a tremendous burst of waters from the mountains, a few years ago. The torrent hurled down immense and numberless blocks of stone, which tore up a fine meadow and carried with it a mill and several houses: the river has since changed its course. Here are several ivy-covered cottages, which would gratify the artist. One of them would entice me twenty miles to see it.

Next morning, after taking leave of Mrs. Griffith and Miss Williams, whose politeness to me demand my warmest acknowledgments, I set out across the hills for Aber, under the oppression of a scorching sun. For the space of six miles, I met with nothing to diversify a scene, barren and uninteresting, till I came to two upright stones, called y Ddeu-faen, from which the pass takes its name, Bwlch y Ddeu-faen. Many are the conjectures respecting their origin. Tradition says, that a great giant and giantess, on their way to Anglesey, met a man on the spot with a wallet upon his shoulder, of whom they inquired how far it might be to Anglesey. The man replied, that it was so far that he had worn out all the shoes which filled his wallet, in his journey from thence. On hearing this, the giant, with much ease, put down the stones, his body occupying the space between, which, I should suppose, can be no less than one hundred and fifty yards: the giantess also dropped her apronfull of small stones, which, in a large heap, lie close to one of the two larger ones, and is called Barclodiad y Gawres, or the Giantess's Apron-full. This huge fellow and his wife, it seems, were going to reside in Mona, with the first inhabitants, and the stones were intended for stepping-stones to cross the Menai, which separates the island from the continent. But this absurd story must give place to more rational opinions. It is, with more propriety, conjectured, that these stones were placed at the head of the graves of some persons distinguished for valour or virtue. The heap of stones, or Carnedd, was opened a few years ago, with a view of finding treasure, and a large stone chest was found, which is yet to be seen, but without any article within that might lead to a discovery of its original use. The circumstance of a chest being there, however, marks it to have been a place of sepulture, as skeletons of men have been discovered in similar situations. These stones, indeed, are not now without their use, as they serve for guides and land-marks to those who travel this dreary pass in winter, when a strong north wind forms a drift of snow under the rising ground, which is contiguous to them.

Pressing forward, I gained the summit of this pass, and on my right was the rugged top of Penmaenmawr, which, from this point, is so much subdued, that it communicates no terrors to the exalted mountain-traveller, though its northern precipice presents horrors to the passenger on that side. On its summit are the ruins of an irregular British fortification, of great strength; and, according to Mr. Caswell (who, at the request of Mr. Flamstead, took its latitude), on a point of elevation above the sea of no less than five hundred and fifteen yards.

Sir Dafydd Owen, an eminent poet, in one of his very humorous poems, describes the hermit of Penmaen, who, in Henry VIII's time, lived on or near this rock; and asserts that he had been robbed by one Thomas *Goch* and his companions. The poem concludes with a catalogue (most humorously given) of the "*good things* found in this *cell of mortification* and *penance*."

From thence the sea and the island of Anglesey appeared, as in a map, beneath me. A little further I came in sight of a rock, called (I believe) Maes y Gaer, which looked like a mighty fortress, impregnable against the attack of the most powerful and obstinate enemy. I now descended into the vale of Aber, amidst scenery perfectly picturesque. The waterfall here is perpendicular, and of great height; and falling into a basin below, makes its way through a craggy bed, till it is swallowed up in the bay of Beaumaris. The artist will be pleased with a sight of this picturesque hollow, especially when the bridge, and a most enchanting group of houses, come in view. It embraces, also, some noble rocks, on each side of the river.

At the entrance of this hollow from the sea, is an artificial mount, once the site of a castle, where Llywelyn the Great occasionally resided. William de Breos, son of Reginald, a baron of the time of Henry III., by the chance of war fell into the hands of Llywelyn. William, during his captivity, is said to have been in favour with the princess: a circumstance which, after his ransom, came to the knowledge of Llywelyn; who, the following year, 1229, inveigled him into this palace, with the pretence of celebrating the feast of Easter. When the banquet was over, the prince, with the countenance of an injured man, reproached Breos with his crime, and caused him to be instantly hung on the acclivity of a contiguous hill. One of Llywelyn's bards accidentally meeting the princess (who then knew nothing of the affair), addressed her in Welsh, of which the following lines are a translation :—

BARD. "Tell me, wife of Llewelyn,
What would you give for a sight of your William ?
PRINCESS. "Wales, England, and Llewelyn to boot,
I would give them all to see my William."

Upon which the bard pointed to her favourite, suspended on a tree.

I now came to the neat little inn at Aber: but it is necessary to remark, that it would be all lost time for the artist to follow my steps from Caer-hûn. The road and scenery is much preferable from Caer-hûn to Conway, and from thence by the seashore, under the huge Penmaen to this house; which he should not pass without seeing the hollow and fall just described.

Availing myself of the opportunity of an ebb-tide, I crossed the Lafan Sands* in the country fashion, barefooted, and keeping in view the white house opposite, for four miles. Here I found a grotesque group of fishwomen asleep, and lying like so many porpoises basking in the sun. Unwilling to allow the opportunity for amusement to escape me, I stepped over one, and standing in the midst, with all the vigour my lungs were capable of, I set up a halloo; and the scene that followed must have set in motion the risible muscles of the merry goddess, had she been present. They raised a concert of the most discordant sounds I ever heard, one crawling one way, a second another, a third running off, while a fourth, unable to move, owing to her extreme corpulence, cried out for help, "A boat, a boat, for Heaven's sake!" Thus they were put in a terrible uproar, supposing the surrounding tide ready to overwhelm them. I soon calmed their fears; and after making the usual signal, a boat put off, and we all got over to the opposite shore in high glee.

The landing-place here is a projecting gravelly bank, anciently

* These sands are more properly called Traeth Telafan, and Wylofaen, or the Place of Weeping, from its having been overwhelmed by the sea in the time of Helig ab Glanog, and the inhabitants, in consequence, shrieking and making a great lamentation.

called Penrhyn Safnes, and afterwards denominated Osmund's Air, from the following circumstance:—A malefactor of the name of Osmund, on his way to execution, jocularly told the populace that the appearance of an individual going along the strand, need not occasion so much disquietude of mind as was so apparent in their countenances, "*for he was only going to take the air!*"

The Tyrers, a family who have long held this ferry under the corporation of Beaumaris, are, much to their credit, extremely careful of the passengers over the sands; and it is hardly necessary to say that the passage should never be attempted on the approach of night, no accident having ever happened to those who cross at the proper time, when the wind is not too high; of which the stranger may be correctly informed at the village of Aber, which he leaves when he enters on the sands.

A walk of half a mile brought me to Beaumaris*. This is the county-town of Anglesey. It is populous, has some good houses, and is compactly built. It has of late years been a place of great resort for Irish families, who fled hither from the incivil commotions of that distracted country. These emigrants contribute much to the enlivening of the neighbourhood. The town lies so low, that it is scarcely two yards above high-water mark; yet it never suffers from the liquid element in the most furious tempests. Its situation is very pleasant, commanding the fine range of mountains from Caernarvon to Conway, together with that awful and sublime pass called Nant Francon,

* The name, Beaumaris, is a compound of the two French words *beau*, (fair), and *marais*, (marsh). The castle was built on a place called *Bonover* marsh, therefore Edward I. called the town Beaumaris.

which, when viewed from hence in lowering weather, is so truly tremendous, that from its appearance, as I suppose, it has acquired the name of the Devil's Kitchen. Lord Penrhyn's grounds look well from hence. Northwards are the rocks of Great Ormeshead and Puffin island.

The castle is in a very low situation, and on a level with the town; a circumstance very unusual in Wales. Its remains are considerable, and discover very great strength. Its area is a surface of one hundred and ninety feet, having small obtuse angles, rendering its shape somewhat octangular. It was erected by Edward I., in 1295, and had an envelope, which is now imperfect. It was originally surrounded by a fosse, supplied from the sea: which answered the purpose not only of defence, but of a canal for the convenience of small craft, to unload their cargoes on the quays: and part of this canal existed a few years since. The form of this castle is far less handsome than those of Conway and Caernarvon. The towers are ten in number, and are low and heavy in appearance, as if strength, which Edward deemed necessary to curb the spirit of a martial people, and not beauty of architecture, had been his object. The governor's apartments were in the extremity of the area. The hall is seventy feet long, and twenty-three and a half broad, and has five windows in front. The approach seems to have been through a sub-hall, by a flight of steps. Within the walls on one side is a beautiful chapel, in form of a theatre, the sides ornamented with Gothic arches, and the roof supported by ribs springing from elegant pilasters, between each of which is a narrow window, and behind some are small closets, gained out of the thickness of the wall, probably allotted to the officers, or persons of rank. A narrow gallery runs the whole space of the castle-walls.

The entrance faces the sea, and near it is a long narrow advanced-work, called the Gunner's-Walk.

The first governor was Sir William Pickmore, a Gascon Knight, appointed by Edward I. There was a constable of the castle, and a captain of the town. The first had an annual fee of forty pounds, the last, of twelve pounds three shillings and fourpence; and the porter of the gate of Beaumaris had nine pounds two shillings and sixpence. Twenty-four soldiers were allowed for the guard of the castle and town, and fourpence a day to each.

The constable of the castle was always captain of the town, except in one instance;—in the thirty-sixth of Henry VI., Sir John Boteler held the first office, and Thomas Norreys the other.

The castle was extremely burdensome to the country, quarrels were frequent between the garrison and the country people.—In the time of Henry VI. a bloody fray happened, in which Dafydd ap Evan ap Howell of Leoydiarth, and many others, were slain.

From the time of Sir Rowland Villeville, alias Brittayne, a reputed base son of Henry VII., and constable of the castle, the garrison was withdrawn till the year 1642, when Thomas Cheadle, deputy of the Earl of Dorset, the constable, put into it men and ammunition. In 1643, Thomas Bulkeley, Esq., soon after created Lord Bulkeley, succeeded:—his son, Colonel Richard Bulkeley, and several gentlemen of the country, held it for the King till June, 1646, when it surrendered on honourable terms to General Mytton, who made Captain Evans his Deputy-Governor. In 1653, the annual expense of the garrison was seventeen hundred and three pounds.

Edward I., when he built the town, surrounded it with walls, made it a corporation, and endowed it with great privileges, and lands to a considerable value. He removed the ancient freeholders, by exchange of property, into other counties. Henlŷs, near the town, was the seat of Gwerydd ap Rhys Goch, one of the fifteen tribes, and of his posterity till this period, when Edward removed them to Bodlewyddan, Flintshire, and bestowed their ancient patrimony on the corporation. It sends one member to parliament. Its first representative was Maurice Gwyffydd, who sat in the seventh year of Edward VI.

There is very good anchorage for ships in the bay which lies before the town; and has seven fathom of water even at the lowest ebb. Vessels often find security here in hard gales. The town has no trade of any kind, yet has its custom-house, for the casual reception of goods. The ferry lies near the town, and is passable at low water. It was granted by charter to the corporation, in the fourth of Queen Elizabeth. I find an order from Edward II. to Robert Power, chamberlain of North Wales, to inspect into the state of the boat, which was then out of repair; and, in case it was feasible, to cause it to be made fit for use, at the expense of the bailiwick; but if the boat proved past repair, a new one was to be built, and the expense allowed by the king. It appears that the people of Beaumaris paid annually, for the privilege of a ferry, thirty shillings into the Exchequer; but by this order it seems that the king was to find the boat. After passing the Channel, the distance over the sands to Aber in Carnarvonshire, the point the passenger generally makes for, is four miles. The sands are called Traeth Telaven, and Wylsfaen, or the Place of Weeping, from the shrieks and lamentations of the inhabitants when it was overwhelmed by the sea, in the days of Helig ap Clunog.

The church is dependent on Llandegvan, which is the gift of

Lord Bulkeley. The former is called the Chapel of the Blessed Virgin; yet in ancient writings one aisle is called St. Mary's Chapel, and another that of St. Nicholas. In the first is a beautiful monument of a knight and his lady in white alabaster, placed recumbent on an altar-tomb. It had been removed to this place on the dissolution, from the religious house at Llanvaes, and the memory and names of the persons represented lost.

A barbarous custom in the feudal system prevailed in this island, and possibly in many other parts. Here was exemplified the power of a lord to sell his vassals and their offspring, as he would the cattle of his estate. It was done in the township of Perthaethwy, many years after the reign of our princes. The deed of sale in this instance is not extant; but I find among Mr. Rowland's manuscripts three specimens, of which the following is the full form of the cruel usage.

"Ednyfed Vychan ap Ednyfed, alias dictus Ednyfed ap Arthelw ap Davydd ap Gryffyd et Howel ap Davydd ap Ryryd, alias dictus Howel ap Arthelw ap Davydd ap Gryffyd, Liberi tenentes Dm Regis villæ de Rhandir Gadog, *&c.* dedimus et confirmavimus Willimo ap Gryffydd ap Gwilim armigero et libero tenenti de Porthamel, *&c.* septem nativos nostros, viz. Howel ap Davydd Dew, Matto ap Davydd Dew, Jevan ap Evan Ddu, Llewelyn ap Davydd Dew, Davydd ap Matto ap Davydd Dew, Howell ap Matto ap Davydd Dew, et Llewelyn ap Evan Coke, cum eorum sequelis tum procreatis tam procreandis ac omnibus bonis catellis, *&c.* habend, *&c.* prædictos nativos nostros, *&c.* præfato Willimo Gryffyd ap Gwilim heredibus et assignatis suis in perpetuum. Datum apud Rhandir Gadog, 20 die Junii, an. Henr. 6ti. 27mo.

I took a walk northwards to see the remains of Lleiniog-castle;

I found it completely enveloped in brush-wood, and with some difficulty ascended the artificial mount upon which it stands. Its figure is a quadrangle, having in each corner the remains of a round tower, three of which are pretty entire. This very small castle (for one side of the area I believe does not exceed fourteen yards), surrounded by a fosse, was erected in 1098, by Hugh Lupus, earl of Chester, and Hugh de Montgomery, earl of Shrewsbury; or, as the Welsh ironically call them, the Fat Hugh of Chester, and the Red Hugh of Shrewsbury. When Magnus, king of Norway, attempted to land here, one of his men, an expert bowman, shot the earl of Shrewsbury in the eye; and Magnus, seeing him in the agonies of death, cried out, "Leit loup!" Let him dance! A punishment merited for the cruelties committed by him and Lupus on the poor inhabitants. Lupus, after this disaster, quitted Anglesey, and spent his rage upon the promontory of Llyn in Carnarvonshire, which was thus made desolate for seven years; from thence he returned to Chester, where he died.

This fort was garrisoned, and held out for the parliament in the civil wars, by Sir Thomas Cheadle*, but in the year 1645 it surrendered to Colonel Robinson. I returned and passed Fryers, the seat of Sir Robert Williams, Bart.: it is a house not regular in its form, and its situation low, being nearly on a level with the sea at high water; Sir Robert, however, seems to

* Of this family was the facetious and playful Dr. Rowland Cheadle, rector of Beaumaris in 1647. He once drew a lady of the name of Price for his Valentine, on February 14, and sent her this couplet:—

"Good Madam, would the man, who you thus meets
"In these small papers, meet you in *whole sheets*."

have spared no expense; and by a judicious management of the surrounding grounds, has rendered it a comfortable and handsome residence. Close to the road and house are the remains of the monastery of Llanvaes: whatever might have been its appearance in its original state, it is certain, that at present, it holds forth no temptation to the artist: it has been converted into a barn, and is precisely of that same common appearance. It was erected by Llewelyn ap Jorwerth over the grave of his Princess Joan, who died in 1240 (and whose coffin formerly served for a watering-trough, but has lately been removed from its state of degradation, and placed under an elegant Gothic building, in a beautiful situation in the grounds at Baron-hill); and was consecrated the same year by Howell, Bishop of Bangor, and dedicated to St. Francis; a few years afterwards it was burnt, when Madoc raised an insurrection in the country; at which time Edward II. saw the sufferings of the brotherhood, and refused to receive the taxes due to him. At the dissolution, Henry VIII. sold it, together with the farm of Cremlyn Monach, tithes, *&c.*, to one of his favourite courtiers. The son of a Danish king, Lord Clifford, and others who fell in the wars with the Welsh, were buried here.

"With all the future glowing in her breast,
There England's royal daughter chose to rest,
On Menai's shelly margin sought repose,
When life should draw its troubles to a close;
And then, directed by a husband's care,
The roof monastic rose, and frequent prayer:
Now Harvest's annual treasure fills the dome
That once resounded with the rites of Rome!" *Beaumaris Bay.*

Leaving Beaumaris, a pleasant walk of three miles led me to Tros y Marion, the comfortable residence of the Rev. Mr. Lewis.

E. Pugh del.^t T. Cartwright sculp.^t

PRINCESS JOAN'S COFFIN LID.

Published 15 Novr 1814 by E Williams Strand.

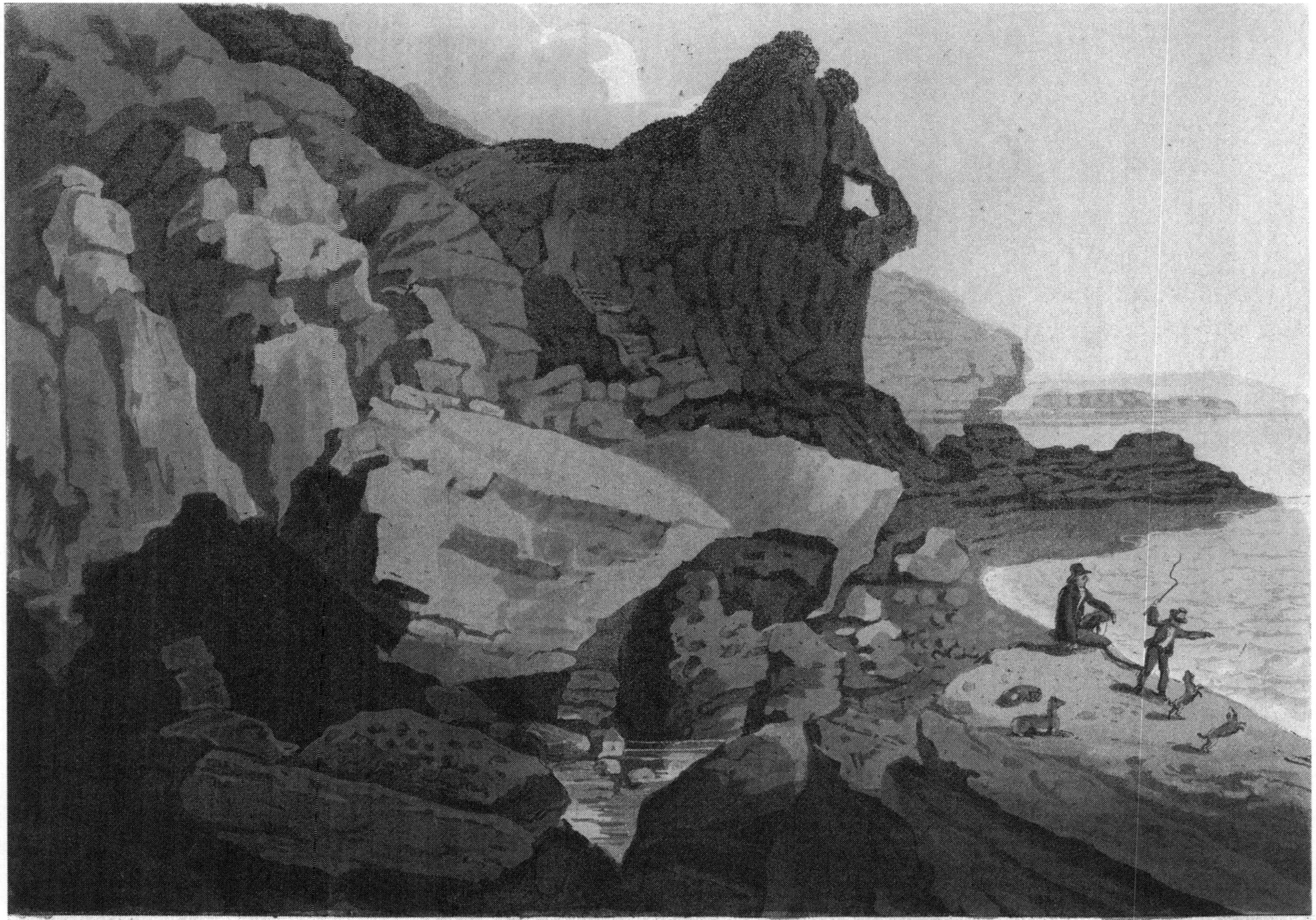

E. Pugh del.^t T. Cartwright sculp.^t

BISHOP'S THRONE ANGLESEY.

Published 16 July 1813 by E. Williams Strand.

Here I proposed to commence an examination of the cliffs around the island. Strangers, and particularly artists, who visit the Carnarvonshire mountains, are so prepossessed against Anglesey, owing to its low and uninteresting appearance, that they very seldom think it worth their while to spend a few days in it. From some slight information which I received respecting its shores, I was determined to make the circuit of the island. Mr. Lewis very obligingly ordered his boat, and we sailed several miles on the coast, amidst abundance of fine scenery. The whimsical rock, called the Bishop's Throne, is certainly an excellent subject: its form is an irregular cone, so perforated by time that it requires no great stretch of imagination to fancy it the throne of a prelate*, preaching to the fishes. The amazing fragments of rocks, or rather blocks of stone, that lie so disorderly on the shore, are covered over with an incrustation of small shell-fish, resembling cockles, which strongly adheres to them. The shore is very rude, and terrific to navigators, and many of its rocks are fine and picturesque, rising to a great height.

"Here sea-gulls scream and cormorants rejoice,
And mariners, though shipwrecked, dread to land."

These craggy prominences afford shelter to that wily animal the fox; and the best dogs find great difficulty to unhouse him. While we were looking for a proper place to land, one of these rogues started, ran several hundred yards, and eluded the utmost speed of some fine dogs that followed a young gentleman on shore.

We proceeded a little way up the country, to see Arthur's Round Table, a piece of ground of about two acres, considerably

* Saint Anthony of Padua.

raised above the main land, which nature has walled round with a solid rock. There are evident marks of its being once a fortress of strength, supposed to have been a British post. It is surrounded by two rows of unchisseled stones. The area shews slight vestiges of buildings. It is excellently situated as an exploratory fort, and probably might have been such, when the northern invaders troubled this country, the sea being open to the eye to a vast distance. The ancient name of this impregnable post is Din Sylwy. It is, according to the other name it bears, circular; Arthur preferring the circle for the form of his board, that no disputes about precedence might arise at the public entertainment of the ancient military sport, the Tournament*.

The next day I visited Priestholm island, or, as it is sometimes called, Puffin island. The entrance into it is broad, which indicates the island to have been a place much resorted to in former times; but on gaining the summit, I was a little surprised to find so desolate a place, extending three-fourths of a mile, and literally half covered with those indolent birds called puffins. They lay one white egg † each, sometimes on the bare rock, but generally in rabbit-holes, and in burrows made by the males. They appear about the 5th of April, and continue till the 11th of August, or two or three days after. Male and female sit alternately, and the absent bird goes in pursuit of food. These birds did not attempt to avoid us by flight till we were within the distance of two or three yards. Their endeavour to raise themselves from the ground seemed very awkward, and was attended with much apparent difficulty: but

* See Nevin.

† It is thought they do not breed till the third year.

when fairly on the wing, they flew with velocity. We walked to the extremity of the island, the boatman frequently shoving his arm up to the shoulder in the burrows, and bringing out the young puffins, to examine whether they were ripe, or fit to take. Lord Bulkeley is the proprietor of the island, which is farmed to this man and one or two others, who take the young birds when not yet able to fly, pickle, and put them in barrels of twelve inches long; thus they are sold at about three or four shillings per barrel, sent to different parts of England, and are accounted a great luxury. In the same manner are the large Penmon oysters treated, and sent away in small casks, and are also esteemed a rarity. One circumstance respecting these birds is remarkable. On leaving the country, they do not wait for the unfledged birds of the latter hatches, which fall a prey to the Peregrin falcon, that waits for them at the mouth of the burrows.

I was shewn the grave of two unfortunate mariners. At the head is an upright stone, with this inscription:—

"Bar. Stout, Belonging to the Sally, died in the small-pox, Nov. 3d, 1767. N. B. The ship was cast away here."

I was not a little mortified to find that the best of arguments, money, was unable to prevail on the boatman to take me round the island, as he alleged that the current would retard his return, if not prevent it till the next tide. I was therefore obliged to take a cursory view of this rocky shore, which is very bold: but am persuaded, had I had the good fortune to go round, its attractions would have repaid me for my trouble. The tremendous and massy blocks of stone that lie so rudely on the south-west shore, some raised upon others to a great height, seemed dreadful to approach. They have a good effect when opposed to the rocky cliffs above, full of cavities occasioned by the dislodgment of these stones, and they contribute much to render this side a subject for the pencil. I believe I may rely upon the information afterwards communicated to me, that the stranger will not count it lost time to sail round, and the best way would be, to hire a proper boat, *&c.*, at Beaumaris.

" ———— in yonder peopled rocks,
To whose wild solitude, from worlds unknown,
The birds of passage transmigrating come;
Unnumbered colonies of foreign wing,
At Nature's summons, their aerial state
Annual to found, and in bold voyage steer
O'er this wide ocean, through yon pathless sky,
One certain flight, to one appointed shore;
By Heaven's directive spirit here to raise
Their temporary realm, and form secure,
Where food awaits them copious from the wave,
And shelter from the rock, their nuptial leagues;
Each tribe apart, and all on tasks of love,
To hatch the pregnant egg, to rear and guard
Their helpless infants, piously intent." MALLET.

This island was originally (and is yet by the natives) called Ynys Seiriol, from St. Seiriol, who resided upon it in the sixth century. Priestholm is its other name, from its being occasionally visited by the priests of Penmon, on the opposite shore; holm being the Norse word for island.

Having left the island, we floated over the place where, tradition says, one Helig Voel ab Glanog, a chieftain of the sixth century, had great possessions, extending far into this bay; but which were suddenly overwhelmed by the sea. It is said that at very low ebbs ruined houses are yet seen, and a causeway, pointing from Priestholm-island to Penmaenmawr. This causeway, indeed, is easily visible; the boatman placing me right over it, and keeping the boat's head to the tide, enabled me to examine it well: but, though so clearly seen as to appear near to the surface, the man assured me that it could not be less than two or three fathoms below it. It seemed to be about nine feet wide, well built, with large massy stones cut into forms, of a light warm grey colour, in all respects like those on the sides of the adjacent isle. From the certainty of the existence of this causeway, we may venture to give credit to the existence of the remains of Helig's houses. Helig, after the awful visitation just related, embraced a religious life; and his twelve children followed his example.

Arriving on the Anglesey shore, I went to see Penmon priory, founded in the sixth century, by Maelgwyn Gwynedd, king of Wales. Idwal, son of Gryffydd ab Cynan, prince of North Wales, was Prior in thc year 1140. This Gryffydd ab Cynan left legacies to many religious houses: to that of Bangor two hundred and forty pence; and to this priory, one hundred and twenty pence. To the reader these may appear small donations, but it is said that these two sums are "more than equivalent to one hundred and fifty guineas at this day." Llywelyn ab Jorwerth refounded this house, which he took care to fill with monks of the order of St. Benedict; and, in the sixth year of her reign, Queen Elizabeth presented it to John Moore. At the dissolution, its revenues were estimated at 47*l.* 15*s.* 3*d.**

The ancient refectory of the priory, though so much in ruins as to disappoint the artist, may yet afford pleasure to the

* Dugdale Monast. ii. 338.

antiquary. The mansion-house at one end is attached to it, and at the other it is connected to the parish church, forming three sides of a square court, which, over a parapet wall, looks to the east.

The serious mind who may visit the refectory, will easily be led to contemplation on beholding a room which at one time received and fed the hungry monks, who now, for ages past, have bid adieu to all sublunary pleasures, of the monastery, and the world.

> "Y llwybrau gynt, lle bur gan
> Yw lleodd y Ddulluan."
>
> JEUAN BRYDYDD HIR, *a Poet who flourished about* 1440.

> "Where erst ascended Music's grateful tones,
> The moping owl in nightly discord moans." LLWYD.

To Mr. and Mrs. Lewis, of Tros y Marion, my warmest thanks are due, for their very kind attention, and to the former particularly, for the promptitude with which he several times accompanied me in his boat to view the shore. Taking my leave, I directed my steps towards Gorslwyd, in the parish of Llandonna, to see Jane Williams, alias Shane Bwt, or little Jane; who, among her poor neighbours, is a reputed witch. Overtaking a woman on a common, I requested to be directed to Jane's house. The woman expressed her surprise that I should like to visit her, and earnestly cautioned me to take the utmost care not to offend her, for that she could, at pleasure, overwhelm me in numberless difficulties. "A twelve-month ago," continued she, "a young man in this neighbourhood felt the fatal effects of a quarrel with her, the enchantress having doomed him to perpetual drunkenness, who, before this brawl, was noted for sobriety." I endeavoured to impress on this woman's mind the

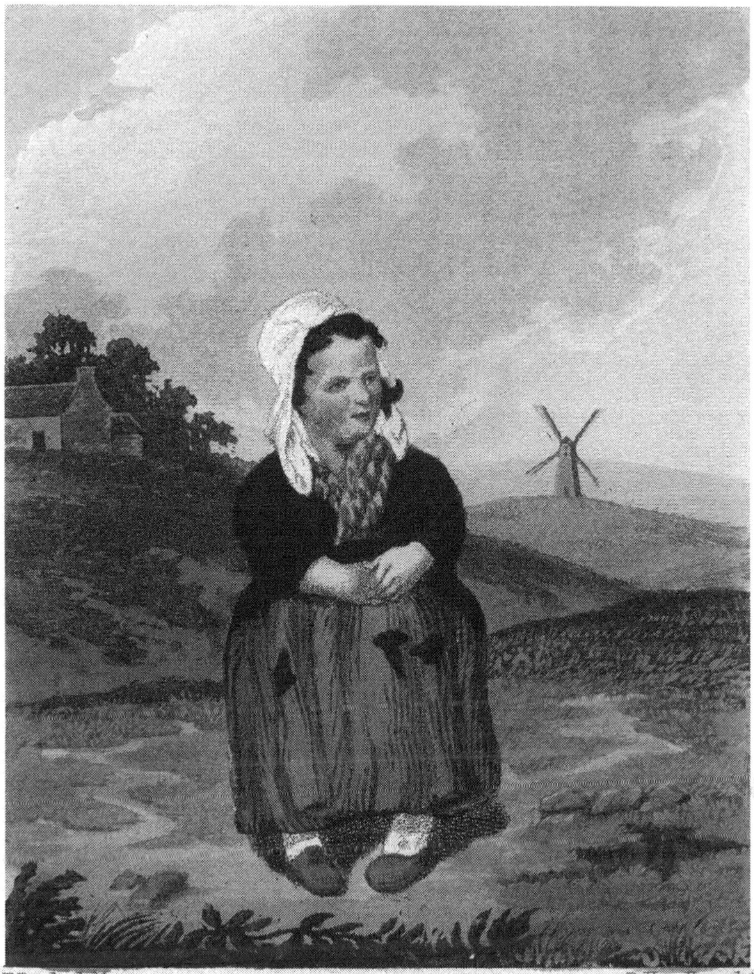

E. Pugh delt. R. Havell sculpt.

SHÂNE BWT.

Published 25 February 1815, by E. Williams, Strand.

evil of such reproachful aspersions, and the necessity of chasing away such absurd opinions. She had probably imbibed them in the neighbourhood, where prejudices generally run high against those poor objects to whom the great Designer and Modeller of the human figure, for reasons too deep for the scanty powers of our minds to fathom, has thought proper to deny those just proportions and symmetry of body which generally belong to man. On knocking at the door of Jane's cottage, which we soon reached, it was opened to us by an old woman, whose head and shoulders, bearing a downward inclination, bespoke extreme age, and who very civilly requested to know my business. I told her that I should be glad to see her daughter Jane. "Sir," said she, "Jane is not at home, but I will send this boy to fetch her." During a space of twenty minutes, I was in conversation with the good old woman and her second daughter, who is a young married woman, well grown, and very handsome. On my observing that all I wanted was a portrait of Jane, they seemed much pleased at the thought: the daughter, however, hoped it was not intended, by this portrait, to do any thing which might hurt the feelings of an already distressed family. I replied that, on the contrary, it was my intention to serve them. They were perfectly satisfied. A little boy now announced the arrival of Jane, who made her appearance, and was so bashful, that it required some persuasion, on her sister's part and my own, to prevail on her to stand steadily while I sketched her: however, she behaved very well. Her portrait, attached to this work, will convey to the reader a better idea of her person, than I am able to express with my pen. Her height is forty-four inches, her age forty years. On her left hand are two thumbs. She lives upon the charity of her benevolent and enlightened neighbours, with whom indeed she is a favourite.

Her father, who has been dead some years, was less than she is; and it is said of him, that when bringing home upon his shoulders a load of fuel from the common, strangers were often puzzled to make out so strange a sight as a moving stack of fern, without the least appearance of any living creature to convey it. This cot stands exactly on the lower road from Beaumaris to Amlwch and Paris mine, over the Red-wharf sands.

Proceeding along this road, I came to these sands, and, being low water, I crossed them for the distance of two miles and a half. The shore here is low, and without interest; and though the great lime-stone quarry is extensive, and of much height, it holds no temptation to the artist, as it is not at all broken to his wishes, and its side resembles a wall of great elevation. Crossing another small bay, I came to a public-house at Penllech. I was now hungry enough to enjoy a dinner, but, upon inquiry, the house afforded nothing better than poached eggs, and the old national treat, a Welsh *rare-bit*. I was handed the bottle of brandy, which, diluted, proved an excellent cooling drink in a hot day. Nor Captain Gadd's nor the Brass Knocker *, with all their variety of dishes and delicacies, or their choice of liquids, could rival the feast I enjoyed at this humble cot. Fine weather, added to the pleasure of a view of an extensive sea, fixed me to the spot for two hours; after which I proceeded, and now and then turning out of the road to see the shore, found a continued flatness for several miles. Passing Llanallgo, and near Dulas, I met an aged woman, whom I addressed in

* Two celebrated eating-houses in the purlieus of Chancery-lane and Carey-street, so named by some East-India officers, who frequented them.

Welsh, and inquired if I was on the road to Amlwch, she said I was on the right way to that place. Eying my portfolio under my arm, she asked, why I carried such a large book.—I replied for my amusement on the road.—" Did you bring it a long way, sir?" " From London." " From London," said the old woman, eagerly catching hold of my arm, " From London, sir! God bless you, sir, do you know John Thomas, was he well? O call at his mother's house, which is on your way, and how happy will she be to hear from him."—Owing to the rapidity with which she spoke this, I found it impossible to say, I did not know John Thomas, and she proceeded, and said, that John Thomas was a most clever young man, whose merits and indefatigable industry in his master's service, were justly appreciated by him.—John Thomas was become the head man in the shop, and so well has he secured the confidence of his employer, that John only knows the value of his effects, which are solely under his command.

CHAPTER II.

Paris Mines.—Amlwch.—Llanelian.—Cromlech.—Llanrhyddlad.—Skerries Light-House.—Hugh Rowland.—Holyhead.—Wakes.—Caves of Mynydd Twr.—Accidents.—Packets.—Roman Work.—Penrhos.—Cromlechs.—Aber-Ffraw.—Fine Scenery.—Malldraeth Sands.—Bodorgan.—Newborough.—The Metropolis of the Druids.—Cromlechs no Altars.—Mistletoe.—Plasnewydd.—The Welsh Youths neglected.—Bangor Ferry.—Cadnant.—New Road by the Menai.—Llandysilio Church.—Tre yr Carneydd.—Gwyndy.—Ancient Prisons.—Llanerch y Medd.—Bodofon Mountain.—Bed of the Tudors.—John Davies.—Plaspenmynydd.—Owen Tudor and Catharine of Valois.

I REACHED Amlwch just as our hemisphere was putting on her night-cap:—The country I had passed affords no variety to amuse the traveller; it is very bare of wood, nor do good houses frequently occur: if this road is at all desirable, it must be on account of its being contiguous to the sea. On visiting the copper-mines in the morning, about two miles from hence; I found, that since I was there last, which was about five years before, the internal part had very much altered its appearance; the great and lofty pyramid of copper ore had been destroyed, and also the arch, which at that time was a grand object, has been since converted into pans, kettles, and penny-pieces. When these were standing, this chasm presented a more formidable appearance, and an aspect much more picturesque than at present; it still is sufficiently grand to entice strangers to visit it from all parts of Great Britain. To professional painters, this vast hollow is very little known; but I can, with the greatest confidence,

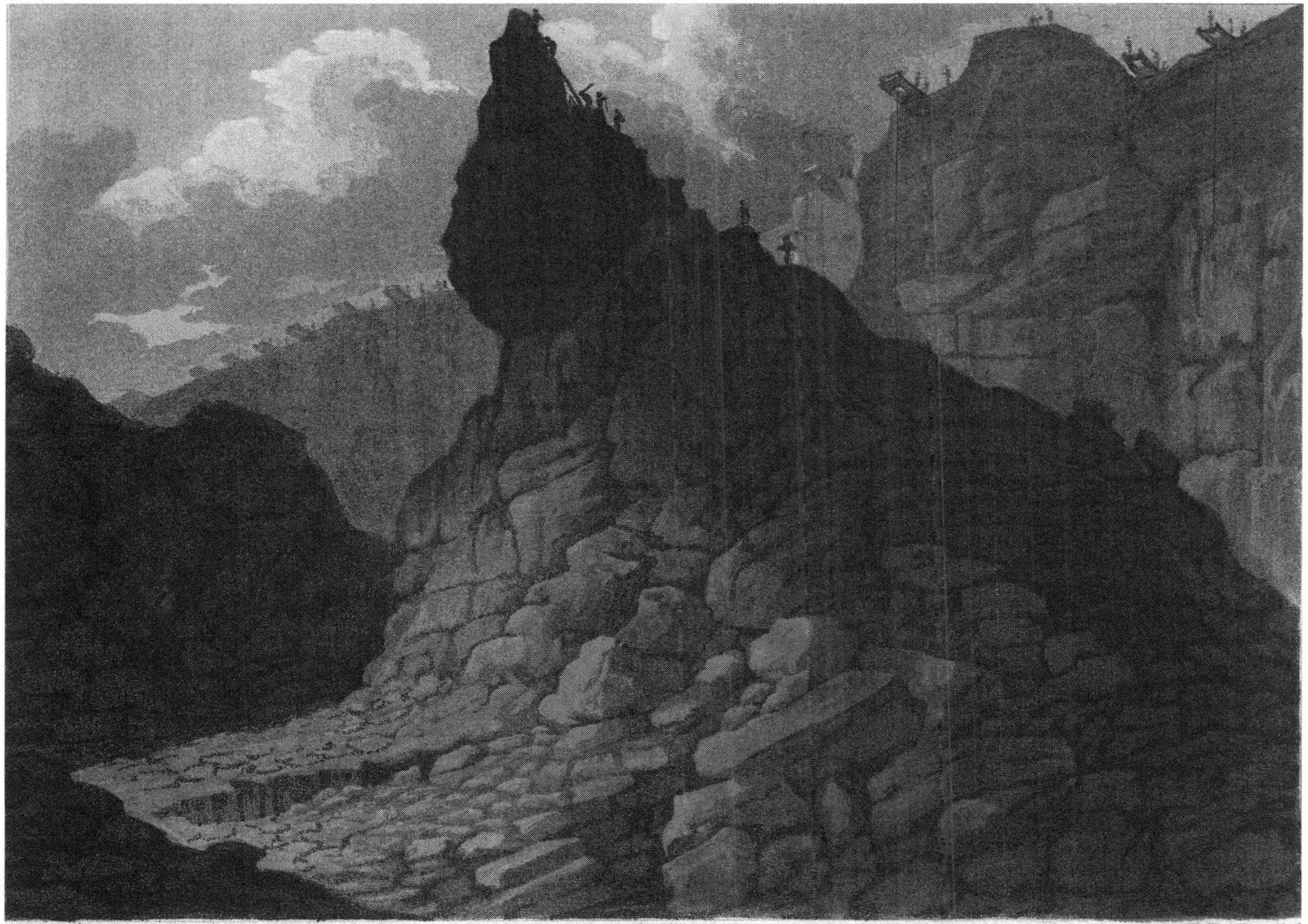

E. Pugh delt. I. Havell sculpt.

PARIS MINES IN THE YEAR 1800.

Published 15 January 1814, by E. Williams Strand.

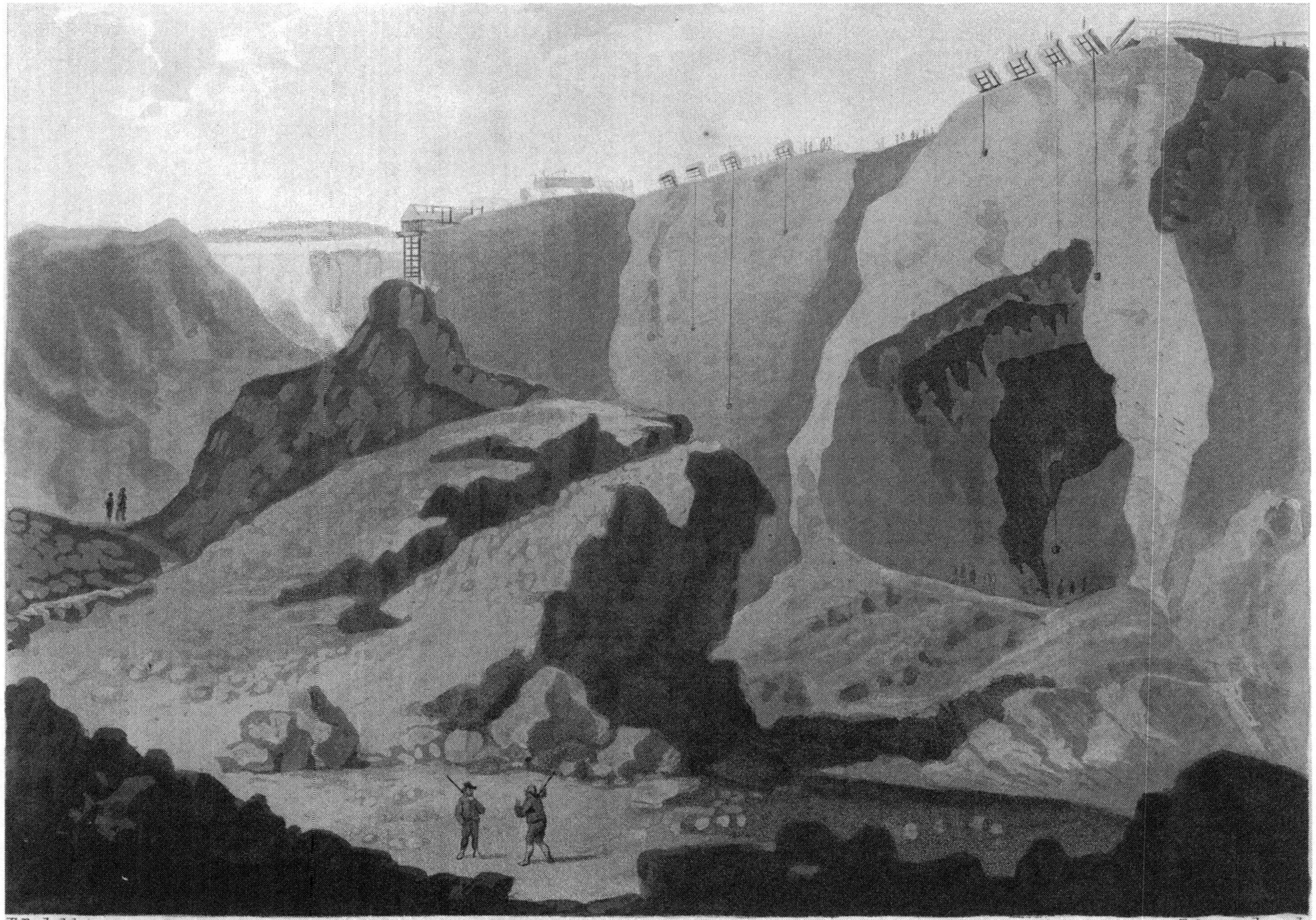

E. Pugh del. T. Cartwright sculp.

PARIS MINES IN 1804.

Published 15 June, 1813 by E. Williams, Strand.

recommend those who are alive to, and know the value of, scenery so sublime, to spend a day or two there.—The great cave, so long as it may retain its present form, is a subject by itself; but the mine will afford the artist a variety, and if he be a man of taste, he will feel highly gratified with the sight. It is necessary for those who descend to take a guide with them, for, from the frequent blasting of the rocks, they will otherwise be in danger, from the situation which they may be in, the workmen not being able to see them. A view of the hollow from above is rather defective, it should be viewed from below:—Even ladies, with trifling assistance, may easily go down. Nothing can impress upon the mind a greater awe than this mine, and all produced by manual labour of thirty years. The circumference of the chasm, is about three quarters of a mile.—The different works above will afford amusement to strangers. On returning to the inn at Amlwch, I found the room allotted to me for breakfast occupied by a number of farmers, for it was market-day. I dined in a corner of the room, and not being known to the party, I soon perceived the conversation, which was in Welsh, turn upon the stranger, who was thought to be English; I was not displeased to hear myself the subject of their jokes, for the unpremeditated wit, so familiar to the Welsh, rather gave me pleasure than offence.—But the Rev. Mr. J. . . . . s had better not have shewn such prompitude in satirical remarks upon a stranger and his faithful dog, for which his genius was so ill calculated; and probably he will not forget the rub he received from a generous little farmer, who soon cooled the fervour with which he attacked them. The afternoon was occupied in a walk to the celebrated Llanelian-church, two miles from Amlwch. Its exterior is handsome, having a battlement round; it has a wing consisting of a small square room, said to have been built by St. Elianus, the patron saint, surnamed Garmaid, or Geimiad, or the Bright. He was a popular saint, to whom numbers flocked to implore his assistance in the cure of various disorders, and they made him great offerings, which were deposited in a chest called Cyff Elian. With the money thus collected, three tenements were purchased, which still belong to the living. These offerings were made at a well, the water of which the patients made use of; it lies half a mile from the church, at the foot of a rock close to the sea;—some parts of the walls that surround it still remain. Amlwch, or *the winding loch*, is a straggling town, raised upon rocks, which prevents it from being built on any regular plan. The port, at the lower extremity of the town, is a busy spot; here is a good dock, made at a great expense, and excavated out of the solid rock. The artist will also find amusement here and upon the craggy shore. Quitting Amlwch early in the morning, I made for Llanrhyddlad. This side of the island is in a high state of cultivation, and by manual industry, every vacuity between the rocks produces the finest crops of grain of all kinds. I passed the small port of Cammaes, and leaving the public road, turned off about a mile to see a Cromlech, near a house so called; it consists of a few upright stones, upon which is laid one of immense size, but owing to some of its supporters giving way, one side of it declines towards the ground. Half a mile off, are the remains of another, which when perfect, must have been handsome; the coping-stone has been carried away, there are three upright stones, standing near nine feet above ground, triangular-wise. Immediately on leaving Cromlech, in a field below the house, I heard a rustling in the grass, right in my path, and pressing it with my foot, a prodigious snake reared its head in a menacing posture; I presently felt the twirling motion of its tail under my foot. With three blows from my umbrella I laid him motionless on the ground, and then conveyed him to the wall hard by, where I found he measured just one yard. My nature is not qualified for deeds of blood, and I have frequently wondered how I could destroy a creature, which though armed with the means of self-defence, yet did me no injury:—Its beautiful marks and colouring, added to its dying agony, made me hasten away from a sight rendered pitiable from a momentary, but warrantable impulse of cruelty.—The residue of this day's walk was not diversified by any one circumstance that could interest the stranger. To the farmers of the neighbourhood indeed, the superabundant crops must have been a grateful sight. I now descended to the little village of Llanrhyddlad, and though personally unknown, I was received by Mr. and Mrs. Williams with that cordiality that has always been the distinguishing character of the Welsh gentry On signifying my intention of prosecuting my journey at noon the next day, an embargo was instantly laid on my person for a longer time. The following morning Mr. Williams's three sons volunteered their services to explore the coast with me: we had not far to go before the shore burst on the sight with a considerable degree of grandeur; the scenery improved much as we neared the level of the sea:—with the exception of the incrusted rock, called the Bishop's Throne, this shore is greatly superior to that near Tros y Marion. The scenery about Carnel's Point is fine, and continues to appear so down as far north as Llanrwydrys.

In every stage of the tide this shore is so rough, that it cannot be passed on foot, and a boat is not easily procured; the rocks are of great height, very much broken, frequently pointed, and in great variety of parts, with fine cliffs jutting nobly into the sea. The Skerries light-house, with the ridge of rocks called the Cardinals, are seen from hence to great advantage; the Skerries has had a light-house on it ever since the reign of Queen Anne, and was, until lately, lighted with coals, at the expense of about £150 per year;—it was last year considerably raised. The building cost rearing £3000. The expense of lighting it with oil, and other charges, is about £1000 annually, and it now produces an average of £4000 per annum to the proprietor, Morgan Jones, Esq., of Cardigan, South Wales. About eighty years back it was purchased for £200. This is a clear demonstration of the amazing increase of the trade of Liverpool, since that period. The light impost on all vessels that pass this light-house, and arrive at Liverpool or Chester, is paid at those places according to their tonnage.

The church of Llanrhyddlad, *or of Free Grace,* contains nothing worthy of notice, save a plain blue slab, commemorating the decease of a worthy man, in the following words: "Underneath lie the remains of Hugh Rowland, late of Ty-mawr, gentleman; he died 14th December, 1781, aged 105." When this gentleman was near 90 years of age, he was requested to serve on the grand jury at Beaumaris. His horses being all busily engaged in the harvest, he performed this Herculean task on foot, a distance of about twenty-five miles, without the least bodily inconvenience. Appearing somewhat uneasy in court, one of the counsellors civilly requested to know the cause of so much apparent disquietude. "Sir," replied the good old man, "in compliance with the mandate of the court, I was obliged, contrary to those feelings which every man ought to possess at

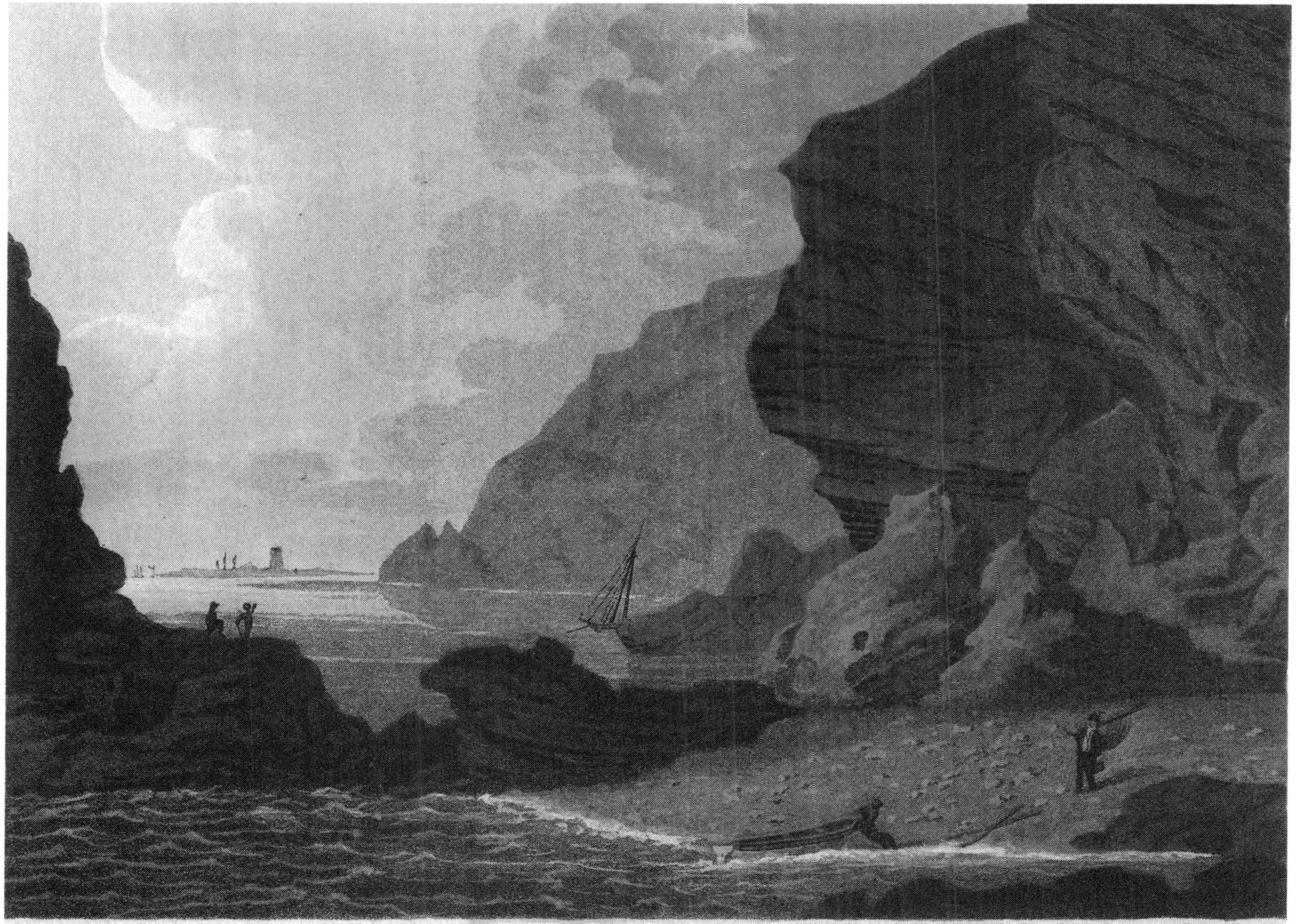

E. Pugh del.t I. Havell sculp.t

THE SKERRIES LIGHTHOUSE.

Published 15 April 1814 by E. Williams Strand.

such a critical time, to leave a young wife, hourly expected in the straw, and my mind is so tortured with the thoughts of being absent from her, who engrosses all my care and affections, that I long to be at home." This speech excited a great deal of admiration in the judges and the court, and he was the same day at liberty to return to his beloved spouse, whom the venerable enamorato met with all the warmth and affection of a more vigorous age.

Mr. Williams's residence is very pleasantly situated on the rise of a hill, and commands a view of Holyhead, and that noble rock above it, called Mynydd Twr: towards the north is seen the Isle of Man, with the boasted hills of the Manks, called Penny-Pot and Snaffield mountains, the latter being five hundred and eighty yards perpendicular height from the surrounding sea. With this mountain and a continued line of hills in view, the house also receives interest from a fine prospect of the sea, frequently exhibiting numerous shipping on the wing for different parts of the globe.

Immediately on quitting Llanrhyddlad, I came upon the grounds of Carreg Lwyd, the seat of Mr. Griffiths, surrounded with wood; the exterior of the house makes a good appearance, but the northerly winds have here similar effects as on the noted wood of Margam Park, in Glamorganshire, and defeat, in some measure, the care and expense evidently employed in the cultivation of the plantations; the nipping influence of these, and other ungenial gales, I have observed on all the coast of the island, except on the south-east side. On all sides, however, planting is greatly neglected in Anglesey; nor (the dread of these nipping gales excepted) have I heard any reason to justify or to excuse this general neglect of the landed proprietors, so injurious to their interests. In some parts we see trees, by the sides of good houses, as shelter, in a flourishing state; evincing at once the power of the soil, and that it is friendly to such cultivation; exertion and a little expense seem only to be wanting. To this want of spirit is owing the nakedness of an island, which at one time was covered with wood; and on that account was called Ynis-dowyll, or the Dark-island. I was told by a gentleman, who seemed to know much of the nature of trees, that were some efforts made to plant quick growing trees in the centre of the island, their success would be certain; and such groups would afford shelter to others, that might be planted in succession, even to the sea-side.

The shore from hence to Holyhead is very tame, and offers nothing for the pencil; the country falling in easy slopes to the verge of the sea. Passing through Llanfachr th, I entered the London road at Llanynghenedl, and came to a common, called Towyn y Capel: near the road is an artificial mount, and on its summit the poor ruins of St. Ffraid's chapel. Mr. Pennant supposes that the mount was originally the site of a small fort.

I arrived at Holyhead the day before the wake, when great preparations were making for the amusements of the week. The following day, by an invitation, I dined at Mr. Jackson's family table, where all the rarities of the season were displayed. The landlord's friends, present, were numerous and respectable, and the cheerful glass went round to every loyal and national toast; here was no compulsion to inordinate drinking, nothing was done or said which could offend the eye, or hurt the feelings of the most rigid, inflexible moralist; on the contrary, the mirthful joke, the ready wit, and the harmless song, created an hilarity that pervaded the whole company. To their honour be

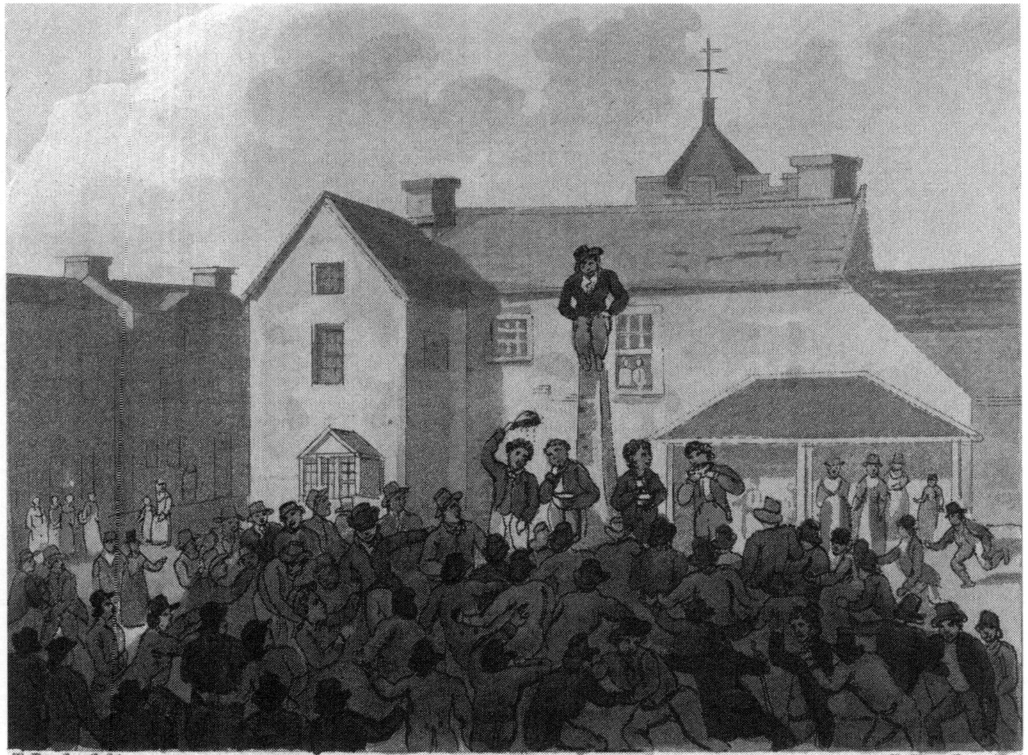

E. Pugh del. *R. Havell sculp.*

HOLYHEAD WAKE.

Published 16 February 1816, by E. Williams, Strand.

it remarked, that the guests, breaking up at an early, but an honest, hour, divided in small parties, and took their walks in the neighbourhood; heedless of the absurd fashion of the times, which prescribes a listless continuance at the table of epicurism, after the just appetites of nature are satisfied.

I have but too often seen it observed by tourists, that the Welsh are an "unpolished and ignorant people;" if at all ignorant, it must be ignorance of those fashionable dissipations, the never-failing promoters of diseases, incident only to the *great* and fashionably *wise*, who take so much pains to secure them; so far as the Welsh are ignorant of such *finished*, such *elegant* refinement of manners, may they ever remain so!

> "Where ignorance is bliss
> 'Tis folly to be wise." GRAY.

The evening presented a scene to me as singular as it was laughable. A collection had been made by the first people of the town, for prizes for different feats of activity, *&c.*; the market-place was greatly crowded, and at seven o'clock, four lusty lads, candidates for three prizes, began the sport of eating hot hasty-pudding immediately from the fire. To see the gestures of the boys, the anxious examination of each other's basins, their blowing into their own, now dipping in their fingers, and then applying them to their mouths, and using every method that fancy could suggest, to despatch their contents, would have made a cynic laugh. I saw determination in the eye of one lad, who seemed resolved upon triumph; and who, in a few minutes, held up his reversed basin in the air, with a shout that begat a general one from the crowd; which was immediately followed by another, for the success of the second competitor; and, shortly after, the third boy was complimented; and received, with the others, a prize proportionate to his abilities; and the tardy fourth, though not entitled to any thing, obtained a small present.

In the retreat, an Irish gentleman, who had placed himself on the higher steps of the obelisk, owing to the pressure of those above him, fell upon the shoulders of a choleric little Welshman; who, fancying an affront, resented it Mendoza-like, and the Hibernian very judiciously retired, to prevent a scene that might easily have followed from the effects of ancient animosity, and a rooted antipathy, that still exist between the Irish and Welsh.

The next morning Mr. Jackson politely offered to conduct me in his boat round the Head, accompanied by a gentleman of Liverpool. We set sail, and for several miles I could discover nothing of the picturesque on the shore, till turning an angle of the rock, my expectations were raised; proceeding a little further, between a small island and the main land, a sight prodigiously fine, which I was not prepared to meet, even by all the encomiums I had heard bestowed upon it, burst suddenly upon us. This was a small bay, the sides of which are composed of rocks of amazing height, in which are several caves of great dimensions, accessible to boats, I may say, to sloops of any size. We entered many yards into the one called the Parliament-house, the full extent of which we could not discover; on one side of it is shewn a piece of rock, taking an upright direction, called the Throne. There are a great number of cormorants, gulls, guillemots, razor-bills, and other aquatic birds, that constantly visit these caverns, making a disagreeable gabbling noise; as if in some mighty debate concerning their

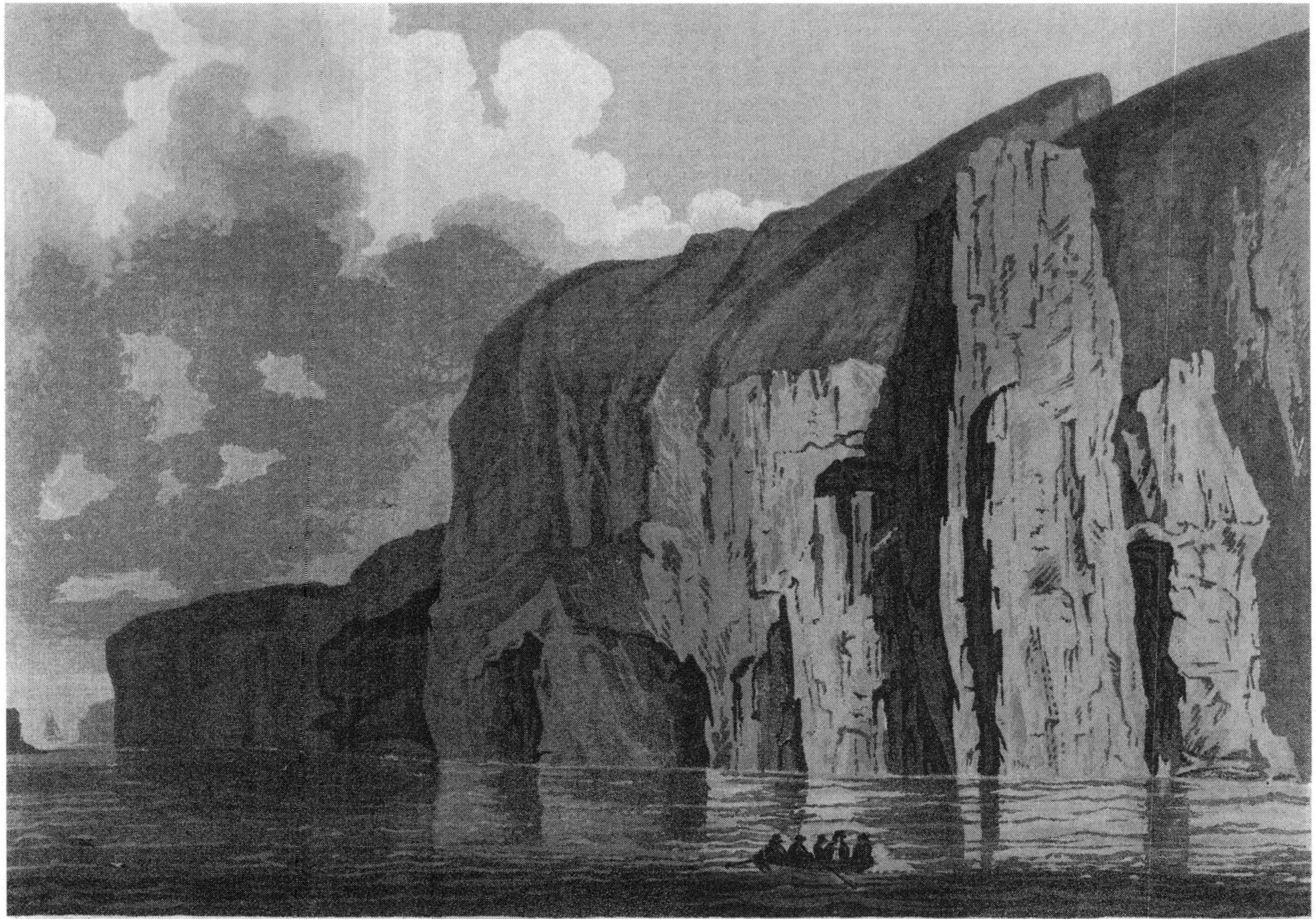

E. Pugh del.^t — I. Havell sculp.^t

CAVERNOUS ROCKS NEAR HOLYHEAD.

Published 15 Novr 1813 by E. Williams Strand.

civil polity, the better regulation of their fishery, or of some other affair of moment. From this circumstance, this cavern has taken its name. It has been observed by some wit or other, that the *cormorants* represented the bishops, the peregrine *falcons* the lords, the *razor-bills* the commons, and the *gulls* the people.

The different mouths of these caves form pictures by themselves. A part of this rock, from its singularity, deserves a minute and very particular description. It cannot be mistaken for another, as it is the only one of the kind ; it shoots up from the sea perpendicularly to the amazing height of the hill above, and gives completely the idea of the vast square tower of a cathedral, in the Gothic style. Two of the sides, a considerable way up, are supposed to attach to the hill, the other two are fronting the water, in one of which is the grand entrance into the cave, with a sharp pointed arch, not inelegantly turned, and which very much resembles a work of art ; on the right of the other, in what the fancy might call a part of the cathedral, is an arch equally picturesque, which communicates with the first. What adds to the effect of this rock, is its bearing visible marks of decay and age ; the heavy blocks of stone which seem as if laid on by art, are in several places disunited, so as to appear every instant in danger of falling. The mind which is impressed with religious ideas, cannot contemplate this piece of natural curiosity without the strongest feelings of awe and admiration of the Author of all nature.

Some years ago a melancholy accident happened here. Two young men had agreed to descend these rocks above the caves, in pursuit of the young birds ; they had ventured so low that a step further appeared to lead to inevitable destruction. One of them had the temerity to hazard this step, in hopes of securing his bird. While his friend held him by the hand, he was by an unlucky slip of the foot precipitated to the gulf below, which terminated his existence in this world; the other would have shared the same fate, had he not disengaged himself from his comrade at the critical moment.

In one corner of this bay is a part which loses its character, and becomes considerably less grand. Mr. Jackson pointed out to me a spot in it, where a vessel was wrecked a few winters ago, in a snowy and dismal night. The poor mariners had gained the shore, and had made many fruitless attempts to ascend to the summit, and the traces of their hands and feet are yet visible in the loose soil, *&c.* The boisterous elements rendered all their efforts abortive, and they fell to rise no more.

In quitting this bay we found it impossible to get round a detached rock, owing to the strength of the tide. Between this rock and the main land is a narrow strait, probably two hundred yards long, called Sound yr Unys Flawd, or the Sound of the Flour Island. While the boatmen were lying upon their oars, deliberating whether or not there could be depth of water enough to get through, we had no alternative; for, in a moment, the inter-current sent us in, and we passed like a dart, expecting every instant the boat, which had but a few inches to spare, would be dashed to pieces; the pointed rocks peeping on each side were not a little alarming: we were fortunate, however, in getting safe through this horrible channel. The velocity with which we went, brought us instantly upon a prospect the most magnificent of its kind I had ever seen. This is totally different from the scene we had just left; in every respect it excels it, I mean to say, when viewed by the eye of the artist and

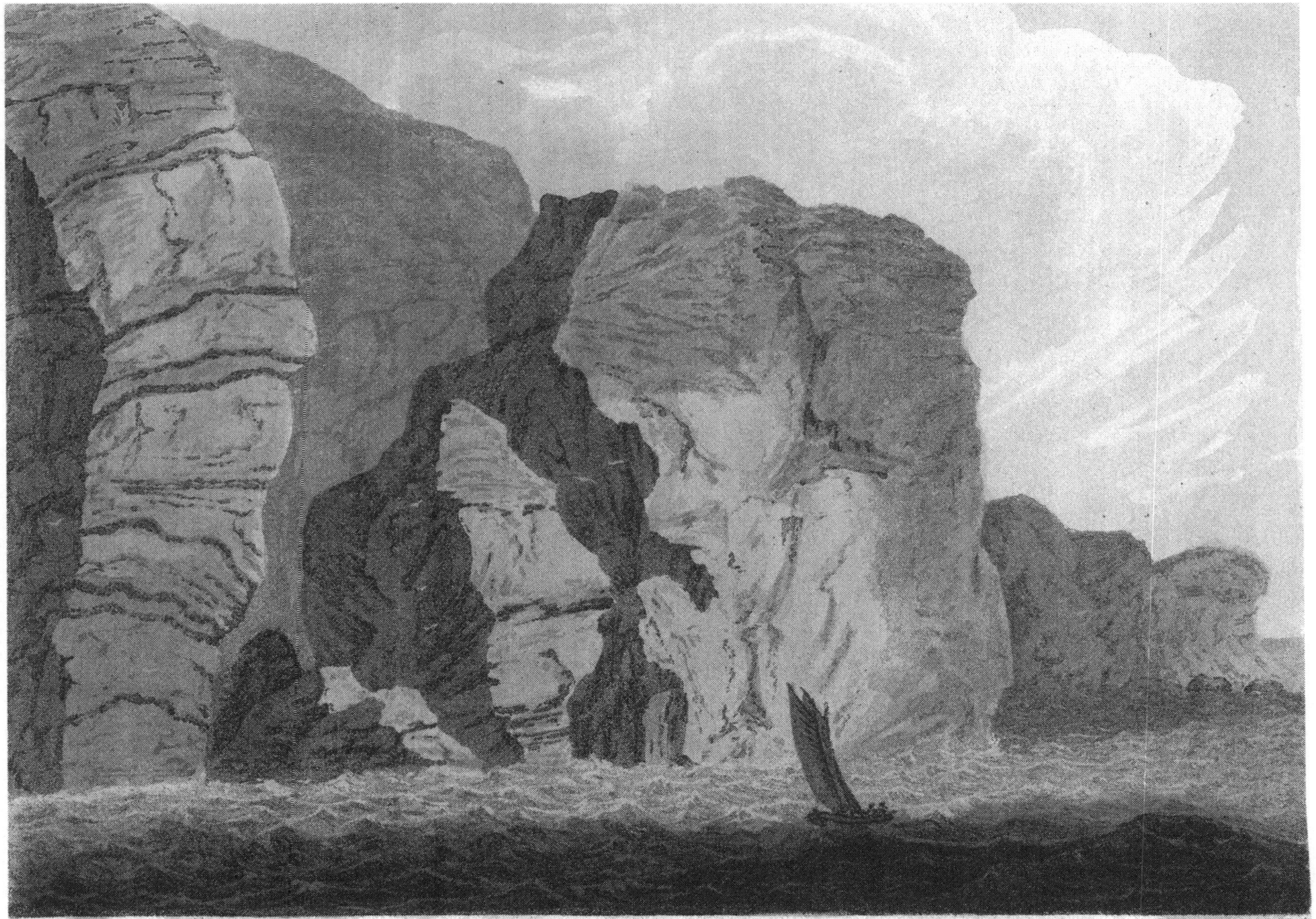

E. Pugh Del.t T. Cartwright Sculp.t

ROCKS NEAR HOLYHEAD.

Published 25 July 1813, by E. Williams, Strand.

connoisseur, this exhibits the rude and the terrific; especially in storms, when may be seen

"A shore where shelves and hidden rocks abound,
Where Death in secret ambush lurks around;
Not half so dreadful to Æneas' eyes
The straits of Sicily were seen to rise,
When Palinurus from the helm descried
The rocks of Scylla on his eastern side."

"With terrible irruption bursting o'er
These marble cliffs, tremendous surges roar;
Hoarse through each winding creek the tempest raves,
And hollow rocks repeat the groan of waves:
Should once the bottom strike this cruel shore,
The parting ship that instant is no more;
Nor she alone, but with her all the crew
Beyond relief, are doomed to perish too." FALCONER'S *Shipwreck*,

The strongest imagination may be challenged, to paint a scene more picturesque. The main rock stands in the rear, shewing a most rugged front, as if it had been shaken and torn by some terrible convulsion of nature; this idea is heightened on observing some fragments starting from the sea, in the perfect shape of mighty buttresses, in support of their mother rock. Some distance advanced into the sea, are several massive appendages which come out very grandly, the whole of this scene, as well as its several detached parts, is finely broken; and, in my estimation of its merits, it does most assuredly deserve the title I have already bestowed upon it. Though this scenery does not exceed two miles, yet it embraces a great many sublime pictures.

The tide is strong here, and it would be advisable for those artists who visit the place, to order an anchor on board, otherwise they will find it extremely inconvenient.

It is observable in many of Mr. Morland's pictures of storms and shipwrecks, that there are many excellent attempts from his own sketches, to shew what he might have thought the awful, and such as suited the subject; but I am of opinion that that admirable artist never visited the rougher shores of Anglesey, and Carnarvonshire; for if he had, he would assuredly have given the preference to these rocks of hard calcareous marble, the breaches of which are so bold, and so sharply cut, as at once to make a difference, with respect to excellence of scenery, decidedly in their favour. These are circumstances he could not recognise on the south-eastern shores of England (where he generally sketched), whose chalky cliffs, from their soft and yielding nature, can never form subjects for the artist, possessing half the romantic character of Mynydd Twr.

On turning into a rough creek to look for an eligible landing-place, we observed a man on the high rocks, who, as Shakespeare says, "seemed no bigger than his head," descending very cautiously by means of a strong rope, fastened on the hill above, to gather the rock samphire. "Dreadful trade!" This is most assuredly a perilous employment, and the person engaged in it cannot be too well rewarded for his courage; for if, by any accident, the rope should break, the man must be instantly hurled to destruction! With some difficulty clambering over great massy stones, strangely perforated by the vortical motion of the tide, and gaining the side of this very romantic corner, calculated to impress dismay on the mind of the most undaunted who are unused to such scenes, we proceeded very cautiously by a narrow ugly path (which seemed to defy the utmost care of one in the party, whose weight of body dictated the necessity of crawling along it on all-fours), and gained the summit. A walk over a barren space of near two miles across the mountain, brought us to Holyhead.

On entering the town, we found it all alive and gay, from numerous parties of people of all descriptions, parading the streets in expectation of a horse-race. The strand was the place allotted for the course, and it was necessary to wait the retreating of the tide, e'er the fun could commence, which occasioned the late hour of seven being appointed for starting. The mode of running was this: two poles were placed erect, one at each end of the course, in a straight line. I soon perceived this was calculated to create a deal of amusement. Two horses were now brought on the ground, and though not caparisoned with the rich and gay furniture of the pampered bloods of New-market—though symmetry might have been wanting, and even the fire and fury of an Hambletonian, or the swiftness of a Childers, of memory renowned in the annals of the turf, yet the racers now under notice were not less famed for their good qualities; and their pedigrees enumerated as many *abs* as they were years old.

Now two jockies made their appearance, not decorated in the manner of more fashionable scenes, but dressed in the style of the stable. The anxious moment arrived; they mounted, started, and went full speed to the pole, through mud and water; the animals stopping suddenly, their riders were consequently pitched upon their necks; one horse feeling the jockey's spurs in his throat, gave a violent jirk, and lodged him safe in his seat, while the other leisurely regained the saddle; and, turning the pole, they set off again with redoubled violence and fury, and this was several times repeated. A greater burlesque upon horse-racing was never witnessed: this was a wished-for effect, and intended to afford amusement to the subscribers; though, by the by, the winner smiling, ironically said, "Let those laugh that win."

Holyhead is a small irregular town, yet well inhabited, and the residence of several genteel families; being the only place of embarkation in North Wales for Dublin It is frequently full of strangers, especially when the wind is unfavourable to the sailing of the packets. These vessels are extremely handsome, very well furnished, and the accommodations always please; the passengers are conveyed to and from Dublin with the greatest safety, and the loss of a packet has not happened for more than a century. There is a light-house erected upon a separated rock at the mouth of the harbour: this and the Skerries light-house are sufficient guides for vessels to come in, in the darkest nights.

The church is embattled and spacious; in it is nothing remarkable, except the following inscription on a marble slab, so honourable to the memory of the deceased, that I cannot pass it without notice:—"In memory of John Owen, of Penrhôs, Esq. a person, who, having never travelled for education beyond the circuit of his native island; yet, by the singular felicity of his genius, attained to such accomplishments, as to be its greatest delight and ornament, for wit; its chief oracle, for civil prudence; a stranger to few parts of useful learning; and that which excelled all, a great pattern of unaffected piety; died at the age of 84, 1712."

Holyhead is so called from the sanctity of the recluse Cybi; its British name is Pen Caer-Gybi, the castellated head or point of Cybi, surnamed Corineus, a son of Solomon, Duke of Cornwall; who having studied a few years in Gaul, was prepared for this see, and to him the church is dedicated. The limits of the church-yard display the remains of works of great antiquity; these are the walls, the masonry of which is well ascertained to be Roman, from the peculiarity of style: the area they enclose is two hundred and twenty feet, by one hundred and thirty; the walls are seventeen feet high, by six and a half thick; the stones are of a blackish grey, and the same with which the neighbourhood abounds.

St. Gybi founded a monastery here, about the year 380; and it is said that king Maelgwyn Gwynedd founded a college here also; this prince was styled Draco Insularis, probably from the spirit he had shewn in protecting the island, and the figure of a dragon carved on the walls of the church may allude to him; others attribute its erection to Hwfa ab Cynddelw, lord of Cwmmwd Llifon, a founder of one of the fifteen tribes of North Wales, contemporary with Owen Gwynedd, Prince of North Wales.

A pleasant walk of one mile brought me to Penrhôs, the agreeable seat of Lady Stanley. Her ladyship, by some late additions judiciously made, and the plantations she has fostered (so encouraging and exemplary in Anglesey), has made it a very desirable residence. It commands the bay of Holyhead, and that part of the island as far as the Skerries, with a fine sea-view. In January and February, 1802, blew some tremendous gales from the north, when two vessels, the Die Liebe, a Dutch galliot, bound from Rotterdam to Ireland, and the Brothers of Liverpool, were wrecked near this house. The first vessel struck at midnight, and the unfortunate sufferers, who consisted of people of different nations, received every attention, and every consolation that their situation required, or that benevolence of heart with an affluent fortune could bestow.

"'Twas thine *, amid the raging of the storm,
To see thy Stanley disappoint the grave:
Tread the dread breach in Charity's mild form,
And bid her Penrhôs ope' its doors to save."

Lady Stanley has now in her possession a portrait of Emma Dolben, her great-grandmother, of which the annexed plate is a faithful copy. This lady was daughter of John Dolben, of Caegwnnion, near Denbigh, Esq., from the same origin as Dr. David Dolben †, bishop of Bangor, in 1631, and Sir William Dolben, Bart. late M. P. for Oxford. She married (about 1650), the Rev. Hugh Williams, D.D., Rector of Llantrisaint, and Llanrhyddlad, in Anglesey, second son of William Williams, of of Chwaen Isaf and Nantanog, in the same county, Esq. By Miss Dolben (not less remarkable for her worth and accomplishments, than for the rank, affluence, and respectability, of her numerous descendants), Dr. Williams had issue, Sir William Williams, solicitor-general, and speaker of the House of Commons in 1684; ancestor of Sir Watkin Williams Wynn, Bart., Sir John Williams of Bodlewyddan, Bart., and the late Watkin Williams of Penbedw, Esq., M. P. for the borough of Flint, and Emma, the lady of Sir Arthur Owen, Bart., ancestor of Sir Hugh Owen of Orielton and Bodowen, Bart. The Viscount Bulkeley is also fifth in descent from Emma Dolben, by Emma, the wife of William Roberts of Cacrau, Esq., and in the same degree, Holland Griffith of Carreg-lwyd, Esq., by Emma, daughter of John Owen of Penrhôs, Esq., great-grandfather to Lady Stanley.

* Lines addressed to the Thrush, in the garden at Penrhôs; a poem in Llwyd's collection.

† Dr. Dolben was Vicar of Hackney. He died at Bangor-house in Shoe-lane, in November, 1633, and was buried at Hackney, where a monument is raised to his memory.

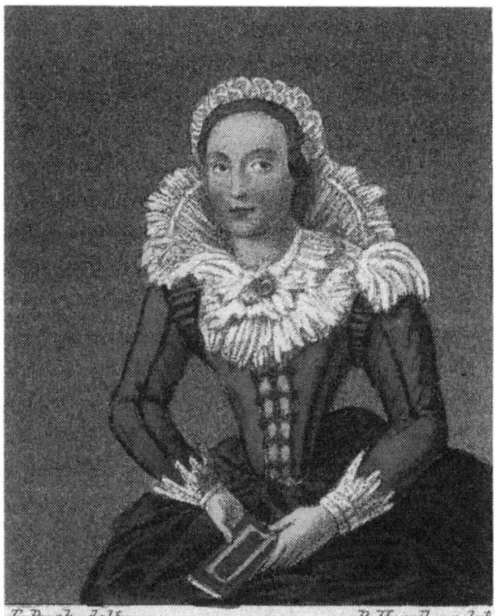

E. Pugh delt. R. Havell sculpt.

EMMA DOLBEN.

Published 15 February 1815, by E. Williams, Strand.

In this part of the island I heard much of the worth and extraordinary abilities of Evan Thomas, the self-taught bone-setter, of Maes, in the parish of Llanfairynghornwy. He seems to have acquired a most consummate knowledge of Osteology; for cases, desperate in the extreme, have been treated by him with expedition and success. His reputation has not only spread through his native country, but has made its way into England, where some unfortunate sufferers have happily experienced his superlative skill.

This very day, in which I have the pleasure to notice this man, I have been informed that a messenger arrived at his house from Shropshire, with a tender of a fee of three hundred pounds for his immediate assistance, which he has accepted. As such a mind must be alive to the praise that he deserves, he must have been much gratified by a translation of the following sonnet; for I find he has no other tongue than the legitimate language of his country.

"Where're Misfortune swells the sudden sigh,
The Muse beholds thy healing presence nigh,
And follows, listens, by thy footsteps led,
To hear the blessings heaped upon thy head.

Nor wonder, Evan, if thy worthy name,
Should henceforth flutter on the wings of Fame:
The Muse shall aid her, as she gives—devotes,
To Virtue's humblest sons, her sweetest notes.

Yes, it shall vibrate on a native s voice,
Thou that can'st bid even Misery rejoice;
With Nature's favour'd precepts only fraught,
With titles, wealth, undeck'd—by Art untaught;
The Virtues love thee—live within thy heart,
Thy country's common blessing, as thou art!"

LLWYD.

To Mr. Jackson my thanks are due for the alacrity with which he offered me his services at different times. To Captain Skinner I am also obliged for his polite attention, as well as for some valuable information with which he favoured this work.

Quitting Holyhead, I left the road to see a double Cromlech, at a place called Tre Jarddur, two miles from thence: the one entire is of an unusual construction, one end of the perpender resting upon an upright stone, while the other reclines upon a stone leaning diagonally on two others. Adjoining this is another Cromlech, that has fallen.

Bidding farewell to Mr. Jackson and Mr. Stephens, who had accompanied me thus far, I proceeded, having on my right the sea-shore for three miles, which on approaching the little church of Rhoscolyn, became bolder. To ascertain its claim to the attention of the painter, it was highly necessary to procure a boat, but I found none on the spot; however, from some points I could discover enough to make me lament that I had not the means of nearer inspection.

Soon after, I entered a pathless common. This coast is, for the space of four miles, nothing but barren sands, and, like the deserts of Arabia, yielding sustenance to neither man nor beast. The stranger in crossing them must be careful to follow the instructions given him: and these are, to make right to a certain house, windmill, tree, or hill; for he has no road to follow, nor can he discover the footsteps of a passenger who has gone by but half an hour before, if there be the least breeze of wind stirring. These sands, in many places, are heaped up in vast hillocks, so yielding as to take a man up to his knees. In crossing those sands, subject to inundation by the tide, near a place called Rhos yn Eigur, I observed at some distance, as I thought an immense quantity of slates, set in order on the shore, ready for exportation; but on coming near enough, I found this side of the bank to be a grey fossil, of the slate kind, peeping out of the sands in sheets, and having the appearance described.

I soon came into Aber Ffraw, or the afflux into the sea of the river Ffraw. Ffraw signifies agitation. My first inquiries were directed to gain a sight of the remains of the palace of the ancient princes of Wales, said by some tourists still to exist; all my endeavours to that end were vain. Some old people told me they recollected having seen, many years ago, a few fragments of the walls, but these had since been used in erecting houses, and walls in the town. There is a small house in ruins, a quarter of a mile out of the town, which it is said some tourists have mistaken for a part of the palace: but it resembles nothing of the kind; and the erection of it could not have been antecedent to the year 1700. The Rev. Mr. Rowlands, who resides here, shewed me a spot crossing the road, where, as tradition will have it, was once a subterranean way to the palace; and yet no steps have been taken to ascertain the fact. Could the passage be found, what may be expected from the discovery?

This was the place fixed on as the chief seat of the princes of Wales, and it is of great antiquity. It was the residence of the wise legislator Howel Dda, or the Good, and after him, Rodric Mawr, or the Great, made it a place of residence for his successors, about the year 870. In his time it was the seat of government also for North Wales, which before was held at Dyganwy. The Saxons invading this island in 877, Rodric, with his brother Gwriad, gave them battle, in which they were defeated and slain. Offering a good landing-place opposite to their shores, the Irish in ancient times, found an easy access to this town, where they committed great ravages.

It is now but a dreary looking place ; the houses are mere huts, and the inhabitants appear poor and needy :—a striking contrast to its ancient state, when it was the occasional seat of government, and dignified by the presence of the princes of Gwynedd. This is not, indeed, to be wondered at; for the grounds around it are a mere waste of sands, not calculated to produce any sustenance equal to the wants of the inhabitants. The place must have undergone a great change during these last nine hundred years, when it was the seat of Rodric the Great.

Near the town is Llangwyfan church, on a rock separated from the main land, when the tide is in; in which case the service is performed at a neighbouring old mansion, called Plas Llangwyfan, in a room which has been consecrated for that purpose.

The only good house in Aber Ffraw, is the clergyman's ; I endeavoured to find out one in which I could suppose the lawyer to live ; but to no purpose : *so I presumed that the good precepts and examples shewn by the former*, had made the residence of the *latter* unnecessary.

At half-past eight, I found the people at the public-house at supper, and preparing for repose after the labours of the day ; my own feelings rendered me not unwilling to take the hint ; after enjoying an excellent supper with a quantum of cwrw da, or good ale, I followed the wholesome advice of these honest folks, e'er the sun had concealed himself for the night. On first entering this house, I was not a little prejudiced against it, but the landlady's very obliging manner and attention dissipated every unfavourable impression. It is not a little famed for being the rendezvous of the followers of the renowned sons of Cush. After the labours and toil of the chase, they are here treated with the greatest rarities of the season, and when the afternoon and evening have been spent in mirth and conviviality, they retire to their respective homes in good time and order. To obviate one great inconvenience, a gentleman of the neighbourhood presented the landlady with a bell, the deep-mouthed tone of which is tremendous, and enough to annihilate the very organs of hearing.

After an early and an excellent breakfast, I pushed on across a desert sandy country of two miles, through the whole of which I could not discover one object worthy of observation, till I gained the hill at Llanfeirian. My attention now was taken up by a scene I had been deprived of for several days, but which was highly improved from this site. I think this the most beautiful eminence in Anglesey. It commands a prospect of nearly the whole of the island; the promontory of Holyhead is seen westward, on the north and north-east are the Paris and Bodafon mountains, and the great stretch of sea from the head, to the extremity of the great Horn of Carnarvonshire, with the triad conic mountain called the Reilf, and Snowdon and his companions, terminating beyond Penmaenmawr. William Jones, who occupies the cottage on this spot, enjoys the best summer situation in all Anglesey. I was not a little pleased with his good-looking daughter, who seemed to take the greatest pleasure in pointing out to me these fine objects; and though familiarized to all the varieties that surrounded her, she spoke of them with a warmth of soul, and strength of judgment, that would have done honour to some in much more exalted situations. I now descended this hill with some degree of haste, in order to gain

Malldraeth sands before the tide could prevent my crossing them, but should have effected this with much less trouble, had not the artless manner and unaffected address of the young woman just mentioned, kept me longer on the spot than it was prudent for me to stay. The tide was making rapid advances and a race with it was necessary, e'er I could gain a safe place to pass over. I walked upon the great embankment, which was thrown up some years since, at the joint expense of a number of gentlemen, who had property in the land to be rescued from the tide. This work cost twelve thousand pounds, and with the losses that followed, it is said, seventeen thousand pounds. In the year 1791 the tide made a great breach at one end, which still remains unrepaired; it happened just at the time when ll was finished, and thought secure, and warranted the immediate cultivation of the land.

> "The bold encroachers on the deep,
> Gain by degrees huge tracts of land,
> 'Till Neptune, with one general sweep
> Turns all again to barren strand." SWIFT.

But it is thought that the breach might easily be made up by another subscription, and better care for the future; for my informant said that it was occasioned by neglect. Another but a successful attempt * would save many hundred acres of fine land, which until that be made, will remain a waste. Mr. Bingley hearing of the state of this embankment, and fancying it impracticable to cross, owing to the breach, gave up the idea of making the circuit of the island; but I can assure the traveller there is not the least danger if the state of the tide be consulted and attended to.

* This has since been done, and the embankment completed.

Having got clear of the sands, I stayed a while to view Bodorgan, the seat of Owen Putland Meyrick, Esq., on the opposite hill which I had just quitted: 'tis a modern structure of stone, and extremely handsome; flanked on one side by an extensive and thriving wood, and on the other with beautiful lawns and grounds well laid out. Mr. Meyrick enjoys from hence a view of the most picturesque part of the scenery described from William Jones's house. The house and grounds of Bodorgan are singularly striking, and at every time of the day, the prospect from them has peculiar interest. When the tide is in, this great region of sands forms a noble bay, which conceals the appearance of barrenness so conspicuous in its absence, and it wants only the presence of shipping, to render it complete. On the other hand, when the tide makes its retrograde movement, the sands, left bare, soon exhibit a novel sight. Frequent parties make their appearance on horseback, and carriages occasionally grace the scene; these perhaps may be succeeded by droves of cattle, sometimes accompanied by very whimsical bipeds.

I soon entered the town of Newborough; a place that some travellers have supposed to give title to a baron of that name; this is a mistake, that nobleman receiving the honour from Newborough in Ireland. This I think a better town than Aber Ffraw, but it looks strangely poor; the church stands a little distance from the town: this circumstance, together with the non-appearance of any two houses, in which I could fancy the attorney and the parson might reside, made me suppose the inhabitants had gone further than those of Aber Ffraw, and had the effrontery to reject both the Law and the Gospel!

This, like Aber-Ffraw, has in ancient times been a seat of the princes; but is now without any remains of their palace.

Newborough, till made a corporation by Edward I. was called by the British Rhos Vair; but from the time of Edward III. it has been uniformly distinguished by its present name. I stayed no longer here than it took me to drink a pint of the worst ale I ever tasted. Descending, I came to a common, where was displayed an *uncommon* degree of spirit in building, and the spot bids fair to become handsome and populous. From hence I had an excellent view of Carnarvon and its mountains. Proceeding downwards, I passed Llanidan, an ancient house, now occupied by Mr. Williams, M. P. for Marlow, and a few fields further brought me to the quiet retreat of Mrs. Goodman. This is the most beautiful part of Anglesey. The lands yield plentiful crops, and are well adorned with wood; their declining sides gently dipping in the straits of Menai, for the distance of nine miles to Beaumaris.

This neighbourhood shews several remains of the monumental stones, altars, and sacred groves, of the ancient druids; and hence has been styled by many *classical* ground. Mr. Rowland, in his Mona Antiqua Restaurata, has laboured to prove that Anglesey was the metropolitan seat of druidism; a position which Mr. W. Owen has lately controverted, assigning that honour, without doubt or hesitation, to Avebury in Wiltshire.

A spot called Tre yr Dryw was the Arch-druid's abode, where the remains are yet to be seen. To enumerate and describe all the relics of druidism, now visible in this part of the island, would be endless and foreign to the purpose of this work; and as there are but few readers unacquainted with their history, I shall only touch slightly upon them.

The circles of stones, of which many remain in North Wales, were the temples of the druids, in which they performed their religious rites; they were generally surrounded by fine oaks. A Carnedd is a great heap of stones, sometimes encircled by upright ones. Some years since, one was discovered near Lord Uxbridge's seat, in which a passage was perceived, that led to a room about three feet wide, and seven feet high; in the centre was a rude stone pillar, which helped to support a roof, consisting of one immense stone, which measured ten feet in diameter: on the sides were benches of the same material, with human bones upon them, which, at the touch, dissipated into dust. These edifices were the repositories of the dead. A Cromlech is another species of druidical remains; it consists of three, or sometimes more, upright stones, with one large stone placed upon them; the whole being similar to those rooms found in the Carnedda. It has often been asserted, that the Cromlechs were the altars upon which the druids performed their acts of immolation, or sacrifices of human victims taken in war: but to this opinion there are insurmountable objections. To those who can suppose the sacrifice was performed under them, it is objected, that many of these are too low to admit the officiating priest to go through the ceremony; and if, again, as has been the opinion, it is supposed that this act could have been performed upon the top stone, another potent reason starts up, and says, that the greatest number of these stones, from their sloping and often serrated summits, could never admit either the fire, the priest, or the victim upon them *. The most rational idea respecting them is, that they were, like the Carnedd just mentioned, the sepulchral monuments of the priests and philosophers of the ancient Britons; and no doubt were the origin of our church-yard tomb-stones.

* See also the opinion of Dr. Borlace. Antiq. Cornwall, pa. 210, &c.

The Druids had a great veneration for the oak (derw), from which the appellation, Druid, is derived. The mistletoe, or pren awyr, was also from a very early period highly regarded by them, and at the close of each year they marched in solemn order to gather it; at the same time inviting all the world to the approaching ceremony, exclaiming, "The new year is at hand; gather the mistletoe!" The priest now ascended the oak, and with a golden hook disunited the mistletoe, which was thrown into a white garment spread to receive it. This part of the ceremony ended, two white bulls (the victims) were brought forth and offered to Jupiter; whom they invocated for prosperity on those who had received so estimable a gift.

From the mistletoe, a portion was made, and taken as an antidote to counteract the effects of poison; and it was also esteemed a preventive against sterility. The mistletoe is a plant of a singular nature; it is produced by seed that will not generate in the earth, but upon other trees, where alone it flourishes; the berries, being ripe in the winter, feed the mistletoe thrush; this bird conveys the seed to the neighbouring trees, against the smoothest branches of which he strikes his beak, and leaves the seed (which is surrounded by a viscous matter) sticking to them, and the following winter the mistletoe is formed. The mistletoe is now hardly seen in this country, but the cyder counties abound with it.

The tenets of druidism in Britain, it is justly supposed, were coeval with the first inhabitants, and the ingenious Mr. Llwyd is of opinion, that, "the great body of men, known in different parts of the world by the designation of *Brachmas*, *Celts*, and *Druids*, were members of one great original society, nearly in unison with respect to their leading principles: these were, the unity of the Deity—his perfections and attributes—the transmigration and immortality of souls—the origin of the world—and its tendency to dissolution *." When Suetonius landed in flat-bottomed boats in this neighbourhood, at a place still called Pont yr Yscraphie †, or the Valley of Skiffs, he had to oppose an army in close array, well accoutred, among whom were a great number of women attired in black, running about like so many Furies, brandishing their torches in the air; while the druids, with uplifted hands to Heaven, were calling down its vengeance upon the invaders: but the tactics of the Britons were ineffectual to their deliverance; the Romans conquered, placed a garrison in the towns, cut down the groves of the druids; which, according to the Roman historian (to be received, in this instance, with some distrust), were consecrated to the most horrible and cruel superstitions.

However disagreeable it may be to me, to have so often to notice the extravagant errors which some tourists detail as facts, yet I feel it a duty I owe my country, to arrest those mistakes in their progress, and to counteract the prejudices people must imbibe from the perusal of their works. That, at present under observation, has, as might have been expected, raised the just indignation of my countrymen, inasmuch as the relator has bestowed upon them a character, which, for ignorance and want of civilization, is as unparalleled as it is untrue. He says that, "a singular relic of the ancient sacrifice of the druids, is yet remaining in some parts of North Wales. When a violent disease breaks out amongst the horned cattle, the farmers of the district where it rages, join to give up a bullock for a victim, which is carried

* Beaumaris Bay, p. 20.

† Mona Antiqua, p. 99.

to the top of some neighbouring precipice, from which it is thrown headlong down; and this they call "Casting a captive to the Devil." That a people, having for near two thousand years lost all the practices of druidism, and for four centuries been united with the intelligent and civilized English, their laws and religion the same, should, at this distant period, retain a custom (if ever practised) so contrary to common sense, and so opposite to the doctrine of their own church, must assuredly appear very extraordinary to any reader. Though I thought it perfectly unnecessary, yet, to remove every shadow of a doubt, I made the inquiry in each country, whether or not such a custom was known there; and uniformly received for answer, that such a circumstance never came to their knowledge, and that those who promulgated such as facts, must be wholly unacquainted with the inhabitants, their manners, and customs.

I now passed Plascoch, the residence of Sir William Bulkeley Hughes; it is a respectable old mansion, in the style of the reign of Elizabeth, embowered in a most luxuriant wood; the whole wearing an air of antiquity, very suitable to the country it is in. Crossing the public road, I made through the fine grounds of Plasnewydd, the elegant seat of the Earl of Uxbridge. It is of the mixed style of the Gothic and Castle, with embattlements round. The front shews three semi-texagonal towers, between which are two slender Gothic ones, ending with spires. I was taught to expect to see a collection of pictures here; but I was not gratified with a sight of any others, than three or four whole-length family portraits by Mr. Hopner, in his usual fine style. When in the neighbourhood of any good houses, I made it my business to inquire, and get all the information I could, about collections of paintings, and where it was probable that there were any good pictures; but I was continually disappointed. Indeed, a general apathy and want of taste for the arts, and I may add for the sciences, are too observable among my wealthy countrymen; which may account why so few natives excel in them. Talents, in a latent state, may exist among them; but while these are to encounter all the discouragement of neglect, and no fostering hand appear to cherish and hold forth the means of pursuing the bent of genius, they are left like

> "Many a flower, born to blush unseen,
> And waste its sweetness in the desert air."

The superfluous wealth of the country is fully competent to form and sustain a national work, or some institution that might be the means of thus cherishing the buds of native genius, and of giving energy to more matured talents, which may sometimes be found even among the wilds of Penmachno, and the vales of Nantglyn.

Having professed impartiality in the delineation of my countrymen, &c., I must notice a deficiency that exists among the common people.—Mechanism is at a very low ebb in North Wales, and if we except shoe-making, which indeed deserves commendation, all other of the lower arts are not above mediocrity. Here solidity seems to be the only aim of every mechanic, forgetting the recommendatory quality of neatness of finishing: their works are turned out with a clumsy and heavy appearance; but I must exclude from this observation, the performances of those whose laudable desire of improvement incite to the measure of visiting London, to obtain more complete knowledge of their art.

Edifices, of any description, not planned by regular architects, are of vulgar taste, and bad proportions; and their interior inconveniently contrived.

It is common here for a mechanic to blend his own immediate business with various others; for instance, a slater and plasterer, will do the work of a bricklayer, or paint rooms, *&c.*:—a joiner will add to his art that of a house-painter, and perhaps a carriage-builder, a custom highly prejudicial to the acquisition of accurate skill: for the original avocation must be neglected, while the others are only superficially acquired *. So long as this practice is suffered, there can be but little hopes of improvement.

As a stimulation, however, it were to be wished, that a society of gentlemen in each county were formed, to reward such men as should, on the completion of their apprenticeship, spend a few years in London for their advancement in their different occupations; and, on their return, on producing a specimen of their proficiency, be entitled to a sum of money, or an honorary reward.

We frequently hear of the nationality of the Scotch, than whom no people seem to have a warmer friendship for each

* This unavoidably arises from the state of the community. The same circumstances occurred in the days of *Xenophon*.—Εν μεν γαρ ταῖς μικραῖς πολεσιν, οι αὐτοι ποιȣσι κλινην, θυραν, αροτρον, &c. Xenophon's Cyropaideia, B. viii. "In small cities the same persons make a coach, a door, a plow, a table: and oftentimes the self-same man builds houses too; and is content if even thus he get employers enough to maintain him. But it is impossible that a man who works at many things, should do all well. But, in great cities, by reason that many want every particular thing, even one art suffices towards the maintenance of every one; and oftentimes not an entire art: but this man makes sandals for men, and that for women, &c."

"Let one exercise one art, and another a different art; this man study such a science, and that man another: thus the whole cycle, as you call it, may be carried easily into perfection." Harris's Dial. on Happiness. On the Division of Labour,—See *Smith's Wealth of Nations*, vol. i. and *Plato* de Repub. lib. ii.

other; an example worthy the imitation of all countries, and particularly of Wales; when, at this moment, no national institution, no public rewards and encouragement, are held out to stimulate to action the powers of intellect: yet the principality can boast of men of mind, of taste and ability; who yet may feel an interest in experiments, the results of which may redound to the honour of their united exertions; and that we shall not always have to complain, that

> "We learn to prize all countries, but our own;
> Find wit, and art, and taste, and genius, given
> To every happy nation under Heaven,
> Save just at home! there Nature's bounty fails,
> And critic pride o'er patriot worth prevails.
> O! dead to shame, to life's best feelings lost!
> Whose taste can triumph at his country's cost!" SHEE.

But, to proceed in my narrative. A hundred yards behind the house are two Cromlechs, the larger of which is the handsomest and most perfect of any I had seen; the perpender is thirteen feet and a half long, about eleven feet broad, and three and a half feet thick; these dimensions give it a noble appearance. Some time before I saw it, it was supposed that some of its supporters had given way on one side, which greatly alarmed the family; it was, in consequence, propped up with pieces of thick timber, and this has entirely destroyed the effect of that picturesque simplicity, which characterizes these ancient remains: but I really think there was not the slightest cause for this alarm; for the whole appeared to me to be well sustained; at all events, wood was a very injudicious auxiliary to stone.

On quitting these grounds, at the north-east lodge, a woman very neatly apparelled, opened the gate; the child she held in her arms, arrested and engrossed my attention for some time. Of all the children that I have ever seen in my travels over various parts of Great Britain, among the poor, the middle classes, and the rich, my eyes have not yet been blessed with a sight of one so lovely. Its form was so angelic, and its face so divine, that for a moment one might have fancied it had made a transitory visit from the realms above, in order to raise admiration in those below.

> "The lovely babe was born with every grace:
> Such was his form, as painters, when they shew
> Their utmost art, on naked loves bestow." DRYDEN'S *Ovid.*

The road led me directly to Bangor-ferry; an appetite, sharpened by a walk of sixteen miles, and a fast of ten hours, made me sensible of the necessity of going over the Menai to Jackson's celebrated inn, to satisfy hunger. On crossing the ferry, a dispute arose between a military officer and the person stationed here to receive the passage-money, about the payment for ferrying him over; the former alleging, that being on his majesty's service he was exempted from the charge, appealing to me on the subject;—I made answer to the appellant, that as the ferry was private property, I was sure his majesty would be most unwilling to infringe upon the rights of individuals, and I advised him to comply with the demand, lest the service might suffer by delay. In a few minutes after landing, this son of Mars was convinced of his error; for, by the order of a magistrate, his gig was stopped until he paid the money for this and former passages.

At the ferry-house all was bustle. After dining very luxuriously, I recrossed the Menai, and took what is now called the middle road, which is very much elevated; the Carnar-

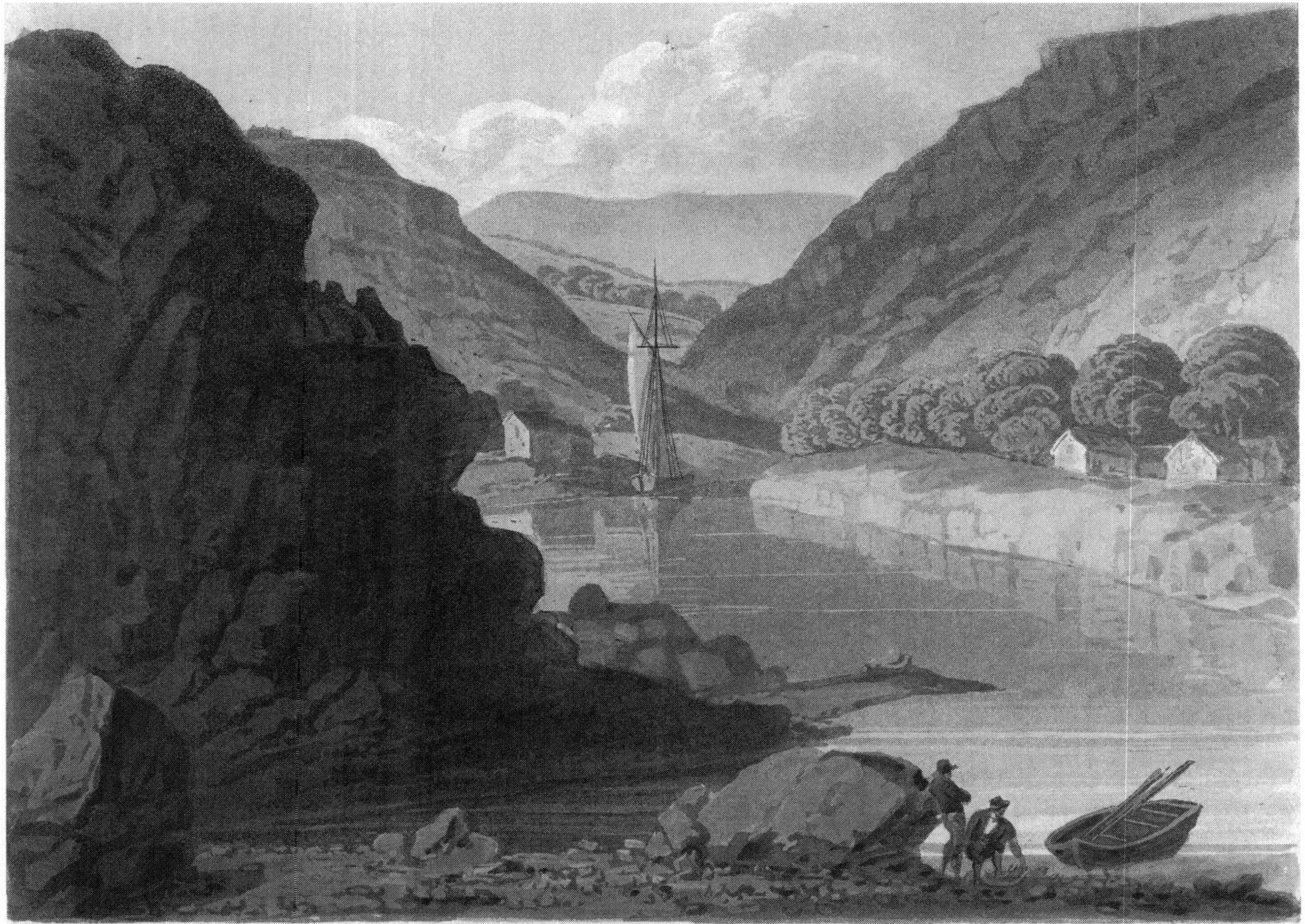

E. Pugh del. T. Cartwright sculp.

CADNANT.

Published 15 May 1813, by E. Williams, Strand.

vonshire mountains on the right. The intervening grounds of Lord Penrhyn, and the country about Bangor, and thence running up the straits towards Carnarvon, with the water and the distant view of Plasnewydd, have charms which can never be forgotten by those who have seen them. Half a mile from the ferry is a creek called Cadnant, noted for being the place where General Mytton landed about September 15, 1648, when he took Beaumaris. There is in and about it much of the picturesque; the cottages on its banks are well disposed, the lines of the hills are well intersected by each other, the rocks on the sides are rough, and add greatly to the effect of the whole; when the tide is in, and the small trading vessels afloat, the picture is much inspirited. On all my former journies to this spot I have admired it, but never so much as at present. The rocks, dispersed in clusters in the Menai, are as singular in their appearance, as they are in the circumstance of having cottages on them. At high water these detached fragments are surrounded by the tide, and exhibit to the stranger a novel sight; from some of them there is a causeway to the main shore, though no security to the cottagers against the encroachments of the flood at high water; who, however, can experience but a transient inconvenience, because, in a very short time after, this stony path is passable. These poor people have very comfortable cabins, each having his garden, producing the most useful vegetables. They enjoy one happiness, which many Londoners would not think too dear a purchase at the expense of a few thousand pounds, and that is, the situation they occupy; commanding constantly the fine scenery that surrounds them, and ever inhaling a pure and salubrious atmosphere.

From the steep at Cadnant is a delightful walk to Beaumaris.

frequently passing by cottages, small farms, and very singular rocks, which engage the attention of the stranger, and retard his progress. Several of these rocks shoot up pretty high, and form excellent subjects for the artist. In warm weather their tops are occupied by cows, goats, and other animals, that get thither by instinct to avoid the tormenting fly, and catch the cooling mid air. One of these rocks is not only singular, but extremely handsome; it is in the shape of a depressed cone, the sides of which are much broken, and are covered with beautiful brush-wood, and a short grass on which goats and sheep love to brouse; this I think is the highest, and has for its distance the noble Nant Ffrancon, *&c.*

A plan has been laid, and a new road completed, close by the water-side, from Beaumaris to Bangor-ferry, at the expense of Lord Bulkeley; the distance is near four miles; and it is to be continued from thence by the water-side to Plasnewydd, a distance of three more, at the expense of the Earl of Uxbridge. This, if carried into execution, will unquestionably be a great public benefit; it will do away the disagreeable necessity of going by a circuitous route to either of those places; and at the same time avoid very great and tedious steeps. One may easily foresee the beautiful ride on this road, close to the Menai; it will, by its actual contact with the water, by the picturesque appearance on each side, with the broad bay of Beaumaris, its shipping continually varying in number and size, and other local beauties, become one of the pleasantest rides in the kingdom.

I now arrived at Beaumaris, having made a complete circuit of the island, a journey I never heard to have been performed by any other traveller. Englishmen on their arrival are always deterred from the undertaking, by the relation of some obstacles that *do*, and others that *do not* exist: the only hindrance in the way is the tide when in, but if the tourist could obtain (and this very easy) information of the precise time of its absence, he might accomplish the excursion with ease and pleasure. The stages are the following:—From Beaumaris over the Red-Wharf sands, to Amlwch, where there is a good inn, is about sixteen miles; in this space he may see every thing worth looking at from the hour of seven in the morning, till night. From Amlwch to Holyhead is about twenty-two miles, in which distance no difficulty from the tide presents itself, as it is a fine turnpike-road all the way, the sea in view nearly the whole time. From Holyhead to Aber Ffraw is about twelve miles: the stranger must inquire the state of the tide at Holyhead, in order to cross the sands at Rhos Colyn. From Aber Ffraw to Beaumaris is about nineteen miles; these stages allow ample time to the *industrious* traveller to examine every curiosity. Of one thing the stranger must be reminded: that he will find but few inns in the intermediate distances, and it would be necessary for him to replenish his sandwich-box before he sets out in the morning; ale and spirits he may get at most villages on the road.

In the morning I set out again, upon an excursion into the interior of the island. Retracing the road I came through the day before, to Bangor-ferry, beyond which a few hundred yards, taking the advantage of the absence of the tide, I entered the beautiful and curious little island of Llan Tysilio, which probably may be three acres of fertile ground. The walls of the church-yard are washed by the tide; the church itself is small, its situation, however, is the most romantic the mind can conceive. When a congregation is convened for divine worship in stormy weather, the waves and the spray come dashing and foaming against the walls of the church, and render the scene solemn and awful in a high degree; the contemplative mind is ready, in the language of Jacob, to say "How dreadful is this place; this is none other but the house of God, and this is the gate of Heaven!" I proceeded half a mile by the side of the Menai, till I came to the pretty cottage, the residence of the Rev. Mr. Owen, whose hospitable disposition would not suffer me to leave his house, without participating in a good dinner. The church here has nothing remarkable about it, except its situation, which, together with that of Mr. Owen's house, is enviable, having in front the Carnarvonshire mountains, and the fine projecting grounds of Vaenol, the seat of Ashton Smith, Esq., and Bryntirion the residence of Mr. Jones. I struck off from hence across to Tregarnedd, the handsome residence of Mr. Grindley. In the greatest part of this day's walk I met with no circumstance of fine landscape that could induce me to use my pencil; it was, however, a pleasing sight to behold the country in an improving state of cultivation. There exists much emulation between the farmers of the north-east side of the island, and those of the south-west side; a laudable rivalry, which should be stimulated by national and honorary rewards; but this must, I am afraid, be dispensed with, and the parties be left to vie with each other upon the score of pride, which may possibly have an happy effect.

At a short distance behind Mr. Grindley's house, is the ancient residence of Sir Gryffydd Llwyd. "This gentleman brought the news to Edward I. of a prince being born to him, in Carnarvon-castle, upon which occasion he was knighted." Sir Gryffydd was the great-grandson of Ednyfed Vychan, who occasionally lived in a "fair house" on the site of the present one, in 1220.

Though Sir Gryffydd, at this time, with the other British chieftains, did homage to the young Prince of Chester, he could not, afterwards, brook the ill usage of his countrymen, who were then suffering under the tyranny of Edward; and felt the necessity of endeavouring to relieve them by force; and, accordingly, between 1316 and 1318, he corresponded with Edward Bruce, King of Scotland, for whose alliance he was anxious; but Bruce's terms being exorbitant, the treaty thus begun fell to the ground. Sir Gryffydd, being a man of a strong mind and great courage, determined alone to undertake the arduous task of freeing his country from the shackles of Edward: at which time he was heard to say, "Gwell marw fel dŷn, na byw fel ci:" *It is better to die like a man, than to live like a dog;* so, in 1322, he took up arms, and with resistless force scoured the country, and overran North Wales and the Marches, taking all the strong holds; but his numbers becoming, as he advanced, greatly inferior to the English, he was subdued, taken, and imprisoned in Rhuddlan-castle, where it is supposed he ended his days*."

This ancient house, as well as Mr. Grindley's, was called Tre r Garnedd, or the Tumulus farm. On Sir Gryffydd's revolt, he put this house in the best state of defence he could, by causing a fosse to be cut around it, of eight yards wide, and four deep, two sides of which are yet in great perfection: and in case he should by adverse fortune be compelled to retreat from hence, he formed another strong hold in the morass of Malldraeth, intended for his last resort, which he secured by a moat round it, filled with the waters of the river Cevni; of this defence also some vestiges remain.

* Vide Llwyd's Poems—Ode of the Months.

Tre r Garnedd has been long deserted. It is in ruins, and a part of it is used as a barn and stabling.

Early in the morning I was most agreeably awakened by the sounds of that feminine instrument, the piano-forte, on which Mr. Grindley's amiable daughter was playing the sprightly national air of Sir Harry Ddu, or Black Sir Harry, which she touched with so much certainty, feeling, and unassuming ornament, that it produced a most rapturous effect upon my nerves. Tregarnedd is a very handsome square house, situated on a gentle eminence in lands highly cultivated, commanding a view of Snowdon and his allies, and other objects equally gratifying to the sight. It is roofed with sheets of copper, a mode originally expensive, but unquestionably durable; this example has induced many gentlemen in the island to adopt the same means of safety from danger by storms, and other casual misfortunes. To Mr. and Mrs. Grindley I am indebted for their united politeness on my present, as well as former visits. I quitted this pleasant house, passing through the neat and increasing village of Llangefni. The road to Gwyndy offers nothing to the artist, the country lying level, and barren of wood, though very productive of corn.

Gwyndy, according to some, *Wine*-house, and others, *White*-house, stands at an equal distance from Bangor-ferry and Holyhead, and nearly in the centre of the island. This house has lately undergone some material alterations; its exterior is handsome, the rooms are numerous and conveniently large. Strangers know the value of the accommodations. Chaises and saddle-horses may be had here for excursions either to the Head, the mines, or to any other part of the Island. At the distance of a quarter of a mile from the house, is an ancient building, now used as a barn, where once lived the sheriff for the county; at one end is shewn a ridge of stone running horizontally along the wall, where was a small room, in which the Sheriff Rhys ab Llewelyn ab Hwlkin held his prisoners in safe custody. Rhys, the founder of this house, accompanied Henry VII. to the battle of Bosworth-field, with his own company of foot; in return, he was sworn, according to the custom of those days, Sheriff of Anglesey for life.

From Gwyndy, along the good road leading to Amlwch, nothing of interest fell within my notice, except the happy appearance of fine crops of corn. Llanerchymedd, or the Plat of the Metheglin, four miles from Gwyndy, is a small but much better town than either Aber Ffraw, or Newborough; here are some smart houses, and a tolerably good inn. The tower of the church is in a dilapidated state, the bell suspended in one corner; and it is not improbable that the next storm may level the whole with the ground. Turning to the right I soon reached Bodafon mountain, the summit of which shews a cavity not very dissimilar to that of Paris mountain; the sides are covered with verdure, and here and there a large rock, exhibiting a rugged front, comes forward with a degree of boldness which gives the whole a very picturesque appearance. On the high peak, next the sea, is a beacon, with a stationary guard; this guard, upon the least alarm of an enemy upon the coast, could give instant notice to the country and its defenders, who, in a few hours would accumulate, and thousands of well-disciplined soldiers be ready, at any point, where their services might be required. Traversing the mountain, I came suddenly to Bodafon, the residence of the Rev. Richard Williams. The absence of that gentleman was to me a subject of regret, as I hoped from his presence to have derived interesting information

Mr. Williams has now in his house a valuable relic, which, until lately, was not known to have been such; it is an ancient bed of the Tudors, made of oak, nearly square, and very low, being only about thirteen inches from the floor; it has four pillars, beautifully turned. The design of the ornamented head-piece is very elegant, and curiously carved; in the centre are the coat of arms and supporters; on each side of which are four Egyptian Termini, supporting the architrave.

Carving was the prevailing mode of ornamenting furniture, three centuries ago: it was fashionable on the accession of Elizabeth (the last of the Tudors) to the throne. "I have seen several beds, the testers of which were decorated with the paternal shields and quarterings of their possessors; and that this was that of the Tudor family, is evident, from the following circumstances: first, the arms are correctly executed, as borne during their government, having their peculiar supporter on one side, *viz.*, the red dragon of ancient Britain, and the favourite cognizance of Henry VII.; secondly, no other family, in this part of the kingdom, could, by any pretext, assume these arms; thirdly, the unbroken location of the family, till the period above mentioned, and the received opinion that the bed was bought many years since, at the sale at Penmynydd *."

The bed came into Mr. Williams's possession in the following manner:—It had been the property of a farmer for a considerable time, but being in some embarrassment, he very unwisely attributed his misfortunes to this bed being under his roof; observing that, "Surely some foul murder had been perpetrated in it," and desired it might be given away. One of his

* Llwyd.

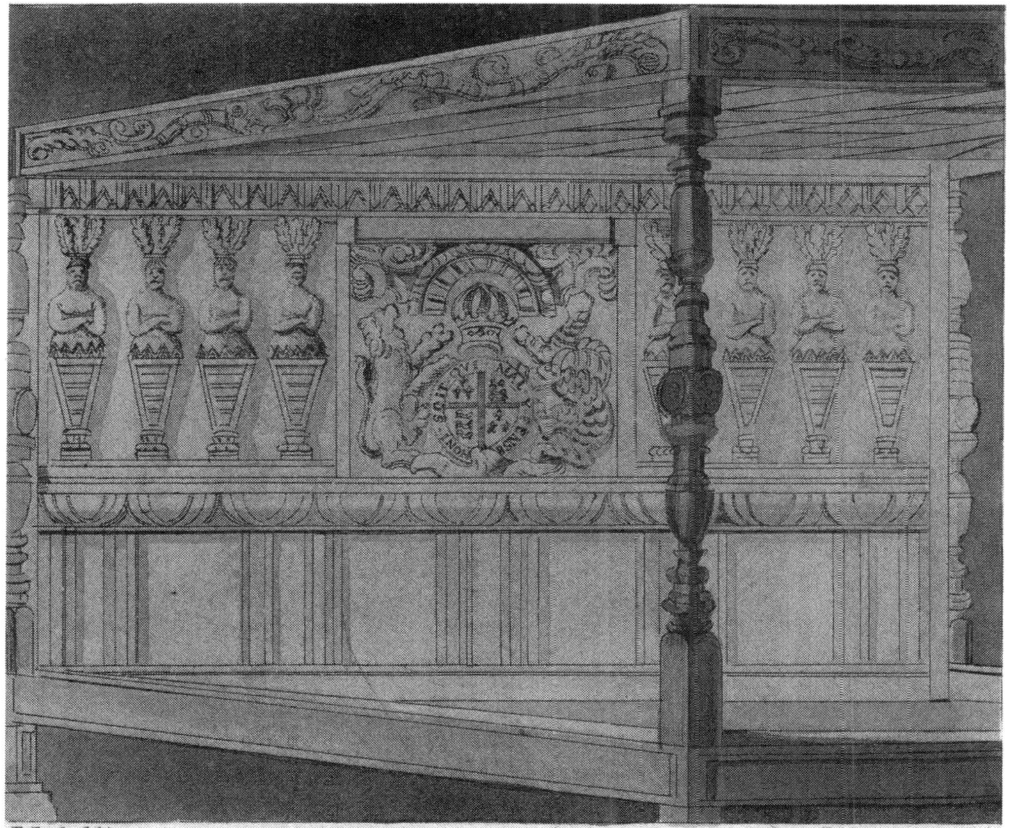

E. Pugh del.t T. Cartwright sculp.t

THE BED OF THE TUDORS.

Published 16 July 1814, by E. Williams, Strand.

cow-boys requested he might take it to his mother; and it was accordingly given to him. Some time after this, the boy wished to part with it, cash probably running low, and offered it to Mrs. Williams, who, though not in want of such a thing, yet as she could serve the boy by the purchase, bought it of him for nine shillings, not supposing, from its odd and unfashionable appearance, that it was so valuable an acquisition. The bed is a little injured by worms, but when the age is considered, it must appear to have been well preserved. It has upon it in some places small marks of gold leaf; whence we may suppose it was gilt in its better days.

The evening being too far gone, I was sorry I had it not in my power to see a man of the name of John Davies, a shoemaker of Penrhos Lligwy, now one hundred and eight years of age, in excellent health, enjoying his sight and hearing in perfection; and having a very numerous family of children, grand-children, and great grand-children.

After very polite attention from Mrs. Williams, I crossed the flat meadowy grounds towards Plas Penmynydd. Perceiving some people burning turf at a little distance, I thought it advisable to inquire of them my way thither. Though at the distance of twenty yards, I felt great heat from the fire; yet, on seeing these people in the midst of it, concluding I could have no apprehension of personal harm, I advanced towards them: but scarcely had proceeded ten yards, before I was involved in a dreadful smoke, which threatened to deprive me of breath. I had now lost sight of the men, and, in my hurry to escape from a situation of so much horror, from a strong easterly wind every moment increasing, I frequently half stumbled on these hillocks of fire; and, but for the guard which my gaiters afforded me, my shoes would have been filled with red-hot sparks, that would have made me dance to some tune. Now an open space appeared, into which I hastened; and there found one man bawling and shouting to a boy, left in this frightful furnace; not at all regarding me, whom he saw out of danger; but, fearing the lad had dropped, he seemed much agitated; who at last made his appearance with his master's jacket in his hand all in a flame, his own apparel being not a little singed. We had to baffle the obstructions of another part to get clear of the whole; this we did by a quick and rapid movement, and received no personal damage from this fiery ordeal. Finding my dog missing, I was under some anxiety for her safety; she however came walking out of this raging fire, seemingly in the greatest agony, and fell down at my feet. Not ashamed to confess so much fondness for a dumb, but faithful, animal, not yet five months old, that I own this sight made me extremely unhappy; and feeling for her, as for a friend recovered from danger, I took her up in my arms, and the pure air restored her in less time than I expected. I was soon however brought into a dilemma; after passing a common, the night became very dark, and, ignorant of my way, I wandered awhile about the country, when coming to a cottage, I was under the necessity of disturbing the repose of a peasant and his wife, who from their bed directed me to a public road, and after much fatigue and trouble, I found myself at Plas Penmynydd, just as the family had retired to rest. One of the domestics however was still up, who had orders to render me every comfortable accommodation which the house afforded.

This house, I presume, is but small compared to what it was in its pristine state, when inhabited by the celebrated Owen Tudor, and it has but little in its outward or inward appearance, that shews its original architecture; yet the little that remains, proves it to have been the abode of wealth. It stands about three miles east of Llangefni, in a pleasant fertile corn country.

Of the Penmynydd branch of the descendants of Ednyfed Fychan, was Owen Tudor; a man of very high birth. Henry the VIIth. commissioned Sir John Leiaf, Guttyn Owen, and others, to inquire critically into his paternal descent; they proved from the chronicles of the Britons, that he was lineally descended by issue male, saving one woman, from *Brutus*, son of *Æneas* the *Trojan*, and that he was son to *Brutus* in five score degrees* Owen was looked upon as one of the most handsome and polite men in the kingdom; his personal charms were so highly valued by Catherine of Valois, queen-dowager of Henry the Vth., as to induce her to make him her husband, in the year 1428. Halle, speaking of her, says "Who beyng young and lustye, folowying more her owne appetyte than frendely consaill, and regardyng more her private affection than her open honor, toke to husband privily (in 1428) a goodly gentylman and a beautiful person, garniged with manye godlye giftes both of nature and of grace, called *Owen Teuther*, a man brought furth and come of the noble lignage and auncient lyne of *Cadwalader*, the last kynge of the *Brittones*." This was a marriage that produced momentous consequences, which, though contrary to the wishes of many, restored the British race of princes to the throne of England. It is said that when Owen was dancing before the queen, among a number of the nobility, he accidentally trod upon her majesty's foot, and fell into her lap. The gracefulness of his manner in

* Wynn's History of Wales, 331.

making an apology, soon procured him a pardon, the queen very pleasantly joking with him, and saying, that so far from offending her, it would only increase the pleasure of herself and the company, if he would again make the same mistake. They were soon after married, and in the course of nine years had three sons and one daughter: they lived happily together till the year 1437, when death separated them, and deprived Owen of his royal consort.

Penmynydd church, near this house, contains a monument of the Tudors; they are recumbent figures, the man is armed *cap-a-pie;* the woman, contrary to all established etiquette, lies on his right side. The body of the tomb has around it several compartments, in each of which is a blank shield. On each side of the heads of the statues, is a little cherubic figure, the whole much mutilated, it being made of gypsum. It was removed to this place, from the monastery of Llanvaes at the dissolution. In an ornamented niche in the wall, it is said, the patron of the saint was buried.

To Mr. and Mrs. Hughes, who are so well acquainted with the true mode of ancient British hospitality, I am indebted for great civility; taking my leave, I returned by the Holyhead road to Beaumaris, without any thing material to relate.

The day following was appointed by the inspecting officer of the district, Colonel Knight, to review the volunteers of Beaumaris, commanded by Colonel Lord Bulkeley, and Major Sir Robert Williams. The corps went through the different evolutions with great precision and steadiness, and seemed to me to be under no embarrassment whatever; this was a circumstance in which my feelings were greatly interested. It was indeed a most gratifying sight, to behold large associations of the peasantry, mechanics, tradesmen, and the superior orders, under the best discipline, advancing in the art of defence and attack towards the summit of perfection, in the utmost subordination, harmony, and friendship; with but one common determination, that of meeting with firmness, and with the invincible courage that has ever been the characteristic of ancient Britons, any enemy who

———— " in social league may dare
On Britain to let slip the dogs of war:
Vain efforts all, which in disgrace shall end
If Britain truly to herself a friend
Through all her realms, bid civil discords cease
And heals her empire's wounds by arts of peace."

Colonel Knight was pleased to bestow the most handsome eulogy on the whole corps; the tributory thanks of which must be due to one of the best adjutants in the kingdom, to whose care and attention, in a great measure, both officers and men owe their skill. The motto of the corps is that of their colonel,

Nec temere, nec timide.

Before I quit Beaumaris, I feel it a duty strongly incumbent on me, to notice the kind and generous treatment and attention I received from a worthy tradesman, Mr. Hugh Jones, whose grateful mind had not lost sight of a trifling service, which, as a man and a countryman, I felt myself obliged to render his son, a fine youth lately studying the arts in London; from a specimen I have lately seen of his, I think I may have ventured, without danger of incurring the censure of better judgments, to have predicted his future excellence, had he met with the patronage promised him.

The Bull is the head inn in Beaumaris, where I found great civility from Mr. and Mrs. Harris, who are capable of supplying their guests with every convenience and comfort.

I now left the island, and landed once more at Bangor-ferry.

CHAPTER III.

Bangor Ferry.—Welsh Harp.—Cattle Exporting.—Bangor.—John Hughes. —Port Penrhyn.—Penrhyn House.—Llandegai.—Archbishop Williams.—Cochwillan.—Coetmore.—Gibson the Painter.—Slate Quarries.—Ogwen Bank.—Nant Ffrancon.—Cwm Idwal.—Cwm Bochlwyd.—Llyn Ogwen.—Capel Curig.—Improved Roads.—Rhyad y Wenol.—Moel Siabod.—Snowdon.—Mr. De Loutherbourg.—Llanberis Pass.—Ynys Etws.—Cady Thomas.—Llanberis Village.—Glydar Bach.—Caunant Mawr.—Dolbadarn Castle.—Carnarvon.—Sir John Owen.—Segontium.—Llanbeblic.—Burials.—Nant Mill.—Llyn Cwellyn.—Llyn y Dwarchen.—Lin y Gader.—Llanfihangel.—Llanllyfni Lakes.—Clynog.—Left Mountains.—Nevin.—Pistill Cliffs.—Tournament.—Perth yn Llŷn.—Llanbedrog.

THE delightful situation of Bangor-ferry, is as well known as as it is justly admired. Mr. Jackson, of late years, has made very great improvements, not only in the building, but in the grounds about, and has rendered it a paradisiacal caravansera, inferior to none within the circle of my knowledge. The very great overflow of strangers in every season of the year, as it lies on the great road to Holyhead and Dublin, gives it the appearance of some of the greatest London inns; but with this difference, that, in the summer season, it is visited by numerous parties of strangers; some of the first rank, and others, who have laid aside the cares of business, for the pleasures of an excursion into the most romantic part of Great Britain.

The sound of the harp, in this house, the indigenious musical instrument of the country, fully accordant with the situation, vibrating amidst water, rock, and wood, has a very agreeable effect upon the ear of a stranger unaccustomed to these pleasurable sounds. Mr. Skrine, speaking of the Welsh-harp, says, "And through the whole of North Wales, it is cultivated with a degree of veneration, and scarce a family exists, in the meanest cottage, without at least one performer." The observation made by Mr. Aikin, is in this instance strikingly verified. The truth is, the harp is by no means now so much in vogue, as it was in former days. When the most distinguished families of landed property, to whom descended the manners and habits of their ancestors, resided constantly upon their estates, with them, indeed, the harp was held in high esteem. It was then, also, customary for ladies and gentlemen to accompany the harp with their voices, in songs preserving the remembrance of the heroic deeds of their forefathers, or in elegies to the memory of departed lovers, or in comic odes descriptive of the humorous and merry turn of mind of some of their deceased or living characters. This is not the case at present; the gentry, in general, seem to have lost their taste for the instrument; its sounds are no longer heard, except in a few of their houses. The intercourse with England, indeed, has long been so general and so close, and the English taste and manners so incorporated with those of the aboriginal districts, as in a great measure to efface them; and the ancient provincial customs and peculiarities, whether estimable or not, are, in a great measure, discarded. Even the copious and nervous original language of Britain, is, among men of rank and fashion, almost lost and forgotten. Among the peasantry and farmers, however, the harp is yet in some esteem; and, I hope, will thus keep the instrument from total oblivion, till some generous effort be made, in higher life, to revive a regard for simple and pathetic music; when the strings of the harp may again be successfully struck in all parts of the principality. In conversation with Thomas Lloyd, Esq., of Marle, near Conway, upon this subject, he once expressed a strong wish to bring the instrument again into general use and fashion: the mode he proposed was, by a small annual subscription from the wealthy, to support the institution, into which such boys should be taken as shewed a propensity for music; a proper master provided, who could give proofs of his musical science, and knowledge of the instrument. From this seminary gentlemen might be provided with youths of merit, taught in a regular and methodical way, to attain the highest skill in performing on this ancient but admirable instrument. Should such a scheme be adopted, Mr. Lloyd intended to present the infant institution with a piece of land *, of several acres, with a building now upon it, which, with some additions, might be rendered a comfortable school. This is so much to the honour of Mr. Lloyd, that I cannot refrain from mentioning it. It is to be wished, that some other liberal and public spirited gentleman, would second Mr. Lloyd in this plan, by which means alone we may yet hope to recover the minstrelsy of Wales.

At Bangor-ferry the small horned cattle of Anglesey are exported for the London and other markets in England, to the number of seventeen or eighteen thousand annually. The method of getting them over is this: a drove is brought to the verge of

* The situation would be a most happy one indeed: it is on Mr. Lloyd's estate, near Mold, amidst rocks, mountains, wood, and water; the best calculated to inspire the young mind with those sentiments, which were so common to the bards and minstrels of old.

the rocks, from whence they are hurried down into the deep, and they naturally make away from the banks where they have been so roughly treated, for the opposite shore, where they arrive in safety; boats generally attending each drove, lest any of the young ones should feel their strength inadequate to the task; 'tis seldom or ever any losses happen in this mode of swimming the cattle over.

An enchanting walk of a mile and a half through the fields, brought me to the small ancient city of Bangor. From the acclivity south of it, there is a most delightful bird's-eye view of the town and the sea, with Beaumaris and the receding shores of Anglesey; and a high projecting rock, on the right, comes in to assist one of the best prospects I had yet seen. I have examined this spot with pleasure: and there are many points about it that may be considered as irresistible temptations for the artist. From the high rocks above the town, is a fine prospect of the surrounding country. Here are yet remaining traces of a great fortification, erected by Hugh Lupus, in order, with better effect, to make his savage inroad into Anglesey: nature seemed to have assisted the projectors in surrounding it with precipices, which must have rendered the fort almost impregnable. There is to be seen a hole in the ground, encircled by a mound, in which is a great quantity of stones, seemingly vitrified. I believe no light as yet has been thrown upon the use of this place; to ascertain the fact, it would be necessary to dig a few yards. In Perfedd-goed-wood, two miles from this spot, is a very picturesque moss-covered mill, enclosed on all sides by wood and rock, in their wildest varieties. A few hundred yards from the town, is the bowling-green, adjoining the Penrhyn arms. The very handsome reading-room here, was built at the expense of Lady

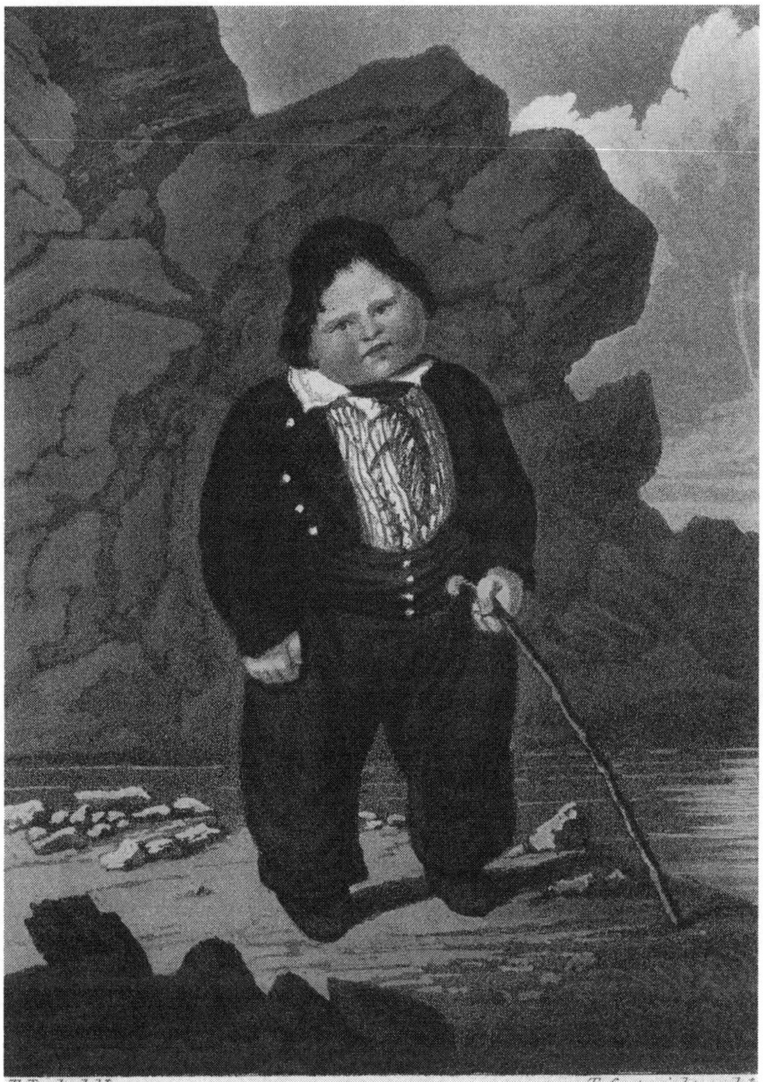

E. Pugh del.ᵗ T. Cartwright sculp.ᵗ

THE INFANT HERCULES.

Published 25 Feb.y 1815 by E. Williams, Strand.

Penrhyn; her ladyship has made a present of it to the book subscribers, who are gentlemen resident in the town and neighbourhood; it commands the finest open prospect that can be conceived; on the right is the entrance into Nant Ffrancon, and thence the mountains terminating with Penmaenmawr to the east; northward Beaumaris, with its bay, and the isle of Anglesey; westward is the town and the beautiful eminences about it. I had here the honour of exchanging a few words with the Right Rev. Prelate of this diocese * (Dr. Cleaver), upon the subject of the beautiful scenery that surrounded us; his lordship pointed out the various picturesque parts of the landscape, with that distinctive judgment, and connoisseur-like phraseology, that at once made me sensible of his acquaintance with, and regard for, the arts. His lordship appears to be about sixty years of age, very frank, easy of access, complaisant, and of finished manners.

In the year 1804, I visited a small farm-house two miles off, called Aber Ogwen, to see a human phenomenon; a boy named John Hughes, of a size so extraordinary, as to attract the attention of all travellers coming that way. As it might be attended with some difficulty to describe his person with accuracy and justice, I have given a whole-length portrait of him, not in the least exaggerated, but in a manner which will stand the test of the strictest examination; his height was four feet two inches and a half, his weight, nine stone, of fourteen pounds to the stone; his age eight years; he was very healthy and of a very florid complexion. This boy has been justly named, by some gentlemen in the neighbourhood, the infant Hercules.

* Since translated to St. Asaph.

Should he live, and grow as he has done hitherto, we may fairly suppose, that by the time he arrives at the age of manhood, he will be one of the greatest prodigies among mankind. His mother is a little woman; his father a tall, but thin man. I was told by the mother, that when the child was born, it was of the usual size, but about the eighth day its nurse perceived a growing alteration; from which time he has continued to increase rapidly to the singular and enormous bulk at which I then saw him.

Bangor cathedral, a heavy inelegant building, has very little in it worth noticing. It has lately been new roofed at a great expense, defrayed from a fund, the produce of a yearly income for that and other purposes of the choir. The following singular epitaph, in the side of the nave, as yet, I believe, unnoticed by any other writer, points to a remarkable rapid succession of bishops in this see; "Here lyeth the body of Robert Hughes, late of Gwedir, gentleman, attorney at law, agent to his Grace the Duke of Ancaster, and to *six successive Bishops* of Bangor, and principal Register of this diocese: he died December 25, 1749, *aged* 44."

The cathedral is dedicated to St. Deiniol, who founded it about 525. It was demolished by the Saxons in 1071, and afterwards rebuilt. Owen Glyndwr ravaged the town, and once more reduced this building into a ruin; in 1532, the whole was again repaired by Bishop Sheffington, whose death put a stop to any further proceedings; and the tower, which was to have been raised much higher, was left as it is now seen. In the choir are two busts, of Bishops Rowlands and Vaughan, made headless, by the fanaticism of the times.

Bangor is but small, and yet one of the prettiest, and certainly one of the cleanest, of all the towns in North Wales. When I first entered it through the church-yard, being accoutred as before described, I was suddenly greeted by three pretty white-teethed, rosy-cheeked, black-eyed nymphs, with "Pray Moses, vat be you got to shell; open your bags, Moses, for we vant some bodkins, sheesors, and oder tings." A plague upon these wicked girls, thought I, they have taken me for a Jew pedlar *. The Bishop's palace lies low, and near the church-yard; it is an old house; the grounds about it, nevertheless, are kept so clean and neat, that the whole is a very enviable spot. The arms of this see are thus blazoned: *Gules*, a Bend; *Or*, *Gutty de Poix*, between two Mullets, *Argent*.

To the Rev. Mr. Davies my grateful acknowledgments are justly due, for a most gentleman-like attention to my pursuits, while under his hospitable roof; and anxious to afford me every assistance, he constantly accompanied me, seemingly gratified by an opportunity of promoting the fine arts; a spirit, I should be happy were I able to say, was more general among my wealthy countrymen. I left this gentleman, and his neat and beautiful cottage, with regret, bending my steps towards Capel Curig. Immediately on leaving Bangor, I passed Port Penrhyn, formerly called Aber Cegin, from whence the slates from Lord Penrhyn's quarry are exported, in great quantities, to London, Dublin, Liverpool, and other places. There frequently lie at the quays, twenty or thirty vessels, of from forty to three hundred tons, taking in their cargoes. The slates are brought from Nant Ffrancon, by a rail-road, a distance of six miles; through the

* I know an artist, who the summer before, in company with a clergyman of Chester, was on his way to Carnarvonshire: when he perceived an old woman running and shouting after him to stop; he did so, and the old dame arriving, nearly out of breath, said, "For G—'s sake, Mr. Abraham! I am almost blind—I want a pair of spectacles!"

whole of which, the declivity, though there are three inclined planes, does not exceed three hundred yards. The expense of making this rail-road was five thousand pounds. When the slates were brought down by carts, his Lordship paid five shillings per ton for carrying: but the present mode of conveyance has reduced the charge to one shilling per ton; and no less than one hundred tons are thus daily conveyed to the port. Near the port is Lime-grove, the handsome cottage of Mr. Wyatt, brother to the learned architect. I passed an elegant gateway into Lord Penrhyn's grounds. The house is in the style of the military Gothic, and has lately undergone some excellent alterations and additions, under the direction of Mr. Wyatt. The situation is on a gentle rise above the bay of Beaumaris, and the house stands on the site of a palace of the ancient princes of Wales. Here is to be seen the celebrated drinking-horn of Piers Gryffydd*, the ancient hero of this house. It is a large bugle, or an ox's horn, mounted with ornamented silver. Such horns were formerly in use with the Danes, Saxons, Scots, and Welsh: they were of different value, as they were used, by the kings, down to their huntsmen and domestics. The officers of the palace were allowed the privilege of drinking out of the royal cup, at great entertainments; metheglin was their favourite drink.

Fill the Hirlas horn, my boy,
Nor let the tuneful lips be dry
  That warble Owen's praise;
Whose walls with warlike spoils are hung,
And open wide his gates are flung,
  In Cambria's peaceful days.

---

* This gentleman, in 1588, sailed in his own ship, and had the honour of partaking with other heroes in the glory of defeating the Spanish armada.

This hour we dedicate to joy:
Then fill the Hirlas horn my boy,
That shineth like the sea;
Whose azure handles tip'd with gold,
Invites the grasp of Britons bold,
The sons of liberty *.

Llandegai church, dedicated to Tegai, a saint, who lived in the sixth century, is of the Gothic order, and accords well with Penrhyn-house; they are both in the full view of the traveller at one and the same time. This is a beautiful little church, and contains the mural monument of the renowned Archbishop Williams; he is represented in his prelatical dress, in a kneeling attitude. His Grace was born at Conway, received the rudiments of his education at Ruthin, and proved to be a man of first-rate abilities. In 1610, the king was so pleased with his preaching, that he appointed him Dean of Salisbury, and in 1620, Dean of Westminster; his shining qualifications now prepared him for another remove of greater importance: in 1621, he was nominated Lord Keeper, in the room of Lord Bacon; and in less than a month afterwards, his majesty made him Bishop of Lincoln. About the year 1640, he was promoted to the see of York, and filled that situation with much honour to himself, and good to others. In the civil wars he experienced some reverses of fortune, sometimes imprisoned, and sometimes personally engaged in the battles between Charles and Cromwell. He was a passionate man, and this hurried him on to commit some improprieties, though these may be palliated by saying that he was impelled to them by most severe and unprincipled treatment

* Part of a translation of a poem of Owen Cyveiliog, the princely bard, after a great victory over the English in Maelorr.

from his enemies, only for persisting with courage, "in all that was right." Retiring to his native country, he died on his *birth-day*, at Gloddaeth, 25th March, 1650, aged 68; and was buried here with great funeral pomp.

Gryffydd Phylip, a native bard, concludes his monody on the bishop with that beautiful idea of Shakespeare, though it is not probable he ever saw a line written by the Avonian bard.

"Fyth weled ei fath eilwaith."
"We ne'er shall look upon his like again."

Two miles from hence is Cochwillan, the ancient abode of Archbishop Williams's ancestors; it is now (as seems generally the fate of such remains of antiquity in this country) converted into a barn; the hall only appears to remain; it has a carved cornice of wood all round, with ornamented ribs to support the roof. Over one of the doors are lions carved in wood, which I presume were a part of the family arms. A little further, on the left of the Ogwen river, is the old house of the Pughs, called Coetmore. I was told I might see some curious pictures and tapestry here, as well as the portrait of the celebrated little painter, Richard Gibson *, and his fairy wife, by Sir Peter Lely; but this, as well as all other pictures, has been removed hence. Whoever may have this portrait in their possession, may rely on it, that they have a treasure. The house has been so much neglected, and in such a state, that to make it respectably habit-able will be a vast expense. On entering, a poor woman with a child in her arms coming out of one of the parlours, met me in the hall: my business being made known, I was told there were no

* See account of Gibson in Walpole's Anecdotes of Painting, vol. iii. p. 34.; and Waller's Poem of the Marriage of the Dwarfs.

pictures, but at the same time, I was requested to walk up stairs for my satisfaction; on reaching the first floor, another poor woman met us with a child also in her arms. Our conversation here being heard, there immediately issued out of all the other rooms, seemingly in great disorder and wildness of look, about twenty more women, with each a child: the sight of all these prolific females with their children, seemed very whimsical; they were very eager to know my business, and on my informing them, one replied, that they then held in their arms much more beautiful and valuable pictures than any I was in search of; an assertion to which I cordially agreed, and they were highly pleased. My inquiries, I fancy, afforded them much amusement; for, on my quitting the house, I could hear a loud fit of laughter. The farmer who lives here (the house being much too large for him) had, it seems, let the rooms to the quarry-men; and thus the odd scene is accounted for.

Crossing the Ogwen again, I came to an apology for an inn, called by the pompous name of the *Hall*, two hundred yards from which is the great slate quarry of Lord Penrhyn. It is a prodigious chasm, but in point of the picturesque, it is of considerably less value and interest to the artist than the Paris mines; yet, even by him, it is by no means to be disregarded, as, by getting to some happy points, he may be highly gratified. The nature of this species of rock, very few are unacquainted with; the colour of it in the first place is unfavourable to a picture, and in the second place, the breaches, possessing no variety of form, are not of that description to produce a good effect. The marks of this rock run upwards, with sometimes a leaning inclination, and sometimes a perdendicular, giving partly the same appearance as slates do when lying at the side of a quay for exportation.

To the contemplative and inquisitive observer, who travels this country for the sake of seeing the wonderful productions of nature and art, this quarry will afford much amusement, as well as exhibit to him eminent proofs and effects of those great and useful powers of mind and body, which the Deity has bestowed on man. The method of conveying the slates from the beds, along the narrow ridges that hang over the frightful precipices, is curious; and though the practice appears big with danger, it is not considered hazardous: a man conducts a four-wheeled barrow loaded along these edges, on a narrow rail-road. When a sufficient number are ready, the slates are conveyed to Port Penrhyn, in eight or a dozen of these little barrows or waggons, and thus one horse will draw many tons. There are two inclined planes at this quarry. The quarries of this neighbourhood are of some antiquity, for we find that "Sion Tudur, who was the Register of the Ecclesiastical Court of St. Asaph, in A.D. 1580, in a poetical address to Rolant Thomas, LL. D., Dean of Bangor from A.D. 1570 to 1588, requests him to procure him a ship-load of slates from Aber Ogwen; which proves that slates were shipped out there, so late as that period*." Lord Penrhyn has lately erected a sawing-mill, where this fossil is sawn into grave-stones, chimney-pieces, *&c.* The slates are large, very beautiful, and agreeable to their sizes, are called queens, duchesses, ladies, patents, singles, *&c.* On the opposite side of the river is Ogwen Bank, a cottage built by Lord Penrhyn. On entering the house, I was requested to write my name in a book chained to the wall, and kept for the purpose of receiving the signatures of all strangers who come to the house. This

* Observations on the Snowdon Mountains, p. 125. Sold by *E. Williams, Strand.*

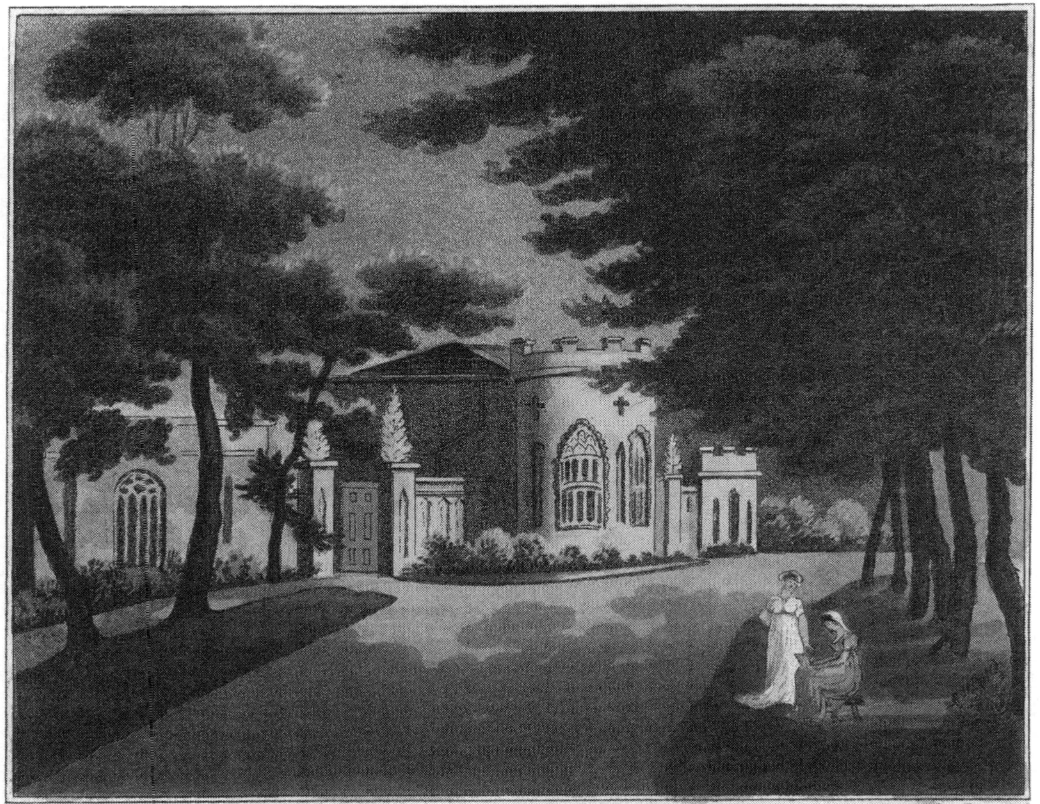

E. Pugh del.t I. Havell sculp.t

OGWEN BANK.

Published 15th Nov.r 1814, by E. Williams, Strand.

cottage is built in the florid Gothic manner, and is one of the prettiest devices that can be conceived. The centre is occupied by a large handsome room, the front of it forming a segment of a circle. The chimney-piece is very beautifully ornamented with a marble tablet, on which are carved the portraits of two favourite pug-dogs and a terrier, upon a hard ground made from the pulverized slate rock, which gives a most agreeable contrast. The side-wings of the house make handsome stabling, and coach-house. Opposite the house is a corresponding bridge over a rough and noisy fall on the Ogwen. Though this little paradise * is justly esteemed as such by all travellers, and by no one more than myself, yet if I might be allowed to give my opinion, I would say, that the gaiety of the house and bridge, accords not with the terrific and magnificent scenery that surrounds them both. Had they been built in the gay and flowery vale of Clwyd, or in the still more remote Vale Royal of Cheshire, they would not have been liable to a remark, which, in their present situation, is strikingly obvious to the feelings of the connoisseur, or to the judgment of the qualified professor of landscape. How nobly accordant with the rocky and majestic environing scenery, would have been a castellated building. It needs not be told, what magical effects are produced in the mind upon beholding Conway, Dolbadarn, Harlech, and other castles in this romantic country; which, if beheld in tamer situations, on the plains of England, would scarcely raise any similar emotion. A row of trees, planted before the house, has rendered it invisible to the traveller on the road. I retraced my steps

* Ogwen Bank.—" The plantations that screen, and the flowers that adorn it, are surprising and exemplary proofs of the power of cultivation, however forbidding the face of Nature:—It is an acre of *Tempe* among the rocks of *Norway*." *Beaumaris Bay*, p. 37.

over the bridge to the *Hall*, and after thanking the landlady, Mrs. Thomas, for her civility, good lodging, and treatment, I made the best of my way to visit the different scenes of this vale of Nant Ffrancon, keeping on the right of the river. I now consider myself as entering upon the most sublime and magnificent scenery in this island.

"We now ascend, and eastward bend our view,
Where Rome's imperial eagles never flew;
The Menai leave—the rocky heights explore,
The Briton's last resource—his mountain's hoar.
Where weeping Freedom from the contest fled,
And Cambria saw her dearest heroes dead.

"Illustrious band! distinguished Arvon's boast:
'Twas your's to lead in Gwynedd's warlike host;
For you (while wisdom dwelt upon his tongue)
Your own Talicsin's sweetest lyre was strung:
For you, in peaceful shades and tented plains,
Flowed from his hallow'd lips th' approving strains."

Beaumaris Bay. p. 28.

A few hundred yards from Ogwen bank is Lady Penrhyn's farm-house, of a bold, handsome appearance. Proceeding, with the Ogwen meandering on my left, I had in front the bold and noble rocks above Llyn Idwal; on all sides finely-broken eminences, jutting out in a manner that captivates the attention, and irresistibly impels the artist to open his portfolio. The nearer the approach to the end of this valley, the more picturesque the effect; and, on the contrary, on looking down towards Bangor, the scenery is by no means so wild.

The fall from Ogwen lake, as seen from the road, I consider as very fine, from the nature of the rocks, down which it rushes with violence, and from its considerable height. On approach-

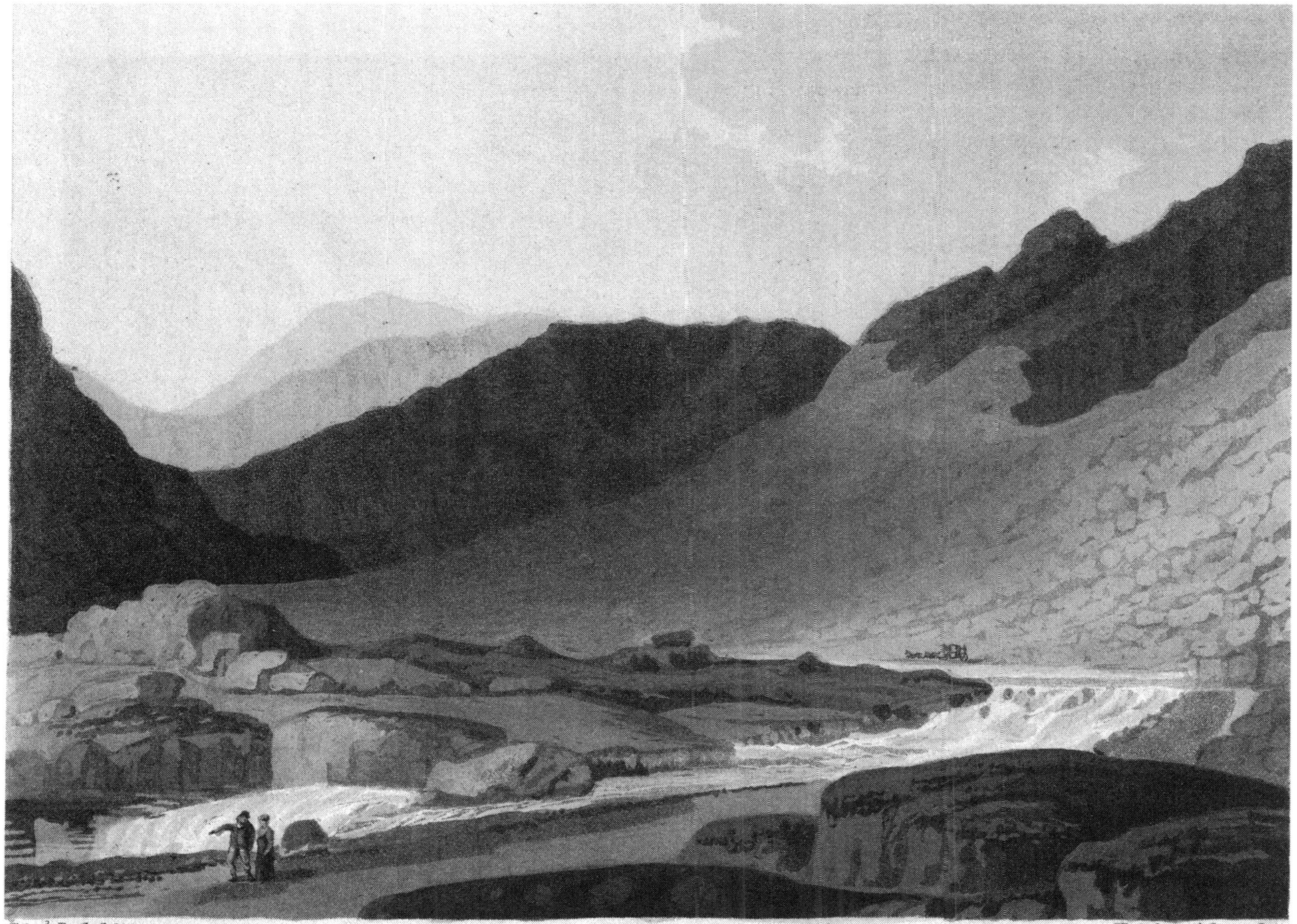

Edw.ᵈ Pugh delᵗ. Thoˢ. Cartwright sculpᵗ.

NANT FRANCON.

Published 30 June, 1813, by E. Williams, Strand.

ing this lake, I observed those stones, so much resembling human figures, on the high rock above the nearest extremity of Nant Ffrancon; called Y-Tryfaen (giving a name to the mountain), or more properly Trifaen*, the Three Stones—the number of the figures, till the fall of one of them a few years ago.

"In Tryfan's steep and craggy womb,
Uprais'd with stones is Bedwyr's† tomb."

From hence I struck to the right to see Llyn Idwal. To visit this with safety, travellers must quit their carriages or horses, and be content to take the foot road. Upon entering this cwm §, strangers have stood aghast for the moment, appearing more like fixed statues than animated nature; the mind is instantly filled with thoughts accordant to the horrific gloom and melancholy that pervade the vast profundity of this British Pandæmonium; the awful and formidable black precipices, that nearly surround this dismal pool, forming a wonderful amphitheatre, mysteriously reared by the magic spell of nature, has an irresistible effect upon the nerves of the most gay and airy; and those who have viewed it with such sensations, as the place is so well calculated to inspire, will not wonder when they are told, that in this hollow was foully murdered a young person of the name of Idwal, from whom it derived the appellation of Cwm Idwal. Idwal was a young prince, and son of Owen Gwynedd, put under the care of Nefydd Hardd, one of the fifteen tribes of North Wales, who lived at Llanrwst, about the end of the twelfth century. Dunawt, son of Nefydd, who perpetrated the horrid deed, as it is said, at the instigation of his

* *Trifen*, would be *three-headed*.

† Bedwyr, an illustrious hero of the Isle of Britain, flourished in the sixth century.

§ Cwm, means a great hollow in the mountain.

father, Nefydd Hardd, or Nefydd the Handsome, was on this account disfranchised, and reduced to a plebeian state. It is said that Rhûn, another son of Nefydd, granted the spot upon which the church of Llanrwst now stands, as an expiatory gift for this crime of his father. Mr. Williams of Llandegai gives an account of another Idwal, son of Cadwalader, the last king of the Britons, who, he supposes, retired hither from the tyranny of Ivor, who had usurped his father's throne. It is very remarkable that the people of this district continue, from time immemorial, to point out the spot where this Idwal was buried; he is fabled to have been a great giant, or gawr; and the rising ground by the side of the lake, several yards long, is said to be his grave, and precisely the length of his body.

This *cwm* is supposed, by the shepherds, to be the haunt of Demons: and that its damned waters are as fatal to any birds that attempt to cross them, as were those of *Avernus*, over which,

> "—— —————— void of light,
> No bird presum'd to steer his easy flight."

From hence I clambered a great height up the rocks, to see the hollow called Cwm Bochlwyd, or Hoary Cheek *. I reached it with some difficulty. This place failed to excite those feelings I experienced on the first approach to Cwm Idwal. This pool † is smaller, and the rocks are neither so high, terrific, nor of such extent, as those at the other; the shores about it are so rough, as to make them impassable. I descended again into the road to Llyn Ogwen. In my way down, I passed some frightful jutting rocks and stones, several of which, I have no

---

Many rocks and hills in Wales, are named after the different parts that form the human frame; as Pen, *Head;* Bron, *Breast;* Braich, *Arm;* Esgair, *Legs*, &c.

† It has some fine fish in it.

doubt, weighed some hundreds of tons, lying upon each other in rude order; my road led me under some of them, and I was not without apprehension, when in the act of passing, lest the least motion of my body should bring them down upon my head. I am of opinion some of these stones are very unsafe to touch, for while I stayed a few minutes to contemplate the wildness of the scenery before me, I sat upon one, which I fancy might weigh four or five tons; it slipped about a yard and a half, but was checked on its approaching a precipice only by a few smaller stones directly in its track. I accounted it a fortunate circumstance, that no massy stones rested upon it, in which case I must have fallen a sacrifice to my incautious procedure. My ears were, just now, saluted with the shrill voice of a shepherd's boy, at a distance on the hills; at the same time, a flock of sheep was making its way towards me, with the shepherd's dog at their heels; mine immediately attacked them in front, upon which the flock divided in two parties; and, facing about, actually drove the dogs out of the field of battle; the boy bestowing a few anathemas on both. My dog here found the refuse of a sheep's carcass, undevoured by Reynard; and it furnished her with a nice mountain meal.

I would advise the artist to get to the north side of Ogwen lake, and up the heights, till he can suit himself with points to his mind; assuring him that Llyn Idwal, with other grand objects, come in very boldly, and if he is so lucky as to be favoured with a murky sky, still clear enough to get the contour of the mountain and rocks, he will not be disappointed. As the new road on the north side of the river is finished, travellers, in this track, will be much more delighted with the sublimity of the scenery all the way down Nant Ffrancon, because the western side of it is by much the grandest. Ogwen lake * is about a mile and a quarter in length, and has in it (as has also Cwm Bochlwyd above) some excellent trout. From this lake to Capel Curig, is three miles and a half, of rather an uninteresting prospect compared with the past. This small interruption gave me a relish for the sublime scene, which, on turning down to the new inn, suddenly burst upon my sight. The evening being fine, I enjoyed from hence a delightful view of Snowdon, uninterrupted by clouds or vapours. It was now too late for much of out-door employment; so I amused myself with examining this poor-looking church. It is somewhat singular, that the parish of Llandegai, beginning beyond that village, is no less than fifteen miles in length †, including Capel Curig, which is chapel of ease to Llandegai, and five other chapels, dependent on the same mother-church. The chapel is dedicated to St. Curig, in the seventh century, celebrated for his learning and holy life: and is well endowed by Queen Anne's bounty. Here is a fair held annually for sheep, on the 28th of September. In full hopes of fine weather for ascending the mountain early, I engaged a guide at the inn, and went to repose for the night. On awaking in the morning, I was much concerned to find that the weather was very hazy; and the mist by noon increased to a heavy rain, which confined me to the house the whole day. The recollection, however, of the beautiful and clement sky with which I had hitherto been favoured, suppressed all disposition to complaint.

---

* Opinions respecting the word *Ogwen* are various; but an idea suggested by Mr. W— seems to carry weight with it: he derives the word from *Eog*, Salmon, and *Gwen*, Fair; so it might be read the Fair Salmon river.

† The whole parish belongs to Lord Penrhyn.—*Observations on Snowdon Mountains*, p. 65.

This inn was lately built from a plan by Mr. Wyatt, but finding it much too small for the convenience of the numerous travellers on this road, Lord Penrhyn ordered an addition of no less than twelve handsome rooms, which are now finished. Here is a large folio book to amuse the stranger, in which it is wished by the landlord, that ladies and gentlemen would favour the public with such remarks on the treatment and accommodation which they experience under his roof, as they may think him entitled to; and I was glad to observe, with the exception of two or three grumblers, who seemed discontented for what the landlord could not prevent, he had met with deserved praise from all. The book also contains some beautiful specimens of poetry, on various subjects; and some to the honour of Lord Penrhyn, to whom the public in general is highly indebted, for one of the greatest improvements the country ever saw, in the planning and execution of an excellent turnpike-road, through one of the roughest and most mountainous countries in Great Britain; where before no animal, but the sure-footed Welsh poney, or the native mountaineer, could travel. This road is now open from Bangor-ferry to Shrewsbury, avoiding the circuitous route through Conway; and thereby saving ten miles, merely in the distance from Bangor to Capel Voelas. Another road is now making from Chester, through Mold, Ruthin, Cerig-y-Druidion, and Capel Voelas, to meet this at Capel Curig; which from hence will branch through to Port-yn-Llŷn, near Nevin, in this county, from whence it is in contemplation to establish packets, to sail to and from Dublin.

Let me not forget to notice the conduct of a man, whom motives of the most honourable sort, induced to embrace a severely toilsome life. The following paragraph is taken verbatim from the book above alluded to. "Evan Jones, the guide at Capel Curig, is one whose good qualities as a conductor, and good character as a man, are highly praise-worthy. He left an easy service, and a kind master, to support his aged parents by great toil and industry. May such virtue meet with its reward! Jones follows the different occupations of a weaver, harper, and a guide; and all of them with deserved reputation."

Having rained incessantly all the second night, the river that runs from the pools here, was swelled to a monstrous height, which gave me the best opportunity of seeing the fall of Rhyadr-y-Wenol to perfection. I therefore pursued the road to Capel Voelas, and about a mile and a half from Capel Curig, passed over a bridge, under which is a great fall, which, were it more compact, and had the assistance of wood, would become interesting to the artist. Proceeding about two miles, I found the fall of Rhyadr-y-Wenol lying on the edge of the road, and a small wicker-gate leading down to it. It is to be wished, that the gentleman whose property it is, would order a commodious foot-way to be made; so that ladies, as well as gentlemen, might see it to advantage; at present it is hazardous to approach it. The noise is heard from the road, but the wood prevents a view of the fall till seen from below. The sight was excessively grand; a mighty torrent rushing down a precipice about eighty or a hundred feet high, between two wood-covered rocks; exhibiting, in my estimation, subject for a noble picture; the roaring noise was too much for me to bear. Though I was forty yards distance from the fall, the spray was so great, that the paper upon which I was sketching, became completely wet. There are two places to view this torrent from, one below another, exhibiting different aspects. Though the Niagara cataract in

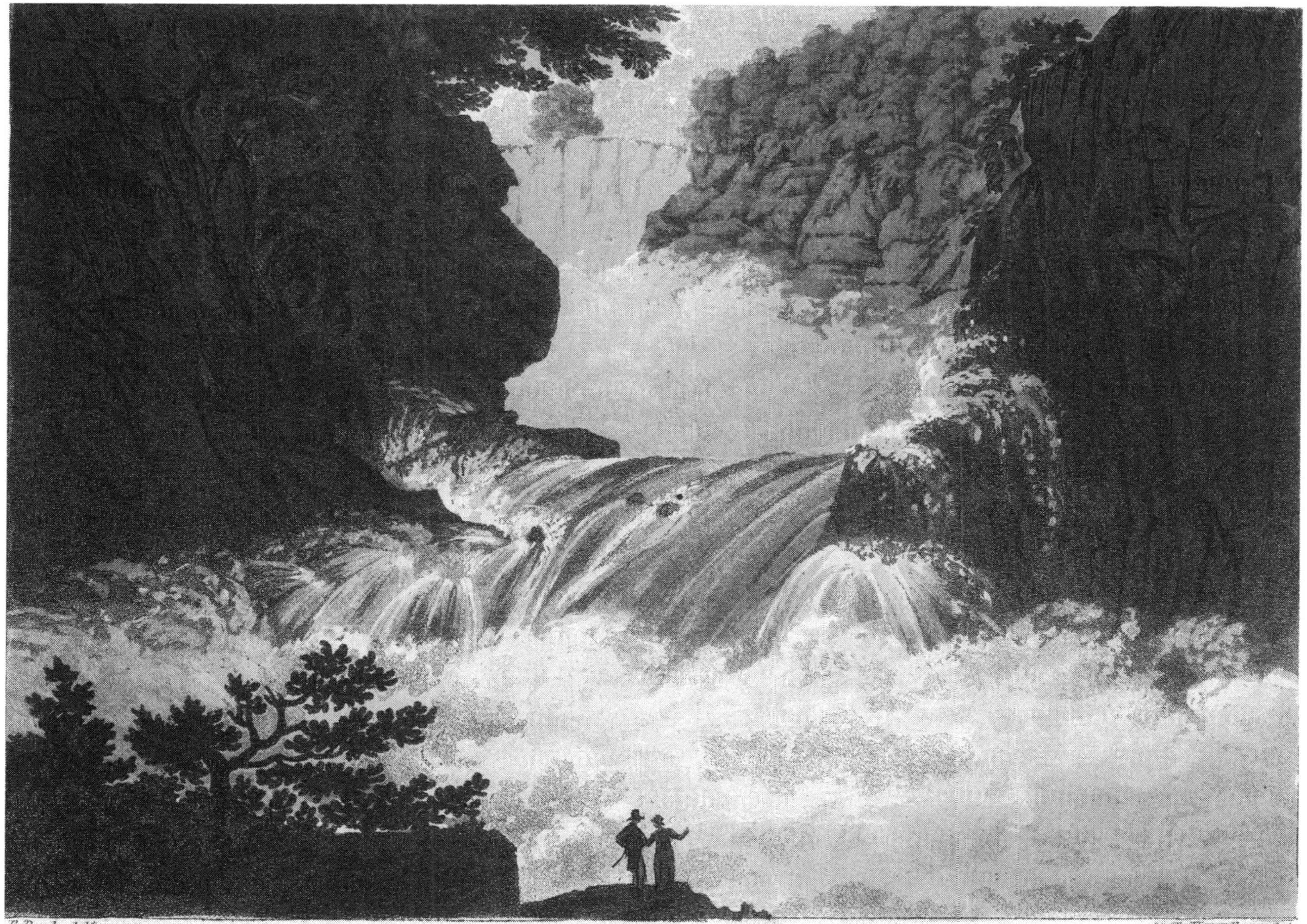

E. Pugh del.t T. Havell sculp.t

RHAIADR-WENOL.

Published 16 April 1814 by E. Williams Strand.

Canada, so celebrated by travellers, is of great breadth, and no less than one hundred and sixty-two feet fall, yet, so far as I can judge of it from pictures, it is not by any means so picturesque as the one now under notice. I returned for some distance by the road I came, and then climbed up the mountains towards Llanrwst, in order to ascertain the picturesque appearance of Snowdon from thence. In my way up, I passed several rustic cottages and farm-houses, so situated, with a rock or mountain behind, as to render them individually very picturesque. I did not perceive that the lines of Snowdon varied much, but the foreground did frequently, and as often discovered rocks that stood out very boldly, or cottages united with other objects, that made it unnecessary for the painter (though an allowed liberty) to compose a foreground of his own. The mountain from hence is excessively grand, and from no point whatever can the view of it be excelled. I had placed myself under the garden-wall of a farm-house, when I was suddenly assailed by a relentless storm; which, with the ferocious clamours of the farmers' dogs, made my situation unpleasant. Finding that the elements had resolved to wage war against me this morning, I made the best of my way down the mountain to the inn, half-drowned; towards the evening, however, there was a short cessation of hostilities in the air, and I embraced the opportunity of clambering up to the summit of Moel-Siabod *. The top of this mountain, like that of its neighbours, is stripped of verdure.

* Moel signifies bald-headed: Siabod seems not to have a meaning; but Mr. Williams supposes, that the *b* ought to be excluded, and the letter *d* take its place, in which case it would stand thus, Moel-Siadôd, properly meaning, " A mountain whose head is crowned or covered with new-fallen snow.

On the south side, the view of the precipice from its brink, is enough to stupify the senses, and almost to petrify the whole animal system, so that I found it necessary to keep aloof. The wind blew fresh from the east, and the country in that point was open. I could distinctly make out the ridge of mountains in the vale of Clwyd, and others as far south as Cader Ferwin in Merionethshire. It was a grand and novel sight, the sun strongly shining upon those distant objects, and on most of the intermediate varieties of hills, rocks, and water; with a dark cloud forming a gloomy canopy above me, throwing a shade and obscurity all around, which contrasted admirably with the splendour of the eastern distance. Snowdon itself was likewise involved in an almost impenetrable cloud, from the body of vapours that sluggishly moved along. It was altogether, to me, awfully fine. The sun was now sinking towards the horizon, and tinged the whole atmosphere with his setting colour. I anticipated the glowing exhibition, and prolonged my departure from the mountain till his rays had lost their influence on our hemisphere. In about half an hour the whole had attained a depth of red, that must be incredible to any, but to those who have been eye-witnesses. Snowdon seemed a dreadful mass of fire, and the clouds which hovered upon his top, and about his base, the consequence of it: the utmost fury of the burning Etna (barring the ill effects of it) could never have displayed a scene more sublime. Glydar mountain on the right, and the other extremity of Moel-Siabod, being detached from Snowdon, received but a small degree of red, as if reflected from him: a circumstance which added greatly to the magnificence of the scene.

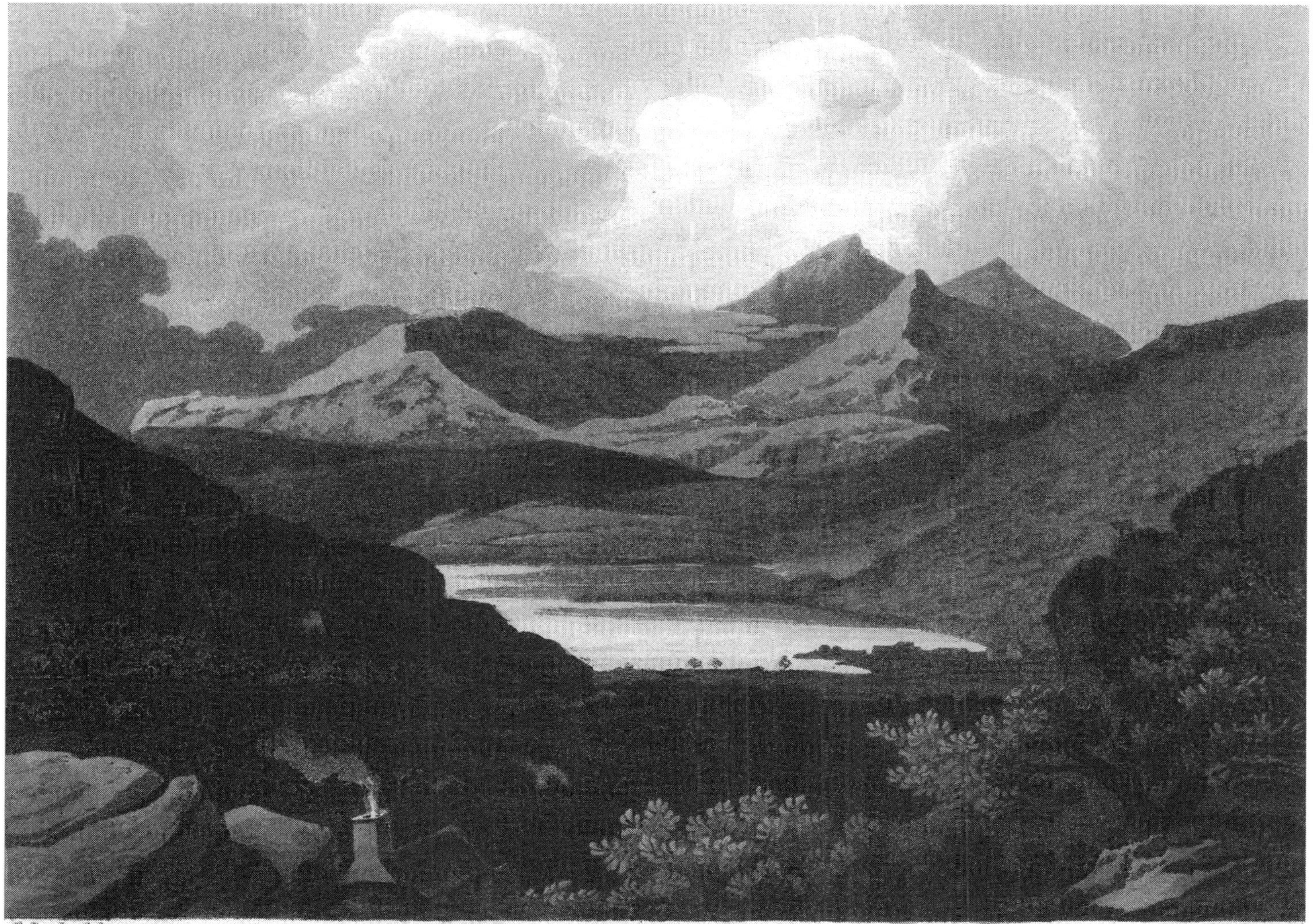

E. Pugh del. I. Havell sculp.

N. EAST VIEW OF SNOWDON.

Published 15 Nov.r 1813, by E. Williams, Strand.

"——————— and now the beamless sun
Sets as in blood; a dreadful pause ensues,
Deceitful calm, portending fiercer storm,
Sad night at once, with all her deep-dy'd shades
Falls back and boundless o'er the scene; suspense
And terror rule the hour."

MALLET'S *Excursion*, Canto i. line 363.

In the exhibition of 1804, P. I. De Loutherbourg, Esq. R.A., submitted a picture to public inspection, the subject of which was taken from the first two lines of "Gray's Elegy written in a Country Church-yard." The tongue of criticism was loud at the time, and scarcely any were to be found, who did not lavishly bestow upon it most unworthy blame. Thus, ignorant of the changes wrought in the terrestrial, as well as in the celestial region, by a fluctuating atmosphere, enhanced by the extreme brilliancy of a setting sun, they presumed to censure a master-piece of art, highly creditable to the hand that executed it. This gentleman having made several excursions into these parts, is intimately acquainted with the effects produced by a luminous sun-set, in a country whose mountains are so frequently charged with moisture, which at particular times flies off in evaporation, and causes an uncommon glow of colour.

Regardless of the distance to the inn, I remained till I could scarcely see my way through bogs and over precipices, and was soon left in total darkness. The night, justifying Mallet's observation, proved excessively stormy, with torrents of rain, which in the morning scudded with violence through the two lakes.

After staying here three days and nights, without the least prospect of weather to ascend Snowdon and Glydar Bach, I set off for Carnarvon by the side of lakes. Two miles on the road, I observed on my right, high on the side of a hill, an object that caught my fancy not a little. It was an immensely large stone completely formed like a shoe. It would not be difficult to devise a story respecting this stone, similar to the legend of the Giant Idris. Imagine, then, that a famous giant called Cawr-y-Eryri, or Giant of Snowdonia, having tried a pair of shoes, and finding that they did not fit him, swollen with passion, threw them after poor Crispin, as he was making his escape down the mountain; who, receiving a blow from one of them, was killed upon the spot: the shoe that gave him the mortal wound, lies at the bottom near the road, but very much disfigured by its journey; the other having met with no injury. Soon after, I came to the junction of Nant Nanhwynen with Llanberis Pass, and the valley I had just quitted. The foot of Snowdon from hence is very rugged, and is an excellent situation, in which to study rude nature. The peep into Nant Nanhwynen from this point, is very rich. I turned to the right into Llanberis Pass; at first it was rather tame, but after walking half a mile, it began to improve, and by degrees it opened very finely indeed; the gloominess of the morning added to the gravity and grandeur of the place. But for the small rain that fell, I should have spent the day here. This pass is one of the noblest scenes that the imagination of the artist can conceive; the landscape painter may find subjects to employ him for a considerable time, and those of the most picturesque kind. The amazing projecting rocks on the right, which seem to support the sides of Glydar mountain, are wonderfully grand, and finely broken; with deep fissures running sometimes perpendicularly, sometimes horizontally, and so often varying in their outline, that the artist is arrested by fresh subjects every fifty yards. Some of these great rocks project frightfully, and from the loose manner in which they are supported and propped up, the passenger goes by with dread, and great uncertainty of their remaining safe in their beds, till he is out of danger. I stayed awhile to gaze on what appeared to me, to be awfully grand; but which perhaps may lose much of its interest if viewed in fine weather. The place I mean is called Ynys Etws; it is a small cwm just above a mount of considerable height. The sullen gloom that overspread this cavity, with a noisy cascade above, and the sweeping clouds that skimmed the sides of the precipices, rendered the place, in idea, like the Devil's council-chamber. While I was looking at it, I saw a woman standing at the door of a solitary cottage, at the foot of the mount; the river being impassable, I was under the necessity of requesting she would come near; and, on my signal, she approached me with her arms a-kimbo. Her appearance was very singular, and not until I gained better information, could I be persuaded that she was not a man in female habit. Her voice was strong and deep-toned, and her shape masculine to a degree; the shoulders being broad like those of the male, while the *glutei muscles* contracted so, as scarcely to enable her to keep on her petticoats. She seemed to cultivate a beard with some care, which had already grown bushy through age. Her name is Cady (Catherine) Thomas. She lives by herself in this dreary spot, and holds a small farm of a few acres, which she manages without the assistance of any other person; her stock consists of two or three cows, a few sheep, and two little ponies; the latter used for plowing, herself performing the office of both plowman and driver. Until lately she had a sister who lived with her, in every respect like herself, but the ever-busy god played with her guileless heart, and, happily, her lover also acknowledging the same pleasing ascendancy, led the *tender fair one* to the hymeneal altar: but poor Caddy, notwithstanding her resplendent charms, seems devoted to celibacy. This neighbourhood has of late years been a little noted for extraordinary women. In 1788, one Margaret Evan lived near Llanberis; she was esteemed the best shooter, hunter, and fisher, of her time. She kept a dozen dogs, and with them destroyed more foxes in one year, than all the combined hunts in ten; to make up a finished character, she was an excellent fiddler, a good joiner, and the best wrestler in the country! The rock, called Dynas y Bod, or the Kites' Fort, standing nearly central in this pass, is a very picturesque bit; still lower down is Cwm-Glas, a solitary farm-house situated under and amongst stupendous hanging cliffs, piled there as it were to sustain the ponderous weight of a side of Snowdon. The amateur must be highly gratified in going through to view all these wonderful works of nature.

Llanberis, at the north-west entrance of the pass, is a small moss-covered hamlet, situated in the midst of a very beautiful little valley, at the base of the two Glydar mountains on one side, and Snowdon on the other, and nearly on the verge of two beautiful lakes. The church, in which is nothing to attract notice, is dedicated to St. Peris, a son of Helig ab Glanog, "a saint and cardinal" about the middle of the sixth century. From hence I intended to ascend Glydar Bach, but the guide, who keeps the public-house, assured me the day was by no means favourable; and that the mist would prevent a sight of the stones, at the distance of but a few yards. I much lamented my not having seen these amazing blocks, which, I have been informed, are so extraordinary, as to be well worthy the notice of every traveller; the view thence being little inferior to that from the summit of Snowdon. Maurice Pritchard, the guide and amen-man of the parish, is a civil old creature, and well acquainted with the country; he is often employed to collect alpine plants, which are to be had in great variety in this neighbourhood.

It would be a great accommodation to travellers, if a good house were built in this village*; and the road improved and made passable for carriages from Carnarvon, to meet the new road from Bethgelert to Capel Curig. In this case, strangers might make a pleasant excursion round the romantic base of Snowdon, and meet with comfortable resting-places at the close of very convenient intervals. The present public-house, belonging to the Earl of Uxbridge, is much too poor to afford the traveller either refreshment or comfort. In the spirit of improvement, now so prevalent, his Lordship's liberality may, ere long, be induced to supply these accommodations, so much wanted in this part of the country. Quitting this place, I proceeded on the left of the lakes, to the fall called Cennant mawr; the body of water that came tumbling down was very great; which, with the rugged sides of the rocks, and deep chasms below, made it, upon the whole, a fine subject.

Dolbadarn-castle, on an eminence above Llanberis lakes, consists of a single round tower of amazing strength and boldness; and is rendered truly picturesque by its various grand accompaniments. The entrance into it being blocked up with large stones, I can say nothing of the internal part. Standing alone, and at a distance from any other building, it has a solitary but very striking effect from the shore below Behind is the rise

* Mr. B—— proposed that Dolbadarn Castle should be turned into an inn; but why should the solemn effect of this tower, situated as it is, be destroyed by the addition of a trumpery modern building? the whole would then evidently become a contemptible hetero geneous mass, highly disgusting to every lover of antiquity.

towards the summit of Snowdon; and the magnificent recess of Llanberis Pass completes the noble and animated scenery. This tower was, no doubt, erected to guard this pass, but was occasionally used as a state prison; for we find that in 1255, Prince Owen Gôch was confined here after his defeat by his brother Llewelyn ab Griffydd. Near is a copper mine, which some years since was found to yield much ore, but its operations were afterwards discontinued. It is now worked again with some advantage, by Messrs. Roe and Co. The slate quarries belong to Thomas Asheton Smith, Esq., but are farmed by Messrs. Ellis, Wright, and Co.; they produce fine slates, a little differing in colour from those of Lord Penrhyn; these are shipped off at Carnarvon and Moel y Don, a few miles below the lakes. The copper ore and slates are conveyed along the lakes, and then carted to their destination

The road now became intolerably bad and in vain did I turn several times a considerable way out of it on each side; I could observe nothing yet unnoticed, till I ascended the hill, when I gained a fine prospect of Anglesey, the Menai, and the turrets of Carnarvon-castle. I reached this latter place very wet and much fatigued. The town I found greatly thronged with strangers, which gave it an air of gaiety I had not observed since my arrival in the country. The castle is well known to many of the artists, as a noble specimen of military architecture; the towers are polygonal, and very bold and broad; from which issue turrets of the same description; and the whole rises up majestically on the verge of the Sciont, a river that flows from Llanberis lakes. The exterior of the castle appears pretty entire, except on the north-west side, where a few fractures are seen, that improve it in the eye of the painter. The same observations with regard to the artist, will attach to this place as to Conway. There are several points that were never tried, or at least, that I have never seen either on canvass or paper; and an immense number of paintings and drawings of it, have come under my observation. Though some houses and walls are interposed, the castle, nevertheless, makes a fine appearance from the sea before the town; and, in my opinion, receives no little importance from those objects lying between: especially as some of them are coeval with it, and tend considerably to increase the picturesque effect. The Rev. Mr. Warner has represented this castle as being inhabited: his words are, "But it does not produce those lively emotions in the mind, which edifices of this nature are apt to excite, from the circumstance of its being kept in *nice repair*, and inhabited." From this description, one would imagine that the old castle having been painted and white-washed, and sashes put in the windows, had become the residence of some respectable family; but the fact is, that it is *not* kept in repair, although the founder (it is said) left an annuity for that purpose; but possibly it is better laid out. With regard to inhabitants, there may be, under the walls of the court-yard, a small portion tenanted by an old peasant: but (my attention being wholly engaged by the ancient walls that surrounded me) this partial inhabitance escaped my notice; but the appearance of the whole, instead of repressing "those lively emotions in the mind, which edifices of this nature are apt to excite," tends to increase them, by reminding us, not only that man himself, but the most permanent of his works, are liable to decay. Upon entering the grand gateway, under which is the statue of its founder, Edward I., under a huge, massive, but noble tower, the stranger is convinced of Mr. Warner's error, by observing an empty court-yard, with walls and towers, shewing visibly the injuries of time. The area within the walls, is about one acre, grazed by sheep and other animals. The Eagle-tower had on its top, an eagle carved in stone: but, lately, two men contrived to hurl it over the parapet to the bottom, in spite of a strong iron rod, that went through the different stones that composed it. Edward I. was the founder of this castle, which stands as a magnificent monument of his taste and power. The king seems to have been in no little haste to erect a strong edifice, that should keep his newly-acquired subjects in order, for this castle * was completed in one year, by the labour of the peasantry, at the expense of the chieftains of the country: a task which must have been oppressive in the extreme. Eleanor, who is represented as an amiable and an affectionate queen, retired hither; and on the 25th of April, 1284, was brought to bed of the unhappy Edward II. The king had promised that the Welsh should have a prince of their own, who could not speak a word of English; which promise he kept, literally, though he still completely duped them, by pronouncing, on the birth of this child, that he was the first Prince of Wales, of the English line.

Mr. Pennant, according to tradition, says, that this prince was born in a little dark room in the Eagle-tower, "not twelve feet long, nor eight broad." Although it be well known that royalty, in those days, little consulted its own ease, being contented with lying even in straw beds, *&c.*, yet the very confined area of this room was by no means calculated to accommodate her majesty, and her numerous female attendants, on that oc-

* The architect's name was Henry Ellerton, or de Elreton.

casion ; and, in this instance, conjecture seems stronger than tradition, and points out a large room, near this closet, with a fire-place, and a handsome window: which appears, in every respect, more suitable to the exigency of the case. The establishment for the castle and town was the following: a constable of the castle, with a salary of forty pounds per annum; the captain of the town had twelve pounds thirteen shillings and four pence. The constable and captain had allowed them twenty-four soldiers for the defence of the place, whose wages were four-pence a day. The porter of the gates of the town, had annually a fee of £3 10*s*.

In the year 1294, happened a great insurrection of the Welsh, under Madoc; who, taking advantage of the fair time, and putting many English to the sword, took the castle, and that of Conway; and, at the same time, reduced all Anglesey to subjection.

In the time of civil discord, when Lord Byron was governor, the place was besieged by General Mytton, to whom it surrendered on honourable terms, in 1646. Sir John Owen in his turn besieged the general, but hearing that a parliament force, under Colonels Carter and Twisleton, were on their march to relieve the garrison, he withdrew a part of his force to attack them; but was defeated, and made prisoner :—after this North Wales submitted to the parliament.

Captain Taylor, who personally contended with Sir John, received £200 reward out of his estates. Sir John was brought to trial, with four noblemen, and all were condemned to lose their heads. Sir John, when the trial ended, made a low bow to the court, and gave it his humble thanks; some person near him asking what he meant, he raised his voice and replied.

"That it was a great honour to a poor gentleman of Wales, to lose his head with such noble lords, for by G— I was afraid they would hang me." Many advocates appeared in favour of the Duke of Hamilton, Earl of Holland, and Lords Goring and Capel: but no one stepping forward in favour of poor Sir John, Ireton instantly became his advocate, and proved successful; and Sir John alone was saved. He retired to his estate in this county, and died in 1666, and was buried in Penmorfa church, where a monument perpetuates his memory.

When we reflect upon the great bustle that pervaded the gay court of Edward, and contrast the scenes of those days with the present deserted state of this castle, the mind naturally turns melancholy on the reflection.

"Ple mae Edwart, plwm ydych!
Gwr a wnai y Gaer yn wych:
Mae ei ddelw, pe meddylien.
Wych yn y porth, uwch y pen;
Ynteu yn fud hwnt yn ei fedd;
Dan garreg dew yn gorwedd."

SIR D. TREFOR.

Where! ye now astonished cry—
Where does mighty Edward lie?
He that gave these ramparts birth,
When prostrate Cambria lean'd on earth;
Here still his image, rais'd on high,
Attracts the thoughtful curious eye;
But he, long humbled from a throne,
Far distant lies beneath a stone.

Translated by MR. LLWYD.

Over the principal entrance-gate into the town, is the town-hall. The county jail is situated near the castle; the assizes for the county are held here. The evening and Sunday promenade is on a beautiful terrace on the north-west side of the town, where the beaus and belles taste the refreshing breezes that skim the briny flood. Near the custom-house, which is on the quay, is a ferry over the river Sciont, to a walk through the wood, where strangers will be pleased with the views. The walls around the town are very entire, and I was informed that £300 only would be necessary to make them as good to walk upon as those of Chester. Close to the town are the remains of the ancient Roman Segontium. They consist of a few fragments, standing two or three yards out of the ground, covered with ivy; and from them the plan of the city is discovered to have been a parallelogram. A quarter of a mile further is Llanbeblic, the parish church of Carnarvon, dedicated to St. Peblic, a saint of the fifth century; where the inhabitants of that town hear divine service in their mother tongue, and bury their dead. The church-yard is thickly bespread with grave-stones. Being upon so *grave* a subject, I shall give the reader some account of burials in Wales. The decease of any person is announced by the parish bell, the day of the burial also being known, the neighbours meet on the night preceding the interment at the house where the deceased lies, which, on such occasions, is termed Ty Corph, *i. e.*, the Corpse's House. The coffin, with the remains of the departed, is then laid upon stools, or a table, covered, if married, with black cloth; if single, with a pure white sheet; upon which are placed three lighted candles; each person, on entering "the house of mourning," very devoutly bends the knee before the corpse, repeating in a low whisper, the Lord's-prayer, or any other established or extempore supplication, the momentary ebullition of the sorrowful heart; after this, to those who are smokers, pipes and tobacco are tendered: originally intended to destroy any baneful effluvia that may arise from the corpse; a custom, perhaps, on such occasion, better avoided than continued; by which, however, no immorality is produced, as little or no liquor is drank. When the assembly is complete, the parish-clerk stands conspicuous, and reads through the burial-service, the people being very attentive, and they conclude the service with singing psalms and hymns: but as Methodism has increased greatly of late years, it is now very common for a man of that sect to make an impressive oration on the melancholy event; after which, the people depart to their different homes. It must be observed, that this ceremony is common only to the mountainous parts; but is falling off fast, and is nearly obsolete in the eastern counties of the principality. It is called Gwylnos, or Vigil; in other parts it is improperly denominated Padrua, a corruption of Paderuace, or Pater-nosters. In the afternoon of the following day, the burial takes place: when three, four, and frequently five, hundred people assemble, to accompany the remains of the deceased to the grave. Two or three are employed to hand around cakes and hot-spiced ale, to the company; and, to those who choose them, pipes and tobacco; and if the deceased was respectable or wealthy, a dinner is provided for those who come from far. The procession now commences, and at the conclusion of the service in the church, and ere the corpse is withdrawn from it, the people walk up to the communion table, when they present the officiating clergyman with a piece of money, proportioned to their means, which they lay on the altar; and this is called an offering; the total of the money thus collected, depends on the deceased's connexions in life; sometimes it is eight, ten, twelve, or more pounds. The coffin is now conducted to the grave, where it is deposited; and, while the grave is closing, the clerk receives his offering upon his spade, which, in general, amounts to about one-fourth of that of the clergyman. The company, after this, retire to a public-house; and each spends three-pence or six-pence for ale.

Though the people all know, that the custom of offering is a remains of a popish superstition, they continue it only as a respect due to the memory of the deceased. In the prayer before the corpse we may, perhaps, recognize a prayer for the soul's repose; and in the offering to the priest, a contribution for the deceased person's absolution, and a speedy release out of purgatory.

But to return:—Carnarvon is governed by a mayor (who is also the governor of the castle), one alderman, two bailiffs, a town clerk, and two serjeants at mace; its burgesses, with those of Conway, Pwllheli, Nevin and Crikieth, send one member to parliament; Sir Robert Williams, Bart., is their present representative.

The marine trade here is chiefly in slates, exported to different parts of the united kingdom. A few small vessels from sixty to one hundred and fifty tons each, were on the stocks; and did not appear to me to be inferior in make and strength to what I have seen in Liverpool and London. Carnarvon is a handsome, smart town; the streets, though narrow, are clean, and strangers frequently prolong their stay to enjoy the beautiful rides in the neighbourhood. It is become a fashionable bathing-place, with every convenience for the purpose. The English service is performed in a small chapel in the town, formerly a chapel to the garrison. There are two or three good inns, but the hotel built by Lord Uxbridge, seems to take the lead: from its external appearance, the stranger would take it for a gentleman's seat, rather than an inn. The accommodations are excellent, and every attention is paid to the comfort and convenience of the stranger by Mr. and Mrs. Wakeman. Carriages and saddle-horses may be had for excursions to Snowdon, a distance of eight miles. After staying here a few days, I embraced the first opportunity of a favourable change of weather, and made for Bethgelert. For four or five miles, the road to Bethgelert is uninteresting; when it descends into the beautiful little vale of Bettws Garmon; the church of this straggling little village is dedicated to St. Garmon, the celebrated saint, who, with Lupus, commanded the Britons, when they completely vanquished the Picts and Saxons near Mold. It stands at the foot of Moel Eilio, a mountain of considerable height. Beyond the village is Nantmill and its waterfall. By reading a late tour, I had been led to expect something great in this fall, but it by no means surprised me by any traits of the picturesque. It is scarcely eight feet high, and too much scattered to form any power of stream equivalent to the noble jutting rock above it; nor does the figure of the mill agree well with the surrounding magnificent scenery. On the left of the road is Plas yn-y-Nant, or Hall in the Vale, romantically situated. It is the occasional residence of Sir Robert Williams. I soon came in sight of Cwellyn lake, about one mile in length; a fine piece of water, containing not only the common trout, but the red-bellied char, in season about Christmas. Here I had a sight of a soft and gradual ascent to the apex of Snowdon. On the south-west side of the lake, at the lower end, is a huge hanging precipice, called Castell Cidwn, the Den of a Voracious Animal, from the circumstance of its having anciently upon it a fortress that

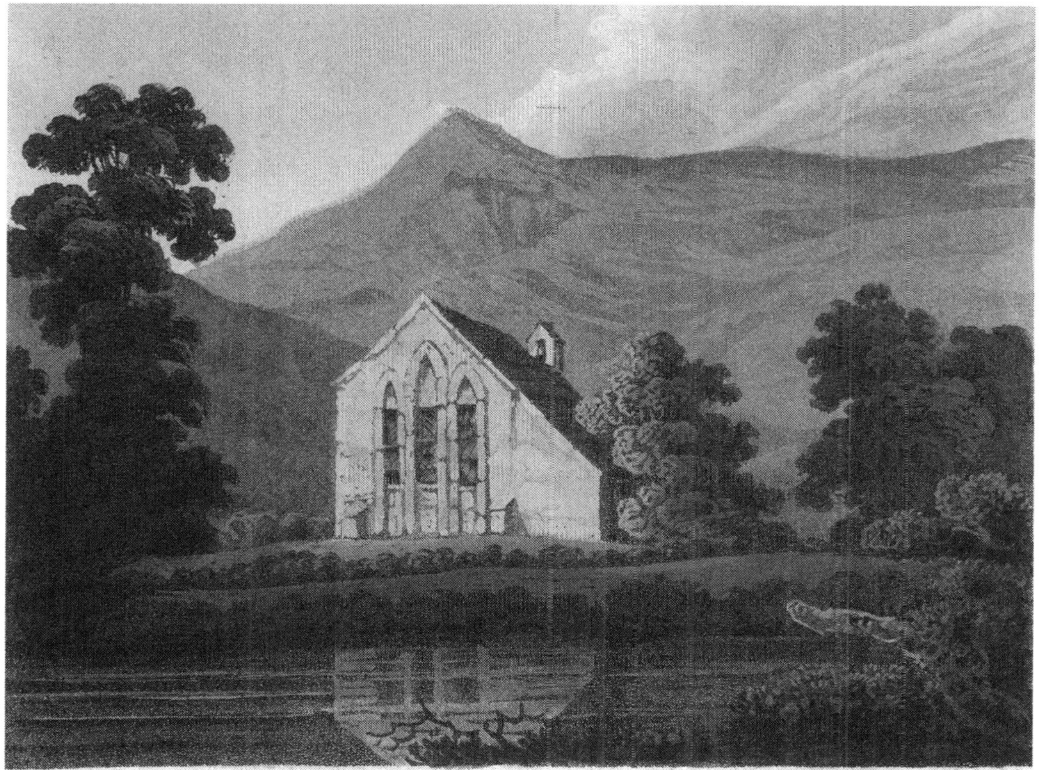

E. Pugh del.t T. Cartwright sculp.t

BETHGELERT CHURCH.

Published 15 July 1814, by E. Williams, Strand.

overawed this mountain pass; of which, however, there is not a vestige now remaining. Further on is a small public-house, kept by a man who is a very intelligent guide to Snowdon; here I intended to have ascended, had not the guide gone up with some gentlemen an hour before. Altering my course, I went by the south-east end of the lake, some miles up the mountains, going by several very fine impending rocks on each side of a romantic pass, till I came in sight of Llyniau Nantlle. Here the opening over the lakes, with a view of the sea, is fine. I would advise the artist to make this deviation from the main road, even beyond these lakes to a little village called Llanllyfni, where he may be accommodated with a bed, and civil treatment. Returning by the same way, I came to a pool called Llyn-y-Dwarchen, or the Lake of the Sod. Camden speaks of a "wandering island" on this pool, and even Giraldus, so far back as 1188, mentions it by the title *Insula Erratica.* It is very remarkable that this island is yet in being. From the best information that I can get, it has suffered no diminution in size: its soil is peat (the nature of the soil on these mountains), covered with a very long grass. This islet is probably eight yards in length, and four or five across. The people here say it is a certain prognostic of fair or foul weather, as it floats to the one or the other end of the pool. When I saw it, it lay at the south end, foreboding, as I presume, the beautiful weather with which I was afterwards favoured. A boy, who lives close by, amuses himself by swimming to it; and, taking the helm, he steers it to any part of the pool he pleases. This piece of water, I believe, is about three-quarters of a mile round, and is situated at the feet of two bold rocks. The inhabited house, contiguous to the pool, has a stone inserted over the door, upon which is a Welsh inscription, implying that it was erected and dedicated to the service of God. Leaving this place, and coming again into the road, I passed another lake called Llyn-y-Gader, or the Lake of the Fortress, a beautiful expanse of water, surrounded by a congregation of wild rocks; and I then descended the hill into the romantic vale of Bethgelert.

Early in the next morning I made up the mountains, westward of the village, following an uncertain, rough footpath, from whence the craggy base of Snowdon, and the much admired pass of Nant Nanhwynen are seen to great advantage. Snowdon was cloud-capt all the day. Ascending still higher, I perceived the Merionethshire rocks and mountains, standing up boldly to my view. I walked to many situations on these heights, all of which offer suitable positions to the painter, for sketches of much interest; and so various are the important points, that I could have remained here during a whole day. Nothing can look more dreary than the abodes of the indigent farmers and peasantry on these great elevations; the land, cold, poor, and boggy, produces very little of any sort of grain or other esculents. This unproductiveness arises either from their obstinacy in persevering in the old injudicious system of managing their land, or from an ignorance of a better method of culture. It has been asserted, that shallow drains, and a seasonable irrigation of their fields and meadows, from the numerous rivulets constantly rushing from their mountains (a practice pursued with success in different parts of England and Ireland), would produce here a most beneficial improvement; and that, while such a management of their land would ensure to them good crops of hay, an earlier sowing of their grain would also bring them an earlier corn-harvest, and enable them to house it in better order. These mountaineers are a hardy race, and accustomed to fare which an Englishman would think meanly coarse. Their bread, made of barley or oats (rarely of wheat), is generally eaten with buttermilk, salt, butter, cheese, and potatoes. In winter, they live much upon dry salted mutton, and smoked rock-venison, or goat, which is called Coch ar Dden, or the Red upon the Withe, being hung upon a withe constructed of the twigs of a willow. They are very sober, ale not being in their bill of fare, and milk and water allaying their thirst just as well. The luxury of ale-brewing is confined to the more wealthy farmer. Thus the hardy inhabitant of the mountains runs his race through life; and, though his meals are coarse and short, "his employments are warranted, his sleep certain and refreshing, neither interrupted with the lashes of a guilty mind, nor the aches of a crazy body." From their childhood accustomed to ramble upon the mountains, to look after their cattle, these people are by habit inured to the utmost inclemency of the weather; their employment, however, though requiring hardiness, cannot be said to be very laborious. As they are great economists, they go bare-footed in summer, to save the article of shoes, the wear of which would be rendered more expensive upon their rocky territories. On meeting their friends, the mode of salutation, "Pa sit mae galon? or, How is thy heart? Pa sit mae yr wraig ar plant? How are thy wife and children?" is expressive of simplicity and affection. When they meet at public-houses, which they seldom do but on some particular occasion or merriment, they will, at every round, drink the health of the person who next receives the mug. These customs are also common to the lowlanders all over North Wales. Though these people, as well as those of the vallies, are, from necessity, cautious and close in their bargains; they are by no means the characters described by a late tourist, who represents them as arrant cheats. That there are dishonest characters in this country, no one will attempt to deny; and where, it may be asked, is the country without them?

In passing hastily through a district, on meeting a tricking fellow or two in his way, is a tourist from thence justified in concluding and representing the whole population to be of the same description? From the detected aberrations of a few, in the mean arts of cunning and fraud, are all the rest, without further inquiry, to be indiscriminately branded by a wanton dash of the pen? Are the fidelity and truth of the delineation which has long exhibited sincerity, honesty, and charity, for the predominant features of the Welsh character, to be thus at once brought into suspicion? Where did a certain gleaner, in the collection of his ingenious reveries, pick up the notable discovery, that "it is the settled usage of the principality for the trading part of the people to overreach strangers, in their little marketings and bargains with them?" The occasional frauds of "little marketings and bargains," he might apply, perhaps, with equal propriety, to any part of the kingdom. In the description, therefore, of local manners, he ought to have refrained from all such random and public defamation; which, instead of embellishing, could only, as he should have known, deform and dishonour his page.

When I had gained the summit of these hills, I traversed them in vain in different directions; as the clouds, gathering thickly around their tops, obstructed from my view every thing that was interesting in the scenery. Descending into a dreary valley, I passed on by the side of a lake a mile long; and a dull walk over marshy ground of three miles further, brought me to Llanfihangel, a little village pent up in an angle, formed by some bold cliffs, with a good river, rushing down from the mountains over one of the roughest beds that I had yet seen. The numerous large and massy stones, lying in grotesque groups near the water, with the savage appearance of the precipices, an old bridge, a small church, with some wood scattered about, and a few rusticated houses, furnished a scene altogether highly gratifying to the eye of a painter. Feeling a want of refreshment, I inquired for the public-house, but was informed that the village enjoyed no such luxury. A farmer's wife, however, kindly inviting me to partake of what her table afforded, the fare, though coarse, was very grateful to an appetite rendered voracious by the keen air of the mountains. This good woman, in the course of our conversation, with a modest apology, inquired what could induce me to travel through a trackless country, where it was difficult even for the natives to find their way? She observed that, sometimes strange people were seen at Bethgelert, with large books (portfolios) making maps of the country; that they would often ascend Snowdon for the purpose, it was supposed, of ascertaining places of landing on the sea-shores, and it became necessary for the natives to be a little watchful over them; she however intimated, that I was exempted in her mind, from any suspicions of this nature. I replied, that those who were seen with books, *&c.*, were probably gentlemen professing an art admired by all the world, and were, I might venture to say, all of them loyal subjects to the king; but that it was nevertheless proper to have an eye upon all strangers, lest any foreigners, with some treacherous intent, should make their ingress amongst them; and, under the pretence of drawing views, *&c.*, might the more easily accomplish their designs.

I left this good creature with many thanks for her civilities, and pursued my way over some fertile land to Dolbenmuen, a small neat hamlet, where the Rev. Mr. Holland's cottage, contiguous to the church-yard, makes a figure amid the wildness of the country. This place is on the confines of Llûn, which comprehends all that flat part of Carnarvonshire, extending from Penmorfa northwards to Llanllyfni, and stretching thence between twenty and thirty miles south-west towards Bardsey Island; thus forming what is termed the Horn of Carnarvonshire. It is a fine corn country, lying nearly flat, with a very gentle rising from the sea; and is rather bare of wood, which is cultivated only as shelter to a few gentlemen's houses. From hence the country on my left was one continued plain, and on my right very hilly, but of that spiritless sort, that uninteresting smoothness of surface, which will always fail to amuse the lover of the picturesque.

I now arrived at the village of Llanllyfni. The summer before, Mr. Webster, a very respectable artist, and a friend of his, amusing themselves near this place in making sketches, were exposed to most unpleasant treatment from the quarry-men, who entertained the suspicions expressed by the good woman of Llanfihangel. The door of the public-house being locked, I waited for some minutes for admission. In the meanwhile I perceived a number of men collecting in the street; at the same moment, the man who belonged to the house made his appearance at some distance; and a lad ran to inform him that a stranger was at his door. "Is he an Englishman, a Welshman, a Frenchman?" was the question in Welsh: the boy replied, he was thought to be a Frenchman. O then! returned he, by G—, he shall not stay in our house. The door however was opened, and I entered a small parlour. This man, though unable to speak English, perceived, I believe, that my dialect was not foreign; with a great deal of suspicion, however, he viewed me from head to foot. I then, in English, requested some refreshment, and repeated the request; but received no answer Finding that my English was not likely to procure for me the comforts of the house, I thought it more prudent to alter my mode of proceeding. I went, therefore, into the kitchen, into the midst of the people, who by this time had crowded in; and, after some silence on my part, finding myself the subject of their conversation, and that the general opinion was rather unfavourable to me, principally on account of my portfolio, I suddenly turned round, and replied with some severity in their own language, to an observation which one of them had just made. It was not a little laughable to see the alteration in the people's looks at this moment; they instantly left the house, expressing their satisfaction on finding that I was not likely to be a spy. I was now assured that I should be accommodated with a bed, and with every necessary which their house afforded. The fracas of Mr. W. and his friend with the countrymen, arose merely from their ignorance of each other's language. This part of Wales is very little known to travellers; and the native poor are without the means of attaining even to a superficial knowledge of the English tongue. Most, if not all, of these men, were probably born on the spot. and having a sort of adhesive quality in them, a strong attachment to their native soil, with a high regard for each other, they scarcely ever travel beyond the circuit of a few miles from home. From these circumstances, they become from principle jealous of travellers, and especially of artists, who are seen (as they term it) *lurking* about the mountains, making *maps of the country, &c.* This jealousy of strangers is by no means peculiar to this part of the country. In the summer of 1803, Mr. V—— and another artist, being on an excursion to the north of England, were frequently interrupted by the country people. At last their presence in a certain neighbourhood, created so strong a suspicion of disloyal intentions, that they were under the necessity of submitting to be interrogated by the magistrates: one of whom, after deliberately fixing his spectacles to his nose, insisted on examining the drawings. The scene which followed was amusing. This *genius* saw in every sketch, either batteries, guns, bulwarks, trenches, castles, or camps. With great facility he turned cart-routes into defiles, trees into revolutionary banners, stones into military horses, gates into ammunition-waggons, cottages into prisons, and ferry-boats into men-of-war. Had it not been for the other magistrates, who saw better, judged more wisely, and knew a little more of the arts than their purblind brother, these gentlemen might have been committed to jail.

The lakes above this village, with the noble rocks on each side and with Snowdon in front, form one of the finest objects in the country. The late Mr. Wilson, R. A., chose this scene for the subject of a picture, which by connoisseurs was esteemed one of the most excellent of his performances. The print which was engraved from it by Woollet, is, as I believe, now become scarce. Excepting the tripartite mountain, called yr Eifl, and not as the English say, Rivals, I could discover nothing in all this extensive part of Carnarvonshire that was likely to attract either the painter or the mineralogist. Willing, however, to sacrifice a part of my time to try to discover some cliffs on the shores, I made towards yr Eifl, every now and then looking at Snowdon, which was perfectly uncovered, and appeared majestically towering above the lakes of Nantlle. These, with alternately some trees, a cottage, or a rock in the fore-ground, and an intervening opposition of a flat, and the little village which I had just quitted, completed a landscape exquisitely fine, though, from the remoteness of Snowdon, consisting more of the elegant than of the picturesque. I presently came to the delightfully situated village of Clynog, embosomed in wood; the church of which is of the crucifix form, and is a large, unhandsome, heavy pile, with an interior not very remarkable for cleanliness. It is, however, noted for the tomb of St. Beuno, who was a descendant of Cadell, Prince of Powis, and uncle to St. Winefred: he founded a college here in 616. It was formerly believed by many, that if a diseased person lodged one night on Beuno's tomb, he would find a radical cure, but that he must first undergo ablution at the saint's well near the village. The experiment, as I understand, is now no longer tried. One part of the church is occupied as a school, the master of which is an old sailor, who retains his old professional habit, and seems eager to impress on the infant minds of his scholars the necessity of becoming, at least, as knowing as himself, by that cogent argument the birch, which he wields with as much alacrity perhaps as he ever saw the cat-o'-nine-tails used at sea. The inns here I found to be comfortable, and the charges truly moderate. Leaving Clynog, I proceeded with the sea on my right for four miles, the shores sloping gently to the water.

Llanhaiarn is a poor village, from whence I struck up to one of the summits of the Eifl mountain; which proved to be very high and tiresome to climb: but I was amply repaid for my trouble by a sight of the greatest British military works in the principality. The outward walls form an irregular area of eight or ten acres, within which are a number of other walls, no doubt once the habitation of the soldiers. This citadel, I presume, from the immense thickness of the walls, must have been considered as a place of great strength in those days, when the use of gunpowder was unknown; but it discovers much ignorance of the science of military architecture, both in its construction and its design. The stones seem not to have been chisselled, and have been heaped up one upon another in a rude and unskilful order, without the aid of mortar, or of any other cement to give their union durability; and, in their original state, nothing but their thickness and weight could have given them that stability which rendered them impervious to the attack of an enemy. The other summits of this mountain, exhibit similar species of fortifications. From sights like these, the traveller may form a juster notion of the persevering spirit of our ancestors in the defence of their country, than he would from volumes of histories of the ancient Britons. Further on is Nant Gwrtheyrn, or Vortigern's Valley, whither Vortigern fled from the rage of his subjects. He was a man of unprincipled character, and is called in the Triads, one of the three disgraceful men of the island, for forming one of the three treacherous plots against his country;—for bringing in, and uniting with, the Saxons; for putting Constantine to death, and for driving into exile two of his brothers, Emrys and Uthyr. He called a meeting of the British and Saxon chiefs, on the mountain called Caer Caradoc, when the massacre of the long knives took place. The two other plots were executed by Avarwy and Medrod. Vortigern is also styled one of the three greatest drunkards of Britain; for he obtained his wife, Alis Rowena, daughter of Horsa the Saxon, in a fit of intoxication at the expense of the Isle of Thanet. His family, with those of Avarwy and Medrod, were for ever after stripped of all their privileges.—He was the eighty-second king of Britain. By his last marriage he had a son called Gotta, on whom he unjustly settled the crown; and thus the Britons were dispossessed of the sovereignty of the island. He died about the year 481; and, as it is related, in a manner which discovered the signal vengeance of Heaven; for he and his castle were destroyed by lightning. Tradition, confirmed by the singular discovery of a stone coffin, in which the bones of a tall man were found, has handed down the fact of his having been buried in the valley called by his name, and in a tumulus styled, from time immemorial, Bedd Gwrtheyrn, or Vortigern's Grave.

Quitting the mountain, I came by a good, though a dull road to Nevin, a small town, with a harbour for about fifty vessels of from forty to sixty tons, which belong to it; and are principally employed in carrying slates from Carnarvon, *&c.* to Liverpool and other places. Within a mile of the town is Ty Mawr, and near it a stone pillar with monastic carving upon it. The worthy landlord, Mr. Jones, relates, that this stone had for a length of time been neglected and taken up from its present and original site; and when his mother was on her death-bed, she expressed a wish that it should re-occupy its former situation, saying, that, until this was effected, she could not die with comfort; and that it was an act of the greatest impiety ever to have disturbed it. Two miles above the town is a house called Pistyll, near which are some grand cliffs that continue some distance on the sea side, with some considerable caverns, of a wild and savage appearance. Adjoining the town, is what the inhabitants call Mount Pleasant, where they assemble on fine Sundays, to view the sea and other objects which are not within the prospect of their houses. This mount, as I am convinced, is a *tumulus*, and it is about fourteen yards in diameter. Lord Newborough, and other gentlemen.

whose lands came in contact with it, were then, I understood, contesting their right and claim to it in some of our courts of law. But it would be desirable that the court should come to a speedy decision; as, otherwise, all the contending parties may be finally disappointed, and the rightful proprietor not obtain a particle of the litigated soil; the mound being continually dug and carried away by an inhabitant of the town, for the purpose of enriching his own garden.

Here, in 1284, Edward I. celebrated his conquest of Wales; and in compliment to his new subjects, held a Round Table, dignified with dance and tournaments:—

"Where throngs of knights and barons bold,
In weeds of peace high triumphs hold,
With store of ladies, whose bright eyes
Rain influence, and judge the prize
Of wit or arms; while both contend
To win her grace, whom all commend."

The chief nobility of England, with a number of foreigners as well as the inhabitants, attending, must have rendered this meeting memorable. Though it is well known that our hero, Arthur, held his Round Table in honour of one of his victories, yet it is supposed that the custom prevailed before his time. The festive board at which Arthur's company sat, was circular, to prevent any disputes on the subject of precedency. In Nevin church is the following inscription, on a tablet in the wall:—"Here lieth the body of Ellin Wynne, of Saython, the wife of John Parry, of Nevin, gent. She died the 30th of January, 1679, aged about 100." This custom of the wife's retaining her maiden name after marriage, is no longer in use, although it was common in that age. A mile from hence westward is Porth-yn-Llŷn, a safe station for small craft. A new road was lately made, from Pont Aberglaslyn, through Penmorfa and Criccieth, to this harbour: where it is in contemplation to build a town, and to improve the port. Leaving Nevin, I passed on and came to Saython, the residence of Mr. Williams. This gentleman being from home, my scheme of visiting Bardsey Island proved abortive. There are no public accommodations whatever in this remote part of Llyn; and it is therefore necessary that the tourist, if he wish to visit this dwarf island, should secure a retreat in some gentleman's house in the neighbourhood. From hence I steered towards Pwllheli, and met with nothing novel, till I came to Llanbedrog, a village in a romantic creek on the south-east side of Llyn. The church and the parsonage lie in this bottom on the verge of the sea; sheltered on one side by a declivity of fruitful corn land, and on the other by a high black rock, forming a promontory, that with a great degree of boldness darts forwards into the sea. Colonel Wardle has a handsome house in this secluded corner, commanding a view of the bay of Cardigan, of Harlech-castle, Cader Idris, *&c. &c.* Continuing my walk over the sands and crossing a ferry, I arrived at Pwllheli.

CHAPTER IV.

Pwllheli.—Aber Eirch.—Llanstyndwy.—Two Cromlechs.—Criccieth.—Wreck of Fowls.—Penmorfa.—Mephitis.—Tan yr Allt.—Cyfnicht.—Falling of the Rocks.—Pont Aberglaslyn.—Salmon-Fishery.—Chrystal.—Snowdon.—Nant Nanhwynen.—Merlin.—Bethgelert.—Tan y Bwlch Hall.—Falls on the Cynfael.—Festiniog.—Moelwyn.—Maentwrog.—Rhyadr ddu.—Llantechwyn Lakes.—A Solo.—Harlech.—Bardic Circles.—Cwm Bach.—Drws Ardydwy Pass.—Pistill y Caen.—Fall of the Mawddach.—Dol-y-melynllyn Fall.—Llanelltid.—Cummer Abbey.—Nannau.—Rhyadr Elugog.—Oak.—Goats.—Sources of the Dee.—Llanuwchlyn.—Overflow of the Twrch.—The handsome Girls of Meirion.—Llyn Llymbren.—Elise.—Llyn Dyfi.—Bogs.—A whimsical Scene.—Fuel.—The Murder of Mr. Lewis Owen.—Llan y Mowddwy—Tydecho.—Mallwyd.—Dr. Davies.—Dinas Mowddwy.—Cwm Cowarch.—Bwlch Oerddrws.—Caerynwch.

PWLLHELI is a market-town, with a safe harbour for small vessels; and the principal employment of the inhabitants consists in building such vessels for the coasting trade. The exportation of corn forms a principal branch of their traffic; that article being very abundant in this part of the county. The imports are what are most wanted in the country, coals, grocery, *&c.* From the spirit of building already shewn, there is very little doubt of the place soon becoming very respectable. The town and grounds near it have nothing striking in them, both lying nearly level with the sea.

The black prince made this place a free borough, in compliment to Nigel de Loryng, one of the gentlemen of the bedchamber; on whom he bestowed this town and Nevin, in reward of services performed in Gascony, and at the battle of Poictiers. At the Crown and Anchor I found good accommodations, and moderate charges. Setting out early in the morning, I pursued my journey along the public road, and the country seemed gradually to improve. The little village of Abereirch, or the Port of the Coffins, is well situated. In the church-yard is a tombstone with the following inscription: "Here lies the body of Ellis Pritchard, mariner, who died the 24th of January, 1785; he served his king and country in thirteen naval engagements: died of a malignant small-pox, aged 28." Seldom has it fallen to the lot, even of old age, to have had so many battles with the foe.

The country now wore an aspect of the greatest beauty. Finely decorated with woods, frequently interspersed with rocks, here and there visible through their openings, and the little, but picturesque, castle of Criccieth peeping between, with a partial view of the sea; it presented the most interesting sylvan scene I had witnessed in Carnarvonshire. Llanstundwy is remarkable for its situation, lying in a woody bottom, with the noisy river Dwyfor passing by, which, after heavy falls of rain, rises to such a height, as sometimes to threaten the village with destruction. It has happened, and not unfrequently, that whilst the clergyman and the friends of the deceased, were performing the sad last offices for the dead, torrents of water have rushed down from the hills, overflowed the church-yard and the village, so as to render it difficult for them to escape. Were it not for so unpleasant a visitor as a deluge, the inhabitants might think themselves, with respect to local situation, unrivalled. Leaving the road, I made up into the country and passed Trefan Hall, the handsome mansion of Mrs. Roberts. In a meadow, a mile from hence, is a Cromlech, called Coeten Arthur, or Arthur's Quoit, fabled to have been thrown by him from a mountain in the vicinity of Bethgelert. It is very handsome and perfect, shewing no signs of decay whatever. The perpender is a huge stone pointed at the ends, and swelling gradually to the centre, it measures in thickness about three feet; the circumference is about thirty. It is raised about four or five feet from the ground by four supporters. Having gratified my curiosity at this Cromlech, I made for a farm, a mile off, called Ystym Cegid, where I had the pleasure of beholding another, the most beautiful of any I had seen in my journey; the farmer, however, through a natural propensity to render any thing useful that may *lie on the ground*, has converted it into a sheepfold, by filling up the interstices with stones, very dissimilar to those originally erected to support the coping-stone, or the Cromlech: I have left them out, and the annexed print will shew its prior appearance. The coping-stone takes a triangular form, its thickness is about eighteen inches every where, and it measures thirty-six feet round; it is raised so high as to allow a person on horseback to go underneath. This also is called Arthur's Quoit; which (to carry on the story) we may suppose to have been thrown by the same hand; but, owing to a slip of the foot, in the moment of exertion, it went wide of the mark at least one mile.

Leaving this Cromlech, I came by a dull unfrequented path to Criccieth. This is a very poor place: and the only object it offers to the traveller, is its castle; which stands upon a rock, much elevated above the sea, and commanding an extensive

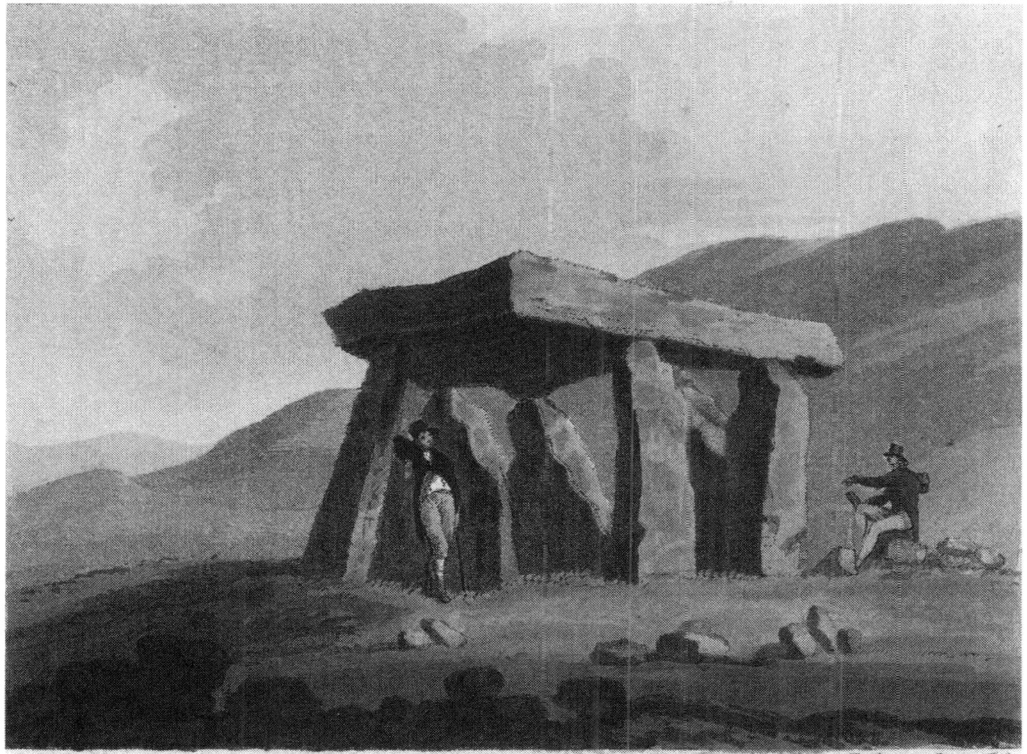

E. Pugh del.^t T. Cartwright sculp.^t

A CROMLECH AT YSTIM CEGID.

Published 25 May 1814, by E. Williams, Strand.

prospect across Cardigan-bay, with Harlech-castle in front. The two circular towers (between which is the entrance) are, with the other broken parts of the building, good subjects for a sketch. The building of this castle is attributed to Edward I., but the square insides of the two rounders, in front, with the other square towers and courts, seem to make this opinion doubtful. Though all Edward's castles vary in their construction and ground plan, yet this is by no means of that species of architecture of which he was so fond, and he, probably, did no more than alter and repair it.

Sir Howel y Fwyall, or of the Axe, so surnamed on account of his prowess in battle with the pole-axe, was the hero, as the Welsh say, who took the French king prisoner, at the battle of Poictiers (though the English assert that Denis de Morebesque was the man), under the command of the black prince. The prince knighted him for his valour on this occasion; gave him the rent of the Dee-mills at Chester for life, and made him the constable of this castle; which afterwards became his residence. The prince also ordered, as a perpetual memorial of his services, that a mess of meat should be served up before the pole-axe, which Howel had wielded with so much honour, and for which reason it became his armorial bearing. Eight yeomen attendants guarded the mess; and, after exhibiting it before the knight, it was bestowed on the poor; this continued till the reign of Elizabeth.

In the year 1776, an astonishing wreck of sea-fowl happened on this coast. The strand for miles was covered with dead birds; with many thousands of razor-bills, puffins, gwillemots, and kitty-wakes; and with these, who are accustomed to visit our rocks in the summer, were mingled equal numbers of turrocks, birds that retire to distant countries to breed, such as gannets, barnacles, wild-geese, scoters, orent-geese, and tufted ducks. The frost of that winter had been extremely severe, and perhaps a storm had overtaken them and had occasioned this extraordinary catastrophe: the perpetually resident birds of the country, unable to withstand the extreme cold, shared the same fate.

One mile from hence, at a place called Pentre yr Velyn, I heard a mendicant sing a most excellent Welsh song, very unfavourable to Buonaparte's views of landing his myrmidons on the shores of the principality. A little further is Penmorfa, a neat little village, at the foot of a high rock, that overlooks the Merionethshire coast across the estuary of Aberglaslyn; in this church is the monument of Sir John Owen. This neighbourhood, in the winter of 1694, was visited by a remarkably noxious phenomenon, a *mephitis*, a destructive sulpherous vapour, resembling a pale blue flame, floating on the surface of the ground, for three weeks. It rose from the marsh called Morfa-buchan, and crossed over a channel of nearly eight miles to Harlech. Sixteen ricks and a barn full of hay, and another of corn, fell sacrifices to this fiery vapour; and the grass was so infected, that horned cattle, horses, sheep, and goats, that grazed upon it, died. It seems that one extraordinary quality of a mephitis was wanting, for men, women, and children went into the midst of it, without feeling the least inconvenience. It moved by night only, and was easily repelled by great noise, such as the discharging of guns and sounding of horns. It appeared the next summer, but less frequently, and with diminished force.

Half a mile further is Tan-yr-Allt, the lately-erected handsome house of William Alexander Maddocks, Esq., member for Boston. It is upon an ascent of considerable height, and in a wild situation; among rocks towering into the clouds. The nocturnal rest of any person, not possessed of strong nerves, might easily be disturbed by the thoughts of the impending fragments that seem to threaten immediate destruction to this house; but there is very little doubt, that Mr. Maddocks has taken the precaution to examine all points; and, notwithstanding the menacing appearance of danger, that he has pitched his tent in a place of perfect security. The look-out from the house is exceedingly grand; having in front that vast collection of picturesque mountains of Merionethshire, with the rocky margin of the sea, and the opening into St. George's channel. The ivy overspreading these rocks is inconceivably beautiful, and gives them the resemblance of some mighty strong bulwarks overgrown with that plant: Mr. Maddocks is, very properly, careful of its preservation.

The great embankment on the Traeth-mawr, or the Great Wash, was raised by the same gentleman, by whose superior genius, and a spirit rising above all difficulties, three thousand acres of land were rescued from the possession of the tide; and now promise, under a judicious management, to become very productive. This vast work was executed with a rapidity unequalled in history; it was completed in two years at the expense of £40,000.

Sir John Wynne of Gwydir, in the year 1625, conceived the great plan of rescuing this and the lesser wash, called Traeth-Bach, from the tide. In this important scheme he implored the assistance of his ingenious countryman, Sir Hugh Middleton, to carry it into effect. Sir John introduces his letter thus:

"Right worthie Sir, my good cousin, and one of the great honours of the nation,

"I understand of a greate work that you have performed in

the Isle of Wight, in gaininge too thousand acres from the sea. I may saie to you what the Jewes said to Christ: We have heard of thy greate workes done abroade, do somewhat in thine own countrey."

Sir Hugh wrote an answer; and that part of his letter that more immediately relates to this business, runs thus: "Touching the drowned lands near your lyvinge, there are manye things considerable therein. Iff to be gayned, which will hardlie be performed without great stones, which was plentiful at the weight as well as wood; and great sums of money to be spent, not hundreds, but thousands; and first of all his majesty's interest must be got. As for myself, I am grown into years, and full of business here at the mynes, the river at London, and other places; my weeklie charge being above £200, which maketh me verie unwillinge to undertake anie other worke: and the least of theis, whether the drowned lands or mynes, requireth a whole man with a large purse."

Lodge, Sept. 2d, 1625.

This scheme of Sir John's failed, and it was left to be performed, in the greater part, by Mr. Maddocks.

"The late Sir Archibald Grant of Monymusk, in Scotland, planted in his own lifetime upwards of forty-eight millions of trees; the present Earl of Fife plants vast numbers: General Gordon, of Fyvie, planted three millions of different forest trees in one single enclosure, all on barren soils *."

Mr. M. has caught the spirit of these gentlemen, and has already planted above a million of young trees, which, in a few years, will cover the denuded surfaces of these hills. He has

* Traveller's Companion from Holyhead to London.

also further improved this estate and neighbourhood, by erecting a pretty town with a convenient inn; a church endowed by himself, and a large cloth manufactory. The place has the privilege of a weekly market, and two or three annual fairs; and is named after the founder, Tre Maddoc, or Maddock's Town. Lately also, has been established here, an annual horse-race, early in the spring, when the town is greatly crowded.

There are many men of fortune, not only in the principality, but in the whole of the united kingdom, who, in point of means, are competent to follow the example of Mr. Maddocks; and from the opportunities which offer themselves in all parts of the island, they stand inexcusable. Is it not a self-evident remark, that the improvement of estates is not a doubtful speculation; but a safe and certain profit, which, whilst it advances the income of the improver, betters the condition of the country? The latter remark obviously challenges the patriotism of the rich landed proprietors. It were to be wished, that those who hazard their thousands upon the skill of a pugilist, the fleetness of a racer, or upon the more doubtful success of a generous bird, whose life and feelings are wantonly and barbarously sported with, would change their amusements for the more rational, honourable, and useful employment of their talents and fortune, in ameliorating the condition of their landed property; in encouraging the industry of the poor; in giving vigour to the polite arts, and in stimulating the spirit of scientific genius. But to return to my subject. The Porth-yn-Llyn road is here finished, and runs under y Craig Wen, or the White Rock, that frowns frightfully upon the passenger. These cliffs are little, if at all, inferior in roughness to those in the pass of Llanberis; their forms are variable, shewing very shattered and indented surfaces; and the stranger to such scenes of wildness, if he loiter on his way, will be seized with some apprehension of danger. These rude and savage appearances continue four or five miles, with an arm of the sea and Aberglaslyn river on the right. The distant objects come in very happily, either up towards the land, or when viewed towards the sea. That picturesque rocky mountain called (I believe) the Nicht, soars into a noble semicone, apparently scooped by some convulsion; which, with the lofty Moelwyen, the marginal crags below, and the tide, make a very sublime picture. There are several instances of the falling of rocks in this country. I have selected one on this spot for a plate, with a prodigious stream of stones, which may give the reader an idea of the danger to travellers, if often repeated; but very few examples of the kind occur in a century. I now came in sight of Pont Aberglaslyn, frequently and undeservedly called (by the English only I believe), the Devil's Bridge; but it is destitute of those horrors which generally accompany our notions of his infernal majesty.

This bridge, joining the two counties of Carnarvon and Merioneth, built on rocks, is of one arch of thirty feet chord, under which the united waters of the Colwyn and Glaslyn pour themselves into the tide, a little lower down. The scenery near and about thc bridge, is awfully grand; and the stupendously high precipitous sides of the cliffs, which seem hostilely to approach and frown upon each other, are strongly marked with indentations that still render it, though much hackneyed, a favourite subject of the pencil. Whether it be owing to a wish to avoid the fatigue of climbing the steeps here, or to any other cause, I know not, but it is certain that the numerous prints of this spot, already published, are nothing but mere

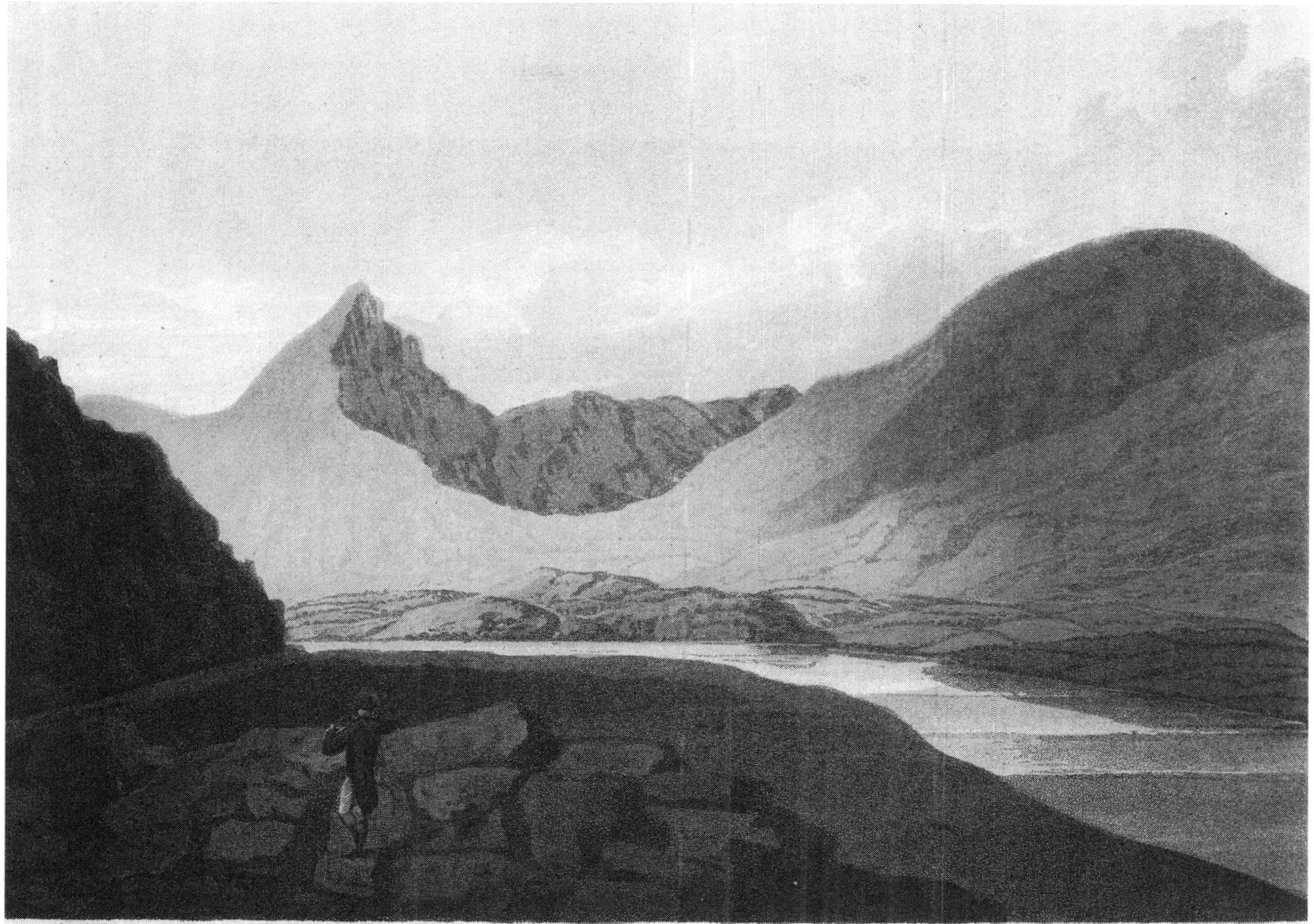

E. Pugh del.t T. Cartwright sculp.t

THE CNUCHT.

Published 15 October 1813 by E. Williams Strand.

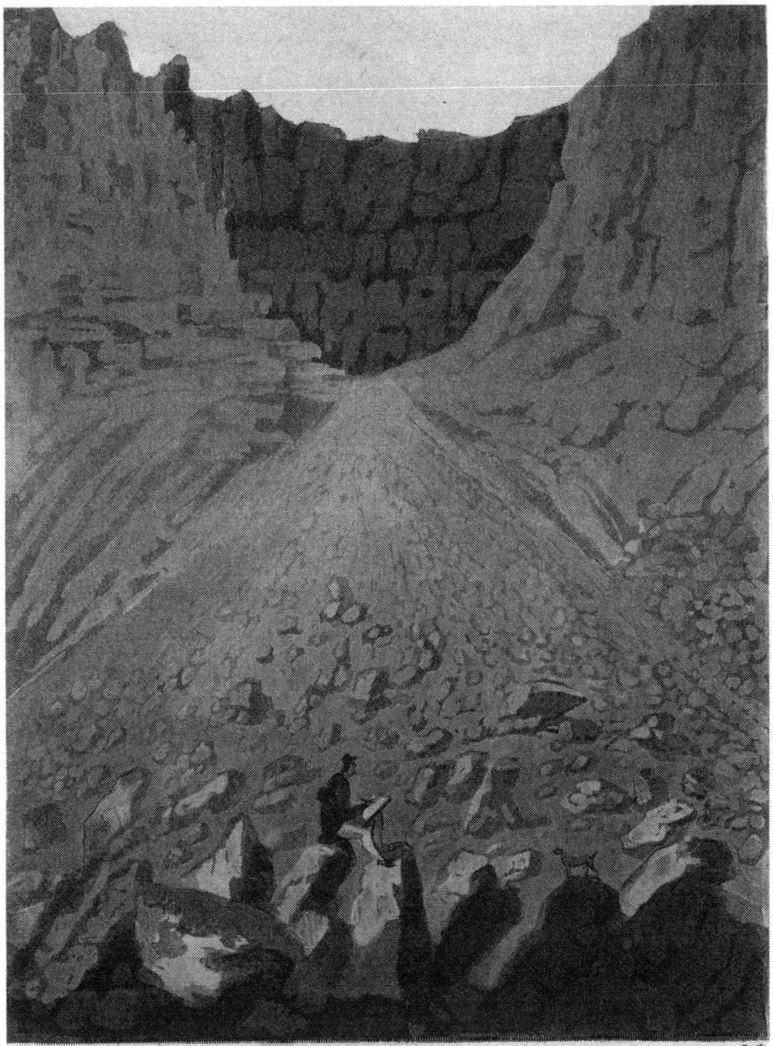

E. Pugh delt. T. Cartwright sculpt.

A FALL OF ROCKS.

Published 18 July 1814, by E. Williams, Strand.

duplicates; the bridge and the bed of the river, constantly introduced into the foreground. By this time I had learned to bear much toil, a lesson which I found to be extremely useful. I ascended these sides, however difficult, and found the entrance of this pass, with a downward view of the river from amongst wood and dislodged rocks, to excel any thing that I had yet seen from the bottom. The Salmon-leap here is too well known to render any further remark necessary, than that it was once a royal wear, in the time of Henry IV.

In my progress up this pass, I was not a little disappointed to find its grandeur and splendid appearance, suddenly die away into the domestic valley of Bethgelert. Here I saw four men with long barbed spears, who were frequently up to their waist, pursuing the salmon through the deep hollows in the bed of the river Glaslyn.

Bethgelert is a small village, placed in the midst of some meadows, and at the conflux of two rivers. Surrounded as it is by high mountains, and rocks of great asperity of countenance, it is already pretty well known to travellers, both for its romantic situation, and from its vicinity to Snowdon.

The old guide to Snowdon, as I was sorry to find, had become superannuated. He speaks English, and is well acquainted with the mountains, their names, and etymology; he is also a connoisseur in fossils, and particularly in the mountain-crystal, or as the Welsh call it, Cerrig-grisial; of which he has some fine specimens of great value. These stones are very transparent, resembling glass, and have generally four, five, six, or more, sides, and though they have hardness enough to mark glass, yet they are said to be too brittle to be formed into articles, either of ornament or use. This, however, is most certainly an error:

for those pieces which are found of pure water, will submit to the operations of the lathe; and I have seen very beautiful seals, *&c.*, made of them. The guide, who succeeded this intelligent man, is ignorant of the English language, and is every way unfit for the office. I therefore suggested the necessity of changing him for a better; and, I hope, that, before this time, he may have been superseded. At nine o'clock in the morning, I set out for Snowdon, having for my companion a fine intelligent young man, whose natural, unaffected politeness of manners, though bred among the mountains, surprised me not a little. We ascended by the west side; and the morning looking gay gave me great pleasure. But before we had got up two-thirds of the mountain, a sweeping cloud dashed along, and we instantly lost sight of the summit. Nothing intimidated, we pushed our way over a narrow ridge a few hundred yards long, and just wide enough for three abreast; on each side of which is a headlong fall, a quarter of a mile in depth; a terror to many, unaccustomed to such situations, but which, however, may be ascended with ease and safety.

When we had gained the apex of the mountain, we were circummured with impenetrably thick mist for the space of an hour. Now a few rays of light passed over our heads, which, I observed to my comrade, were a happy omen. "O, Sir, replied he, 'tis but like a flash in the pan, that leaves our condition but the worse on its disappearance." Presently another gleam of light, and then awful obscurity; and so alternately for a few minutes. This quick succession of vivid light and profound darkness, was not altogether very pleasant upon so elevated a situation: and though, in my own opinion, it portended good, I could not help remarking to my companion, that I wished his *flashes* might not produce *fire* and *thunder*. At this instant the clouds entirely left the mountain, and the noble illuminator of the universe displayed before me a scene, the most awful and magnificent my eyes ever beheld. This summit being the greatest in altitude of any in Wales, and converging to a point of but eighteen feet diameter, gives the visitor an opportunity of seeing, in good weather, an almost unbounded expanse of land and sea. I could distinguish the high mountains in the Vale of Clwyd, eastward, and others stretching to the south, where the famous Cader Idris makes a fine appearance: thence to the westward, across St. George's channel, where Ireland may be seen in any part of the day, if the atmosphere be clear. Towards the north-west, the island of Anglesey, in beautiful aerial perspective, lay beneath me without the least appearance of those protuberances of hills and rocks which I had wandered over. The Isle of Man was also visible; and more to the right, the shores of the north of England and Scotland. The nearer objects of rude shapeless mountains that surrounded me, took up much of my attention. The two Glydars, Moel Siabod, and beyond them the rocky heights above Llanrwst, were bold features. The fine assemblage of the mountains of Merionethshire, towering above each other, and shewing their caverned sides, were also objects of admiration. Westward is Moel Hebog, and the fine opening with the lakes at Llanllyfni, Ewelling lake, and the mountains forming the pass of Bettws Garmon, though depressed from the height on which I stood, becomes a charming piece of scenery, when viewed from the side, half a mile below the summit. The artist, with a good guide, will find on the several sides of the mountain, some fine subjects for the easel; and though I had not the good fortune of another opportunity of ascending it, I have since learnt, that the following places are worth the toil of clambering to them: the precipices of Cwn Brwynog, Llyn-y-Madrod, and Llyn-Coch. The ancient name of Snowdonia was Creigie'r Eira, or Snowy Cliffs or Mountains. The British name for the highest peak of Snowdon, is Y-Wyddfa, or the Conspicuous, and it signifies also, the Monument; the other peak, but a little lower, is called Crîb-y-Distill. Snowdon has four limits or buttresses, and between each a noble cwm, or hollow, in all of which, one excepted, are one or more lakes. The cwms on the eastern side of Snowdon that front Capel Curig, are called Cwm Llyn Glas and Cwm Llyn Llydaw, and are the most picturesque: in these are two lakes. Camden, probably following the error of Giraldus, has very much mistaken the climate of Snowdonia, unless it has undergone a great change since his time; "And yet (says he) harbour they the snow; for all the yeere long they be hory with snow, or rather with an hardened crust of many snowes felted together." But in our days snow is rarely seen, even on the Wyddfa itself, later than May or the beginning of June. The height of this monarch of the mountains is from Carnarvon Quay 1189 yards one foot; 298 feet higher than the celebrated Skiddaw of the North of England. Leland says that, in his days, stags were so numerous on Snowdon, as to be a pest to the farmer, whose corn they often destroyed.

In Elizabeth's time the whole of these mountains was a royal forest; which was extended even to the counties of Merioneth and Anglesey, to gratify the favourite Dudley, who had been appointed its ranger. This nobleman's insolence to the inhabitants of the forest, was more than could be brooked. He tried to bring many freeholders' estates within the boundary; juries were empannelled; but the commissioners

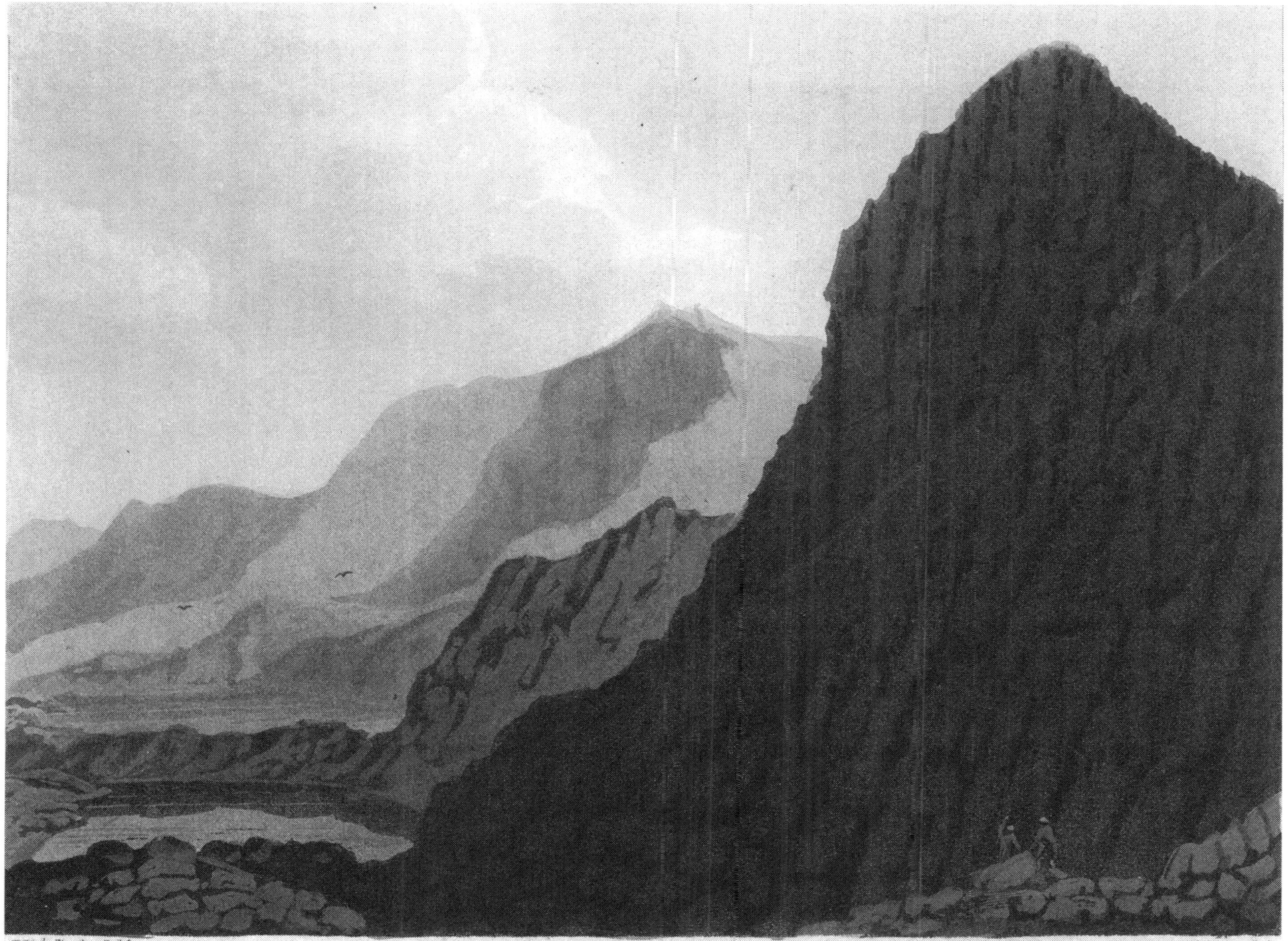

Edwd. Pugh del^t.

Thos. Cartwright sculp^t.

CWM LLYN LLYDAW & CWM LLYN GLAS

with the high Peak of Snowdon.

Published 30 June 1813 by E. Williams Strand.

rejected their returns as unfavourable to the earl; these honest jurors, however, persisted, and found a verdict for the country. But in the year 1578, he succeeded by a packed jury, who appeared in his livery, blue, with ragged staves on the sleeves; men, who, ever after this nefarious act, were stigmatized with the title of "the black jury, who sold their country." Sir Richard Bulkeley, of Baron Hill, who, with Sir William Herbert and others, had superseded a prior commission, resisted this oppression with equal firmness, and laid these odious grievances before the queen: whose regard for her loyal subjects, the Welsh, was evinced by the recalling of the first commission by proclamation at Westminster in 1579. The earl being worsted, sought the life of Sir Richard, and accused him of being concerned in Babington's plot;—"Before God," said the queen, "we will be sworn upon the Evangelists, he never intended us any harm;" and kissing the Bible, said "We shall not commit him; we have brought him up from a boy." So this generous patriot, by his excellent and manly conduct, overthrowing every malevolent design of his enemy, came out of this fiery trial as pure as the pellucid crystal of Snowdon, to which, after this digression, I return.

Snowdon has always been held by the ancient Britons as sacred, as was the double-peaked mountain of Parnassus by the Greeks. Some of the inhabitants yet say, that it has the quality of inspiring any person who sleeps upon it with the spirit of poetry (awen) or of afflicting them with madness. There is in Cwm Brwynog, on the side of this mountain, a large stone, and upon it another smaller one, which the people call Maen dû yr Arddu, or the Black Stone of Arddu. It is said that two young men of the neighbourhood, by agreement, which originated in a frolic, put its power of inspiration to a trial, and slept upon it one fine summer's night. When they awoke one fancied himself mad as a bedlamite; and the other, all in raptures, notwithstanding the blows he received from the hardy fists of his infuriate companion, began to manufacture penillim, or stanzas, by the wholesale. The poet was afterwards nick-named Huweyn Sion y Canu, or Hugh John the Poet, or Singer. We now perceived, westward, a collection of vapours rising from the sea; which, though partly dispersed before, they successively reached the mountain, in part gained upon us, and gave us much annoyance; and we were now, as on our arrival, enveloped in a disagreeable chilling moist. The evening advancing, and this wonderful panorama being closed for the day, we descended between the two peaks into Cwm Llyn Glas, by a zig-zag path, or, more wonderful to say, a horse-road, formed in one of the greatest precipices of the volcanic sides of the mountain; and it would be difficult, perhaps, to persuade a stranger that it was ever passable. It is, however, no less a fact, that horses come down this way, and return by the same road with their burden of ore.

My guide now begged that I would view a certain spot, where happened the following accident, in the winter of 1804. A man named Williams, having been promised a jug of honey at an apiary east of this mountain, to avoid a circuitous road, came this way to receive his present, accompanied by two young men of his acquaintance. Much snow had fallen during the preceding night, and drifted to that side of the hollow which has the path, and consequently the footing was rendered slippery and unsafe. Williams, who was the foremost man, suddenly disappeared: his companions arriving at the spot, and observing the aperture which his body had made in the snow, called out aloud; but receiving no answer, they concluded that he must have perished, and sorely lamented his fate. They now proceeded cautiously to the bottom, to endeavour to discover his mangled remains, if haply they could reach the spot; for they could not, from the nature of the horrid-looking place, encourage the least hope that he could survive the fall of nearly three hundred yards. But on nearing the ground, what circumstance could have excited their astonishment more, than the sight of their friend, safe, and unhurt? for we cannot consider a little lasceration of the hands, occasioned by his catching hold of the pointed rocks in his way, as, in such situation, of any concern. But here I have to record a strange instance of the perversion or infatuation of the human intellect.—Williams, instead of exhibiting joy and gratitude on his wonderful deliverance, seemed to be sensible only of the loss of his jug!

After walking down a considerable distance, I could not perceive that I was leaving the peak, owing to the high prodigious perpendicular fall of it; and not until I had gone two miles from the summit of this path, could I believe that I was got completely clear of this tremendous steep into the crater below. We passed the copper-mine, where I saw a small quantity of good ore at the mouth of the shaft, but nobody on the spot. This work goes on but slowly, and I am not able to solve the question, whether it will ever prove advantageous to the speculators or not. But one thing is evident, that it ought to turn out very rich to enable the adventurers to make a fortune; for the expense of conveying the ore over the rough sides of this mountain, to a convenient port for exportation, must be very great. The highest peak rising perpendicular from the lake, is supposed to be one fourth of a mile high*. We now descended some steep rocks to the lower lake (Llyn Llydaw), by the south side of which we followed a dreadful horse-path. I saw here three dark grey gulls hovering over the lake, which, it is said, they never quit: hence it is sometimes called Llyn yr Adar, or the Lake of the Bird.

I stayed awhile on the spot to view the grandeur of this vast, tremendous, and noble amphitheatre. The cliffs that project and cut each other on all sides of the lake, are objects of considerable importance and admiration; and the greater steeps above, shooting their pointed tops to the sky, and exhibiting their black and dismal hollows, softened into grey by the influence of the intervening air, look grand and picturesque beyond conception †.

The guide from Capel Curig conducts his charge along one of the serrated sides or supporters of Snowdon, above this cwm; but, on returning, he should by all means come down this romantic horse-path to the bottom, by the sides of the lakes, to give strangers an opportunity of contemplating the awful works of nature which encompass them. Should the highest peak happen to be

* Mr. Evans of Llwyn y Groes, once informed me, that as he was going to the top of Snowdon, his guide fell into a conversation with a shepherd on the opposite branch of it, nor did they make any extraordinary exertion to be heard; the distance between them was two miles.

† Artists who visit this country, are, I fear, in general, utter strangers to the interior of this, and other cwms; and are too apt to be contented with their distant appearance; which, at the same time, must be confessed to be highly interesting in a fine picture; but it must also be allowed by those who have taken the trouble of seeing any of them near at hand, that the internal part of them, but of this in particular, possesses great and valuable combinations of parts and circumstances that render them fit for grand and magnificent pictures.

cloud-capt at the time, it would afford them additional subject for meditation, for in that case the cheerful light of the sun being denied, a gloominess of aspect would pervade this vast hollow, which could not fail to beget in the deep-thinking mind, the greatest respect and veneration for the Author of their natural wonders, and a ready acknowledgment, that

———————————" Holy are His ways,
His works unnumbered, and to all proclaim
Unfathom'd wisdom, goodness unconfin'd." MALLET, 608.

" Once, alas! the warbling shade
Round the raptur'd mountain grew:
Once the hand of Nature spread
Woods magnificent to view.

Desolation now appears!
Ruin holds these drear abodes:
Now beneath the weight of years,
Lo! the tottering mountain nods." *Genius of Cambre.*

After walking three miles from the peak, which is supposed to be the length of this hollow, we descended a very abrupt and rugged rock into the new road, from Bethgelert to Capel Curig, and, turning to the right, into the enchanting vale of Nant Nanhwynen. The day drawing to a close, I deferred the pleasure of investigating its charms; and having dedicated to Snowdon more than twelve hours, I now made the best of my way to Bethgelert.

Nant Nanhwynen, a valley six miles long, being an object of moment for me to examine, I set off early the next morning for that purpose. The entrance into it at Bethgelert is, for some distance, much compressed, with the turbulent river Gwynen issuing from Glaslyn Lake high up in the hills, pursuing its course through the whole vale. Opening by degrees, it first exhibits only a few small farms : but at the entrance of the first lake called Llyn y Dinas, or the Lake of the Fort, the scenery begins to improve. Here the insulated rock, named Dinas Emrys, has an easy ascent to the top. In ancient times this rock was called Dinas Faraon, or the King's Fort: but it has for many centuries gone under the name of Dinas Emrys, or Ambrose's Fort, where the said noted *Merlinus Ambrosius* resided: celebrated in our annals as a magician and a prophet. It is probable that, in that age, he may have attained his reputation for supernatural powers, by an eminence in science as an astronomer and mathematician. Tradition says that he penned his prophecies here, though he was a native of Carmarthen in South Wales. Among the many prophetical denunciations of his, traditionally handed down to posterity, is the following, foreboding the destruction of his native town by an earthquake and inundation ; never, we hope, to be verified :—

" Caerfyrddin, cai oer foreu,
Daear dy lyngc, dîvr yn dy le."

" Cold—cold the morn—more chill than snow,
Engulf'd by earth, and sinking low,
The waves thy site shall overflow."

Vortigern, on his introduction of the Saxons into the country in 449, unable to withstand the fury of his enraged subjects, meditated to build in this place an impregnable fortress. The materials collected for the purpose, suddenly disappearing one night, the astonished prince called on his magicians for their advice. They accordingly attended, and one advised him to sprinkle the building with the blood of a child who was born of a virgin, without the assistance of a father! The kingdom was searched in vain for this extraordinary production: till one day, an emissary listening to some boys at play, heard one of them call another " An unbegotten errant knave." The mother of this unbegotten errant knave, in obedience to the king's mandate, brought the child; and related, that he was the offspring of a *Bwabach*, or an Incubus, who had taken advantage of her while asleep between two of her sisterhood; herself being a nun and a princess. This fable she invented to save her honour; for the child's father was known to be a noble Roman of the same name. The boy, on finding himself doomed for a sacrifice, confounded these magicians with the ingenuity of his answers; and, explaining to them the cause of the king's disappointment, and the mode of remedying it, he gained his liberty. There is now not a vestige of this structure remaining, save a heap of stones, which might possibly have been employed in it. This beautiful eminence was well adapted for a man of Vortigern's mind and character, who wished to be safe from the resentment of an enraged people. Some have imagined that this Merddin Emrys (or Merlin) was the architect of that stupendous work on Salisbury plain called Stonehenge, erected, as it is said, on the spot where before stood a conventional circle: the Welsh to this day call it Gwaith Emrys, or the work of Ambrosius, for the purpose, as some assert, of commemorating the plot of the long knives. Passing the first lake, I beheld the scene, which I had left, open very finely; that towering rocky mountain by Bethgelert, called Moel Hebog, with his denuded and shattered sides, shooting his head aloft with much self-importance, as if in effort to rival Snowdon, as seen from Llanllyfni lakes.

This is a singular coincidence: in each of these views there is a fine piece of water, and on each side high and craggy eminences; which, at the end of the lake, dart forth rocks, meeting across the pass, of very picturesque appearance; and in the opening beyond these is a very majestic grand mountain. The only existing difference is, that Snowdon has two heads, and Moel Hedog but one. In every other respect the similarity is so great, that a person acquainted with both, might, during the least absence of mind, think himself at Llanllyfni when at Nant Nanhwynen, and at Nant Nanhwynen when at Llanllyfni. The scenery now began to look more wild and improved every step I made, till I reached the end of Llyn Gwynen, or Gwynen lake; where was exhibited a rude and most disorderly assemblage of water, rocks, woods, and mountains. The great and stupendous cliffs, appendages of Snowdon, continually varying in form, with others of very fantastic shape dropping from the opposite heights, and meeting so as apparently to deny the traveller a passage, have a noble effect; which is still heightened by the addition of hills in the mid-ground, and others receding finely into the distance. It is needless to expatiate much upon the allurements of Nant Nanhwynen*, as they are already known to the painters: but it may not be improper to notice a neglect of which some are guilty in not ascending the heights on the south-east side of the vale. I returned by that side, frequently climbing up these elevations, where I was continually delighted with the magnificence of the scenery; especially so, when looking across the vale, and between the rough openings of the adverse steeps up Snowdon, which often display cascades of a great height. There is a handsome house built by Mr. Vawdry, on the south-east side, in the

* All the farms in this valley belong to the following gentlemen;—Richard Parry, of Warfield, Esq.; Sir Thomas Mostyn, Bart.; Sir W. W. Wynn, Bart.; Sir Robert Williams, Bart.; Wynne, of Pengwern, Esq.; and Maurice Owen, Esq.

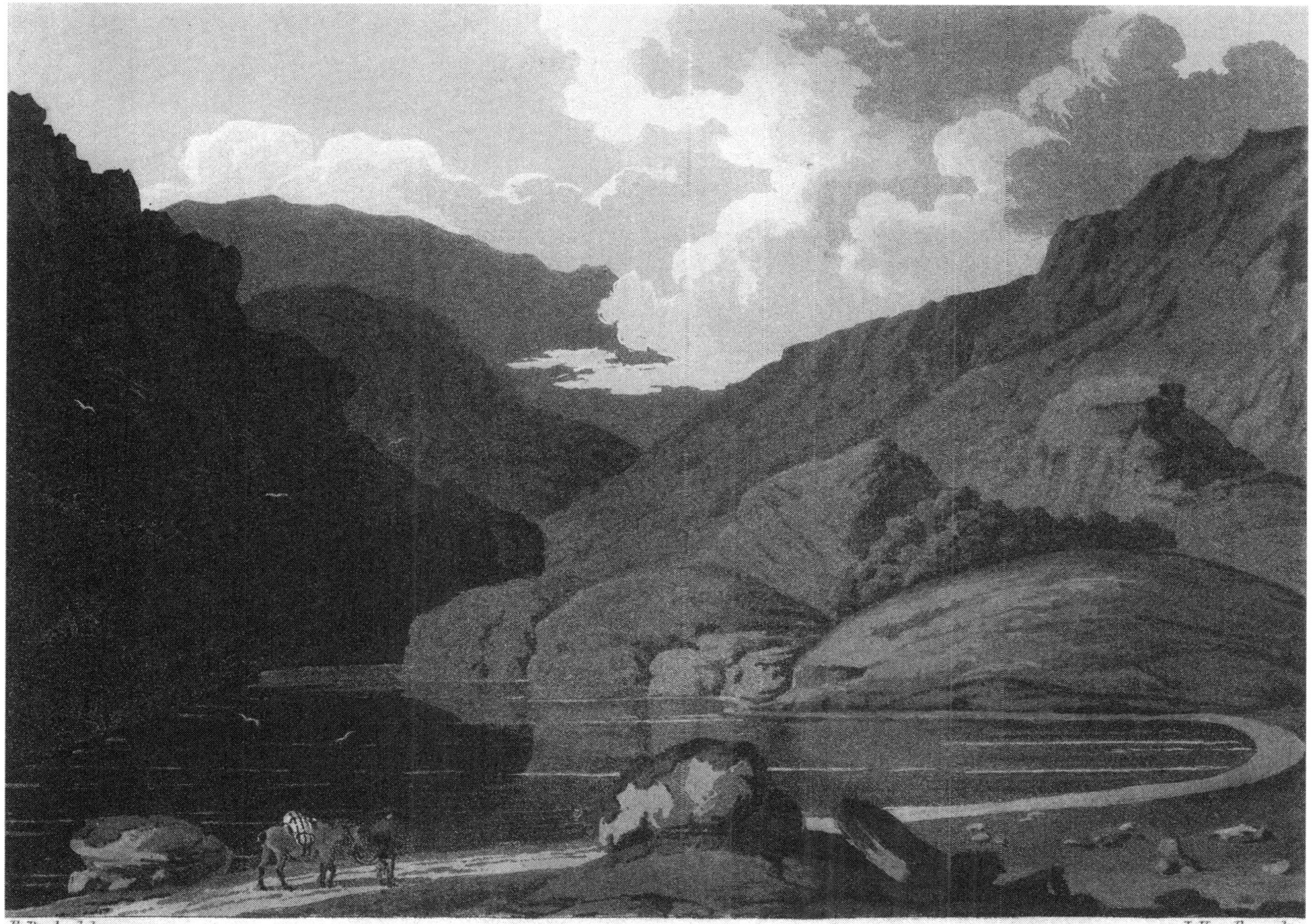

E. Pugh del. I. Havell sculp.

VIEW IN NANT NANHWYNEN.

Published 15 Novr. 1813 by E. Williams Strand.

most luxuriant part of this pass, and where it is well wooded; but if this edifice had been situated above, on a more elevated ground, its prospects would have been better.

Bethgelert is variously spelt, and the meaning of the word is still doubtful: the etymology of it, however, is by some thus made out. Bedd means a grave, and Cilert, or Gelert, a dog's name; and to this is added a traditional story, which, as there is some reason to believe, really arose from the act of which it relates*. Prince Llywelyn ab Jorwerth going out a hunting one morning, missed his favourite dog, nor did he appear in the chase: on Llywelyn's return, however, his dog, with his mouth all bloody, welcomed him with every indication of friendship. When his royal master got into the house, he perceived that his child was missing; and, upon this, he sheathed his sword in the dog's body, suspecting him to have destroyed the infant. But on searching a room where the babe had been laid to sleep, he was found, unhurt and smiling, under the bed-clothes; and, by his side, a monstrous wolf, dead, and torn to pieces by the favourite greyhound who had rescued his young lord. Llywelyn grieving much for his hasty deed, erected a tomb to the memory of this much-lamented dog; as some say, where the parish church was afterwards built; but as this does not agree with the religion of those days, it is more likely, and the supposition much more rational, that, if such was the fate of the dog of Llywelyn, he must have been buried in a hillock, now the site of a cow-house, two hundred yards from the church; which, to this day, is called Bryn-y-Bedd, or the Hillock of the Grave.

* There is an eastern fable related at large in Miss Hamilton's Letters, Vol. I. p. 87, in no way differing from this, except, that the instrument of the mischief is there stated to have been a serpent.

This was a conventual church, which belonged to a priory of Augustines; and was dedicated to St. Mary. It suffered by a casual fire in 1283 ; but the damages were repaired by Edward I. Of this religious house there is not a vestige standing: the church, indeed, has some arched doors, which some suppose led to the monks' habitations; if so, the church itself must be the remains of this religious building. Near the church is an old house, said to have belonged to the priory, in which is shewn a pewter mug, called Bethgelert pint, measuring two quarts. It may be filled with ale, at the request of any person who chuses to try his power of swallowing the contents at one draught: and if he should succeed, he will not only have the honour of being regarded as a first-rate guzzler, but will be entitled to the liquor gratis; the charge being placed to the lord of the manor's account, and deducted by the innkeeper from his rent. But if the person fails, *he* pays for the ale. Bethgelert has two inns; the most fashionable one is the Goat, lately built: but I preferred the old one, that I might enjoy those quiet undisturbed hours, which artists well know how to appreciate.

Mr. Bingley, when here, complained of having been teazed by fleas all night, and the servant made this quaint answer, "Dear me, Sir, if we were to kill one of them, ten would come to its burying." I slept in the same house several nights, very comfortably indeed, and without the mortification of being tortured by one of these insects. I fancy, therefore, that the whole of the nation were on a visit to a very distant burying, or had "gone to that bourne from whence no traveller *(or flea)* returns." The accommodations which I met with in this mountain-inn were very good; and the pretty little widow, Mrs. Parry, with her civil attention, seems to have learnt the art of pleasing her uncle's customers. I now left

Bethgelert for Tan-y-Bwlch, and passed over Pont Aberglaslyn. On this road is the old house of Havodgarregog, once the residence of Rhys gôch Eryri, Rhys ab Davydd, bard to Owen Glydwr, who died about 1420, at the advanced age of 120 years, and was buried at Bethgelert.

I kept on the lower, or new road, and met with nothing of importance in my way, till I came to a precipice, called in the Celtic language by a most significant term, Carreg Hill Drem. I know of no English equivalent for it: but it signifies a Rock of a Frowning or Threatening Aspect. A new road however, from Aberglaslyn-bridge, now passing beneath its projecting sides, renders its appearance so much more terrific, that I am not certain that even the Welsh language, with all its energetic powers, can describe it with justice and propriety.

I would advise the artist to go by the old, or mountain-road, from Pont Aberglaslyn to Tan-y-Bwlch: it is, certainly, not so pleasant to the thirty-per-cent plodding traveller, but most assuredly it will give greater satisfaction to a man of picturesque taste, as it has great varieties for him, being so intervolved with the mountains; and he will frequently be pleased with vistas of the sea, *&c.* Warned by the waning day, I hastened my pace through the romantic village of Llanfrothen, down the precipitous wood-covered road, to Tan-y-Bwlch-inn, which I found to be well stored with roving parties on their perambulation of the country. This, by all accounts, is become a comfortable house: but finding it crowded with guests, I passed over a handsome bridge, a quarter of a mile, to the little inn of Maentwrog; where I found more civility to the foot passenger. Next morning I visited the different falls of the Cunfael, and others in the neighbourhood. Three miles up, at the remotest part of the valley, is Festiniog, where I procured a guide to the river, which I found deeply immured between lofty hills; its bed is overhung with branching oak, and other wood. The ugly precipices on each side seem resolved to deny the stranger a sight of the falls; but by perseverance, we overcame every difficulty, and I was amply repaid for my trouble, by an exhibition no less whimsical than it was picturesque. It consists of an insulated rock of the grey shaly sort, standing erect in the centre of the river, forming a quadrangular pier. This by tradition is called Pwlpit Haw Llwyd, or the Pulpit of Hugh Llwyd; a singular character and poet, who, about the year 1600, lived at a house, yet standing, on the banks of this river. It is reported of him that, at different times, when particularly warmed with poetic fervour, he would ascend this rostrum to arrange his ideas, and commit them in proper order to paper; which, having done, he would recite them with great pathos and effect; and the sound of his voice was heard to vibrate at a distance, along this hollow aqueous amphitheatre. None ever attempted or dared to approach him, on account of the difficulty of descending. He was also believed to be skilled in magic. This is an uncommonly wild bottom. At the distance of a hundred yards, raised high up in air, is a very romantic ivy-coated bridge, called Pont Ddu, or a Bridge in a Dark and Shadowy Situation: occasioned by the depth of the chasm, and the meeting of the collateral branches of the great trees above, under which the river comes rushing down in two falls of great height; but they have the appearance of one undivided sheet, enclosed on each side with black shattering rocks, that cross each other in very fantastic shapes. The scenery above the bridge is good; and below it, occur various instances of bewitching pictures of rocks,

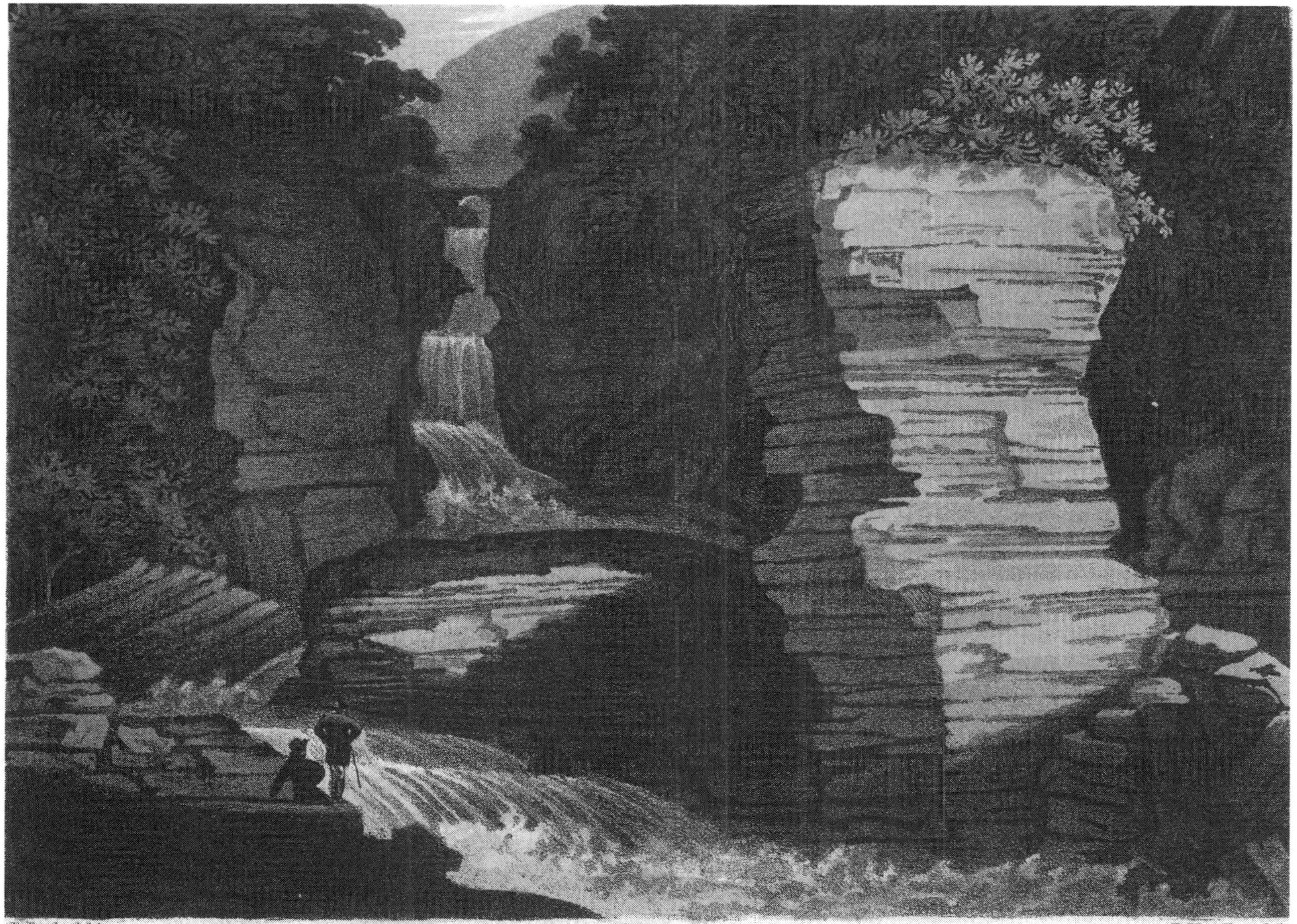

E. Pugh del.ᵗ T. Havell sculp.ᵗ

HUGH LLWYD'S PULPIT.

Published 26 January 1814, by E. Williams, Strand.

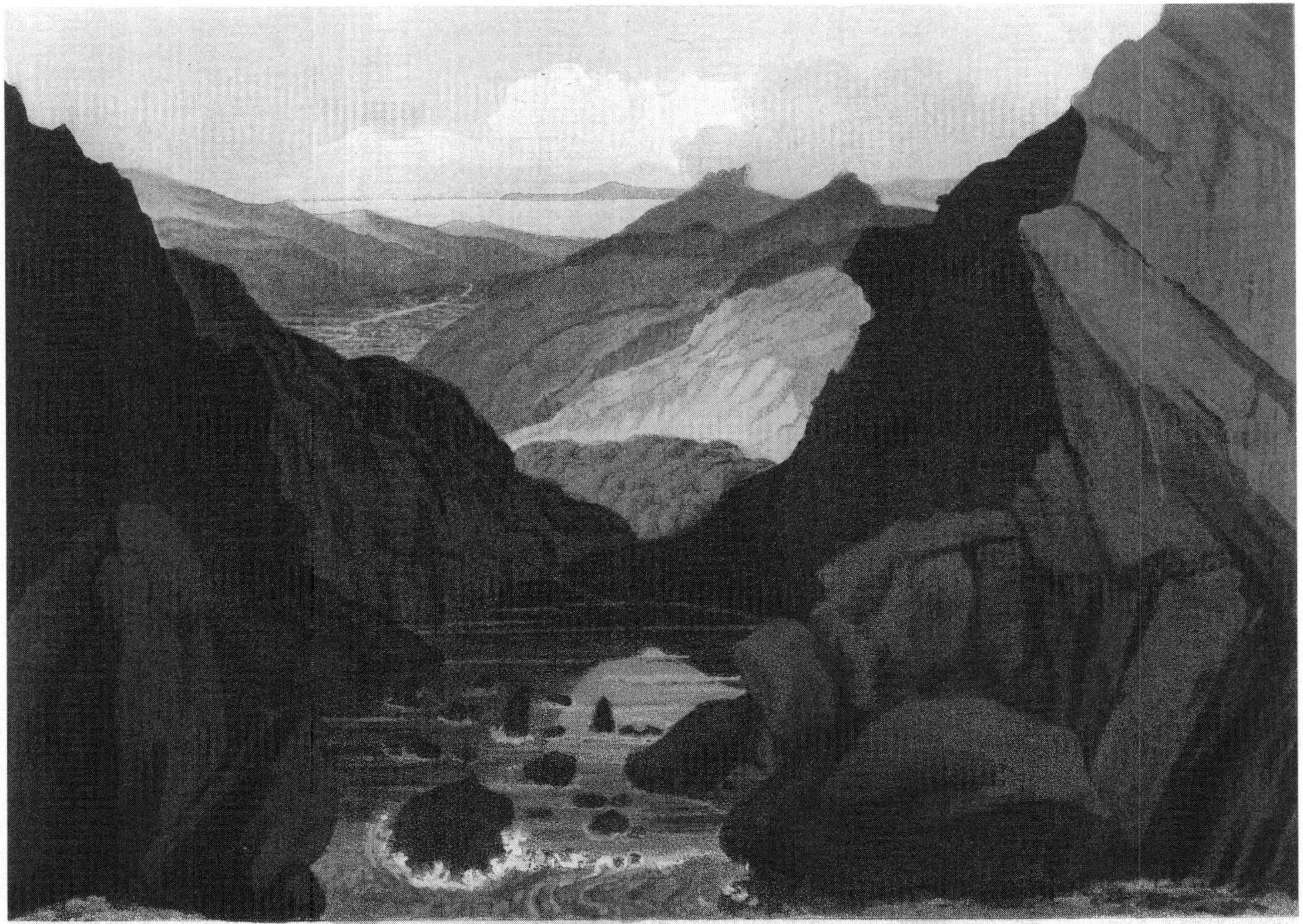

E. Pugh del. I. Hassel sculp.

VALE OF FESTINIOG.

Published 15 April, 1813, by E. Williams Strand.

pools, and falls, all the way to its junction with the Dwy-ryd, the stream in the vale of Naentwrog. I have had occasion, frequently, to lament the impossibility of ladies approaching these fine subjects.

As I proceed, I am induced to point out the spots that are the most hazardous, or the least accessible; after which, I trust that the several gentlemen, whose property they may be, as it would be attended with inconsiderable expense, will prepare a foot-path, so that the fair sex may partake, with their friends, of the pleasure of visiting these grand and picturesque recesses: in return they would secure their thanks, and their smiles.

One mile north of Festiniog is another water-fall, called Rhyadr-y-Fuwch. From the long continuance of fine weather, the rivers were nearly become dry; but viewed after a fall of rain, this cascade, I should presume, must be extremely grand, from the roughness of its sides, and the breaks of the water. Festiniog, or *Place of Hastening*, is a small, poor village. The only attraction the church can have for strangers is its high and delightful situation, overlooking the romantic vale of Festiniog. It was from the adjoining field that Lord Lyttleton was so fascinated with the charms of the surrounding country, that he thus expressed himself to Mr. Bower: "With the woman one loves, with the friend of one's heart, and a good study of books, one might pass an age here, and think it a day. If you have a mind to live long, and renew your youth, come with Mrs. Bower, and settle at Festiniog." The artist should desire his guide to shew him the following places: Rhyadr-y-Cwm, Rhyadr Bod-Losgad, Rhyadr-y-Fuwch, and Caenant Llyn-y-Pyscod; all of which will reward his trouble. The great slate-quarries at a place called Diffwys, in a romantic spot on the mountains, belong to Messrs. Casson's and Co. The slates, fine blue stone, and of large sizes, are exported to Dublin, *&c.*; their conveyance to a quay, a mile beyond Maentwrog, is both tedious and expensive: these gentlemen not being, as yet, possessed of a rail-road, they employ for this purpose about thirty carts, which, certainly, do not *improve* this public road. The rocks called Manod Mawr, and Manod Bach, the great and the little Manod, are noble objects when viewed from good points. Moelwyn is a very majestic top-rock, towering above all others in the neighbourhood, whose skirts are well wooded to the lower end of the vale, which is terminated with an opening into St. George's channel.

The artist should inquire the road to Dolwyddelan, and proceed along it for two or three miles: and on ascending the mountain he will have some good views of Snowdon. On his return to Maentwrog he should make up to the top of Moelwyn, where

"—— The bleak hill sand barren mountains rise,
And spread their ample bosoms to the skies;
While in the mighty distance seen below,
The gloomy vales, the lake's wide waters flow."

In descending towards Tan-y-Bwlch, he will meet with a number of curious and picturesque cottages, which are oftener in the clouds than out of them. After a pleasant excursion of a day and a half among these mountains, I returned to Maentwrog. Mr. Thomas, the landlord of this inn, very obligingly became my guide through the extensive grounds of Tan-y-Bwlch Hall. I do not remember a walk in which I was more interested; the waterfalls, though not great, are pretty bits, rushing down the dingles. Pursuing our ramble, often over ugly precipices, which, though terrific to some, only added to my gratification every step; we at last gained the fine lofty summit of these woody heights; when opened to my view a noble expanded scene, over the Traeth Bach, and Traeth Mawr, with several attendant circumstances, making up a whole of an enchanting prospect:—

> "From this hoar hill, that climbs above the plain,
> Half way up Heav'n, ambitious, brown with woods
> Of broadest shade, and terraced round with walks
> Winding and wild, that deep embowering rise,
> Maze above maze, through all its shelter'd height,
> From hence the aërial concave without cloud,
> Translucent, and in purest azure dress'd;
> The boundless scene beneath, hill, dale, and plain;
> The precipice abrupt; the distant deep,
> Whose shores remurmur to the sounding surge;
> The nearest forest, in wide circuit spread:—
> Solemn recess, whose solitary walks
> Fair Truth and Wisdom love; the bordering lawn,
> With flocks and herds enrich'd; the daisied vale;
> The river's crystal, and the meadow's green—
> Grateful diversity; allure the eye
> Abroad to rove, amid ten thousand charms."
>
> MALLETT's *Excursion*, Canto I. line 88.

After feasting our eyes during a considerable time, we descended to Tan-y-Bwlch Hall, the fine mansion and residence of William Oakley, Esq. The prospect from it is beautiful, commanding the vale below, with the woody hills; and from the return looking towards the sea, there is also an agreeable view. The handsome and extensive meadows below the house, owe their existence and improvement to the judicious and skilful management of Mr. Oakley, who rescued them from the immersion of the tide; which is now very subservient, and keeps within the extensive embankments, thrown up at considerable expense. A few years since, this gentleman received from the Society for the Encouragement of Arts, *&c.*, the gold medal, as an honorary reward for so important a recovery.

The church of Maentwrog is dedicated to St. Twrog, who lived in the beginning of the sixth century. The stranger will find attached to one of the angles of the church, a large stone, called Maen Twrog, or Twrog's Block of Stone; which, as an absurd legend tells us, the saint threw from the top of Moelwyn to this place, where it has ever since kept its station. About two miles from the village is a noble fall, called Rhyadr Ddu, or the Black Cataract, beautifully enriched with wood. It is in a broad open hollow; a circumstance which will probably please the common taste, but will not give that delight to the artist, which he receives on the view of others of a form more close and compact. Llyn-y-Gigfran, the Lake of the Raven, on this stream, is a grand chasm, which is worthy of a visit from every stranger who may have a taste for sights like these.

Leaving Maentwrog, I directed my steps towards Harlech. After ascending a very steep hill, I came to Llyn Tegwyn Ucha, or the Upper Tegwyn Lake, taking its name from the parish-church, a fine piece of water, surrounded by high rocks and hills, except on the south-west end, which lies open to the sea. My road led me under the side of a rude rocky mountain, which from its frightful, stony appendants, and other circumstances, appeared not unlike, in aspect, to Penmaenmawr. Llan Tegwyn church is dedicated to St. Tegwyn, a saint of the sixth century; it is pleasantly situated above the sea, and a rich and beautiful valley. As I approached the public-house, the landlord of Maentwrog-inn, and another person, reckoned a good *musician*, gave me the meeting; and, with many civil apologies for stopping me on the road, they put me under an arrest, by an earnest request to be favoured with a solo upon the patent flageolet. The importunate solicitations of these good men, I could not resist: and the beautiful air of "Morfa Rhyddlan," produced flattering compliments on the proficiency, which they were pleased to say, I had attained on an instrument so recently invented. One of these sweet octave flutes (for which I am obliged to Mr. Bainbridge, of Holborn), I found, in my leisure moments on my journey, to be an excellent companion: its tones, whenever introduced, never failing to please. I found it particularly well calculated to give effect to the native airs; especially to those of the plaintive and melancholy cast, played in the minor keys. The flageolet, whose gamut and semi-notes are very easy of attainment, is already become fashionable, as a beautiful accompaniment for that feminine instrument, the piano-forte.

I had now a prospect before me, the different lineaments and beauties of which required some time to study. Right below me was the handsome lake called the lower Llyn Tegwyn; and still lower down, enriched with varied green, and impending cottages on its acclivities, a well-wooded valley; intercepted from the sea by a further extent of land, with some fine uplifted rocks. On the left, the great and precipitous eminences fall off, in beautiful aërial perspective, to Harlech, whose castle breaks the horizontal line of the sea. This neighbourhood is furnished with many good subjects for the painter, and is right on his way from Tan-y-Bwlch to Harlech. Leaving the road, I struck through the wood to Glynn, an old mansion, the property of the Porkington family, of Shropshire. In proceeding through an avenue of tall elms and beech, I was suddenly obliged to halt. Two bulls presented themselves in attitudes that left no room to doubt their hostile and ferocious purposes; and a groan and a roar now and then evinced their painful sensations, which tended the more to increase their mad and jealous rage. I approached to within the distance of forty yards; but as I always hold it as a maxim that to meddle officiously with other folks' quarrels (unless sanctioned by reason and prudence) is not only unwise and disagreeable, but in many cases, even unsafe, I declined interfering in this furious contest. Making my retreat, therefore, through the woods, I declined to witness the encounter of these two bullies, and soon reached Harlech, or High Cliff. This, once a place of importance, is now a very poor village; and though immediately contiguous to the sea, having no harbour, *&c.*, it derives no advantage from it whatever. The neighbourhood is rocky and barren, scarcely affording food for sheep; a circumstance which gives it a naked, cold, and uncomfortable appearance. The castle is a noble object, situated upon a rock of great elevation above the sea, which washes its western base; and on this side it looks triumphant and severe on all below. This building is square, having an area of nearly an acre, and at each angle a strong and handsome round tower, from all of which, once issued turrets of like form: but some of them have fallen; while those which remain add greatly to the picturesque effect of the whole. The west front stands upon a horrid precipice, which is very strangely marked with fissures and indentations to the bottom. There is an entrance on this side to different barriers; although one would suppose, from its invulnerable appearance, that it could need no such precautions.

In the land front of this castle, is a grand gateway entrance, between two round towers, guarded by portcullises, and a foss continued to the western angle. This seems to be the only side, in which, in the days of its erection, it could be susceptible of breaches. The interior front elevation is a specimen of bold architecture, more of the Roman than any other, and similar to the fine inside front of Beaumaris-castle, which every traveller of taste must view with pleasure.

In ancient times this fortress went by the name of Twr Bronwen, from Bronwen, or the Fair-bosomed, a lady remarkable for her beauty and heroism. She was sister to Bran ab Llyr, King of Britain, who was the father of the celebrated Caradoc, or Caractacus. It was afterwards called Caer Collwyn, from Collwyn ab Tangno, one of the fifteen tribes of North Wales. Of the ancient castle, traces are very visible, upon which the present building rests. This structure was erected by Edward I., about the year 1282. Dafydd ab Jevan ab Einion, a friend of the House of Lancaster, and a man as much distinguished for his valour, as for his handsome person, and great stature, possessed this place in 1468. William Herbert, Earl of Pembroke, imitating Hannibal's military course over the Alps, after a march of almost insurmountable difficulties over the tremendous rocks of this country, from which, in one place particularly *, he and his soldiers had to climb and precipitate themselves, invested the castle; but Sir Richard, the great hero, his brother, conducted the siege, and summoned the British commander to surrender.

* Called to this day, Lle Herbert, Herbert's Track.

"With brazen voice, was Einion call'd,
To quit the post of glory:—
With brazen voice, the chief replied,
That Fame could tell his story*."

Einion returned for answer, that he had kept a fortress in France so long, that all the old women in Wales talked of him; and that he would keep this so long, that all the old women in France should hear of him.

"At length came Famine, fellest foe,
That ever fac'd a hero;
She came to Herbert, as a friend,
On Einion frown'd a Nero*."

Thus unfortunate, the gallant Einion yielded, but on honourable terms. There is a trait in the character of Sir Richard, on this occasion, singular and romantic. Sir Richard, perceiving in his opponent a noble and warlike disposition, engaged to intercede for his life with his cruel and ungenerous master, Edward IV. The king refusing his request, Sir Richard told him, with some warmth, that his Highness might take *his* life for that of the Welsh captain: for that he would certainly replace Dafydd in the fortress; and the king might send whom he pleased to take him out a second time. This threat succeeded: but the grant of this life was Sir Richard's only reward for his great services, and, to a man of his turn of mind, it was no mean one†.

After the battle of Northampton, in 1460, that spirited Amazon, Margaret of Anjou, the faithful queen of the mild Henry VI. fled to Coventry; from whence she retired and

* The Castle of Harlech—a Poem by Llwyd.

† Life of Lord Herbert, 78.

found an asylum in this castle. After staying here a short time, she went to the north of England, where she collected force enough to wreak her vengeance on her greatest enemy, the Duke of York, at the battle of Wakefield.

In the time of the civil wars, the garrison, counting only twenty-eight men, under the command of Major Hugh Pennant, defended the place with spirit against a large force under General Mytton, to whom, in March, 1647, it surrendered on good terms; and it had the honour of being the last place that held out for King Charles I.

From hence is a fine prospect of all Lyn, with Pwllheli and Criccieth-castle, and, more easterly, Snowdon and his lordly associates. Seven years since, Anwyl, the civil master of the public-house here, employed some men to cut peat in the marsh just below the down. It being usual to go pretty deep, at the depth of two yards the men struck their spades against some hard impenetrable substances, and, upon further perseverance, they were found to take a circular direction; when their investigation led them ultimately to the unexpected discovery, that the place had been at one time or other, a lime-kiln. It was full of the common calcareous stone; about one half of the contents was properly reduced to calx, while the other seemed to have suffered no change; and, what is very remarkable in this case, there were not the smallest remains either of coal, or wood, or any other burning material, intermingled with the stone. Anwyl, perhaps unfortunate for discovery, did, to use his own emphatic words, " chwalee yr cwbwl," *i. e.*, scatter the whole, and now not a vestige is left, save the impressions of the spades. The pulverized half was used to manure the fields, and the other to make walls. Query, Could this have been a kiln to prepare lime for the building of the castle? and, if so, may there not be more on the spot? It appears very probable that this kiln was overwhelmed by some sudden convulsion of the sea, which might at the same time have thrown up those vast hills of sand that run across, between the sea and this immense marshy ground.

The member of parliament for the county is always elected at this place. The present member is Sir Robert Williams, Bart. of Nannau. The castle, though it has nothing near at hand to second it, save the rock upon which it stands, makes a fine picture with Snowdon and other mountains in the distance, and the extensive flat between. But, with respect to composition, it must give way to Conway, Carnarvon, and Dolbadarn castles, as it is unsupplied with that variety of objects so happily blended in those landscapes.

I left this place the next morning with a young guide across the hills. About a mile and a half from Harlech, I saw a bardic relic, stones set circularwise, where the ancient bards held their meetings. These meetings were held in conspicuous places in the open air, and while the sun was above the horizon; for their laws forbade their performing these ceremonies in his absence. The premier Bard stood in the centre, by the side of a large stone. This circle was denominated Cylch Gyngrair, or the Circle of Federation; and the middle stone, Maen Llog, or the Stone of Covenant. The dress of his order, by which the Bard was distinguished, was a robe of azure blue, unicoloured: it was an emblem of truth, and typical also of the conduct he must follow, in assuming, amidst the storms of life, all the serenity of an unclouded sky. The Druids were the second order, and were dressed in white. The Ofydd, or third order (the first into which the candidate was admitted) wore a dress of green. The Awenyddion, or Disciples, wore a variegated dress of blue and green; green, blue, and white, being the bardic colours. While the Bards stood, bare-headed and bare-footed, within the circle, the ceremony commenced by sheathing a sword, and laying it formally on the stone of the covenant. After this, the bardic traditions were recited. The Bards, under the title of Beirdd ynis Prydain, or Bards of the Isle of Britain, were held as the heralds of peace: accordingly out of respect to them, no naked weapons were shewn in their presence; nor were they to become parties in any dispute, either political or religious. If a Bard but presented himself between two contending armies, they would instantly desist *.

From these heights is seen a noble view of the British Alps. Proceeding over some rough precipices, I came down to Cwm-Buchan; the weather was too fine and gay to meet this romantic spot with that degree of reverential regard, which in a dull and murky state of the atmosphere, it is so well calculated to inspire. Here is a small lake, over which hangs a high rock, called Carreg y Saeth, or the Rock of the Arrow; on the verge of which are a maen hîr and garnedd. From the name, it is not improbable that this rock might formerly have been a station for sportsmen, to watch and intercept the wild deer, which were very numerous here in ancient times.

The inhabitants of the two small farms in this hollow, were busily occupied in getting in their scanty crop of hay. One can-

* The time of the Druids and ancient Bards is generally supposed to have been tinctured with much ignorance and superstition; but who would not wish that we had now men of such singular powers, to stop the rapine and slaughter in Europe?

not but commiserate what appears to be the comfortless condition of these poor beings in the winter. Shut up from society, and from all free communication with the surrounding neighbourhood, they seem left to brood upon the inclemency of the weather, the forlorn state of their cattle, and their own melancholy mountain-imprisonment. But while the sanguine philanthropist is indulging in these commiserations, the simple native smiles at the recital of such imagined privations and seclusions, and happily feels little of their inconveniences. On the side of this cwm is a house where formerly lived Mr. Evan Llwyd, who could justly boast of being the descendant, in the eighteenth degree, of Bleddyn ab Cynfan, a prince of North Wales and Powys, who was slain in battle in 1072. The form of this pedigree is as follows;—Evan ab Edwart, ab Richard, ab Edwart, ab Humphrey, ab Edwart, ab Dafydd, ab Robert, ab Howel, ab Dafydd, ab Meirig Llwyd, or Nannau, ab Meirig Fychan, ab Ynyr Fychan, ab Ynyr, ab Meiric, ab Madoc ab Cadwan, ab Bleddyn, ab Cynfan, Prince of North Wales and Powis*. An ingress into this place is difficult, and the departure from it, attended with equal trouble, over uneven grounds and rocks, to the entrance of the grand pass, called Drws Ardydwy, or the Door of Ardydwy. This is, indeed, a very wild, bold, and picturesque passage, formed by two sterile lofty and rocky hills. To the lonely traveller it presents a most gloomy aspect: the rocks, from their black mossy coverings, seeming to have agreed with the heights above them, to render the place fit only for the abode of Melancholy. The sides are broken into great masses of rocks, whence heavy blocks of stone precipitating, fill the pass; and without a stratum, in which a single blade of grass can

* Pennant's Tour.

grow, the whole is a dismal wild. The fineness of the weather, and the splendour of the sun seemed to have but little influence on the aspect of the place; the dull black heath conspiring to give an air of sullenness to these impending moss-covered rocks. They are frequently of very fantastic outline, though their horizontal strata rather lessen the picturesque of their appearance. This pass continues for near a mile and a half. The horse-road through the whole of the place is a great curiosity: it is formed of stone steps, and the passenger ascends and descends regularly, as if he was going up and down the stairs of a house. Those who visit Harlech markets, *&c.*, seated on their sure-footed ponies, pass this way; and these valuable animals bring them home in safety through the darkest nights, and over a road which, of all I have ever seen or can imagine appears to be the most dangerous. Making my way through some boggy grounds, I came to a farm-house called Drws Ardydwy; on entering which, a young woman approached me with a countenance full of good nature. On requesting a draught of milk to allay my thirst, she instantly complied, and ere I could well seat myself, a table was spread before me, as by magic, with all the best eatables, *&c.* the house afforded, consisting of two sorts of bread, butter, cheese, and butter-milk; the common fare of these contented and happy mountaineers. The whole of this was done with all the ease imaginable, and with a welcome and kindness peculiar to the hearts of my country-women; and which for ages have distinguished, and I hope ever will distinguish, them, in their hospitality to the stranger. I am convinced that nothing would be more practicable to a native, a master of his native language, whose appearance does not create a suspicion of character, than to travel over Wales, free of all charges for eating and drinking, let his situation in life be what it may.

On taking my leave, I offered some apologies for the trouble I had given this good-hearted girl, on which she promptly replied, that the only trouble she felt, was in consequence of the words I thus had just dropped.

Crossing the road from Tan y Bwlch to Dolgellau, I struck up the country to the fall, Pistyll y Caen, or the Spout of the Caen, situated in the hollow of a rock eighty yards in length, taking nearly an oval form; the sides of which are covered with oak, ash, and birch, except immediately close to the fall, where the rock is bare, perpendicular, and mural, an unfavourable circumstance in such a picture. The fall, in height about seventy feet, pours down in one undivided sheet, which, with the roughness of the banks and of the bottom, makes it a grand and striking object for the eye, or the pencil of taste. At the entrance, a bridge made of the trunk of an old oak, is placed over the rude and terrific black channel of the river; the path over this cascade is not very safe for the steps of the timid fair, though a very trifling expense would make it dangerless.

On leaving this place, I turned a few hundred yards to the left, to see a fall of the Mawddach, in a wild and romantic dell. This fall, from the roughness of the abrupt precipices over which it rushes, and the interruption of the water thrice in its descent to the pool at its foot, a depth, I should suppose, of about seventy or eighty feet, forms a very picturesque scene. To those who are familiar with the pictures of Salvator, these rich moss-covered rocks and banks, and the gold-tinged foliage, will be very observable. In the summer months, the distance from Dolgellau, about seven miles, over a pleasant road, and through a charmingly wooded country, renders an excursion to these falls so highly delightful, that no one should neglect to visit a spot where

> " Torrents loud, impetuous cataracts,
> Through roads abrupt, and rude unfashion'd tracts,
> Roll down the lofty mountain's channell'd sides,
> And to the vale convey their foaming tides." BLACKMORE.

Returning by the side of the Mawddach, I saw Mr. Maddocks's house, now occupied by Mr. Woodcock, at Dol-y-Melynllyn, or the Holm of the Yellow Pool, embosomed in a fine rich and extensive wood. I kept up the hills a considerable height, for the purpose of ascertaining from thence the figure and character of Cader Idris: but a lowering sky disappointing me, I returned and crossed the Mawddach again into the public road; following which, a short distance, I came to Rhyad Ddu, or Black Cataract, in the grounds of Dol-y-Melynllyn, on the furious river Gamlan. This is another celebrated fall, that gave me as much pleasure in the contemplation of it as any I had yet witnessed: but an insufficient quantity of water at the time, rendered it less sublime than if better supplied. The character of it is bold, and receives much consequence from the beautiful lichen and the variegated green of other trees spread about, and with the jet-black rocks that lie in rude order, above and below, makes up a whole perhaps not excelled by its neighbouring rivals. This species of stone is observable for several miles on this river, and on the Mawddach, into which it soon precipitates. The stranger would not be a little amused if he followed the stream a little way, to see the hollows in it, and the massive stones strangely perforated by the whirling motion of the water.

The declining day, with a thick mist, warning me to seek

shelter as soon as I could, I made a rapid movement along the road to Dolgellau. In this state of the weather, I could not direct my thoughts to individual objects; and only know, that the road led me under the noble woods of Dol-y-Melynllyn, and that on my left ran the turbulent Mawddach, through a beautiful and well-wooded valley.

The flood-gates of heaven were now set open, and every object shut from view for the night; whilst in an half-drowned condition I made my entry at a public-house at Llanelltid. The fatigues of the day's journey, over the roughest grounds I had yet seen in Wales, acted as a most powerful soporific when I retired to rest.

The following morning opened with a most splendid sun-rise. It was the sabbath; and the church (dedicated to St. Iltutus) was soon crowded with a congregation composed of the farmers, tradesmen, and the poor of the neighbourhood. They appeared very pious in their devotions, shewing every deference to the pastor, whose well-known abilities has ensured to him a full and constant attendance; and whose urbanity and decorous deportment in life, make up a character of general admiration. This village is very handsome, and the view from it delightful. Cader Idris stretching in great length from north-east to south-west, and the middle space occupied by an extensive tract of meadowy and marshy land. A few hundred yards off is a handsome bridge of several arches, close to which were a few vessels of from sixty to one hundred tons each, on the stocks. This may be considered as a novel sight; for when the tide is out, and no water seen, the shipping appear amidst wood and meadows, twelve miles distant from the sea; and one would be ready to wonder, how such hulks could be made to float, in a place seemingly land-locked. A quarter of a mile from this bridge is Cymmer-abbey. The choir of the church, in which is a specimen of Gothic architecture, in numerous remains of arches, pillars, *&c.*, is disproportionably and extremely narrow. The east end presents a handsome window, consisting of three lancet lights, and over them three others, mantled with ivy. This is, on the external of the building, utterly hid by a shed erected by the farmer: but were this and a part of the ivy removed, it would make an agreeable picture. Time and weather have committed great devastation in this monastery; and have left little for the antiquary, and not much for the artist. The adjoining farm-house exhibits the remains of the refectory, *&c.* This was an abbey of Cistercians, founded by the two princes, Griffydd and Meredydd, the sons of Howel and Conan, about 1198. Llywelyn granted it a charter in 1209, which gave to Esau, then the lord abbot, and the other religious men of the house, great latitude of right over the sea, lakes, and rivers; over birds; wild and tame beasts; over mountains, woods, things moveable and immoveable, and over all things under and upon the land so granted; and it further gave liberty of digging for all descriptions of metals and hidden treasures.

Its revenues, at the dissolution, were valued, according to Dugdale, at £51 13*s.* 6*d.*; according to Speed, £58 15*s.* 4*d.* Returning through an avenue of tall and venerable sycamores, I pursued my way up the mountains towards Nannau. From these heights, the scene became more and more expanded, the the flats beneath were spread like a map, while the peaked heads of Cader Idris shewed their magnificent fronts, rising to an amazing altitude above the valley. Nannau-hall is the residence of Sir Robert Williams Vaughan, Bart., M. P. for the county; a gentleman whose suavity of manners, and attachment to his country, have secured him the esteem of all. The perpendicular height of the spot, upon which the house stands, is 639 feet, from high-water mark. In dull murky weather it is commonly obscured by clouds, which linger on their way over these hills: but though at this vast height from the vale, it is still situated in a hollow; a circumstance which gives it an air of solitude, not ill-adapted for the residence of a recluse, who wished to retire from the busy world to the enjoyment of devotion and peace. The hills on each side guard it against storms. A vista, at the back, in some measure takes off from the gloom; it is a peep between the hills, over a small lake, to the grand scenery about Dol-y-Melynllyn. On ascending the heights a few yards, the noble prospects of Cader, *&c.*, just described, came in view. The house was lately erected, and what may be wanting in design, is amply made up by the durable quality, strength.

The next morning I began an excursion of fifty miles. The country for two or three miles was rather dull, till I reached Pont-Newydd, a very handsome bridge of one arch, of large span, over the river Arran. Keeping up the hills (an arduous ascent) I came to a water-fall, called Rhyadr Elugog, until now unknown, and therefore unnoticed by any other tourist. This is very difficult of approach, but I was sufficiently compensated for the trouble of descending, by a most extraordinary sight. The body of water that comes down an uninterrupted fall of about seventy feet, between the compressed sides of two dismal black rocks, was not great: but yet the picturesque scenery of a wild rough bottom, makes it valuable. The wood that covered the high rocks, nearly surrounding the fine chasm below, was completely metamorphosed. The winter of 1804 produced a heavy fall of snow in this neighbourhood; and the pressure was so great upon this wood, that the younger trees, from their flexibility, soon yielded to the ponderous weight, and were consequently bent, curled, and twisted into a variety of fantastic forms. Though they had suffered the severity of such a change, their foliage however was healthy and gay. I left them in the everlasting act of most courteous and ceremonious compliment to each other across the stream, like so many ladies and gentlemen courting and bowing on meeting in the open air. Crossing the Arran again, I made up to Blaené, the residence of the Miss Jones's on the opposite hills. These ladies have a tree on their grounds, remarked for its great singularity. It is a large oak, of whose very bulky body scarcely any part but the bark remains. Within grows a noble birch, already so large, as to fill the venerable trunk "almost to bursting," making its way through the remaining branches of the old tree, and covering a prodigious space of ground. This is not all; for upon one large horizontal branch of the oak, are two very beautiful ash saplings growing very upright, but whose fate will be certain on the demise of their foster-mother. Close to the house is rather a good waterfall, but too low to excite much interest: were it not defective in this, every other circumstance about it would render it a good subject for a drawing. These ladies live on a delightful spot, adorned with wood and other local beauties, and yet raised so high as to command great and prominent objects. Cader Idris, being fore-shortened, makes an ostentatious display of his pointed tops; the interval is so filled up by mountains, wood, water, and valley, as to render the situation equal to any in the neighbourhood.

After paying my respects to these very obliging ladies, I returned to the vale below, where, at the distance of two miles, I took up my abode for the night at Drws yr Nant, or the Door of the Vale, a small inn, and deficient in those conveniencies which we find in houses on roads better frequented. I had for supper some potted venison, as they are pleased to call it; but which in reality is potted kid of peculiar taste, very agreeable to most palates. Goats are not now so numerous in this country as in former times: but it is evident, were some attention paid to the rearing of them, the farmer and the nation would be benefited. This useful animal is so hardy, that it prefers the rock before any other situation, and will not quit it in the severest weather. It feeds on heath-tops and furze as its proper aliment: but when these are covered by the snow, it will contentedly brouse upon the rock moss. The goats' propensity to nibble trees and plants is well known; and from its disposition to hurt the vine, one of the trees consecrated to Bacchus, the goat was slain in the sacrifices made to that deity. A fattened goat is excellent eating: it is otherwise valuable to the farmer, the skin sells at from seven to eleven shillings each; the tallow might, from its whiteness, make beautiful candles; and the hair also is useful for various purposes.

I set out in the morning late, the rain preventing an earlier walk The road led me up for two miles along a fine woody vale, through which the river Arran makes its way, murmuring between its shady banks in frequent meanders, that rendered it often agreeably visible through the wood. The scenes on this road are of the same cast as those of Doly-Melynllyn; the dingles and the acclivities of the mountains, being loaded with heavy timber. Leaving the road, I ascended to a considerable height among the hills, from whence I had a delightful view of Cader

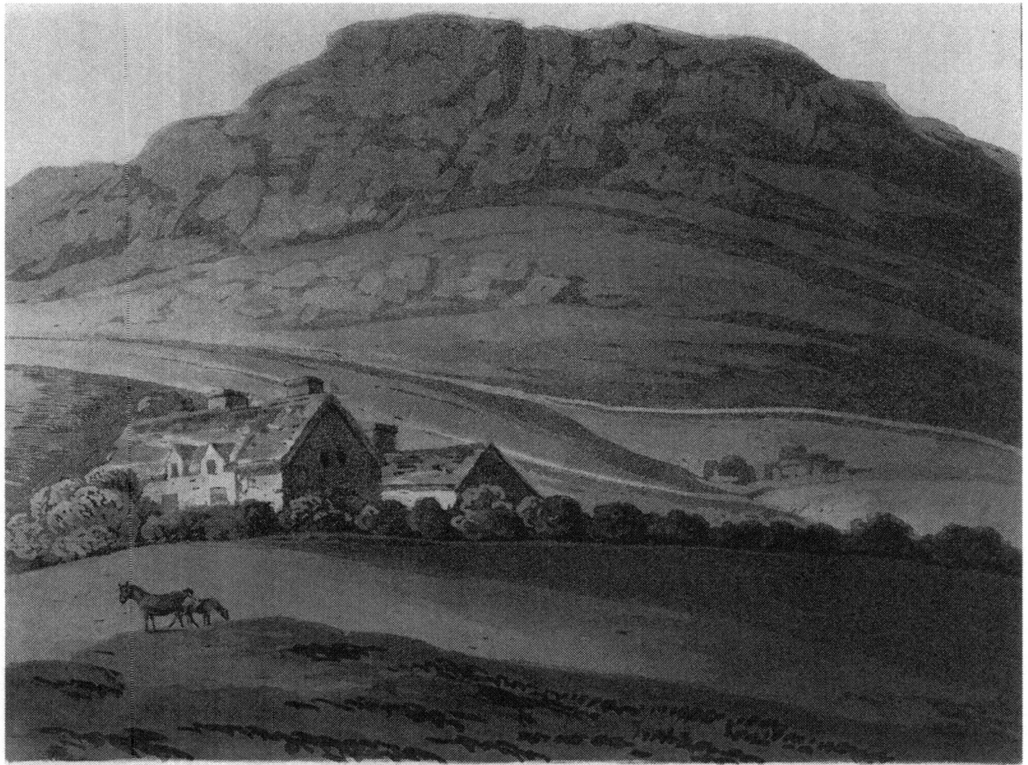

E. Pugh delt. T. Cartwright sculpt.

THE SOURCES OF THE DEE.

Published 26 May, 1814 by E. Williams Strand.

Idris, which became an object of great interest, with the intersecting lines of wood and mountains, and the variable inequalities of the near grounds.

From lower situations, not distant from the road, the scenery is also fine; the woods below are well grouped with cottages, and other accidental circumstances that come in very happily. Following the road a little further, the country began to open, but exhibited a barren and unfriendly soil. Close to a small farm-house called Pant Gwyn, the property of Sir Watkin Williams Wynn, Bart., are two small springs, the sources of the celebrated river Dee, that loses itself beyond Chester, in the Irish sea. There is no respect paid to them, as they lie exposed to the treading of cattle, hogs, geese, &c.; the flow of water is small. Spencer *, by some mistake, supposes the Dee to arise from a spring under Arran Benllyn, the stream from which is now called the Turch: but these springs are unquestionably the source whence Deva rolls his wizard stream.

The house is noted for an instance of singular curiosity †. In rain, the eves-drops fall from one side into the Dee, and from the other into the Arran, taking quite opposite courses. In the adjoining plates are represented the appearance of the sources and the house in one view.

A short distance from this place is the famous old well, called Ffynnon Brynnon Bryn yr Eirch; which, from the fragments of

* Fairy Queen.—Book I. Canto ix.

† Another rarity of the kind, and spoken of by travellers, is seen near Burtatingen, in the Austrian territories, near the Black Forest. A chapel is so situated, that the rain from one side of it falls into the Danube, and from the other into the Rhine.

walls about it, one would suppose was once in high estimation. Here I got the first near view of Llyn Tegid, or the Lake of Tegid, probably so called from a chieftain of that name, who lived on the spot, in the fifth century: it is a grand piece of water, stretching four miles longitudinally. The surrounding country, though hilly, is yet tame compared with the scenery I had just left. Llanuwchlyn, or the Village above the Lake, is poor: but it afforded me lodging for the night, at the public-house kept by Maurice Roberts. Near the village are to be seen the effects of a dreadful commotion of the elements.

The little river Turch, or the Burrower, was swelled to such a degree by a sudden fall of rain during a thunder storm, that it rushed from the mountains, and brought with it many stupendous and massy stones, that now lie on a rugged flat, which, before this circumstance, was a beautiful meadow; and on which, at the time, a number of cattle were grazing, many of whom were swept away by the current, and lost. It came down so suddenly and unexpectedly, that the people had scarcely time to save themselves. Eight houses and a bridge were carried away, with other subsidiary buildings, and every moveable article which stood within the sweep of the torrent. A part of one house, with an old woman, was observed floating upon the lake, and brought to land; and a looking-glass was found standing upright upon a bed, which a little before was made use of by a young woman to adjust her head-dress, preparatory to her appearance in the dance at the fair held on that day. This happened on the 20th of June, 1781, and lasted from four to six in the evening. It was difficult for me ascertain which of these stones was the largest; but I measured one, and found it to be, in its length, forty feet, and in its girth thirty-three; and hence the reader will form a pretty correct idea, as to the weight of these vast bodies, thus hurled along the narrow channel of this river.

The whole of this rapid inundation lasted but two hours. The consternation at the fair may easily be conceived; and the people were unable to return to their homes until the flood abated. A venerable old man, an eye-witness of the whole, whilst the knitting-needle passed nimbly through his fingers, related to me all the particulars; and his account was afterwards fully confirmed by some gentlemen in the neighbourhood. Groups of people, of all ages, are here to be seen busily employed in knitting woollen hose, a staple commodity, forming the greatest part of the commerce of this county of Merioneth, which, with the exception of the skirts of other counties bordering upon it, engrosses the whole of this trade. They have brought this article to such a degree of perfection and fineness of texture, as to have no rivals. The Shrewsbury merchants, and others, employ agents for the purpose of purchasing the stockings, which are afterwards sold in London, and in other large towns, at various prices, from three shillings to twelve shillings a pair. This is a source of useful employment, and a happy mode of procuring a livelihood for the poor, whom it is common to meet on the roads, travelling upon other business, busily at work with their knitting-needles; and no conversation, or any slight occurrence, can divert them from this object of their industry. I now pursued my route towards the hills on the Mowddwy road, and coming to a little cottage on the road-side, I went in to inquire my way to the mountain, called Arran Benllyn. An old woman and her daughter, a beautiful brunette, readily gave the information I wanted: and, in return, inquired if I travelled that rough mountainous country without a companion? I replied that I did not; and that I had a little lady who followed me wherever I went; upon which they both with great earnestness requested I would bring the lady in, to partake with me of what refreshments their cot afforded: my further intimation that my companion was a *black*, produced a smile of surprise on the daughter, followed by a slight distortion of her beautiful features. " What, Sir," replied the mother hastily, " black,—a black-a-moor wife!" On my telling her she was not my wife,—" O naughty man," she rejoined,—" but in the name of all that's good, where did you find such a thing? and, if you must have a female companion, why did you not get one of your own colour?" I replied I could not procure one of that colour. " I am afraid" said the good old woman, lifting up her hands, " there are but too many of them to be found in the world; but," continued she, " poor blacks must eat and drink like other folks; so if you please, bring her in." I accordingly called my little negress, Miss Wowski*, who made her appearance readily in the middle of the floor. The old woman and daughter perceiving the deception, fell into a convulsive fit of merriment, and good humouredly said, it was no wonder I should love so pretty and so loving a little creature. Such are the sentiments and genuine good feelings of the country poor, that to perform acts of kindness to the stranger, becomes to them a luxury unknown to the haughty rich. This county, for ages, has been celebrated for its beautiful women: and this very beautiful girl brought this celebrity to my recollection, and inclined me to bow to the testimony of so many witnesses, who declare, that

* My black dog.

"With Meirion's daughters, matchless maids
No country yet contended;
Not all Circassia's countless charms
To Beauty's palm pretended."

The late ingenious and learned Mr. Lewis Morris, confirms this testimony in such bewitching terms, as set all translation at defiance;—

"Pwy sy'n ymyl dwyn vy ngho!
Morwynion bro Meirionydd."

Making up through some fields by a farm-house, I met a venerable old farmer, near ninety years of age, just returning from the mountain, where he had been in search of some lost sheep. He insisted upon his son's attending me to Llyn Llymbren, a small lake under the side of Arran Benllyn. This hanging rock is very high, rather curving inwards, or bending its top over the lake, as is commonly the case with these lofty heads. It does not strike the stranger with so much awe as some lower precipices, from the circumstance of its colour being light grey, while that of the others was black, and their nature shelfy, consequently forming uneven and rugged surfaces. This lake has in it some good fish. The haziness of the weather prevented my ascending the mountain. Taking my leave of my guide, I pursued my way along the side of the rocks, and overtook three shepherds who were collecting some wanderers from the fold. They shewed me the noted path along the precipitous side of Arran Benllyn, which, it is said, one Elise followed on horseback. The story is related three different ways: but that which is generally told, and gains most credit, is this.—A man, of bad character, mounted a horse which he had stolen from the plains below, and to prevent the possibility of being overtaken, should his theft be discovered, ventured upon this desperate path with the beast, which he afterwards sold at a distant fair. The path is observable as a small line, running obliquely on the craggy side of this mountain; and ever since it has been denominated, Llwybir Elise, or Ellis's Path. I kept in company with these hardy men for a considerable distance over these boggy hills, through an increasing mist: when at the verge of Llyn Dyfi, a handsome lake under the high peak of Arran Mowddwy, the drizzly rain prevented my seeing the precipice; the partial glance of whose grey side, which I caught for a moment, only served to increase my wishes. But it was totally shut from view; and the shepherds assured me that there were no hopes of the weather clearing up during that day upon the mountains*. This was to me a great mortification, as it was my intention to ascend to the summit of one of the highest mountains in Wales, from whence I could have been gratified with a sight of Snowdon, Cader Idris, and a vast assemblage of mountains that surrounded me. This lake is a fine piece of water, and is the source of the river Dovey, or Dyfi, or the Profundity. It was now my wish to descend the mountain into the Mowddwy-road, to get safe to which, the shepherds advised me to keep by the side of this rivulet. I did so for some time, but perceiving it taking a circuitous direction, difficult to follow on account of deep fens, I endeavoured to make a chord line, to meet it below, but in attempting this, I literally found, that I had got out of the mud into the mire; for I frequently sunk in

* The shepherds in this, as well as all other mountainous countries, are, of all other people, the best prognosticators of the weather; this they have partly acquired from their forefathers, and partly from a habit of studying the different appearances of the sky, when the wind is from certain quarters. This faculty of foretelling the weather, is among them reduced almost to a certainty, grounded upon the observations of past ages and the present.

bogs up to my knees, and the further I went, the worse I fared, verifying the proverb, "The furthest way about, the nearest way home." Regaining the stream, I judged it best, therefore, to keep by its side; and soon coming to the very romantic hollow called Llaethnant, I saw at some distance below me some rocks of very strange forms; and, from the circumstance of the intervening mist, I formed them in my imagination into ramparts, bastions, towers, and arches, so completely, as for the moment to suppose them real. But, on approaching, a clearer atmosphere enabling me to see more distinctly the objects around me, I was soon convinced of my mistake. The artist will here find opportunity for employment, as in clear weather the Arran is a noble feature, and the foreground is enriched with wood, water, and other very favourable circumstances. On coming to the public road, I met a woman, who seemed at the first to be much struck with my appearance; and soon after burst into a hearty fit of laughter; and, as I always consider a duet more agreeable than a solo, I kept her company for the moment. The nether part of my dress, from the bogs I had walked through, being one patch of mud, and the rest of my clothing being extremely wet, had, it seems, made the whole appearance so ludicrous, as to produce this laughable effect. Addressing the woman in English, I begged to know my way to Llany Mowddwy; pronouncing the name after the English idiom. She appeared greatly distressed that she was not able to understand me, and looked about her to see if there was any one near, who could answer my question, at the same time repeating in her own vernacular tongue, "Gwynn fy myd, pa bae rhyw un yma a fedrai roddi i'r gîvr da, hyspysiad am yr hyn y mae ef yn ei ymofyn:" "I wish to Heaven there was some one near, who could answer this dear man, and give him the information he wants." This is one of the many instances I have met with on this very journey, disproving the assertions of some English tourists, who represent the character of the Welsh to be morose and uncivil. Whenever such appearances occur, we may more candidly conclude it to arise from their ignorance of the language in which they are addressed, or, in the case of some slight knowledge of it, from the apprehension of ridicule in any attempt to speak it. Whenever I have introduced myself in the language of England, whether in towns, or even among the mountains, where perhaps not a person could be found that could in reply tell me the hour of the day, I have always been received, even among the poorest, with due respect. I had now come into a winding valley, on each side of which the numerous mountains stood like so many bulwarks, but were of a character totally differing from all I had hitherto seen. They did not appear to be so high as those of Carnarvonshire, yet they were, in general, more precipitous, and, what on that account is not a little singular, covered with soil, and a soft downy grass, beautiful to the eye, but possessing few of those traits which the artist contemplates with pleasure on the sides of Snowdon, Glydar, *&c.* This deficiency is however amply remedied by what Snowdonia is defective in, wood. The stranger, though easily admitted into this hollow, will wonder how it can be possible to find a passage out; yet, at every turn or curve, he will be most agreeably surprised to discover an egress as open to him as his entrance into it.

These hills present a sight as singular in appearance, as the operation itself is hazardous in execution. The inhabitants know no other common fuel here than peat or turf. This they cut, in

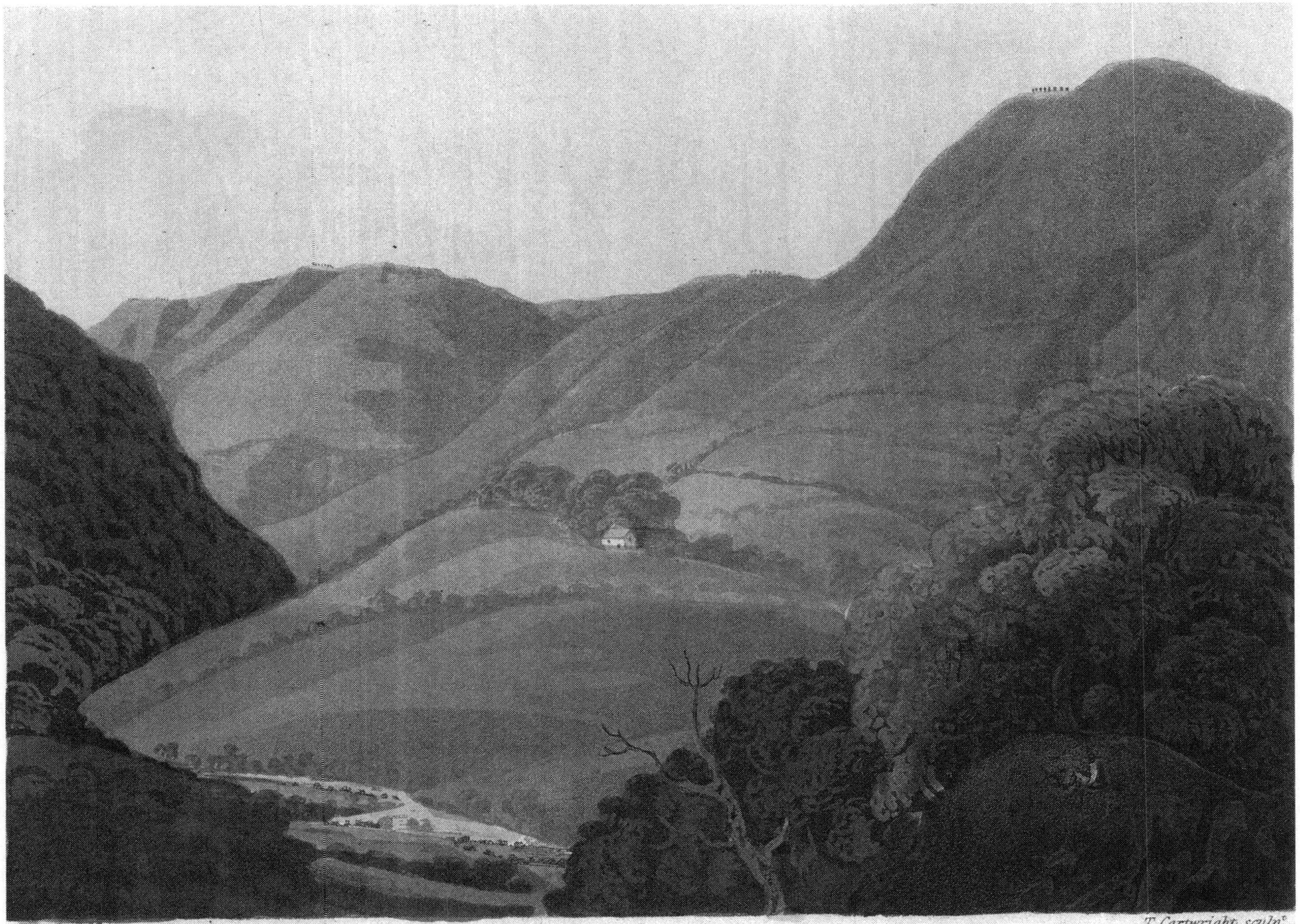

E. Pugh del.^t T. Cartwright sculp.^t

THE GREAT PEAT MOUNTAINS.

Published 26 March 1814, by E. Williams Strand.

summer, on the summit of these mountains; and bringing it to the edge of these great elevations, the people pile it up in the shape of stacks, in which form it remains some time to dry ; when it becomes ready for removal to the proprietor's home. The stacks are arranged, twelve, fifteen, or twenty in a line; and some strangers, once seeing a number of people and horses in constant motion, busied in their erection, fancied them so many batteries for the purpose of defending this pass, should Mr. Bony-party (as the Welsh people call him) venture into these parts. The mode of bringing them into the valley is this: A vehicle called Glwyd-fawn, or a Hurdle, is constructed of two thin boards, about six feet long, placed parallel to each other on their edges, which are shod with iron, and about three-fourths of a yard asunder: thin hazel rods are run through the boards at right angles with them, and three inches from one another, for the whole length of the boards ; this forms the bottom : at the ends and sides are placed plaited rods, through which is drawn a rope across and lengthways over the turf, for its security. A man now places himself before the hurdle, and throwing a rope attached to it with a loop over his head, sets off for the bottom, a distance of half a mile at least, with a velocity hardly credible : the chief difficulty is to guide the vehicle, for, if the man is off his guard in this respect, the whole may fall upon and crush him severely. In the run down, they sometimes overturn, and occasion a deal of trouble, but a serious accident seldom happens. As these turf stacks are very numerous, it is a source of entertainment to the traveller, in the month of September, to see the rapidity with which the men continually descend. The hurdles have made bare the tracks, and the people ascend by a green zig-zag path, with the hurdle upon their shoulders.

It is recorded, that, in 1555, this neighbourhood was disgraced by the cruel murder of Lewis Owen, Vice-chamberlain, and Baron of the Exchequer of North Wales, on his return from the discharge of his duty at Montgomery assizes. After the wars of York and Lancaster, daring banditti, chiefly felons and outlaws, hovering around this neighbourhood, infested the country, committing various outrages; and, amongst others, perpetrated this atrocious deed in open defiance of the laws. They went about in large armed bands, and for a long time continued to rob, burn, and murder, with impunity: the honest inhabitants were obliged to secure their habitations at night, in the strongest manner they could; their houses, being generally built on the steep sides of the hills, gave these miscreants easy admission through the chimnies, which were often not more than two feet from the higher ground; to prevent their entrance, families fixed scythes across them, some specimens of which, it is said, are still to be seen. In my road, having the curiosity to examine a house of this description, I looked down the chimney; but instead of the weapon described, a far more pleasing object appeared; a young female, cooking a joint of mountain-mutton. I asked her, in a loud tone of voice, my way to Mowddwy; she gave a shriek, and withdrew: but instantly recovering from her surprise, with a smile, smartly answered, " straight forward !" I replied, that if I did come straight forward, I should spoil her broth; when, in merry mood, she appeared at the door, to give me that information, which, in fact, I did not want. Llanymowddwy is a small village, incapable of affording refreshment to the weary traveller: the church is dedicated to St. Tydecho, a noted saint, who flourished about the close of the fifth century. We are informed by Dafydd Llwyd ab Llywelyn, ab Griffith, Lord of Mathafern, in a legend in verse of this illustrious bard, that Tydecho came hither from Armorica, when the country was overrun by the Saxons, and led a most austere life in this sequestered spot, lying upon the bare stones, and wearing a shirt made of hair. Maelgwyn Gwynedd, when a youth, being offended with the saint, seized all his oxen: but on the following day, wild stags were seen performing their office at the plough, and a grey wolf dragging the harrow after them. Maelgwyn was much enraged at the sight, and brought his milk-white hounds to chase the deer, himself sitting on a blue stone enjoying the sport. When he attempted to rise, he found himself firmly fixed to his seat; and, ere he was liberated from it, he was obliged to ask pardon, and make reparation to the saint. It is also related of this wonder-working saint, that he converted the Dufi near his house, into a stream of milk, to supply the necessities of the poor; and the place ever since has been called Llaethnant, or Milky-brook. The following couplet perpetuates the tradition:—

> "Tydecho dad di-duchan
> Ai gwnaeth yn llaeth at y llan.

"Tydecho's power of performing miracles," say the Catholics, "was not a whit inferior to that of Narcissus II. the Bishop of Jerusalem, who is said to have turned water into oil to supply the church lamps."—BACON.

I passed a very picturesque hamlet in a dingle, and went through Dinas Mowddwy, to the inn at Mallwyd, kept by Mr. David Lloyd, who very obligingly accompanied me the next morning, on an excursion in the neighbourhood. Mr. Lloyd seems to be well acquainted with those features in a landscape, that are suitable to the ideas of a painter. He brought me to the mountain-river on his farm, which exhibited some excellent rude scenery. Its bed is rough, and the rocky precipices on each side have much height, and are happily broken; their lines frequently intersecting each other, render them perfect pictures. The wood on each side forms beautiful canopies, which is the character of this river for some distance. It resembles those scenes I have already noticed on the Cunfael: but there are two or three spots here, which, in my opinion, surpass any thing which I saw there: the fine breadth of light and shadow occasioned by an afternoon sun, must make any painter enamoured with the sight. The cascade by the Wear has no height: nevertheless, it wonderfully assists the dark hollow below it, from whence this fall is but partially seen, as the branches of oak cut it very agreeably. It is not possible for ladies to see these hollows without careful attendants. Mr. Lloyd shews one of them, where the following accident happened: A horse and cart were employed a short time back in the field above one of these chasms, when by some mismanagement the poor animal, with his load, was hurried down through the bushes, and over some dreadful rocks to the bottom, and though the cart was dashed to pieces, the horse escaped unhurt. How to get him from hence, seemed to be an insurmountable difficulty, but one probable place presented itself, to which the animal's head was turned; and, by means of a few spirited lashes behind, he shot up like a dart, to the surprise and astonishment of every one who witnessed the novel circumstance.

The scenery about Mallwyd's ivy-coated bridge, is very fine; but differs from every thing which I had hitherto seen. The character of it is sylvan and very bold, frequently presenting to the traveller such massy fore-grounds as characterize the pictures of Salvator. Ascending the sides of the hills, I found the prospect open in a fine and picturesque manner. Though the mountains, as I have observed before, are destitute of those characteristics which so much distinguish the highly famed protuberances of Carnarvonshire, yet the noble woods, and the richly decorated flat beneath, more than counterbalance the absence of craggy eminences and rillets. The communion-table in Mallwyd church, is made of a blue-black marble, taken from the bed of a river just below the bridge: the marks in it are two or three degrees darker than its own colour; and, were it capable of a polish, it would be very valuable for its great beauty. This was a present from Mr. Mytton, of Halston in Shropshire, in 1737. It is somewhat remarkable, that this communion-table stands in the centre of the church; in the same situation as the one which preceded it, had occupied in the time of Archbishop Laud. The Archbishop had ordered it to be removed to the usual station, at the east end; but Dr. Davies, the then incumbent, in defiance of Laud's orders, subsequently removed it again to the spot in which it has ever since remained *. The church-tower is constructed of wood, and the date 1640, with a Latin inscription, has been perforated in it with the auger. Over the porch are suspended a rib and a bone of the spine of a whale, caught in the Dovey many years ago. A little beyond the church is the rectory-house, once the residence of the learned divine Dr. John Davies, a son of a weaver of Llanferres, Denbighshire; who had the livings of Mallwyd and Llan-y-Mowddwy. He was author of several eccle-

* Dr. Davies, it seems, was a strict church disciplinarian; for I find that the Rubrick orders, that the table shall stand where morning and evening prayers are appointed to be said, *i. e.*, in the body of the church; so that the present mode of fixing the communion-table in the eastern extremity of the chancel, seems an infringement of the established rules.

siastical writings, and his memory will be ever respected by his countrymen for his literary productions, and for his indefatigable industry in collecting the works of the ancient bards; he died in 1632. The pavement before the door, made of remarkably small pebbles, is rather a curiosity: the initials of the Doctor's name, wrought into it, have stood the brunt of one hundred and eighty years, and are yet in perfection.

Mallwyd-inn is singularly situated, standing in the two counties of Merioneth and Montgomery, and paying taxes to both. Quitting this comfortable house for Dolgellau, a walk of two miles along this rich undulating valley brought me to Dinas Mowddwy, which the day before I passed unnoticed. This is a large village, but poor; and strangers never stay here, but go on to Mallwyd-inn, although the situation of this place is very desirable at the junction of the Dovey and the Cerris. Dinas means a fort or a city; but why Dinas Mowddwy was ever so denominated, I do not know; for one fact is certain, that it has not the least appearance of either, nor has it any ecclesiastical insignia, not even a church to give a little colour to the title. Though a late tourist (Mr. Evans), by some odd mistake, has told us, that, "at Dinas are a fine church and bridge," the traveller will find there neither the one or the other. Craeg-y-Dinas, that towers above the town, is not only lofty but nearly perpendicular. Mr. Pennant relates a frolic of his youthful days, in climbing to the summit of this mountain, "to enjoy the *pleasure* of darting down again in one of the peat sledges:" but afterwards, when on his tour, he surveyed it with horror. The place for such a feat is singularly frightful.

At a short distance is Moel Benddu, a very steep mountain; which I ascended, to get a sight of Cwm-Cowarch. This cwm is unknown to the artist. It would be advisable for those who may visit it, to enter from the Bala-road, a little above Dinas. The hollow has great character, though it suffers materially by comparison with some of the cwms of Snowdon; however, there are several good points here; and as a whole it makes a picture. Many of these stupendous rocks are perpendicular, with deep and broad incisions on their surfaces, and some of them are more or less inclined, having perforated sides and craggy contours which recommend them to the artist. The openings towards the mountains are objects of considerable interest, because, from these happy circumstances arise that fine breadth of light and shadow, which is beheld with such pleasure, by those who are alive to the merit of a picture, which, in this respect, is well managed. The bottom of this hollow is pasture land, and contains several cottages and farm-houses. From hence is a good view of Paenmaen-du, a noted mountain on the left of Dolgellau-road, with a bridge and a few houses beneath. The summit of this hill from the road is singular: a ruled line of nearly a mile long, without the smallest serration, or the least deviation from a parallel with the horizon, it appears like a beautiful walk or terrace, beneath which is a terrible hollow. The country now began to wear a cold ungrateful aspect, till I gained the greatest height of Bwlch Oerddrws, or the Entrance of the Cold Pass, just above Dolgellau; from whence it opened most magnificently indeed. Cader Idris, completely fore-shortened, shewed its separated sides to great advantage, and, were it not for lessened height, and want of water and wood, it would be as good a subject from hence as from most other points. A mile to the right of this new house of Caerynwch, or the Fort Ynwch, is the summer residence of Richard

Richards, Esq. This is a handsome mansion, too modern, perhaps, in its style for its situation, lately built on an eligible spot, with Cader Idris before it, on the banks of a mountain ripler; the eminences around, affording a great variety of fine views. Descending by a long steep road, I came to Dolgellau, or the Holm of the Groves.

CHAPTER V.

Cader Idris.—Dolgellau.—Llanelltid.—Barmouth.—The Harp.—Anecdote.—Mary Thomas.—Llanegrin.—Towyn.—Mill.—Penal.—The Story of Lucy Llwyd.—Cefn Caer.—Battle of Penal.—Machynlleth.—Owen Glyndwr.—Tarran Rhos y Garreg.—Llanidloes.—Plumlymmon.—Sources of the Severn and Wye.—Caer Sws.—Rhos Ddiarbed.—Penstrywad.—Newtown.—Sir John Price.—Bridget Bostoc.—Vanbutchel.—Castell Dol Forwyn.—Sabrina.—Gwendolen's Cruelty to Sabrina.

THE morning opening finely, I ascended Cader Idris alone, taking the lower Towyn-road for three miles; then, turning towards the mountain through some pretty woody enclosures, I gained the open space under its side; and, making my way over what is called the saddle, got upon a wide and extensive plain; when by a gentle rise of nearly a mile, I reached the summit of the highest peak. Nothing could be more favourable than the clear, beautiful, and unclouded weather which I experienced. The view from hence all around, is inconceivably fine. Northward is Snowdon,

> "—— On whose barren breast,
> The lab'ring clouds do often rest;"

standing up above his compeers, and shewing a noble breadth of front, that seems to overawe, and command respect from them all. Eastward are the fertile plains of Shropshire, and the interjacent mountains of Montgomeryshire: southward is

> "Huge Plumlymmon, from whose endless source,
> Three famous streams sustain their flexuous course*."

Between are the picturesque companions of Cader Idris, exposing to view their torn and distracted sides; and in the extremity of the western horizon, "Hibernia skirts the azure main." The lakes upon this mountain go by the several names of Llyn y Cae, Llyn y Gader, *&c.* I descended several precipices just below, on the south side. The crater here containing the lake Llyn y Cae, is a dismal hollow, and the semi-conic rock above it, with other corresponding ones near, furnish a scene of horror, which, if we can conceive it once to have emitted fire (as it has every appearance of a volcano), well assimilates with the ancient Tophet, the immolating pile of the Israelites †. I stood upon the spot where I thought Mr. Wilson must have sat, to sketch for that fine picture of his, a subject which he afterwards published.

In the first exhibition of the painters in water colours, in Brook-street, Mr. Nicholson's drawing of this cliff, was a fine specimen of his abilities. The east end of this mountain is, by far, the most picturesque, possessing a number of noble and terrific cliffs, which might be taken either singly, or in a mass, and form excellent pictures. Strangers should not be contented with a bare view of the peak; for they would find much gratification in descending to the south-western and eastern sides: but particularly the professor of the arts should descend the south-

* Severn, Wye, and Rheidol.

† 30 Isaiah, ver. 33.

eastern side into the romantic pass which leads to Towyn. This is narrow for a considerable way, and shews nature in her savage dress: denuded rocks appearing in diversified shapes, some pointing upwards, others projecting into the pass in noble masses, as if menacing the stranger with instant destruction. One of these precipices is called Llam y Ladron, or the Thieves' Leap. Tradition says that thieves were punished here, in the same manner as criminals met their fate from the Tarpean rock in Rome. Such a custom among us is not upon record: but, in feudal times, an arbitrary lord might have exercised this mode of retribution for crimes; though for capital offences death was scarcely ever inflicted, because a door was opened for escape by the payment of a fine, often accepted, even in cases of murder, which became subsequently the cause of meditated revenge, quarrels, and bloodshed.

Near the little pool Llyn-tri-Grauenyn, are some large blocks of stone, which, the people say, that the giant Idris finding troublesome, flung out of his shoes to the bottom, where they now lie. Returning up the mountain, considerably below the crater, and setting myself once more upon the peak, to take a farewell view of the noble surrounding prospects, I came down right under this peak by Llwybir Madyn, or the Fox's Path, to Llyn y Gader, the Pool of the Keep, or the Chair of Idris. This path, nearly perpendicular, is about a quarter of a mile to the bottom. Few strangers chusing to try it, it is seldom attempted but by the shepherds: it is, however, perfectly safe; the tread upon loose soil, intermingled with stones, rendering it, indeed, somewhat troublesome, but not dangerous. The pool below is a fine piece of water, which, with the stupendous impending cliffs above it, makes as fine a subject for contemplation as it does for the skill of the painter. Cader Idris is the Seat, or Observatory, of Idris, a noted astronomer of ancient times. He is also called Idris gawr, or Idris the giant; and he, Gwin ab Nudd, and Gwdion ab Don, are celebrated as the three most excellent and sublime astronomers of Britain. When Idris flourished, is not exactly known. The highest point of this mountain is 950 yards above the green at Dolgellau.

Dolgellau is very singularly built: its streets are narrow and unpleasing in appearance, with very few good houses. Its situation is low but agreeable; and it is watered by the rivers Arran and Wynion, over which last is a handsome bridge of many arches. The church is a fresh and handsome edifice, with a roof supported by two rows of wooden columns, not very well executed.

A house now tottering with age, is said to have been the court-house of Owen Glyndwr. From the busy trade carried on in sheep skins and wool, the town is rather populous, containing more than two thousand inhabitants. The armed defenders of the country, called the Cader-Idris company, commanded by Col. Sir R. Williams Vaughan, and Major Edwards, were drawn out on the Marion, and made a respectable appearance; and it might easily be perceived, that great pains were taking to make this corps expert in the use of arms. The jail here is a new substantial building, and in every respect suited to the condition of those confined within its walls. The assizes are held alternately here and at Bala, eighteen miles off. Here is an eccentric old man, not unknown to many of those who have visited this place: he fills the office of a guide to Cader Idris with as much credit to himself, as pleasure to the strangers whom he convoys.

I have given a portrait of him from the life, seated upon his

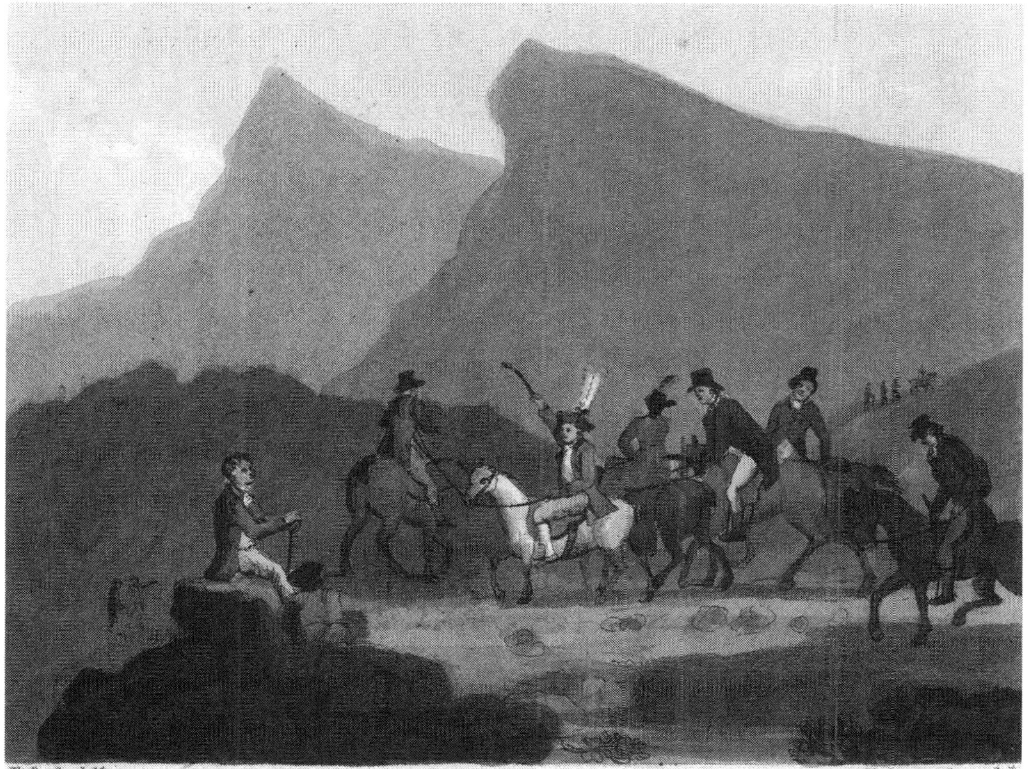

E. Pugh del.t T. Cartwright sculp.t

A VISIT TO CADER IDRIS.

Published 15th Nov.r 1814, by E. Williams, Strand.

poney, conducting a party up the mountain. This, I trust, with the following ludicrous description, will give a just and proper idea of the little fellow :—

"Lege! aspice conductorem! et ride."

"Robert Edwards, second son of the celebrated tanner, William Edwards, ap Gryffydd, ap Morgan, ap David, ap Owen, ap Llewelyn, ap Cadwalader, great, great, great grandson of an illegitimate daughter of an illustrious hero (no less famed for his irresistible prowess when mildly approaching under the velvet standard of the lovely Venus, than when sternly advancing with the terrible banners of the bloody Mars), Sir Rice ap Thomas!!! by *Anne, alias Catherine, daughter of Howel ap Jenkin of Ynys-y-Maengwyn; who was the thirteenth in descent from Cadwgan, a lineal descendant of Bleddyn ap Cynfyn, Prince of Powys. Since his nativity, full two and eighty times hath the sun rolled to his summer solstice †. Fifty years was he host of the Hen-and-Chickens ale-house, Pen-y-Bont, twenty of which he was apparitor to the late Right Reverend Father in God, John, Lord Bishop of Bangor, and his predecessors: by chance, made a glover; by genius, a fly-dresser and angler. He is now, by the all-divine assistance, conductor to, and over the most tremendous mountain, Cader Idris:—to the stupendous cataracts of Caen and Mowddach; and to the enchanting cascades of Dolymelynllyn, with all their beautiful romantic scenery; Guide General, and Magnificent Expounder of all the natural and artificial curiosities of North Wales; Professor of grand and bombastic lexicographical words; Knight of the

* Vide Cambrian Register for 1795.

† He was eighty-two, March, 1805.

most anomalous whimsical (yet perhaps happy) order of hair-brained inexplicables.

"*Mark, Traveller*, what rarely meets thy view,
Thy guide, a giddy *Boy* of eighty-two."

Bryn Adda, the residence of Mr. Anwyl, is in a beautiful sylvan spot, from whence are caught some excellent peeps, and the artist will be highly pleased with the walk. To this gentleman I owe great obligations, for his politeness and good wishes. Leaving Dolgellau, I went by a delightful road, on which, near the ship-yard, is an excellent view of Cader, with an advantage of wood on each side. I passed Hengwrt*, a handsome old house, belonging to Colonel G. Vaughan; and came once more to the public-house at Llanelltid. Since my last visit, I found my bed had been engaged by another; and that no alternative was left to me but that of sleeping in a room, seven feet by seven. On awaking in the morning, I perceived that I had passed the night almost among the dead and buried; being so close to the church-yard, that nothing but a thin wall, full of interstices, separated me from the peaceable remains of poor Jane Roberts, whose cranium must have come nearly in contact with my own.

I left this place for Barmouth. For two miles this road presents several fine pictures, and peeps at Cader Idris across the estuary of the Maw, often between rocks, or by the side of houses, which added much to the general effect. I hailed and got into a barge going to Barmouth, and was highly pleased with the rich and picturesque scenery from the river. Its often varied form raised my wishes of remaining some hours upon the

* This house was the residence of Robert Vaughan, Esq. the celebrated antiquarian, who died in 1667. Of the vast collection of ancient British manuscripts which he left behind, the greater part remains with this family.

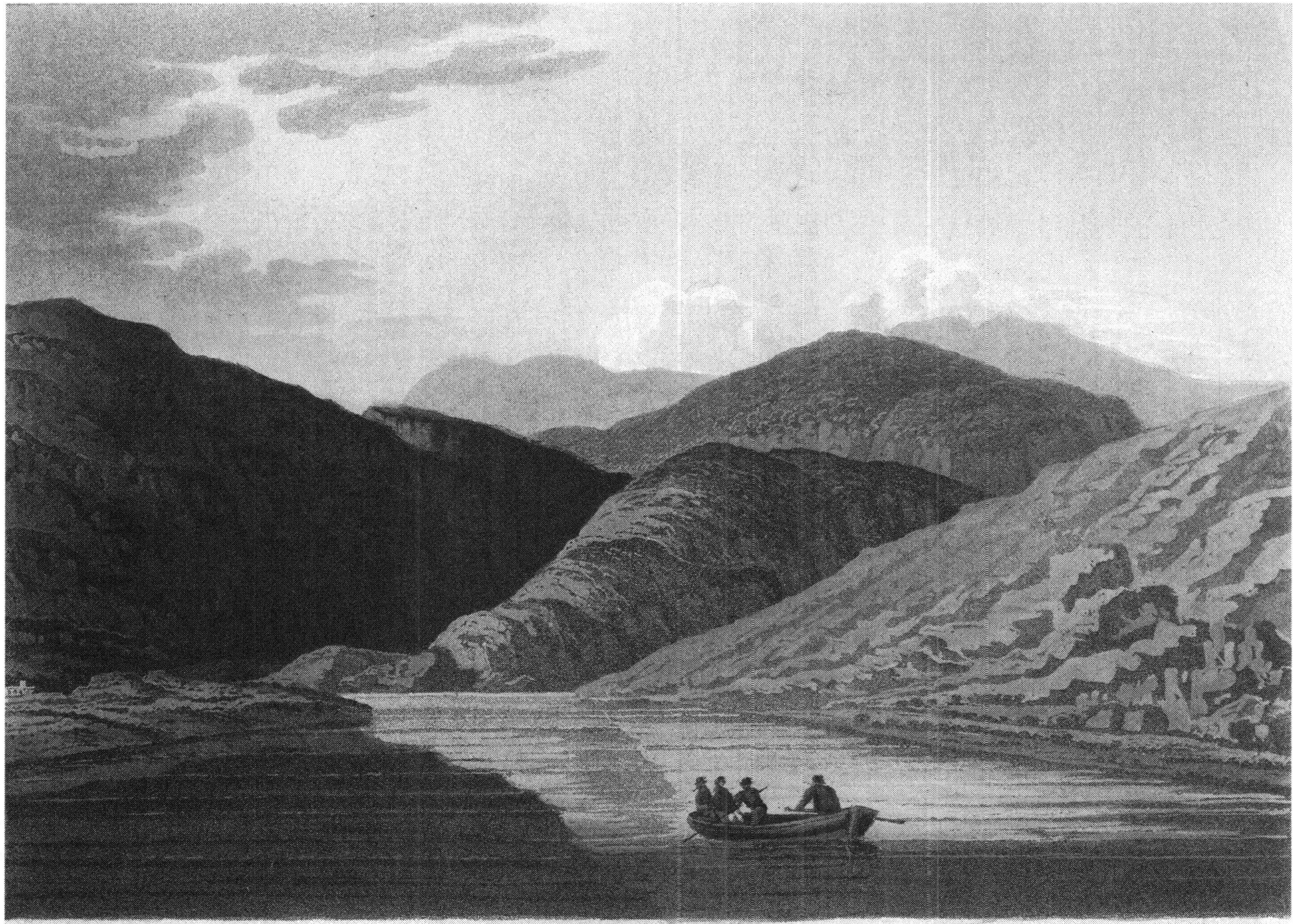

VIEW BETWEEN BARMOUTH & DOLGELLEY.

Published 15th April, 1813, by E. Williams. Strand.

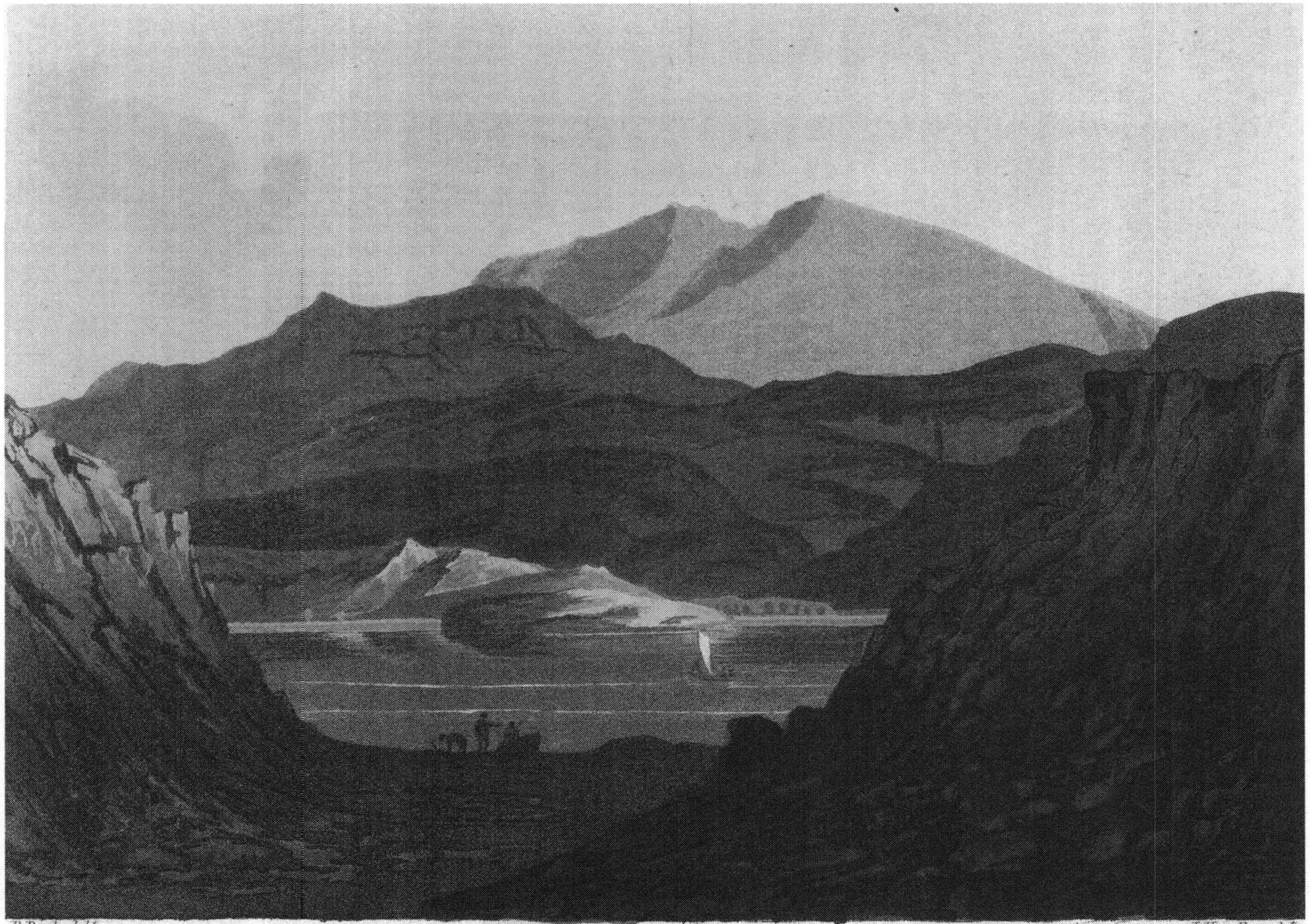

E. Pugh del.t　　　　　　I. Havell sculp.t

CADER IDRIS FROM BARMOUTH HEIGHTS.

Published 15 Nov.r 1813 by E. Williams Strand.

water, but the receding tide pressed the bargemen to urge their way through. Nothing can be finer than the variegated appearances of the land on each side. The rocks, on the left (looking towards Dolgellau) are very high; and parts of them covered with verdure, come sloping down and are opposed by others, highly broken, and of a thousand shapes. On the reverse side are very great craggy eminences, often covered with wood, but more frequently bare; leaving openings and breaches which expose to view the noble peaks of Cader Idris. In front are some fine mountains, falling back one after another to a great distance towards Bala. There are times much more favourable to see the prospects from this river, than that which I experienced. An azure sky is unpropitious to an artist in a country like this; and, though the aspect of it be ever so sublime, yet he is not satisfied without a continual succession of clouds, to throw the subjects before him into various lights and shadows; a circumstance that would not only decisively mark out the contour of the whole of his subject, but afford him opportunities of observing nature under a variety of forms and tints.

On approaching Barmouth from the river, a stranger will be agreeably surprised to see a town, built on the rough precipitous sides of an immense rock, the houses standing one above another to a great height in the air, so that the inhabitants of one house sitting at their door, may look down their neighbours' chimney, and so progressively to the base of the hill. The town was full of people, it being then the bathing season. The Cors y Gedol arms-inn was so thronged with strangers, that my having a bed there depended upon the departure of a gentleman; who, fortunately for me, ordered his carriage, and took his leave. This place, from the fineness and solidity of the sands, with the short distance to the water and every convenience for bathing, is one of the pleasantest water-places in the kingdom; especially, if we take into consideration the delightful rides in the neighbourhood. The number of very handsome houses that have been lately built, and are now building, is an indisputable proof of the great influx of strangers to this place. One unpleasant circumstance is to be noticed, high winds from the sea have covered the streets, in the lower part of the town, with sands: but this might easily be removed, on the completion of the houses that turn their backs on the water; when the intervals are filled up, the streets paved, *&c.*

For a considerable time I had not heard the melody of the harp: this was now amply made up to me by the tasteful performance of a blind young man, lately the pupil of the justly celebrated harper, Mr. Owen. This county, formerly, stood one of the foremost in encouraging this instrument; and even now, ladies and gentlemen who have had the good sense to retain their native language, will sometimes assist it with their vocal powers: thus keeping alive an innocent, useful, and a rational, but an almost extinguished, species of amusement. At fairs and wakes, however, the young people of both sexes will frequently be seen assembled for a dance early in the evening; and when tired of this entertainment, they will all sit around the harp, each man with his favourite lass by his side: where they sometimes dictate to the musician when at a loss, and commence singing penillion or stanzas, alternately: and some men among them are so ready as to produce, extemporaneously, apposite verses, in answer to the last singer, and thus often occasion a great deal of mirth. It is not lawful for any one to repeat a stanza which he has sung before, though as a singer he stood foremost in such a practice; and this would deprive him of the honour of being held first of the song. Good singers never call for tunes, as they are ready with songs adapted to all tunes. Sometimes challenges are given from one parish to another; and their contention is as earnest as that of the nightingale and the woodlark.

In the year 1610, was born at Llanfachnedd near Dolgellau, a boy, whose father was a day labourer. When at the age of two or three years, he discovered a talent for music that surprised all his friends; for, at this early time, he was heard continually to imitate others while singing; and a few minutes trial made him master of the song, which he would give with an air of superior beauty that never failed to gain him great admiration. Some time after this, having heard the harp, he expressed a great desire to learn to play on that instrument, and as harps were numerous in those days, his father found no difficulty in procuring one for him. He accordingly devoted all his time and thoughts to it; and when arrived at the age of five years, the gift of nature in him had risen to such a state of resplendency, as to astonish all who heard him. The minstrels of the country readily avowed their inferiority; and were not backward in confessing him to be the greatest prodigy that they had ever witnessed. The child was uncommonly handsome, his manners polite and lively: he was extremely quick of apprehension; of a ready wit, which, with a degree of sensibility that would have done honour to riper years, he indulged only on proper occasions. He was the very life of the festive board, which he would often keep, for a considerable time, in a roar. His extraordinary abilities introduced him to the first families in the principality. At this age he followed the judges in the North-Wales circuit; his father carrying him occasionally on his back, while another man was employed in bearing the harp. From his tender age, he was not able to screw up the strings of the instrument: but would request a bye-stander to perform this little service, while his ear was engaged in bringing them to a proper state of harmony *.

Barmouth has some trade in woollen manufactures, which are conveyed to Shrewsbury, and ultimately to London, *&c.* A few small craft are seen here, which go freighted with timber and other mercantile productions of the country.

Leaving Abermaw, or Barmouth, I crossed the ferry, and went to a cottage of David Roberts's, called, Tan yr Allt, in Llangelynin parish, to visit a very extraordinary old woman, whose name is Mary Thomas. Mr. Pennant mentions her so far back as the year 1770: but as forty years have been added to her lingering existence, she now may be considered as an infinitely greater curiosity. Her history is precisely this: when at the age of seven or eight years, an eruption, similar to the measles, broke out upon her, which continued to affect her, more or less, at the spring and fall of the year: during this time she kept her bed, and walked out alternately. I questioned her very closely; nevertheless, I perceive that Mr. Pennant's account of her differs a little from mine, respecting the period of her finally taking to her bed: but this is immaterial, as it might have risen from the circumstance of her frequent confinement. At one time, relates Mr. Pennant, "she continued more than seven years without any sustenance of any kind, excepting a little liquid, to moisten her mouth." At the age of fifteen, her complaint returned, with the addition, as it was supposed, of a severe cold, which affected her legs so power-

* Taken from a MS. in the possession of Mr. William Ellis, attorney, Ruthin, written by Richard ap John, of Llanganhaval, in Denbighshire, in 1615.

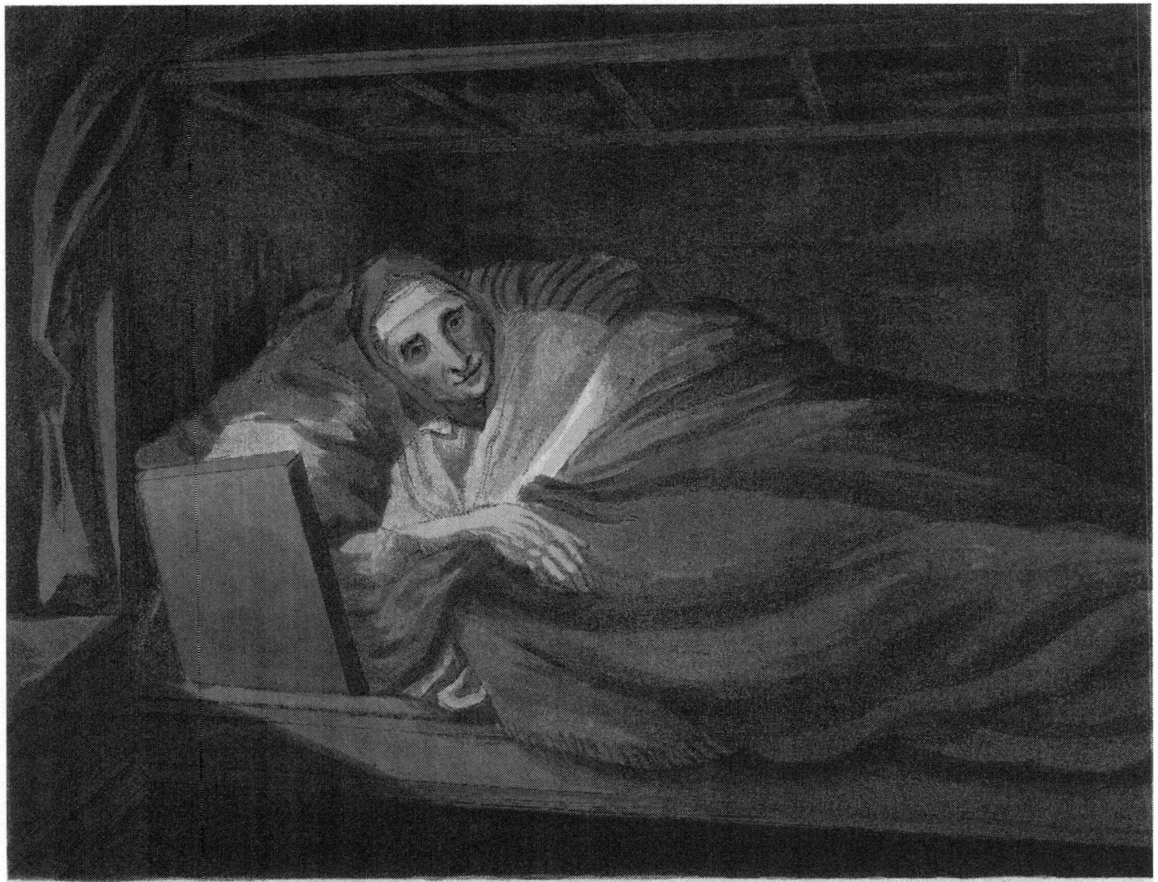

E. Pugh del^t. R. Havell sculp^t.

MARY THOMAS THE FASTING WOMAN.

Published 15 February 1815, by E. Williams, Strand.

fully, as totally to deprive her of their use: consequently she has been bed-ridden from the commencement of the attack. She is now eighty-six years of age, so that seventy-one out of that number have witnessed her pitiable condition. Once a day she *is removed to another bed in the same room, while her own is making. The tendons of the legs are so permanently fixed and contracted, as to bring the *os calcis* nearly in contact with the *os-sacrum*, thus debarring her, at once, of the possibility of extending her limbs, as well as of the power of walking. Having passed so many years, suffering under the influence of the greatest pains, which have baffled the skill and the experience of the faculty in the country, added to the want of such indulgencies as soften the asperities of life, she is reduced to a mere skeleton. The colour of her countenance is pale brown, and her eyes a deep jet, as is also her hair. Her food is bread and milk, of which she takes but a few penny-weights in quantity, and that but once a day.

It has been observed, lately, that she eats more than she used to do, but this has not occasioned, as we might be led to suppose, a renovation of health: the reverse is her experience; for she seldom feels a cessation from sickness, and her sleep is uneasy and disturbed. Mary has lately lost the use of one eye, though its decay was not observable to me. Her recollection is exquisitely strong, and her hearing so quick, that she can hear an out-of-door conversation a considerable distance off. She is so susceptible of cold, that it has been judged necessary to put fire in an iron pot, which is placed in bed with her, but so well secured, as to prevent the least danger by accident, or

* Mary Thomas is since dead.

at all prove a molestation to her. Until very lately she had for many years habituated herself to the singular practice of kneading and baking her own bread. A large dish was placed on the bed by her side, upon which she contrived to knead and form her paste: this was replaced by a tripod wooden stool reversed, which received an iron kettle, full of fire; upon this was also placed an iron pan or plate with the shapened dough; and thus, in due time, she would produce an excellent loaf. Her singular history brings a number of visitors from all parts to see her, particularly the English nobility and gentry, when on their excursions through this country. I am concerned to state that my efforts to learn the name of a nobleman, whose benevolence has made him highly respected here, have proved abortive. He saw this poor object, felt for her, and with a munificence that will do his lordship everlasting honour, sent her necessaries of different descriptions, to the value of fifty pounds. Some time since, his Royal Highness Prince William Henry of Gloucester honoured her with a visit: she seemed highly pleased with the idea of having beheld the King's nephew, and that the royal visitor should have condescended to enter her humble habitation; and she spoke of the prince with a heart fraught with gratitude.

No one having ever published her portrait, she readily permitted me to take her likeness; and I have been so successful, that the accuracy of it may be depended upon. It has been asserted by some people, that Mary Thomas is an artful woman; that her illness has been feigned, to deceive the charitable stranger; and that her abstinence by day, is compensated by her voluptuous appetite being amply satisfied at night; and this was even told me by a gentleman in the neighbourhod. Is it not surprising, that people will so far suffer prejudice to get the better of their understanding, as to deny the truth of an extraordinary operation of Providence, for no other reason than that it appears unaccountable to them? Is it likely, or can it be believed for a moment, that a gay, young, and sprightly girl, at the artless age of fifteen, could have the courage to adopt an austere, rigid way of life: a mode of existence so shocking, that the very soul would naturally revolt from it?—that she would abandon her companions, and those innocent pastimes and pleasures, so congenial to youthful constitutions; and that she would, without premeditation, instantly forego the vast gradation of delights which youth are so apt to picture to themselves, as flowing through life, for the bitter potion of a perpetual imprisonment, and exclusion from all the happiness and comforts attached to liberty and ease? Such a supposition is an egregious absurdity, broached by ignorant and unfeeling minds, without the slightest foundation of truth or probability. The day I saw this woman, these insinuations were fully and satisfactorily refuted by Mrs. Thomas of Llancgrin; who, twenty-five years ago, lived in the same house with her, when a similar report was in circulation: but which Mrs. T. declares to have been utterly void of truth; as such a circumstance as that of her getting up at night for refreshment, or of any such being conveyed to her, must infallibly have been attended with discovery, which never took place.

This and a few other cottages are situated under horribly looking, high craggy rocks, which seem to threaten instant destruction to the whole. Should high winds, lightning, or any other casual misfortune, dislodge some of the heavy masses of stone from their sockets, some fatal event must ensue.

Bidding farewell to this extraordinary woman, I had a dull

and uninteresting walk of four miles over the mountains not an object to be seen capable of affording the least entertainment, excepting two individuals, out of numerous flocks of sheep, who had turned out to settle a quarrel of honour, and decide their pretensions to the attractive beauties of a female, that seemed to watch the eager combat with some fearful and solicitous emotions. The *os-frontis* of one proving too hard for the other, soon decided the affair; and the lady, highly pleased with the decision of the contest, moved off with the conqueror.

I would recómmend the artist to keep the lower road from Barmouth to Towyn, by the sea-side, as he will meet with excellent rocky margins of the sea. Descending these hills, I came in sight of the vale of Towyn, an open and handsome plain, terminating with Cardigan-bay in the south-west. Looking up the vale it narrows, undulating between very numerous and magnificent, but denuded, rocks, among which, a little above the road, is a picturesque one, called Craig y Deryn, or Bird's Rock, from the circumstance of its being the brooding-place of several species of aquatic birds. A party of ladies and gentlemen, lately attempted, from its deceptive appearance when seen from below, to ascend to the nests: but ere they had with great difficulty, reached half way, they were obliged to abandon their pursuit. On viewing the precipices by which they came, their hearts recoiled at the thought of returning the same way; and they were obliged vehemently to halloo to some peasants at work, who extricated them from their perilous situation. The ladies had lost their shoes, and some of the gentlemen their hats, which had tumbled into the crannies of the rocks, where, as I was told, they still remain.

This road from Towyn, through Tal y Llyn to Dolgellau, is

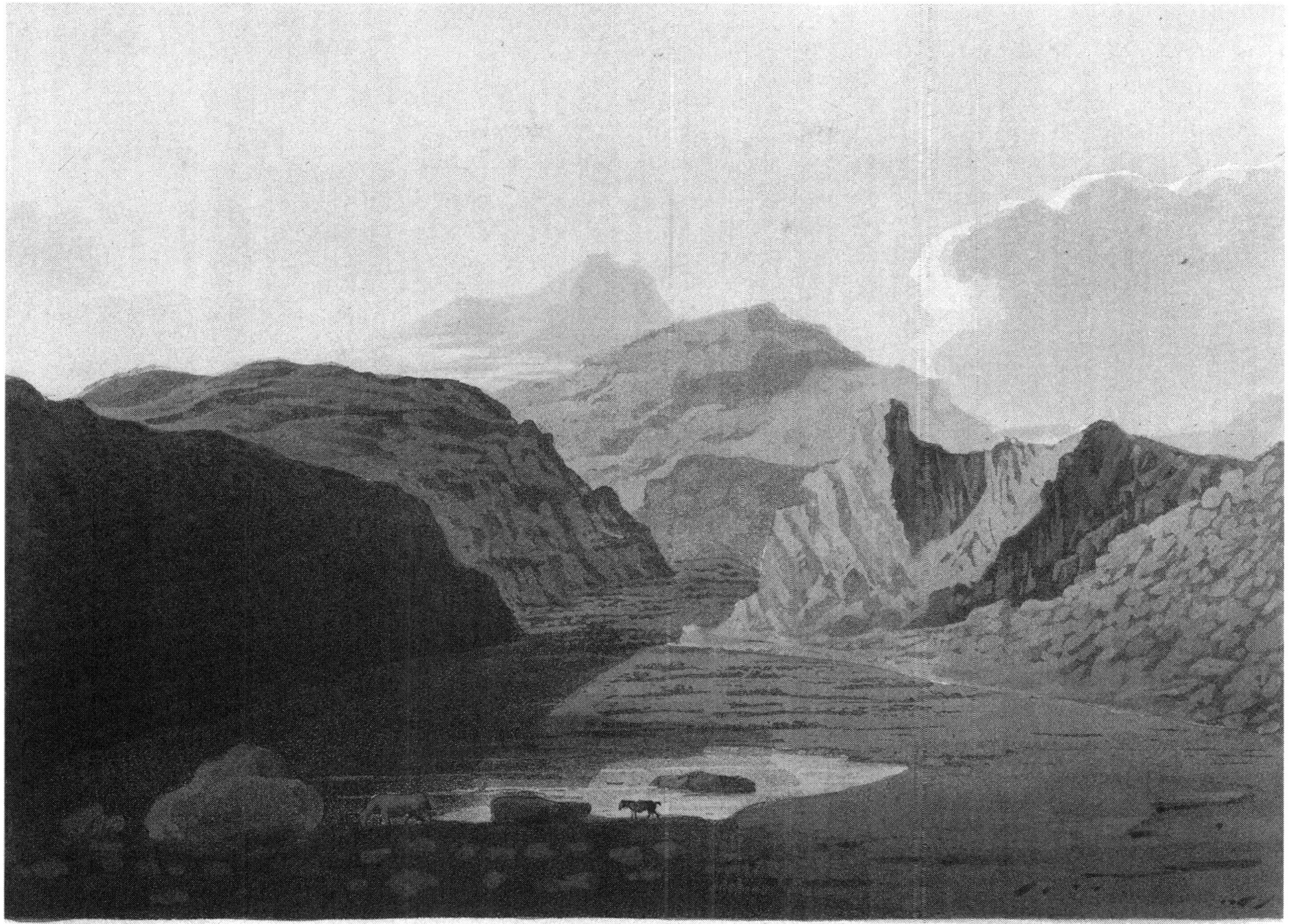

E. Pugh del.t T. Cartwright sculp.t

CADER IDRIS AND CRAIG-Y-DERIN.

Published 15 December 1813 by E. Williams Strand.

extremely interesting to the artist, and the man of taste. Though a little inferior to Nant Nanhwynen, in some respects it resembles it; and is to Cader Idris what that place is to Snowdon. Cader is seen overtopping its rough-hewn unpolished-looking neighbours, and frowning black upon all beneath him.

Peniarth is a noble-looking mansion, commanding the scenery just described: below is Llanegrin, a mean and miserable little village. The houses are of a singular construction; the ends facing the sea are built of stones, rudely placed upon each other, as better calculated to bear the storms from thence; the sides also are built of the same materials to the height of one yard above the ground: and the remainder, to the straw roof, is made of well-tempered mud, intermixed with rushes, which bind and render it durable. These huts have an uncomfortable appearance: but the poor, who inhabit them, find them proof against the most rigid winter's cold. I passed on by the grounds of Ynys-y-Maengwin, the handsome seat of Edward Corbett, Esq., and reached Towyn. This is a small placc, which, in the bathing season, is full of visitors from the adjacent countries of Montgomery and Salop. The church is large and cruciform, and contains several monuments of the family of Ynys-y-Maengwin. A recumbent monumental figure of one of them, in a niche in the wall, has been much neglected; and lower down is his wife in another niche: but, for what reason does not appear, this is closed up, and the monument hid from view. In the church-yard are the remains of the tomb of Cadfan, the patron saint of this church; consisting of three upright stones, which once supported a curious stone with an inscription: but this a gentleman in the neighbourhood (by what authority I could not learn) has lately removed to a grotto of his, in a wood, almost impenetrable, and as gloomy as Erebus. Would it not be better to restore it to its former sacred station, or to the church, which would be still better adapted to it? and he might substitute in his grotto a statue of Laverna, or of Mercury, as more in character with the place. Another part of the church-yard exhibits a tomb of a modern date, to the memory of Hugh Ellis, harper to the family of Ynys-y-Maengwin, who was drowned in the adjacent river Dysyni, on the 5th of August, 1774, aged 66. On the stone are these lines:—

"The Nymphs of the flood, were rutting, plague rot 'em!
With the Genius of Music, when he went to the bottom.
Their care and attention would else have supported
The child of the harp, whom the Muses all courted."

Here are also shown two grave-stones, at the distance of twelve feet from each other. The present landlord of the Raven inn, when at the age of twenty-seven, effected a standing leap from one to the other; a very extraordinary feat of agility.

The country ground is not interesting; and near the sea it is low and marshy: the shores are not prominent, or marked with much character.

The Raven inn is a commodious house, and the charges at it are reasonable. Mr. Owen, the landlord, is very obliging and attentive. His abilities are so well known, that it may seem needless to say, that he is esteemed the first performer upon the Welsh harp in the kingdom. The inhabitants of Portland-place are witnesses, not only of the harmony of his music, but of his mode of producing such effects upon this instrument, as are absolute fascinations.

The next morning I set off for Machynlleth. About three miles on this road is a little mill: the scenery about which is extremely picturesque: but it may, from the smallness of its size, be easily overlooked. On descending the hill to the bed of the river, the rocks on each side look bold: the water, rushing down a fall of fifteen feet, adds greatly to the effect; and the mill (which is seen in this opening receding a little), with the hills beyond it, form a good picture. For five or six miles of this road, the country is dull and tiresome. I was, on this account, induced to ascend a mountain on the left, as was often my custom, to see whether I might find scenery better suited to my views. But I was disappointed; the sight of the summit of Cader Idris with no other circumstance to second it, being an ill compensation for my trouble: on descending again, however, into the road, I found the prospects before me improving. Within half a mile of Penal, is Talgarth, the handsome seat of Lewis Edwards, Esq.; and, in a meadow, close to the road-side, is a tumulus, overspread with young pine. Penal is a little village, pleasantly situated on an extensive plain, open to the sea at Aberdovy. Here lived once, the most amiable, and the greatest beauty of Gwynedd *, the celebrated toast of North Wales, Lleusi Llwyd, or Lucy Lloyd. Her melancholy and romantic death, though highly honourable to her feelings, cannot be read without commiseration. She was beloved and solicited by Llywelyn Goch ab Meriog, Ken of Nannau, a native bard, who received in return her most tender affections. But in an evil hour her father, averse from the match, taking advantage of her lover's absence in South Wales, tried to break off the attachment; and, with that view, he told her that Llywelyn had deserted her, and had married another. The shock overpowered her: she fell down, and instantly expired. Llywelyn returning a day or two

* North Wales formerly so called.

afterwards, hastened to the beloved of his heart: but the sudden surprise of beholding her laid in her coffin so affected his senses, that he fell prostrate on the floor. Recovering, however, he subsequently composed an elegy, in which are pourtrayed, with the feelings of an injured man, and an agonized mind, the character of the most excellent of woman-kind. A recumbent monument of this lady is now in Northop church, in Flintshire; and by the inscription it appears that she died in 1402. Half a mile from hence is a farm called Cefn Caer, or the Back of the Fort, which was once a Roman station. In the walls of the house are many pieces of Roman tile, worked into the interstices: the grounds about also exhibit a great quantity of them; and in the adjacent field may be seen tracings of the walls, approximating to a square. Lately, as the farmer's man was preparing a piece of ground for potatoes, he discovered an ancient urn, with many pieces of gold coin, which were afterwards distributed to different gentlemen in the neighbourhood. To whose reign they belonged I know not: but the excellent historian, Mr. Vaughan of Hengwrt, mentions a coin found here, bearing the name of Domitian the emperor. Near this place was fought the battle of Penal, in the reign of Edward IV., between William, earl of Pembroke, and Thomas Gruffydd ab Nicholas for the house of Lancaster: in which the said Thomas gained the victory. A mile further, the town of Machynlleth burst upon my sight very agreeably, across some beautiful meadows, through which the noble river Dovey flows: these, with the craggy eminences on one side, and the rising grounds on the other, form a beautiful and extensive valley. I crossed the river by a large bridge, which seemed tottering with age, and while a carriage heavily laden with timber was going over, my anxiety was great lest it might press in some of the arches.

The inhabitants of the counties of Merioneth and Montgomery, on whom jointly falls the expense, were then going to build a handsome bridge on the same spot. Those boats in miniature called coracles, are used upon this, and on all the larger rivers in Wales, for the purpose of fishing; their shape is nearly oval, one end being somewhat broader than the other, and the bottom is of an easy round. A seat occupies the centre, where the fisherman sits; and while one hand is engaged with a paddle in guiding the coracle, the other is employed in fishing. This vehicle is constructed of wicker-work, and covered with pitched canvass: and in this respect only do they differ from the ancient coracles, which were covered with skins, or coria, from whence they derived their name. Their weight is from twenty-five to thirty pounds. When the fishermen have finished the business of the day on the water, they carry the coracles home upon their shoulders.

Machynlleth is a large and good town; the three principal streets of which are long and straight, and seem to contend with Pall-Mall for width. The inhabitants display a spirit of building unrivalled in North Wales. The manufacture of flannel is carried on here, and the country about is supposed to contain mineral substances in great plenty, which at present lie dormant. The probable conjecture is, that were some monied people to embark in a scheme for their production, they would be highly benefited by it, especially, as there would be a very easy mode of conveying any mercantile article to Aber Dovey, by a canal of ten miles, from whence it might be conveniently exported by sea. The church is old and craggy, it seems very unsafe for the congregation to frequent; and the place and the people are worthy of a better structure.

Owen Glyndwr held his parliament here: and the house is still in being in which he and his adherents assembled. Its exterior appearance is barn-like, and it is now used as a granary, *&c.*, with the exception of one end, which is occupied as a miserable dwelling-house. Its interior exhibits great age: at the back is a flight of stone stairs in ruins, leading into the great room, in which are carved ribs, *&c.* of timber. Glyndwr convened the states of his country at this place, for the purpose of establishing himself on the throne, and causing his title to it to be acknowledged: he was accordingly crowned, and reached the zenith of his ambition. A most ungenerous and murderous scheme had like to have proved fatal to him, and his cause. David Gam, of Brecknockshire, appeared among the chiefs who seemed cordially to support his title; but, though he had married Owen's sister, he had conceived such a hatred to him, as to resolve to murder his prince and brother-in-law. The plot, however, was happily discovered. He was immediately arrested and imprisoned: and, but for the intercession of Glyndwr's warmest friends and partisans, would have met with his deserved punishment *. On a solemn promise of future fidelity to the cause of Glyndwr and his country, he was pardoned: but afterwards, Owen, on more mature consideration, kept him closely confined till 1412. By another account it is said †, that David was released on his parole of honour, and was bound not to oppose, or in any way to act against Owen, while engaged in the contest with Henry; but that he broke his faith, and again commenced a formidable opposition. David, it is said by Carte, was instigated

* Wynn's History of Wales, 321.

† Jones's History of Brecknockshire.

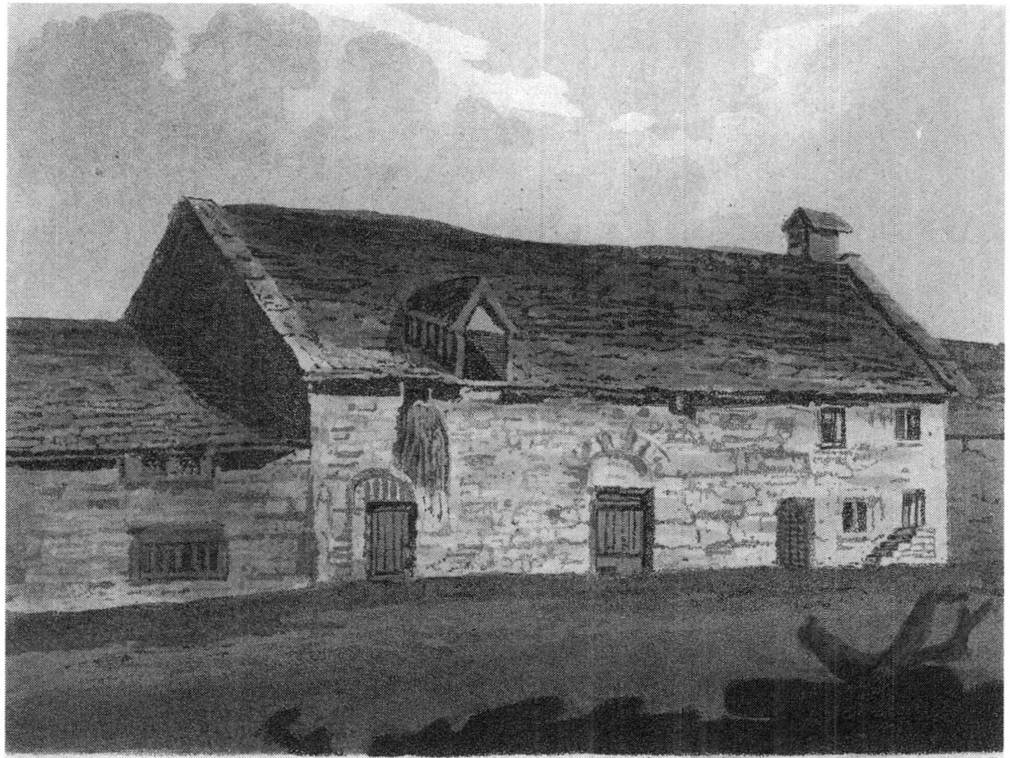

E. Pugh delᵗ. T. Cartwright sculpᵗ.

GLYNDWR'S PARLIAMENT HOUSE.

Published 15 Septʳ. 1814, by E. Williams, Strand.

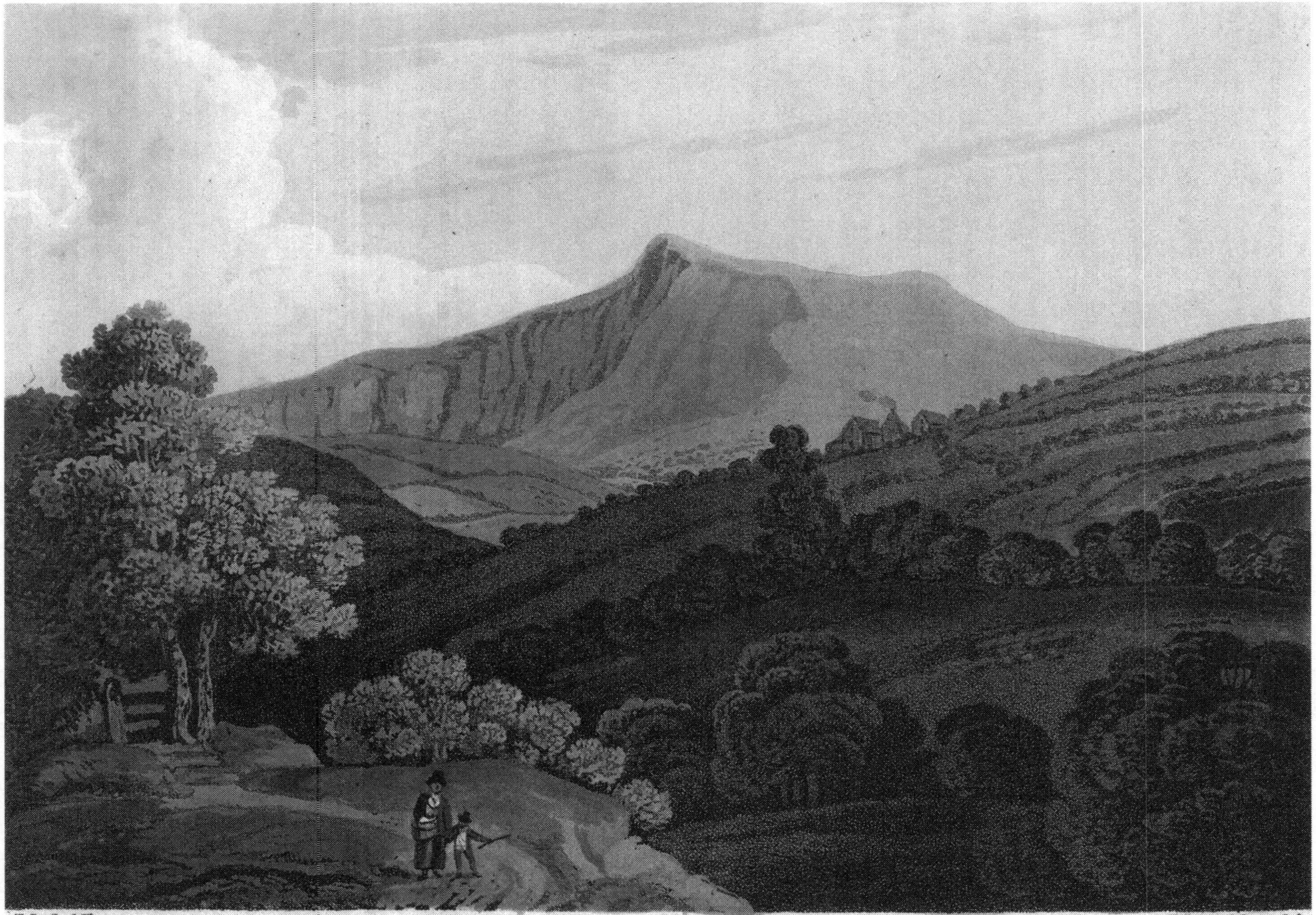

E. Pugh delt. T. Cartwright sculpt.

DARRAN RHOS Y GAREG.

Published 25 October 1813 by E. Williams Strand.

to this treacherous design by Henry, to whose interest he was strongly attached. David was a man of undaunted courage; as was proved in the battle of Agincourt, when he, his son-in-law, Roger Fychan, and his relation, Walter Llwyd, rushed into the thickest danger, and rescued the king, then surrounded by his foes; though David and his relations fell by many mortal wounds at the close of the victory. The king approached them at the moment of death, but perceiving that it was too late to bestow on them the favours he could have wished, he conferred on them the honour of knighthood. Leaving Machynlleth, my road led me across the course (where races are annually held) to Llanidloes. Above the forge, further on, is an ivy-coated bridge, and close to it a cavern, called Hester Mathews's Parlour; and it is asserted by some credulous people on the spot, that the spirit of a woman so named frequently haunts the place.

This country, though mountainous, is destitute of character; the very reverse of the picturesque county of Merioneth. The mountains are of easy unbroken slopes; preserving their coating of the downy kind, rather offensive than agreable to the eye of the professor of landscape. Several times in this day's walk I ascended them, and saw a great sameness around me: but whenever I recognised Cader Idris, the scenery improved. About six miles on the road, my attention was taken up by the best subject for a picture I had this day seen. The mountain called Tarran Rhos y Careg has height, and its sides are precipitous, and somewhat volcanic, much resembling Cader Idris from Dolgellau; and other interesting hills and flats between, with a mountain-stream, render this a picturesque scene. Further on, at a place called Esgyr Galed, is a lead-mine, likely to turn out to the advantage of the proprietors, who live at Machynlleth. On the opposite side of the road, at a place named Tre yr Eglwys, is a factory for preparing wool for the loom. Some distance from hence, as I was viewing the most miserable-looking cottage the mind can conceive, on the right side of the road, I saw a person peeping through his window of twigs, who presently, with his shirt-sleeves tucked up, darted towards me with a quick step as if in a menace, having an awl and a strap in his hand, emblems of his trade, and with looks as wild as ever characterized a maniac, in a loud tone of voice, demanded what I had said; "Nothing to you, my friend," I replied: he then applied his ear close to my head, and repeated his request. Perceiving the poor man to be deaf, I exerted myself to give him satisfaction. "O! Sir," said he, "I am hard of hearing: *I was think* you *was spoke* to me, *undeed*, I beg *pardoon*, Sir." According to the present charges in the country, this poor creature pays a most exorbitant rent, £4 10*s*., for a hut, infinitely inferior to many a pig-stye.

Within three miles of Llanidloes, the scenery on the Clewedog (if I am not mistaken) is not unworthy of notice. In front is a towering hill, rising up perpendicularly from the little valley below: its side is hollow and well marked, and on each side of it are other hills equally interesting, the whole forming an excellent picture. Coming to Llanidloes in the dark, on entering the inn my ears were assailed with the vociferous songs of some English soldiers. Fatigue being generally considered an efficacious opiate, I endeavoured by the suspension of the mental powers, to get rid of so much noise, but all in vain. This night-warbling was succeeded by the most discordant and inharmonious concert of dogs, cats, and pigs; and at the break of day the gabbling of ducks came in as an after-piece, and finished this nocturnal concert, the most grating and offensive to the auditory nerves that I ever heard. I should be extremely sorry to notice this circumstance as operating to the prejudice of the obliging landlord; who is as attentive to strangers, as his accommodations are good, and his charges reasonable; but the whole of this disturbance must be attributed to the noisy sons of Mars, who quitted the town on the next morning. The following night I passed in great quiet. The church of Llanidloes is large and old, the Gothic columns, supporting six arches that run along the centre, have Arabesque capitals, which bear no affinity to either the Corinthian or Composite orders. The roof is finely executed in wood, and the figures on each side evince no common genius in the artist. Three of these represent the Crucifixion: the first supports the hands and feet, nailed to the cross; the second, the cross and ladders; and the third, the nails. The picture of the Lord's Supper might easily be passed over in silence, without disparaging the taste of the spectator, were it not for its history as related here: but I do not vouch for the authenticity of the information, though it comes in the shape of truth. When Dyer, the poet, was on a visit to a friend in Newtown, in this county, it is said that he painted several pictures, of which this is one. A sign painter of this town, who died a few years since, suggested to the parishioners the necessity of retouching it. He was immediately employed; and he has not left any traces of Dyer's painting, with the exception of the ungrateful outline; which, if at all Dyer's, must have been one of his juvenile performances.

The church is dedicated to St. Idloes, who lived in the sixth century; and who is represented by the ancient bards as a man endued with most excellent qualities. At a place called Glanhavren, near the town, is a flannel manufactory; a very considerable concern, belonging to Messrs. Herbert and Brittain. This manufacture is of the most delicate and beautiful texture; and, from the improvements lately made in it by these gentlemen, we may fairly augur that it will become a very powerful rival, in the shape of shawls, to those imported from India, and made of the fine hair of the Thibet goat; which are frequently sold in England for forty guineas each, and upwards. Near this town, at a place called Fryn Du, is a lead mine belonging to Messrs. Lawrance, of Shrewsbury, now in its infancy: but its commencement has already afforded very sanguine hopes of success. This place is small, its few streets are broad, and on account of the singularity of the houses, are rather picturesque. The old mill, now in ruins, with the bridge and the Severn, form a good picture. In the market-place stands the hall, an old wooden building extremely mean in its appearance, and apparently very unsafe for the assembling even of a small number of people. As there is not an article in it worth saving, I would recommend to the inhabitants, upon the first good news of a victory over the fleets or armies of our foes, to make a bon-fire of it, and thus to convert this shabby nuisance into a blaze of loyalty. In this hall, however, is held a court-leet twice a year: but from the bad state of the building, the company retire to the inn to finish the business. Llanidloes, environed by high mountains, from many points offers a good subject for a drawing. Two miles from the town towards Plymlymmon *, that mountain opens finely upon the sight. Its appearance, though not tremendous, assumes an air of gravity,

* The name implies that five rivers take their rise in this mountain.

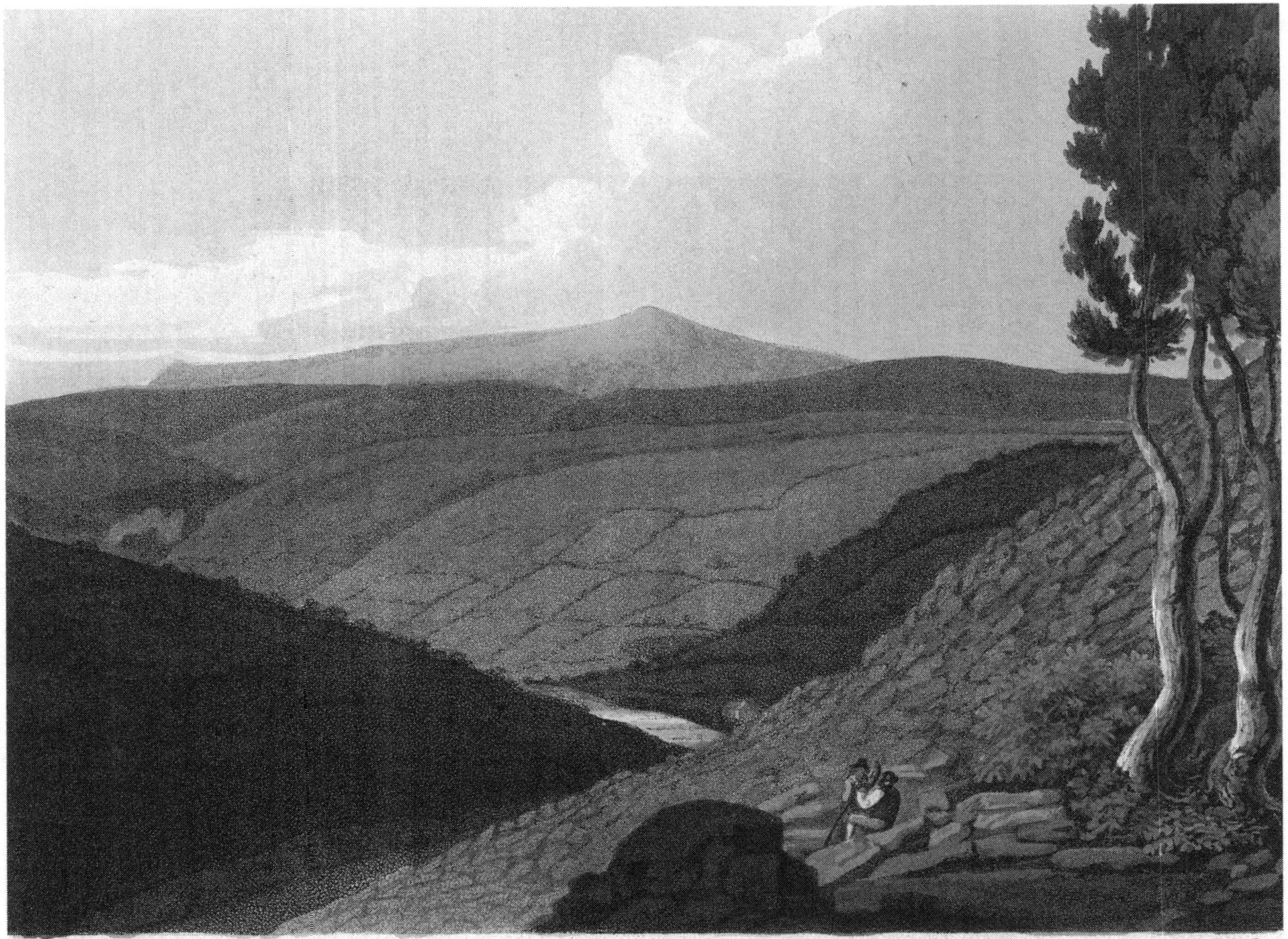

E. Pugh del. I. Hassel sculp.

PLIMLIMMON MOUNTAIN.

Published 15 April, 1813, by E. Williams, Strand.

and rises with dignity above all the surrounding elevations; which, like itself, are smooth and grassy. The view is simple, yet, from the great height of the mountain and its heavy preponderance, sublime: the meandering Severn escaping between the subordinate hills.

On the next day, though looking rather gloomy, I hired a horse to ascend Plymlymmon, a distance of eleven miles, and hoped that the vapours would clear up before I reached the foot of the hill. The road follows the infant Severn, and is so intolerably bad for a horse, that I feel no hesitation in saying, that had I ridden one of those delicate-limbed animals reared in England, I should, with it, have been precipitated to the base of some dreadful cliff: but my native carrier picked his way so well, that I had not occasion once to dismount. Perceiving a man within a mile of the mountain, seemingly unemployed, I tempted him by a small gratuity, to lead me to the sources of the Severn and the Wye, which we reached after a good deal of unpleasant wading through bogs and ditches. I was not a little diverted with a sight of what I had not, until then, witnessed upon any hill. The peat soil here is probably ten feet deep, before it meets a stratum of small slaty fossil. Immense quantities from time to time, have been carried away for firing; and the tracks of conveyance, with the torrents of rain that sometimes sweep down the mountain, form a number of avenues, resembling so many streets, in different directions; while the standing soil is left in the shape of houses on each side, their black thick covering of furze serving as thatch. In fine weather, the walk between them on a hard and excellent footing, must be not unpleasant. The source of the Severn is in a swampy dingle, with a great depth of black soil, or turbery, on each side. It oozes out of an unctuous, soft, clayey matter of a light red colour: the diameter of the spring, which seems but feeble, is about eighteen inches. I observed to my guide that a much greater force of water came down this dingle, and passed the spring: this was occasioned, as he told me, by the drizzling rain through the preceding night and this day; and that some people have even affirmed, that it proceeded from the proper head of the Severn, higher up in the mountain; and, as such, ought to have the honour of precedency. This undoubtedly would easily be granted, but for one cogent reason: the pretender to priority, in dry summers, is completely exhausted, while the other flows with unabated vigour. A mile south of this, is the head of the Wye; which rises out of a bog of about ten yards diameter, from whence the water is not seen to ooze, owing to a covering of a variety of foliage, common to such miry grounds. The river Rhydol rises westward of this, in a lake called Llyn Uygad Rhydol, the Eye of the Rhydol; and empties itself in Cardigan-bay at Aberystwith. The small soaking rain had rendered this excursion very unpleasant, as I could not see an object twenty yards from me; I therefore declined visiting this, as well as ascending the summit of the hill.

At a house at the foot of the mountain (where I left my horse), called Blaen Havren, resides a person, who, like my guide and a few others, makes a livelihood by looking after sheep and horned cattle, sent to them from different places to graze on the mountains during the spring and summer seasons, at three-pence per head for sheep, and a shilling for cattle. At his cottage-door, I parted with David Owen, my guide, who pressed me earnestly to take some refreshment; but being this day possessed of an epicurean appetite, I declined this honest

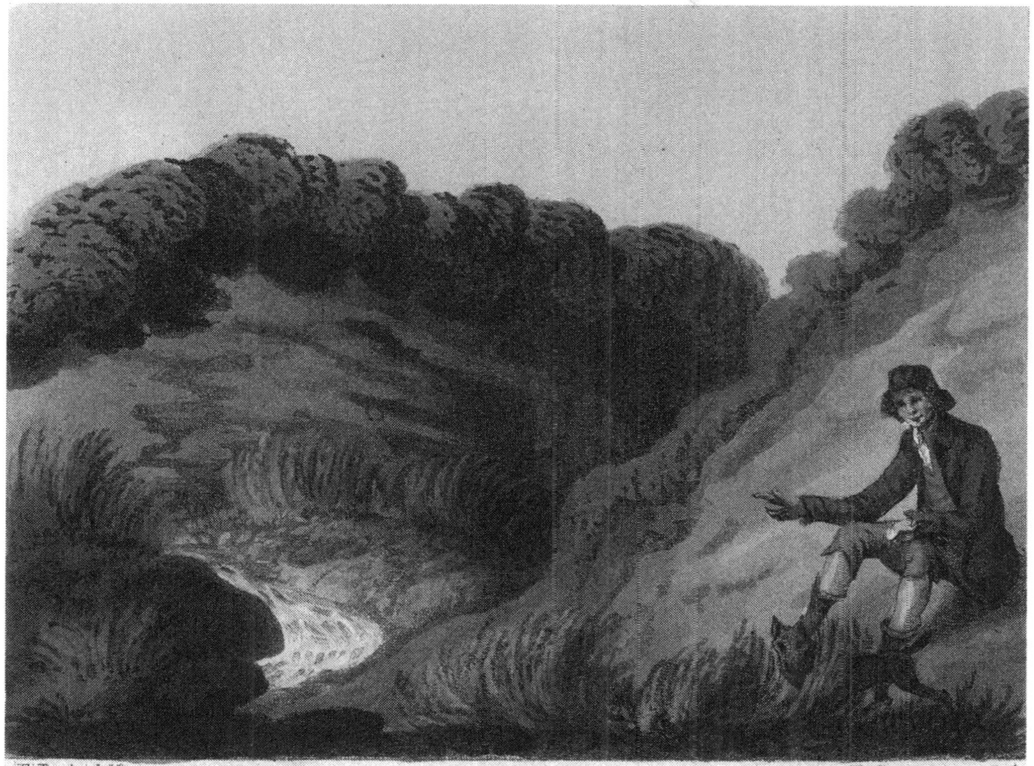

E. Pugh del.^t T. Cartwright sculp.^t

THE SOURCE OF THE SEVERN.

Published 25 June 1814, by E. Williams, Strand.

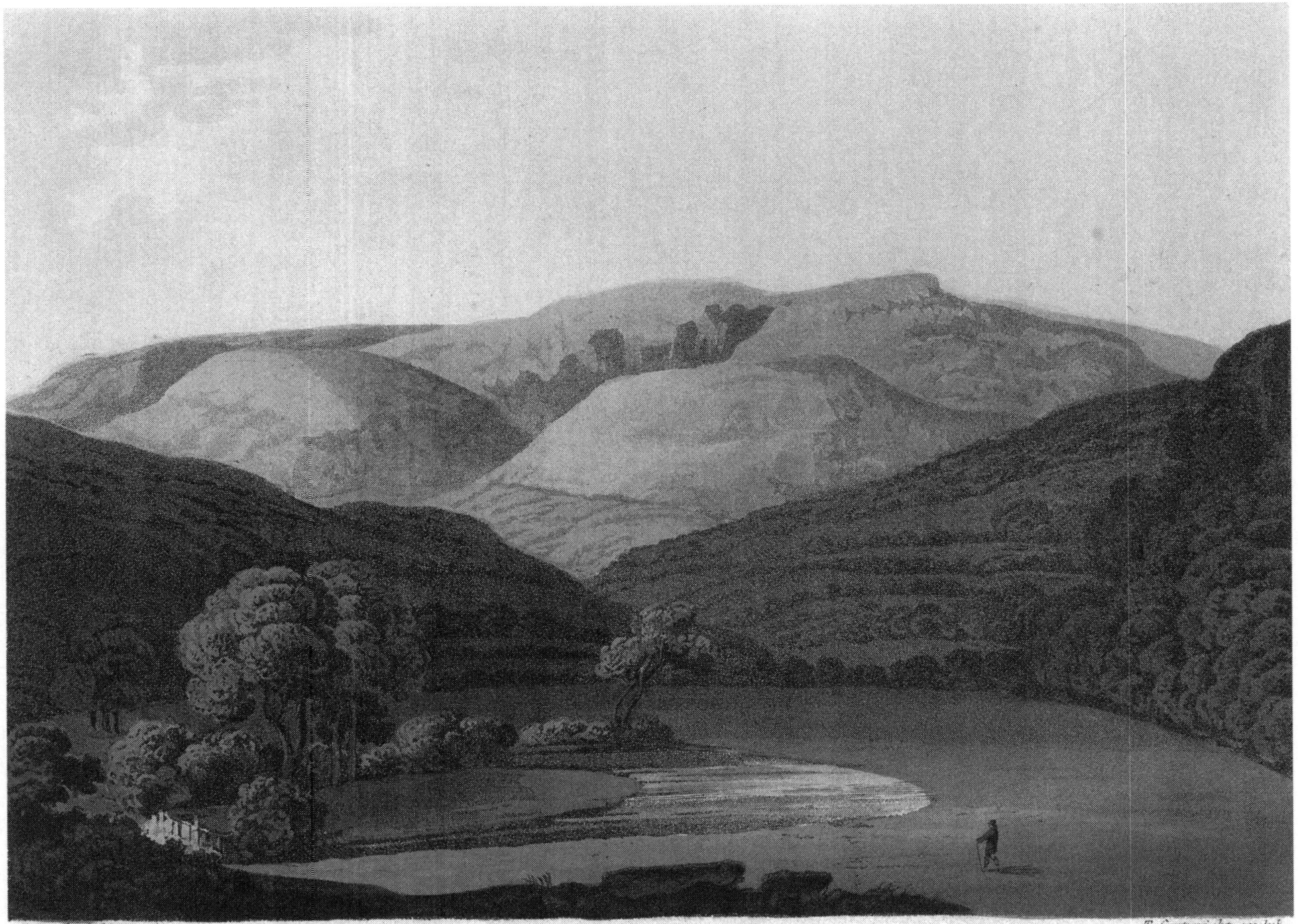

E. Pugh del.t T. Cartwright sculp.t

ON THE SEVERN A FEW MILES FROM LLANIDLOES.

Published 25, March, 1814 by E. Williams Strand.

man's invitation, for the more luxurious table at the Excise Office.

The contrast from a dreary, ungrateful soil, to a more friendly one about Llanidloes, is very striking. In this dingle of eleven miles, might be found a few good subjects for the pencil: but I was unable to ascertain its proper valuation, on account of the mist that obstructed the view.

From Llanidloes to Newtown, the road winds with the Severn through beautiful and well-wooded vallies, which frequently exhibit some bewitching landscapes. It will be necessary for the artist frequently to cross the river to chuse his points, which he will often find easy opportunities of doing. Two miles on this road, crossing the stream, and ascending the mountain, I perceived some fine subjects: and in descending and recrossing the flat to Berth-Ddu, I again saw such views as would induce any artist to follow my track. Llanddinan church is prettily situated upon the Severn, though the village has nothing worthy of notice *. A little further is Caer-Sws, once a Roman station, but now a small hamlet. Tiles and urns are now and then taken out of the earth. There was lately discovered by a blacksmith an urn, full of human bones, half of which were reduced to ashes; and a woman, some years since, whose name was Margaret Morgan, found a number of Roman coins, which she sold for their intrinsic value: traces of the works are still visible. In a house here are inserted in the walls, some stones with Roman inscriptions in alto relievo: but, in the attempt to decipher them, antiquaries have hitherto been puzzled by their

* Opposite to this village, on the summit of a mountain, is Gaer Fechen, or Little Fortress. It was a British post, surrounded with a number of fosses.

ambiguities. Some etymologists suppose the name Caer Sws, to be derived from Hessus, a Roman lieutenant, which the Welsh in old times, pronounced Caer-Hessws, and by contraction Caer Sws. A Roman road, called Sarn Swsan, is easily traced a little way from hence, pointing towards the banks of the Virnwy.

At some distance from the river, and opposite Caer Sws, is Rhos Ddiarbed, or, the Common where no quarter was given. The reason why it is so called, is not known. In the adjacent field is a Roman camp, in which is an exploratory mount, surrounded with a fosse of great depth. In the north part of the fosse is a large area, guarded by a rampart and a ditch: in the lowest part is a *porta*, leading to a rectangular-shaped camp, two hundred yards long by one hundred broad; and in the opposite extremity is another *porta*.

Penstrywad church, on the edge of the road, is extremely small and uninteresting. In the church-yard is a yew-tree of amazing girth: it is hollow, and the neighbouring farmer keeps in it his plough, and other agricultural implements.

From hence to Newtown is a wide expanse of meadow, and corn lands; of value to the proprietors, but of less concern to the artist, than what I had already passed. Nothing is more observable than the gradual improvement in cultivation, and in farm-houses; which contrast strongly with the melancholy and gloomy aspect of those on the hilly or western side of North Wales: the sight of these modern, gayer buildings, exhilarated my spirits. It might be noticed, that the most sprightly parts of Wales are those bordering upon the English counties; as their immediate converse and traffic with England, have made even the common people equally civilized with their neighbours: and an

Englishman will be surprised to find his language as well spoken thirty miles from his own country, as it is in it.

Trenewydd or Newtown, is a large and populous place. Its trade in woollen manufacture is very extensive; and besides, it possesses other sources of inland commerce, carried on by means of the Montgomeryshire canal, which touches at Welsh Pool, Llanymynach, Ellesmere, Chirk, Ruabon, Bersham iron-works, Gresford, Chester, and Liverpool, entering the Mersey near this last town. A spirit of building here is very conspicuous, which points out, demonstratively, the increase of trade and population. This indeed is evident in a greater or less degree, through all the northern parts of the principality, which are contiguous either to an outland or inland navigation; and it is not at all doubtful but that Wales, ere many years pass over, will display an energy of mind which may produce as much local commerce, as any trading part of Great Britain. The church is highly worth seeing, and the stranger is struck in it with one great singularity, that of the walls being all covered with small cards, in good lackered frames, with some portion of Scripture upon each, either of admonition or of example. There are also a number of old knights' mantles, *&c.*, suspended on poles from the walls. The filligre-work, in wood, of the screen that runs across the church, is the most beautiful and rich in execution that I ever witnessed: immense labour as well as expense must have been bestowed upon it; and it is highly worth the attention of the curious. I believe that this work of art has been suffered to remain unnoticed (as far as I can learn) by any other traveller. Here is also a handsome monument, to the memory of the two ladies of Sir John Pryce, and inscribed, of course, with their eminent virtues. The first of these ladies was the grand-daughter of Sir John Powel, one of the justices of the King's Bench, in James II.'s time, who signalized himself in the deliverance of the seven bishops from the tower. On the monument to the memory of Sir John's eldest daughter, aged eight years, are these beautiful lines:—

> " Short was thy time on earth—translated hence
> In the first bloom of virgin innocence;
> Thy dawning virtues, like the morning, bright,
> But just appeared, and sunk in endless night.
> Had Heaven, propitious, but prolong'd thy days,
> To emulate thy virtuous mother's praise,
> Then had the rising age rejoiced to see
> Her bright example copied out in thee."

Sir John Pryce, whose family descended from Elystan Glodrydd (one of the five royal tribes of Wales), who reigned king of the country between the Severn and the Wye, lived at the family seat, near the town, called Newtown-hall. He was a gentleman of good fortune; and though accounted a sensible man, he had, nevertheless, contracted habits of eccentricity, which engaged public notice. He married three wives; and on the death of each of the two first, he placed her in his room in a chemical preparation, by the side of his bed. The third lady very wisely declined the honour of his hand, till her deceased rivals were entombed in the church. Bridget Bostock, of Cheshire, the noted performer of miracles, who healed diseases with prayers, and a lotion of fasting spittle, and to whom multitudes resorted for the benefit of extraordinary cures, lived in the time of Sir John. This gentleman (like Brothers of late) was tinctured with religious enthusiasm; and, believing too much in the efficacy of Bridget's rhapsodies, wrote to her to make him a visit, in order to restore to him from death, his third and favourite wife. His letter runs thus :—

"Madam,

"Having received information by repeated advices, both public and private, that you have of late performed many wonderful cures, even when physicians have failed, and that the means used appear to be very inadequate to the effects produced, I cannot but look upon you as an extraordinary and highly-favoured person. And why may not the same most merciful God, who enables you to restore sight to the blind, hearing to the deaf, and strength to the lame, also enable you to raise the dead to life? Now having lately lost a wife, whom I most tenderly loved; my children an excellent step-mother, and our acquaintances a very dear and valuable friend,—you will lay us all under the highest obligations, and I earnestly entreat you, for God Almighty's sake, that you will put up your petitions to the throne of grace on our behalf,—that the deceased may be restored to us, and the late Dame Eleanor Pryce be recovered from the dead. If your personal attendance appear to you to be necessary, I will send my coach and six, with proper servants to wait on you hither, whenever you please to appoint. Recompence of any kind that you could propose would be made with the greatest gratitude; but I wish the bare mention of it may not be offensive to God and you.

I am, Madam,

Your most obedient

and very much afflicted humble servant,

JOHN PRYCE*."

* The late Dr. Vanbutchell, like Sir John, was very careful of the mortal remains of his

The Severn, having received a few tributary streams, though but twenty-four miles from its source, is swelled into a handsome river. In great floods, the torrents of waters rushing from Plymlymmon, and the other mountains from thence to this place, increase it to such a degree as to endanger the skirts of this town. Three miles, on the ridge of a hill north-

---

wife, and for some years preserved her body in his apartment, immersed in a pickle prepared by the skill of the late Mr. John Hunter.

She is described in a Latin Poem, written by a celebrated Physician—a translation of which is here subjoined, for the use of the curious reader, and particularly the ladies:—

"Here, covered not by earth or stone,
Lies John Vanbutchell's wife alone;
His pleasure, joy, and sole desire,
Quite uncorrupted, and entire:—
Who was preserv'd by Hunter's art,
When Death had shot his fatal dart!
Behold her now, 'gainst Nature's will,
With face so fair, and blooming still.
O husband blest! who in one house
Can still retain one charming spouse;
Can speak to, kiss, and with her toy,
And sleep close by—if such his joy:
Who now exists, not as you see,
The Fates would chuse to have her be;
But—what's more wond'rous—is much sweeter,
More perfect too in limb and feature,
More firm her flesh, more full of juice,
And fitter for domestic use.
O fortunate and envied Van!
To keep a wife beyond life's span;
Whom you can ne'er have cause to blame,
Is ever constant and the same;
Who qualities, most rare, inherits,
A wife that's dumb:—yet full of spirits.

ward, are the poor remains of Castell Dol Porwyn, which can have no charms for the painter, nor will the antiquarian, from its dilapidated state, find any thing to amuse him. It was erected between the years 1065 and 1073, by Bleddyn ab Cynfyn, Prince of Powys; who, by ameliorating the laws of his country, became a popular prince, and beloved of his subjects, till 1072, when he was killed in battle by Rhys ab Owain. Bleddyn was the head of the royal tribe of Powys. The legend of the beautiful virgin Sabrina is well known: she is reported * to have been the daughter of Locrine, King of Britain, by Estrildis, one of the three virgins, or matchless beauties, whom he made captive after defeating Humber, king of the Huns, to whom they all belonged. Locrine (or Lloegrin) was so enamoured of the charms of his young captive, Estrildis, as to divorce his queen Gwendolen in her favour. Gwendolen, however, on the decease of Locrine, assumed the government of Britain; and with unrelenting cruelty pursued the unhappy Estrildis, and Sabrina her daughter, both of whom she caused to be drowned in the river Severn; which, with a slight alteration, assumed the name of the innocent victim. Milton has immortalized her, as the goddess of chastity; and, in his beautiful masque of Comus, has given her story at full length; to which the reader is referred.

This vicinity is calculated to please the eye, on account of its rich variety; but the hills on each side are destitute of character, and devoid of every thing that can be termed grand. The woodiness of the valley may often retard the artist's steps

* Jeffery of Monmouth.

on the river's side; yet he should sometimes leave the road, for the better satisfaction of sketching upon its banks. Quitting Newtown, and a few hundreds of yards from it, I passed the handsome flannel manufactories of Messrs. Wyld and Williams, and a beautiful walk of eight miles brought me to Montgomery.

CHAPTER VI.

Montgomery.—Nantcribbe.—Offa's Dyke.— Watt's Dyke.—Powis Castle.—Rodney's Pillar.—Welsh Pool.—Buttington.—Llanfair.—Can Office.—Dolanog Bridge.—Iron Forge.—Myfod.—Mathrafal.—Allt yr Ancer.—Yew-Tree.—Vale of Llanfechan.—Llanfyllin.— Robbery. —Bodfach.— Gyrn Moelfre.—Llanrhyadr.—Cataract. —Llangynog Mines. —Accident. —Pennant Melangell.—Jorworth Drwndwn.—A Mountain Politician.—A Child Lost.—Grouse.—Cader Fronwen.—An Alarm.—Battle of Rhiw-Waedog Llywarch Hên.—Sandde Hardd.

MONTGOMERY is a neat but small town, where great quiet is observable; and where are to be discovered no indications of the bustling trade of the other places which I had passed through. The castle, standing upon a lofty rock that beetles over the town, commands a most extensive luxuriant country to the east, with Stiperstone and other hills in Shropshire: and on ascending still higher, the prospects improve. Northward is seen the valley stretching beyond Welsh Pool, and bespread with a great many houses, looking most hospitably, and exposing their red and white fronts to the glowing sun. This part of the scenery seems to vie with the vale of Clwyd, as seen from Ruthin. The ruins of the castle are too poor and insignificant for description; and the small remains which are visible, from the circumstance of their overhanging their base, and from other symptoms of decrepitude, but too plainly shew signs of speedy dissolution. From various grounds about the town, however, small as these remains may be, they have the power of arresting the attention of the painter, and the lover of art. At a little distance, where the imagination has sufficient room to supply their deficiencies they become very picturesque, and especially from some points, when the castle, and the town couchant at its foot, are viewed from the fields north of them. A mile eastward of the town, you enter Shropshire: on which side the neighbourhood seems to be abundantly productive in every thing necessary for man, as well as for the sustenance of creatures subservient to him. The county jail is a neat, small brick building, having its courts in front; it stands on an airy elevation, a little lower than the castle; but the assizes are always held at Welsh Pool, eight miles off, to which place the prisoners are conducted for trial.

The hall is rather a handsome brick edifice, and stands, as usual, in the market-place. The church, dedicated to St. Nicholas, is of the crucificial form, with a heavy massy tower. Internally it much resembles an old cathedral, having stalls arranged in the manner of those buildings. There is an extremely handsome monument to the memory of Richard Herbert and his lady, but so much mutilated as to reflect no credit on those who have had the superintendence of the church. Nor is this the only instance of the kind; for, near it lie the disjointed figures of other monuments: heads, legs, arms, and trunks, are huddled up in a corner, the sight of which is hideous, and strikes the mind with an idea of some dreadful carnage on the spot. Surely it would be attended with little expense to place them properly in their original attitudes, in some situation, where they might be preserved, and seen without offence. On quitting the church-yard, my eye glanced upon an inscription on a stone, the effusion of some *profound literary character*, which stands exposed to the *admiration* of all passers bӯ:

To the memory of two children of Maurice and Hester Powel,

"Here lies two branches which was young grown,
Cut off by Death to join the heavenly throne:
Spotless from guilt, the Lord he took we hence,
To reign with Christ, not to return from thence.
Momento Mory."

Adverting again to the castle:—it had fosses excavated out of the solid rock, over which there must have been communications with the building by draw-bridges, though at present there are no traces of any. The parading yard, a flat piece of ground, lies close to the precipice at the end of the castle. The town was founded by Baldwin, then lieutenant of the marches to William the Conqueror, after whose name the Welsh have ever since called it, Tre Faldwyn, or Baldwin's Town. Roger de Montgomery, Earl of Shrewsbury, entered Powysland in 1092, and the castle and town of Baldwin, at that time possessed by the Welsh. The earl then fortified the place, and from that period it has been called by the English, Montgomery. Two years after, the Welsh retook the castle, and destroyed it: put the garrison to the sword, and carried destruction through the county. After this, it experienced various revolutions, the Welsh and English being alternately successful; and during this time the castle was twice destroyed, and twice rebuilt. Henry III. rebuilt it in 1221*: when it was possessed by

* Powel, 280.

Hubert de Burgh, great justiciary to Henry, by a grant from that monarch. In 1231, Llywelyn brought a great army into the neighbourhood; at the sight of which, Hubert was so panic-struck, that he evacuated the castle, leaving it to the exasperated prince to seize and burn*. In 1644, Sir Thomas Middleton of Chirk-castle, laid hold of it for the parliament: but on the appearance of the king's army, he made a retreat to Oswestry, leaving a small garrison, ill provided, for its defence; and the royal forces, five thousand strong, under Lord Byron, laid siege to it: but Sir Thomas, returning with an addition of three thousand men, commanded by Sir Richard Brereton, obliged the enemy to occupy a position on the hill above the castle. The garrison being relieved, a dreadful battle ensued. The king's army descended the hill, and gained considerable advantages; which exasperated the parliament forces to a degree of madness; and making the most violent efforts, the fortune of the day decided for them, in a complete victory over the royalists, whom they pursued for twenty miles, taking fourteen hundred prisoners, and leaving five hundred slain: the loss on the parliament side being only forty slain, and sixty wounded. The castle was then dismantled, and thus shared the common fate of all others.

On a hill, not far from the castle, is an amazingly strong British military station, guarded by four great ditches, *&c.*; the stranger who has never had an opportunity of seeing a work of the kind, will be much gratified.

Goging-stools were of Saxon origin, and by them called Scalfing-stoles: it was an instrument of correction for ladies of dissolute or unguarded lives and conversation; and it is said that

* Powel, 287.

it was often in use here, for, at a very early period, the burgesses had the privileges of the Goging-stool, or Cucking-stool. The naughty lady was placed in it with her hair dishevelled about her shoulders, and with naked feet, as an example to the scolding sisterhood; immersion afterwards superseded this practice. It is a happy circumstance in these our days, that ladies, by their better manners, have rendered these, and all other modes of correction, unnecessary.

The Dragon-inn is a comfortable house, with ready attendance, and reasonable charges. Quitting it, I directed myself towards Pool.

Two miles on the left of the road, is the House of Industry, a handsome pile of building. A little further on the right, and near the road, is Nantcribba, the seat of Lord Hereford: its handsome front looks towards Shropshire, but unceremoniously it turns its back upon the traveller on this road. It is unquestionably well situated, as it commands on all sides a very extensive fertile country. If I am not mistaken, it stands precisely upon the site of Offa's Dyke. This celebrated mound begins on the banks of the Wye, proceeds through Herefordshire, passes Montgomery, and touches upon the road here for a considerable distance; continues its course through Llanynynach, a little west of Oswestry and Chirk, by Ruabon, close by Wrexham; then by Plas Power and Brumbo; crosses the Cegidog river, near Bryn Yorkin mountains, to Tryddyn Chapel, in the parish of Mold, where it is quite lost, at a place called Cae Twse; which, agreeably to Dr. Davies's opinion, means *fractura*, very expressive of the ending of this noted boundary, here suddenly stopped by some cause, of which we must now remain ignorant. At this place (Nantcribba) its breadth is about seven yards, and height about six or seven feet: the dyke or foss is on the Welsh side.

Offa decreed that this interdictory barrier against the incursions of my countrymen, which certainly was of immense labour, should be the boundary of his conquests. But it was soon proved that his mud wall was a scheme, that evinced only the imbecility of his judgment; for on his death, the Britons despised his toils, and, with an irresistible fury, carried their ravages far and wide into the English territories, and superior force only could repel them.

Harold enacted some sanguinary laws, to prevent the recurrence of such inroads; and decreed, that if any Welshman crossed the prescribed limits of Offa, and was found in arms on the Saxon side of the ditch, he should lose his right hand*. Watt's Dyke has been confounded with this: but the ingenuity and abilities of the late John Evans of Llwyn y Groes, Esq. have ascertained the distinction. He proved that Watt's Dyke commenced at the British post at Old Oswestry; continued to Hen-Ddinas, to Golowen; crossed Prys-Henlle common; passed St. Martin's; crossed the Ceiriog and the Dee, below Nant-y-Bela; passed through Wynnstay-park, by Pentre-yr-Clawdd, or the Township on the Dyke, to Erddig; went by Wrexham and Dolydd, Rhôsddu, Croesyneirias, and Gwersillt; crossed the Alyn, went to Rythin in Flintshire; then, by Hope-church, turned towards Sychtyn hills; passed Northop, Nant-y-Flint, through Strand-fields, near Holywell, and below Basingwerk-abbey, where it terminated, near the estuary of the Dee. The space between the two dykes, is, in breadth, from five hundred yards, to

* Leland collect. iii. 230.

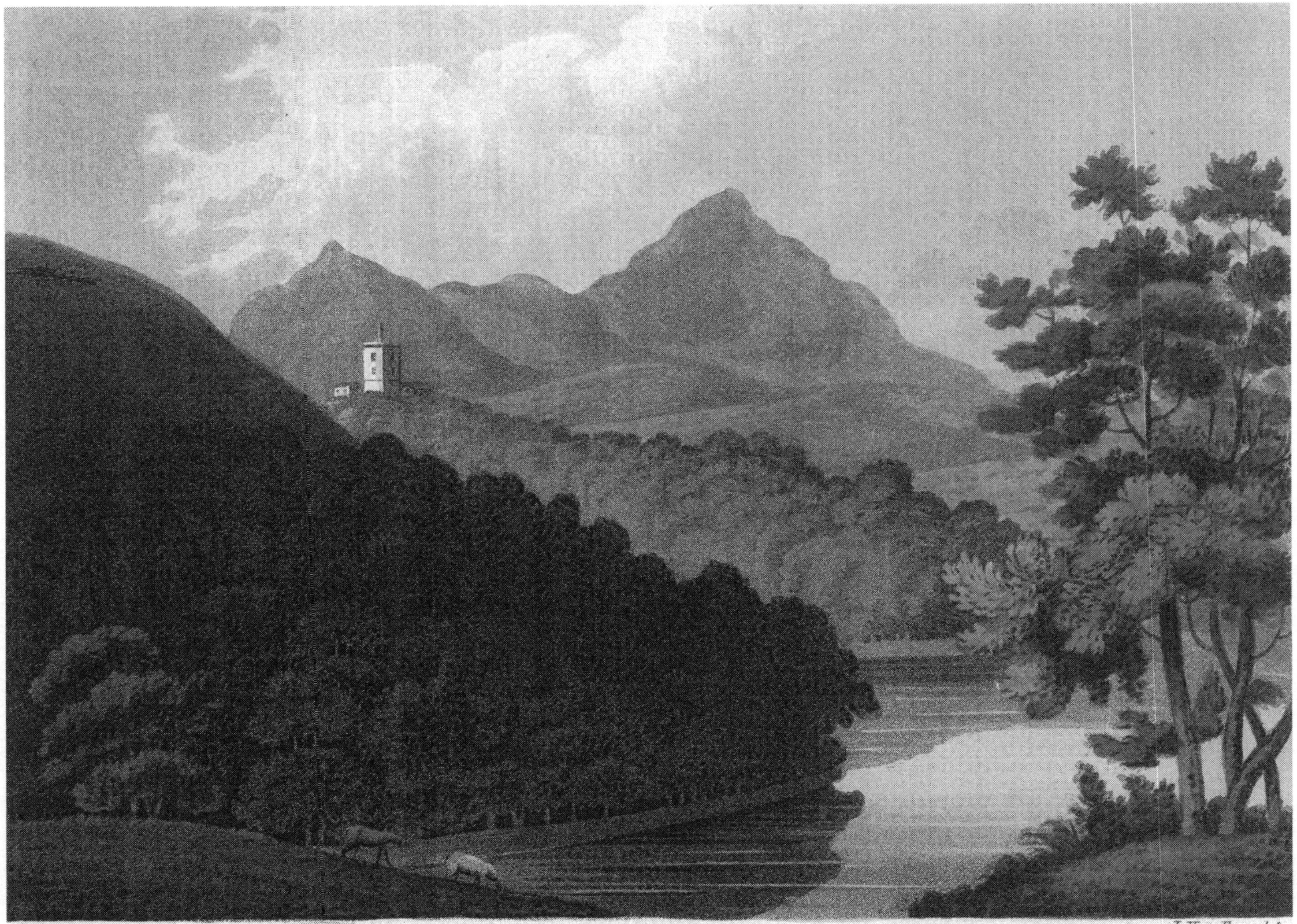

E. Pugh del.^t I. Havell sculp.^t

BREDDYN MOUNTAINS FROM POWIS CASTLE GROUNDS.

Published 25 April 1814 by E. Williams Strand.

three miles, and in length, about eighteen miles. This space was esteemed free ground, where the Welsh and Saxons were permitted to meet, for the purpose of bartering the produce of their labour :—

> "———————— there is a famous thing,
> Cal'de Offae's Dyke, that reacheth farre in length:
> All kind of ware, the Danes might thether bring;
> It was free ground, and cal'de the Britaine's strength.
> Watt's Dyke likewise, about the same was set,
> Betweene which two, both Danes and Britaines met,
> And trafficke still, but passing bounds by fleight,
> The one did take the other prisner streight.
>
> CHURCHYARD'S *Poem*, p. 104.

Three miles further is Glanhafren-bridge, over the Severn ; this is a desirable spot to sketch in, as the Breddyn mountains, of very picturesque appearance, are often seen through avenues of wood ; which frequently line the sides of the river, or open in elegant groups, alternately on rising and level grounds. Sometimes a sudden vista breaks on the sight, exposing to the view a beautiful space of meadow ground, through which Sabrina steals along, and at every inflexion exhibits a sheet, broad and smooth, save when gentle zephyrs softly touch its surface, and occasion those silvery undulations, which some of our modern draftsmen have so successfully represented in their productions.

Though I was well acquainted with the road, I stopped an old dame to inquire my way to Powis-castle. This I frequently did, to have a little confab with my compatriots ; and after addressing her in English, I soon perceived that she had eccentricity enough to amuse me. She instantly faced right about ; and, placing her hands upon her hips, said to herself in Welsh, " God bless me, what shall I say to him ?" then, flourishing her hands alternately in the air, and sometimes pointing to the castle, she talked away with the utmost rapidity, and a mixture of English and Welsh shot out at random, in the most terrible confusion. She continued her honest instructions with the greatest ardour, still keeping her eye on the castle; a favourable circumstance, which concealed from her my ungrateful laughter. Her earnest solicitude to guide me rightly, threw her frequently into the most ridiculous attitudes; sometimes couching to the ground, then suddenly starting up, pointing to one side of the road, then to the other; till being at last exhausted by the multiplicity of her directions, she placed her hands as at the first; and, looking me right in the face, demanded to know, if what she said was intelligible? I returned for answer, in a language better understood by her, that I fully comprehended her jargon: upon which she broke out in a violent passion, at my having pretended ignorance of her tongue. This rage, however, soon subsided into good humour, a strong characteristic of the country. On parting, she desired I would no more play with the feelings of elderly women, as my jokes would be better directed, and more acceptable to the young ones. The grounds of Powis-castle run up from the vale to a considerable height; and the view from their summit is very extensive, on all sides exhibiting a great variety of objects. In different parts of the park are capital studies of trees; the noble and sturdy oak often meeting the eye. The rough and undulating surface, seconded by groups of trees of various species, and grand openings to some distant object or other of importance, render this a place of much consequence to the arts. From several points, the Breddyn hills, with the intervening valley, and the church-tower of Welsh Pool, with other happy circumstances, are very bewitching subjects for the draftsman. Descending, I came immediately upon the castle: yet that is exceedingly elevated above the vale; which it commands southward, as far as Montgomery, and northwards to the plains of Salop, through an avenue formed by the Breddyn hills, and the heights beyond Pool.

The stranger will perceive a monument on one of the northern peaks of these hills, called Rodney's Pillar. It was erected at the expense of the county, as an honourable testimony to the noble and illustrious hero whose name it bears.

Powis-castle is built partly of brick and a sort of red gritty stone: the entrance into it is between two round towers; and two terraces rise one above the other in front of the castle, or rather of the house; for having undergone many repairs and alterations, it retains very little of the appearance which would justify the former appellation. The interior is graced with some noble pictures by Claude, Cuyp, Rubens, Canaletti, Carlo Dolce, Reynolds, *&c.* About the year 1110, the renowned Cadwgan ab Bleddyn, ab Cynfyn, sought refuge here from the persecution of his relations, and began the castle: but while he was intent upon the work, his nephew Madoc surprised, and slew him. In 1191, Hubert, Archbishop of Canterbury, besieged and took it. But soon after it had been fortified, it was attacked by Gwenwynwyn, to whom it surrendered on the same terms that his own garrison had before received; and it was then called after his name. It was afterwards in the possession of his son Gryffydd, who, as it is conjectured, sided with the English: for, in 1233, Llwelyn ab Jorwerth took the fortress, which by him was called Castell Goch, or the Red Castle*. It was after this possessed

* Powel, 288.

by Owen ab Gryffydd ab Gwenwynwyn; and after his demise, by his daughter Hawys Gadarn, or Hawys the Hardy; who, by the recommendation of Edward II. married, in 1268, John de Charlton, styled *Valectus Domini Regis* †: and it continued in the possession of their posterity for several generations. In the reign of Henry VIII. the title became extinct. Sir William Herbert, second son of the Earl of Pembroke, purchased it in the time of Queen Elizabeth, and was created Lord Powis. In 1644, when the castle was in the possession of Peircy Lord Powis, it was captured by Sir Thomas Middleton, who made his Lordship prisoner, and pillaged the place. It is now the property of Lord Clive, created Earl of Powis, who married the only sister and heiress of the late Earl. A beautiful walk of half a mile brought me to Welsh Pool; when an appetite, sharpened by a long ramble of seven hours, demanded some attention. After dinner I strolled about the town. The church, a new and handsome edifice, stands exalted upon the side of a hill; from whence there is a curious bird's-eye view of the town, and its pleasing environs. Within it is a very handsome chalice of gold, which will hold a wine quart.

The assizes for the county are held here, in a new hall, with an elegant front, raised upon columns and pilasters: a very substantial fabric, which stands in the centre of the principal street. The town is well inhabited, and is situated in a hollow between two high hills. On market-days it is a busy place for the sale of flannel, stockings, webs, *&c.*, which are conveyed from hence to the Shrewsbury merchants. The Severn begins to be navigable at a place called Pool Stake, about

* Powel, 217.

three-fourths of a mile from the town, where small craft only can be employed. Before I quit this neighbourhood, I shall take the opportunity of noticing how general it is, to paint the walls of the rooms of public-houses in size, with decorations of festoons, and in pannels ornamented with various devices, strongly mimicking the present mode, so prevalent among the fashionable world; than which nothing can more display a want of taste.

Is it not to be lamented, that preference should be given to the performances of those who follow the meanest, and lowest parts of the arts (it is a question, indeed, whether they belong to them at all), and which are often executed by sign-painters, when the highest and most noble branches of painting are neglected, and suffered to decay?—This is strictly true, when we consider how strangely the finest pictures of the old, as well as of the present masters, have been excluded from the best apartments, and suffer ignoble imprisonment in some dark sequestered garret. This fancy-work, like all others, depending upon the whim of the moment, or the caprice of its patrons, must sometime or other, it is to be hoped, give way: and the more meritorious artists of the united kingdom receive that encouragement and patronage, which are so justly their due. "They require and deserve a noble recompense; the homage of wisdom and virtue; the respect of their own times, and the regard of posterity." Sir Joshua Reynolds, aware of the impolicy of any severe animadversions on the false taste of a people, expressed himself in the following words*: "A national taste, however wrong it may be, cannot be totally changed at once: we must yield a little to the prepossession which has taken hold on the

* 7th Discourse, p. 238.

mind; and we may then bring people to adopt what would offend them, if endeavoured to be introduced by violence." An excellent observation, verified in the grand efforts now making by the nobility and gentry, to revive the sinking arts, and bring them into competition with the performances of the most flattered painters of the ancient schools. May success attend the British Institution, and may its laudable endeavours remove that apathy and neutrality to the fine arts, which for years have distinguished this nation!

Welsh Pool had for its lord the possessor of the castle. Gryffydd, in the year 1355, did homage to Edward, Prince of Wales, at Chester, for the lordship of Powis, by the title of Lord of Pool *, which title was afterwards frenchified into *de la Pole* †. On the other side of the Severn, is Buttington, the Butdigingtum of the Saxons, where the Danes in 894, under Heston, took their station, after traversing a great part of England. They were instantly and closely blocked up by Alfred's generals, and driven to the alternative of eating their own horses, or of perishing. At last, having no other prospect before them than famine, the Pagans attempted to cut their way through the Saxon army: but were nearly all slaughtered, few of them escaping to their own country ‡.

The next morning I left the Royal Oak, the principal inn here, and steering through the meaner suburbs, soon came upon a road, which, though flanked by very high grounds on each side, was not interesting enough to induce me to take out my pencil. Having passed on my right a beautiful retired house;

* Powel, 382.

† Ayloff's Calendar, 102.

Sax. Chr. 94, 95.

a little further on the left, the handsome residence of Mr. Lyons presented itself. This neighbourhood is woody: yet there is a sameness through the whole length of six miles, which renders the road tiresome to the painter. I did not perceive more than two spots that would form tolerable pictures. I now descended a steep hill, to the handsome village of Llanfair, situated in a very romantic hollow, and watered by the Banwy*. The church has little to boast of; on a tablet in it are inscribed these words, "To the memory of Mr. David Davies, who died at Cheltenham; he left by will £20. to the poor of this parish; and directed that sixpence should be given to every poor person attending his funeral, at which one thousand and thirty were present, and received sixpence each." There is a well, close to the walls of the church-yard, much resorted to, and said to be very efficacious in the cure of several disorders. It is exposed to the open air, but, for the sake of decency, ought to be enclosed with a wall, if not covered. The water is opaque, and of a greenish colour: it seemed not to flow, but to be as still as a stagnant pond, and it may probably be fed with the moisture from the receptacle of the dead, which is right above it. The Cross-Foxes-inn, here, afforded me a very comfortable dinner. Requesting to borrow a book of the roads, a young female handed me a volume, entitled, *Rule a Wife and have a Wife*. Conscious of my want of a treasure of this kind, I asked her if she meant this as a challenge, and, on my reading the title to her, her face became instantly suffused with the sweetest of blushes. She went again, and returned with the *Corsican Pirate:* she went a third time, and brought me *Mar-*

* This river, I am informed, is wrongly called Virnwy, another river of that name being in the neighbourhood; its ancient and true name is Banwy.

vellous Tales, and other Strange Things. On my remarking this repetition of mistakes, she replied, with a painful consciousness of her defects expressed in her countenance, that she could not read. Poor girl! however deficient in the acquirements of the school, she seemed to possess Nature's best gift—a heart fraught with modest sensibility.

The country from hence to the Can-office, is at intervals more open, but less interesting than the grounds which I had passed over; though it was in some measure mountainous, it was of such a cast and description, as not to please the eye of the painter. It is pleasant enough however to the commercial traveller, on account of the good road that passes through it. The Can-office is an inn, but from what circumstance it derived its odd name, I have not, with all my inquiries, been able to ascertain; and though some English tourists have made etymological attempts in this instance, they have certainly failed. The house stands alone, and is situated on the banks of the Banwy, near its junction with the Avon Gam, or the Meandering Stream. In the garden is a tumulus of larger dimensions than are common to these ancient remains; it is seventy yards in circumference at the base: as yet it is unopened, but its examination is meditated. It has suffered decapitation, for the purpose of accommodating a certain description of men, stimulated by cruelty, with the *manly* pleasure, and *delightful* opportunity, of beholding the feats of two innocent birds. This is a comfortable house, where I experienced much attention from the landlord, brother to the ingenious Mr. Baugh, who engraved that most correct, full, and excellent map of North Wales, published by the late John Evans, Esq., which was the companion of my journey.

Leaving this place in the morning, and making a retrograde

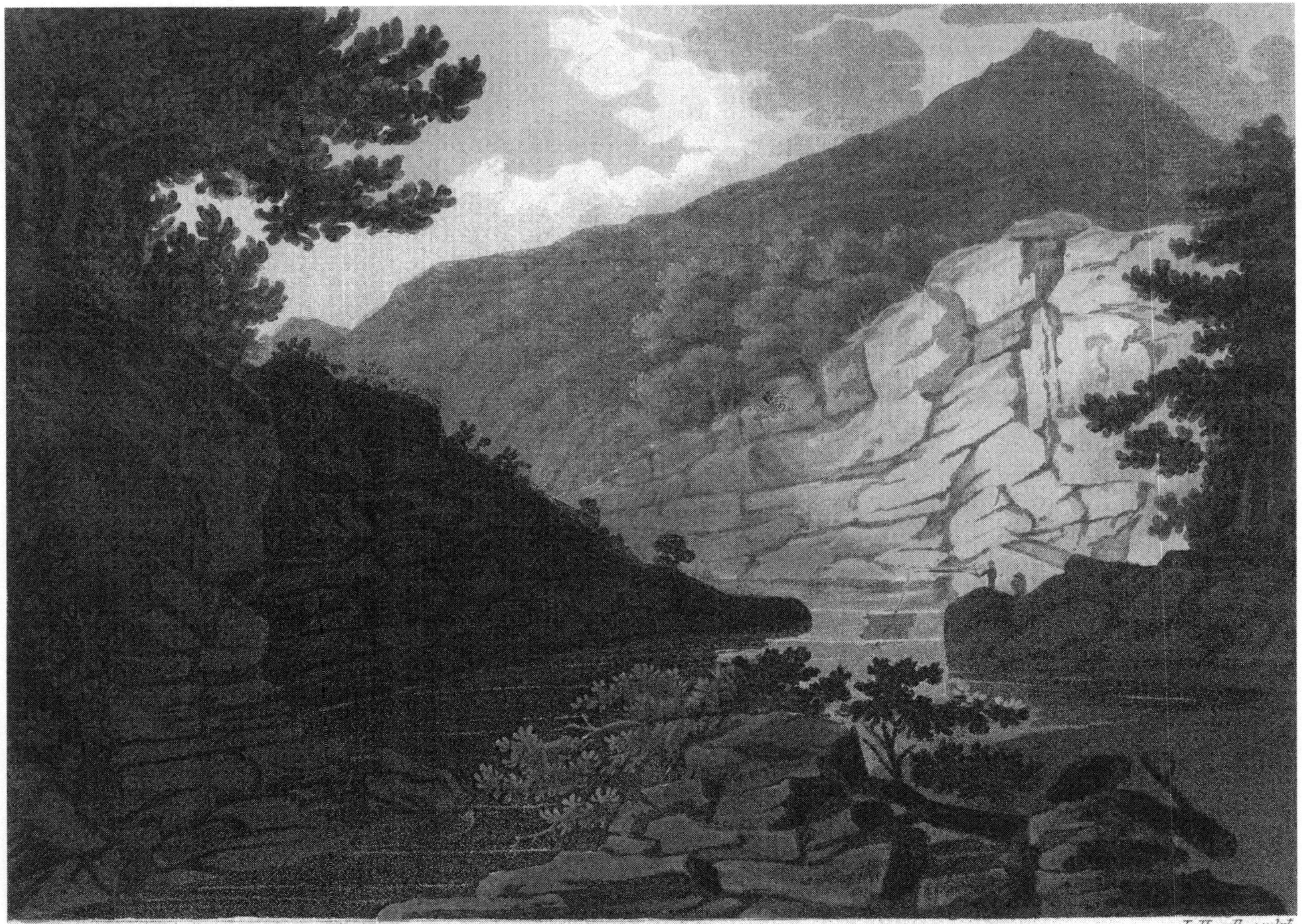

E. Pugh delt. I. Havell sculpt.

VIEW ON THE VIRNWY DOLANAG.

Published 15 January 1814, by E. Williams, Strand.

movement of one mile, to the little church and bridge of Llanersyl, which I passed on the left, and bidding adieu to the public road, I commenced a perambulation of many miles among trackless mountains, rough rocks, *&c.* Proceeding along a narrow lane, I passed a farm-house called Llysyn: in the grounds of which is a tumulus. The river Banwy, taking a circular direction round a hill called Moel Bentyrch, is soon out of sight, and I saw no more of it till near its union with the Virnwy. A walk of several miles brought me over some very dull, unpleasant, boggy mountains and dingles, which better agree with the interest of the plodding grazier, than the views of the artist: the latter, however, has greatly the advantage on ascending the heights above the handsome river Virnwy, where he is instantaneously treated with a prospect, with which he must be highly gratified. I had almost despaired of finding much of the picturesque in this county, till I came upon this spot, where I stayed some time to contemplate the variety of grand features that composed the noble whole displayed before me. Looking down the river, we perceived huge protuberances of rocks, jutting into the centre of the picture, and plunging their craggy ends into the stream. These sometimes are cut or crossed by others from the opposite shores, which are diversified with wood and pasture, in some places precipitous, in others of easy slopes. There are no less than seven detached hills (those in the distance with serrated peaks), overlooking all others, and very magnificent.

Anxious to examine the banks of the river, I descended a steep hill to Dolanog-bridge: the scenery about this spot is truly romantic, and partakes strongly of the character of the best hollows and dingles of Merionethshire. The mountains have great height; and their sides, from their approximation to the perpendicular, have suffered much laceration from time and the weather. The sight of these great falls is sometimes interrupted by picturesque and woody prominences, which create a pleasing variety. I felt a wish to follow the river, and to explore its banks for ten or more miles towards Llwydiarth: having been there only in the dead of the winter, when it appeared to be a very wild spot. Upon consideration, however, I found that it would derange my plan of examining this neighbourhood. The bridge is of one arch, but so light and elegant as, in my opinion, to be little inferior to Inigo's-bridge, at Llanrwst. Below it, the scenery is very grand, the Virnwy flowing down in great breadth, and interrupted by a craggy rock that crosses it at right angles.

This fall of water is probably not more than twelve feet high, but its breadth is seventy or eighty yards; which, with its craggy sides and the body of water that rushes down, makes it a fine subject; but it must be excluded from the picture, if the bridge be introduced. Salmons are caught here, by harpoon-irons being darted at them, on their leaping the rocks. Proceeding lower down on the side of the river, I met at every turn with something excellent. The wildness of the scenery is great; the denuded prominences on one side, and the woody banks on the other, with the river between, making its way seemingly with much labour and difficulty through a wild rugged bottom, are objects that interest the mind of the artist. This scenery, however, I was sorry to find, did not continue long; the prospect then opening with hills, of less spirit and consequence. Upon ascending the rocks, another species of objects presented themselves to the eye; which, on looking towards the bridge,

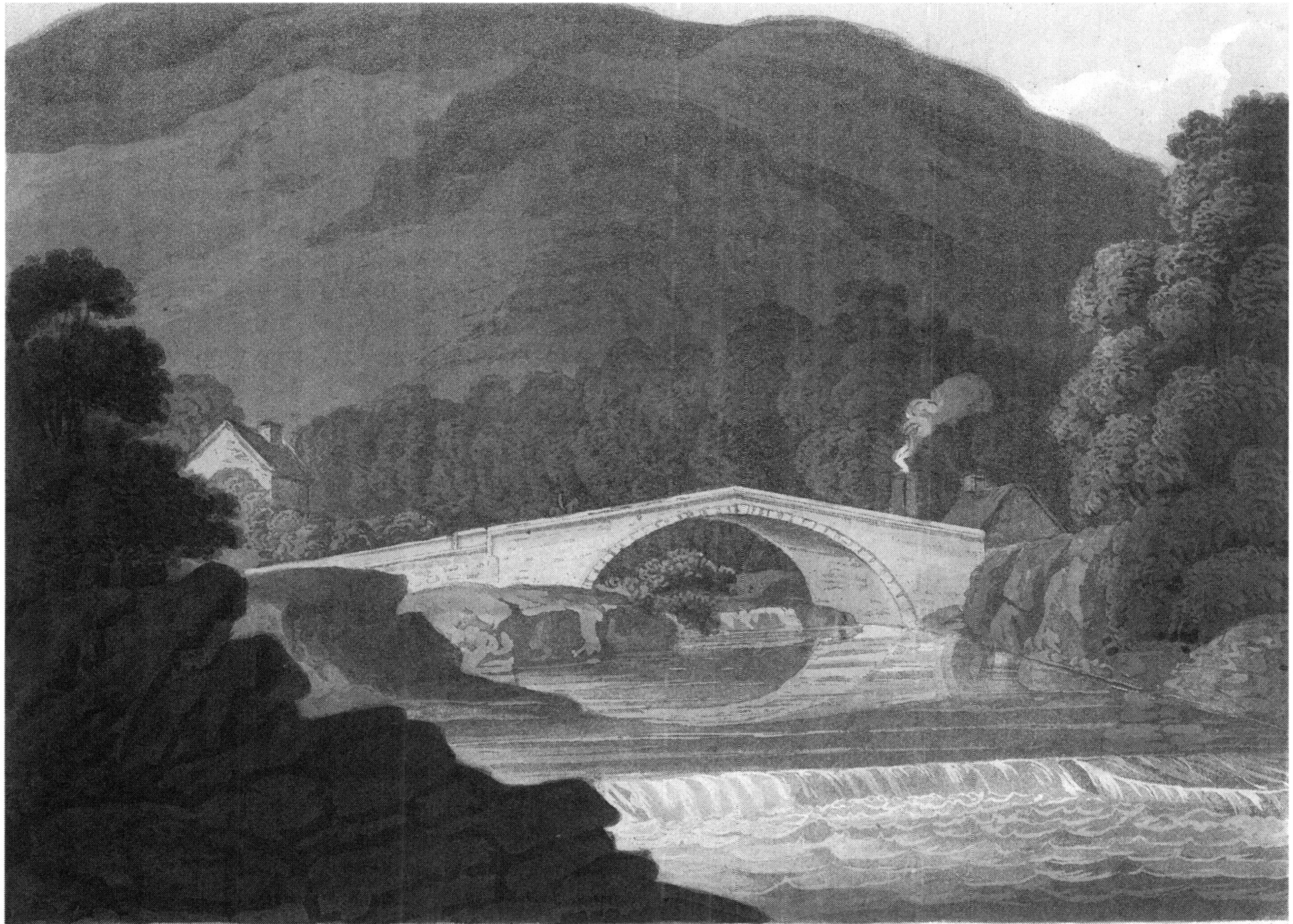

Edwd Pugh Del.^t Thos Cartwright sculp.^t

DOLANOG BRIDGE.

Published 15 April 1813, by E. Williams, Strand.

became as diversified as they were grand. The mid-space is occupied by rocks, wood, and river; while the bridge makes a figure at the foot of a noble mountain, whose summit penetrates the clouds. I came again to the bottom, and passed through a beautiful sylvan glen, extremely enriched with wood, small meadows, and picturesque cottages, which considerably retarded my steps. Quitting this delightful spot, I was again ushered into an open space, that promised me but little for contemplation: but in other respects, it was a prospect very pleasing to the landlord and the farmer, as cultivation seems here to be carried to great perfection.

Crossing the Virnwy, I passed the iron forge, and the flannel factory of Messrs. Jones, Owen, and Mytton: these works are extensive, and employ a great number of men. It is very observable that in this county the manufactories and other commercial works in it, belong to, and are conducted by, the natives; whose public spirit, it is to be hoped, will be copied by others who live more northerly, and who, by attending a little to the nature and properties of minerals, the mode of producing, cleansing, and fusing them, may be the means of highly enriching their country. The Virnwy here has a good character for some distance, and offers some good things for the pencil in small confined spots. I now came suddenly down a steep hill, upon the village of Meifod, most enchantingly situated in a beautiful valley, whose flanked sides consist of lofty mountains, the haughty brows of which rise up with pride into the sky; and from the great mass, frequently rush out craggy promontories, which jut out in very excellent contours, covering many romantic recesses. If this vale be viewed from some situations south-west of Meifod, I am persuaded that it will not suffer much by a comparison with the vale of Festiniog; the latter, indeed, surpassing this only by the circumstance of possessing that famous rock called Moel-wyn, and of its being circumscribed within a narrower space, and thus allowing more of the picturesque to be admitted into the landscape. But this vale of Meifod has a greater variety of parts, which form noble pictures of themselves; and it abundantly excels the other in fertility, without that melancholy appearance that floats over the vale of Festiniog. It is well wooded throughout, which, with the addition of the divine Virnwy, makes it almost an Eden,—a spot of general admiration. There are no good houses in this valley, which to me appeared remarkable, as the situation is the most desirable of any which I have yet met with in my journey; nor do I think that the vale of Clwyd excels it, but in the circumstance of its commanding a view of the sea. It is about seven or eight miles long, and not more than half a mile broad at the end, but it opens by degrees towards the north-east, to two or more miles.

The church stands close to the village, and the surrounding church-yard may bear commenting upon. This piece of consecrated ground was originally intended as a cemetery for the dead: but that so large a space should have been bestowed for that purpose is singular, unless it could be proved that it equally belonged to two other churches that were here in former days. The space of ground which it occupies is about ten or twelve acres. From the great infrequency of burials, nine parts at least of this space are superfluous.

Though this piece of ground was primarily intended to *accommodate the dead*, it now amply *supports* and *increases the living:* for the present incumbent lets it to a publican in the village, for grazing, at the yearly rent of twenty pounds!

The church is dedicated to St. Tyssilio, a prince of Powys, who supported the British churches against Austin, the monk. Tyssilio wrote a history of the church of Britain, and lived in the seventh century. This is the mother-church to Welsh Pool and Guilsfield, and is a place of great ecclesiatical antiquity. Meudwyfod, analogous in sound to the present name, implies a hermit's habitation; and it is reasonable to suppose that, in the early periods of Christianity, it was the residence of some hermit or recluse. Here were two other churches formerly, in the chief of which the princes and great men of Powys were buried.

On the heights above the river, near Mathrafal, are the sites of some British and Roman works; but of which remain scarcely any vestiges.

I took up my abode for the night at an excellent public-house, kept by one Williams. I do not remember to have slept in a better bed; and every article that made up my meals, was of the best quality. The several items charged in the bill were as follow:—tea, six-pence; supper, six-pence; breakfast, six-pence; bed, gratis. That the landlord should derive some pecuniary advantage from his guests is but reasonable: but what must be the comparative profits of those on the public-roads, who charge three times as much, and in a country whose local productions are as abundant and as cheap as on this spot?

On leaving this place I passed a huge rock, called Gallt yr Ancer, or the Steep of the Anchoret, or Hermit; and pursued my way among the mountains, where the hollows between often exhibited proofs of the able skill of the husbandman; but these, however productive to the occupier, have nothing to recommend them to the artist or the stranger; and for several miles was I thus immured amidst a congregated mass of hills, to me barren of all pleasure. About two miles from Meifod I crossed some meadows to see a yew-tree: which, from the road, appeared very formidable, and so indeed it proved on a nearer examination. Not being able to reach the medium thickness, I measured the smaller circumference, which I found to be twenty-one feet. A traditional story, among the country people, says, that in early times there was an attempt to build a church on the very spot where this tree now stands; that the work had commenced, but that the workmen's labour of the day, it became the devil's amusement to undo; and that his sable majesty persisted in carrying the stones placed in the building to the spot where now stands the church of Meifod; and that at length a voice was heard to pronounce, "Ymma myna ei fod:"—"Here it shall be."

The reader will perceive some analogy in sound between this speech, and the name of the parish, of which the latter seems to be a contraction; and the Welsh, of former times, were seldom wanting in invention to turn any names into meanings which might suit their fancy. The poisonous qualities of the yew has been conjectured to be the reason and origin of planting it in church-yards, where cattle might be secure from the taste, which is fatal to them. No tree whatever could have better suited these sacred grounds than the yew, as the best emblem of mortality. Reaching the summit of these hills, close to the house of Mr. Lloyd Tudor, and looking back at the country I had passed, I was not a little surprised to find that those hollows, and the various hills which afforded me so little pleasure while among them, now as a whole, with the mountains, and the vale of Meifod crossing them at right angles, and other remoter objects, become an interesting subject. The situation of this house must be pleasing in the summer. I now descended a steep hill towards a few cottages at the bottom, and deviating from the right road to Llanfyllin, I turned a mile to the east, to view the vale of Llanfechen, and from an acclivity I was enabled to contemplate with pleasure this singular, but beautiful valley. The figure of it is a circle; a circumstance which renders it a curiosity seldom to be met with; and its diameter may be no less than three miles of fine land, in very high tillage, watered by the Cain. By the indefatigable industry of the inhabitants, the sides of the circumjacent hills are covered with corn, and seem to be in an excellent state of cultivation. Just on the point of parting with a person who had conducted me to this delightful spot, and whom I met a few minutes before, a disclosure of names ensued. I could not be less surprised than glad to meet with a gentleman, for whom I had made incessant but fruitless inquiries in the neighbourhood, and whom I had given up all hopes of seeing. That we should unexpectedly meet upon a trackless mountain was not a little singular, as one single minute of time might have kept either of us in the rear, and have deprived me of the pleasure which I derived from my short conversation with the Rev. Mr. Walter Davies, who, as an antiquarian, and for assiduous researches into the history of his country, is well known. Descending the hill into the road, I passed the handsome mansion of Llwyn, the residence of Mr. Humphreys, and immediately entered Llanfyllin, a large and handsome village, which a stranger would not expect to find, involved amidst the mountains. The church is a new brick building. It is very unusual to see edifices of this sort in North Wales, built of any other material than stone, that being common every where, and little expensive. The internal part of the church is good. On the walls are suspended several boards, exhibiting a list of handsome and liberal donations to different charities in the parish. The first benefactor is a Mr. John Maurice, a native of this parish, and a silk-weaver of London. The charitable deeds of the following munificent ladies, are also handed down to posterity with much honour:—"Mrs. Mary Vaughan, of Llangedwin did, among other good charities, settle in trustees, £1116 10*s*., to purchase lands; the yearly rent, *for ever*, to be applied for the clothing and education of thirty-two poor boys, and ten poor girls, who are to be educated in the principles of the church of England. She saw these schools flourish, and gave them her further charitable encouragement. She was the daughter of John Purcel, Esq." "The good lady, Mrs. Strangeways, bought a tenement, value nineteen pounds per annum, for the support of the schools founded by her mother, she also left £1000, the interest thereof to be given to ten poor clergymen's widows yearly: she besides left £700, the yearly interest thereof to be given to twenty poor decayed tenants, and £690 12*s*. 5*d*., the yearly interest to be disposed of in apprenticing poor boys yearly."

To neglect noticing acts of benevolence like these, would be unpardonable, especially as, unfortunately, they are too rare. Happy would it be for every neighbourhood, were the spirit of divine charity more prevalent, to influence the mind of the rich more universally, to turn that portion of superabundant wealth (too often dissipated in degrading ways), into a channel so beneficial to their fellow-creatures.

"Oh! hear that lovely widow's wail!
See her dim eye, her aspect pale!
To Heaven she turns, in deep despair:
Her infants wonder at her prayer;—
And, mingling tears, they know not why—
Lift up their little hands, and cry.
O God! their moving sorrows see!
Support them, sweet Humanity."

Hymn to Humanity.

"Who can all sense of others' ills escape,
Is but a brute, at best, in human shape."

TATE'S *Juvenal.*

While I stayed here, unwelcome news were brought to the family of a young man, who had left the place a few days before, that between Chester and Wrexham, on his way to Liverpool to buy flax, he had been robbed of upwards of six hundred pounds, of which were 400 guineas in gold. Some knowledge of this treasure, it seems, he had unfortunately disclosed on his way, to characters, who probably would have voted it a crime to let slip such a golden opportunity of securing to themselves a glorious series of drunken bouts—heedless of the injustice, or the ruin to the honest tradesman.

I ascended several of the hills in the neighbourhood, of a similar description to those which I shall presently have to notice.

In the reign of Edward II., Llywelyn ab Gryffydd, ab Gwynwynwyn, bestowed a charter on this place, which was confirmed by Edward de Charlton, Lord of Powis, by which charter, the burgesses could apprehend, imprison, and bring to trial, all thieves; and might pursue them for a league out of the town, but no further. If a stranger stayed in the town during a year, paying scot and lot, he became free. It is governed by two bailiffs, annually chosen, who, with other immunities granted by Charles II., were made justices of the peace, within the limits of their corporation, for the time of their being in office *.

The Goat is the only inn of this village, the ale of which, for its good qualities, is proverbial, "Cwrw da Llanfyllin,"—" The excellent ale of Llanfyllin." The house being always full of customers from the town and neighbourhood, the draught is immense at home, and the reputation of this excellence, secures for it an exportation to different parts of England.

> "Genius of Health, thy grateful taste,
> Rivals the cup of Jove;
> And warms each 'Welshman's' generous breast
> With liberty and love."
>
> IRELAND'S *Hogarth.*

It would be more agreeable to strangers, if there were better attendance in this house; though no blame can be attached to the good inactive landlady, who through age, perhaps, is not able to keep her noisy servants in order.

Leaving this place early in the morning, I passed by Bodfach, a snug house, the occasional residence of Sir Edward Lloyd, Bart., M. P. for the borough of Beaumaris. On taking a retrospective view from a steep road, the woody acclivities about the village appeared to advantage. By keeping to the west of the road, the scenery improved; and, though neither rough nor frowning, was excellent in its kind. There is a good road over the mountains; but it commands only a dull uninteresting mountain scenery.

Coming upon the heights that overlook the vale of Llanrhyadr,

* Camden ii. 783.

the prospect becomes more striking and luxuriant, and one hardly knows which part of the vale commands the attention most; all being great and grand. From a farm called Brithdir, the mountain Gyrn Moelfre is seen rising in great majesty above the rest, and it assimilates well with some of the bolder protuberances of Carnarvonshire. With a commanding height, its sides have the appearance of being excavated, and it shews an outline that undulates to a peak. Beyond, are hills subordinate to it, with others, between it and the spectator, well grouped; whilst nearer still, are some precipitous rocks, well marked for the pencil, and, close at hand, a dingle pregnant with wood; making a whole as fine as the scenery about Dolanog-bridge. Descending the hill, I passed through a part of this fertile valley to the romantic village of Llanrhyadr. My first concern was to satisfy an hungry appetite; and I found much better cheer than could have been expected from the external appearance of the house. In the church there is a mural monument to the memory of Dr. Worthington, the resident vicar of this place, about 1750, whose name will be ever respected as a theological writer, and a good man. His "Essay on the Scheme and Conduct, Procedure and Extent, of Man's Redemption," passed through many editions, and is held in high estimation. A Welsh inscription, on the arched ceiling of the church, tells us, that a young man fell from it into one of the seats, without the experience of the least injury.

This church is dedicated to St. Dogfan (son of Brychan), who lived in the fifth century. Doctor William Morgan, vicar of this place, wrote the first translation of the Bible into Welsh. In 1595, he was rewarded by Queen Elizabeth, with the Bishoprick of Llandaff, and was afterwards translated to that of St. Asaph, where he died September 10th, 1604.

The facetious, but learned Dr. South, was also a vicar of this parish. The gothicated ruins in the wood above the vicarage, as seen from the road, have a pretty effect, and might lead the stranger to suppose them the remains of some ancient abbey, were he not informed that they had been planned and executed by the taste, and at the expense, of Dr. Worthington.

A road on the river's side, and through a slightly-wooded glen, compressed into a narrow space by the high hills on each side, brought me, after a walk of four miles, to the celebrated fall, called Pistill Rhyadr. It is seen and heard a considerable distance before you reach it. It falls down the front of a rock, with only one slight interruption, into a black basin below. Its height is more than two hundred and ten feet: a circumstance which most recommends it to the traveller's notice, as it is otherwise unattended with any picturesque qualities, and will by no means bear a comparison, as a picture, with the Mowddach, or Cain. Of this opinion was that judicious critic, Lord Lyttleton, who says, "Upon the whole it gave me but little pleasure, after having seen the Velino." I hope that I shall be understood to speak of it only as a subject of little interest for the pencil, as the stranger will be highly gratified with the spectacle, nor will he think it lost time to ride or walk to it, since the singular arch, formed by the fall through the solid rock, which is very high, renders it an object of much curiosity. The shepherds, in pursuit of their flocks, will sometimes, with much unconcern, walk over this slippery arch; a sight at which a stranger would shudder. Not long since, a female was seen to pass the narrow and frightful ridge, and, looking over the horrible precipice, she inclined her head forwards to listen, at her leisure, to the roaring cataract; while those who were eye-witnesses were almost petrified with apprehension, till she quitted the spot. The hut at the bottom was erected by Dr. Worthington, for strangers to take refreshment in, which they sometimes bring with them from the village. This river, for ten miles from the fall, separates the counties of Denbigh and Montgomery : the village and fall being in the former. Returning through the village, I went to Garthgelynen Fawr, two miles further, the residence of John Lloyd, Esq., whose absence I regretted ; but his lady's kind attention deserves my grateful acknowledgment*.

I spent the next day in a walk about the neighbourhood, and first proceeding along the sides of the hills to the romantic village of Llangynog, discovered from many points on these sides the subjects of good pictures. Keeping my eye westward, the above village with its church, appeared in the distance, with the waters of the Tanad, flowing through a well-wooded vale, the vale, on each side, fortified by high mountains, and those mountains, in many instances, proof against any attempts to render them productive of vegetation. The several rocks on each side, and above the village, are lofty and well disposed, deserving the appellation of picturesque. Their precipices are often nearly perpendicular, and somewhat lacerated; but not in that bold manner, so conspicuous in the rocks of Llanberis. Striking across the meadows, I frequently came upon good landscapes on the banks of the river, which at every curve produced a good peep between an avenue of trees; a rock, or the church, or some other apposite object, presenting itself to view. Not far from the village are some lead-mines, now of very little productiveness. Mrs. Evans, who keeps the public-house, is the lessee. The

* Both are since deceased.

lead-mine at Craig-y-Mwyn, two miles from hence, discovered in 1692, produced to a maternal relation of the late Lord Powis, for a few years only, £20,000 annually: but now the product, after paying a few men for their labour, is inconsiderable. The vein was discovered by accident:—a woman in going up the hill, making a slip, her foot opened a slight fissure in the soil, which exhibited the shining lustre of the ore. Similar discoveries have been made at other places, and in other times, by similar accidental means. The plow brought to light the gold mines of Galicia: the silver mines of Spain were found by the accidental burning of a wood: those of India by hillocks formed by pismires; and the great mine at Halkin, in Flintshire, was disclosed to view by the digging of a ditch.

On the reverse side of the valley, and just over the village, is a slate quarry in the side of a huge rock. I walked up its steep ascent with some difficulty: the excavations are very considerable, and the workmen have so undermined the rock, as to leave it beetling over their heads in a frightful manner. It seems highly dangerous to drive further into it, and it requires no penetration to foresee some dreadful accidents if the work should be continued. The rock being a sort of schistus, its quality of course is not adhesive; and the slightest accident imaginable, perhaps a moderate breeze of wind, may separate large masses of stone, and thus occasion the most distressing consequences. This description of the place I trust will not appear erroneous, when the following has been read: Anthony Hughes, one of the quarrymen, a few winters since, while drilling a hole in a piece of rock preparatory to its being blasted, met with instant death, by the mass dislodging from its socket and falling upon him. Five minutes before the accident, he was warned to quit his situation, but deaf to this advice, he remained to meet his fate; he left a widow and an infant family to lament his untimely death. Quitting the village, I passed other slate-quarries, in a narrow road leading to Pennant Melangell, a valley between the hills, totally unknown to travellers. Because it possesses beauties and advantages denied to similar situations, I shall take pains to describe it. I walked about it in different directions, and venture to say, there is not, in all the principality, a more enchanting retired spot for a summer residence. Its length is probably near three miles. On entering the valley, a huge rock, of a conic form, perfectly bare of covering, presents itself to the left; this is called Moel Dimmor, a contraction of Du-mawr, or the Great Bald-headed Black Rock; its sides are nearly upright, and a little clifted, up which the shepherds will not hesitate to climb in pursuit of their wandering sheep: from hence to the extremity of the vale, are several other protuberances of various and picturesque outlines, permitting between them several little mountain-streams to ripple down the declivities, and unite with the river below. At the semi-circular end of the curn is a waterfall of some height, but, from the scanty supply of water, it seldom makes much show.

The opposite, or north side of the vale, is in appearance somewhat like the other, but being more indulged with the vivifying power of the sun, it is much more fertile. As the beautiful flat is narrow, scarcely a quarter of a mile across, the heights on the south side of course must overshadow a small part of it, in the earliest hours of the day; but the whole valley receives the force of the sun's rays, when they are most conducive to the gentle nourishment of the corn. The north side has several easy and beautiful flowery slopes, but that most to be admired, is at a farm-house, called Llechweddgarth, the occasional summer retreat of Thomas Thomas, of Downing, in the county of Flint, Esq. An aged avenue of pine, elm, and other trees, leading to this house, denotes it to have once been a mansion of respectability. From hence, the general view of this Elysian vale, and the many beauties that surround the house, had an irresistible influence on my mind; exciting wishes, which in a state of poverty, it would have been the vainest arrogance to indulge. The rocks in front, opposed to the rich verdure below, enhance the beauty of the scene; inasmuch as the striking contrast imposes the contemplation of the richness of the one, and the grandeur of the other. The pretty secreted little church, situated in the centre of the valley, is but partially seen; a circumstance that naturally provokes the inquisitive stranger to visit and examine it; its interior is, like most other mountain-churches, plain, and void of that furniture, which characterizes the better sort of sacred buildings in towns, and better peopled districts. On the front of a poor gallery, where the *so-fa-la* gentlemen of the sod try the strength of their lungs, are some curious carvings of hares, *&c.* Here is shewn a large bone, which tradition says was the rib of a great giant: but it requires very little penetration to find out the absurdity of this supposition, for the ribs of the human skeleton, as it is well known to those but superficially acquainted with osteology, are considerably curved, while the one in question is very little bent: a circumstance decidedly in favour of the better opinion, that it must have been the rib of some other creature; the chord line of it is about three feet. In the church-yard is a recumbent monument of Jorworth Drwyndwn, or Edward with the Broken Nose, who was the father of Llywelyn the Great. Jorworth was

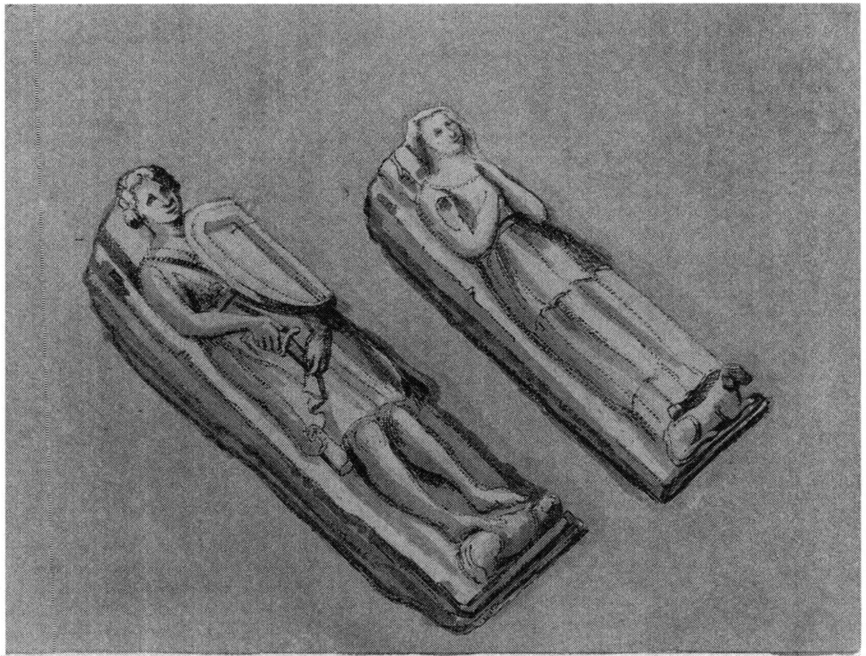

E. Pugh delt. T. Cartwright sculpt.

THE MONUMENTS OF JORWERTH DRWN DWN AND St. MELANGELL.

Published 15 Novr. 1814 by E. Williams Strand.

otherwise deformed in his legs, which the monument well describes. As the eldest son of Owen Gwynedd, he was entitled to the sovereignty of Gwynedd, or North Wales; but, on account of personal blemishes, he was not suffered to reign *, and fled here in 1176, from the cruelties of his contentious brothers; his shield has but faintly upon it this inscription, *Hic jacet Edwart*. We are informed by tradition, that he was slain near this place, at a spot called, after him, Bwlch croes Jorworth. Not far from this is another recumbent monument of a female, which may be fairly presumed to be that of St. Monacella, or as we call her Melangell; from her legend we learn that she was daughter to an Irish monarch, who intended to give her in marriage to a nobleman of his court. The princess having vowed celibacy, to prevent her father's design, fled from his dominions to this retired place for refuge, where she lived fifteen years without seeing the face of man. One day, as Brochwel Ysaythrog, prince of Powis, was out a hunting, his dogs pursued the hare to a thicket, into which, however, they would not venture; the young prince, to ascertain the cause of so strange an incident, penetrated into the woody apartment, and, to his great surprise, beheld a virgin of amazing beauty, earnestly engaged in her devotions, with the object of his pursuit (the hare) under her robes, fearlessly facing the dogs †,

* Powel's History of Wales, 227.

† To make this part of the legend probable, we may suppose this hare to be a domestic one, brought up by the lady, whose presence might have the effect of keeping the dogs away. I know a lady who, a few years ago, had a tame hare, which proved a better turnspit than any dog that preceded it in the office; while it was at play with, and chased about the garden one day, as was usual, by the house dogs, a strange dog joined the chase, and killed it.

who retired to some distance, howling hideously; nor could the sportsman oblige them to seize their prey, and when he blew his horn, it *miraculously stuck to his lips!*

Brochwel heard her eventful history, and gave to God and to her, some lands, as a sanctuary to those that should fly thither for protection. At his request she founded an abbey on the spot, of which she died abbess, at a great age. After her, this church is called Pennant Melangell; her remains were deposited under her tomb, in an oratory adjoining to the church, called Cell y Bedd, or the Cell of the Grave, from whence they have long since been removed: the rude carvings in the church of hares scudding to the saint for protection, perpetuate this legend. These were called St. Monacella's lambs. So strong a superstition prevailed in this country till the sixteenth century, that no person would destroy a hare within the precints of the parish; and, even at a later period, it was believed, that if when a hare was chased, a person should cry "God and St. Melangell be with thee," it would certainly escape.

Mr. Southey intended to give engravings of these two monuments, but was induced to decline it by a subsequent supposition that the one, said to be that of St. Monacella, was in memory of some other lady of distinction. Records do not furnish us with the account of any other lady of distinction whose monument could have here been erected, but allowing Melangell to have been the daughter of Cyvwlch, according to another story *, she was a person sufficiently distinguished to have her funeral rites followed by a monument, the appearance or the execution of which agrees well with the time in which she

* Cambrian Biography.

lived, *i. e.*, in the beginning of the sixth century. Mr. S. is rather suspicious of the history of Jorworth's monument; here appears every circumstance of probability to satisfy the historian; erected upon the spot where he lived and died, and describing those bodily defects which the several accounts of him declare he had, it stands indisputably as the monument of Jorworth. I have already noticed the neglect and careless indifference shewn to ancient remains, in several places in North Wales. To grow tired of complaining would, perhaps, only tend to encourage that palpable neglect, rather than to remove the cause of the offence, which I feel it my duty to attempt, by this plain representation, in hope that the effectual remedy may follow. These monuments being placed in the open air, do not only receive injuries from the weather, but are, every seventh day, exposed to the rudest treatment from the hands of the peasantry; who (thinking more of their Sunday dinner than the instructions of their pastor), while the bell is tolling, apply their large pocket-knives to the sides of the monuments, to give their edge a keenness commensurate with their appetite. The muscles of the right arm of the lady are here already fretted *down to the bone;* and, in a few years, if suffered to remain thus exposed, even the monuments themselves, as well as those whom they represent, will have paid the debt of nature*.

The little river, deriving its birth from the hills above, flows in a serpentine figure down the vale, the road following it through a beautiful avenue of trees. From its various windings,

* As these infractions are great infringements and draw-backs on the pleasures of the antiquarian, it would do him credit to make a parliamentary effort to prevent the recurrence of an evil, which is not confined to Wales.

and for the accommodations of the farms and cottages on the other side, there are many bridges in a short distance. It is impossible to admire too much this little paradisaical spot; it is the Vale of Clwyd in miniature:—

> "———————— Nor that sweet grove
> Of Daphne, by Orentes, and the inspired
> Castalian spring, might with this paradise
> Of Eden strive."
>
> *Paradise Lost.*

In returning, I crossed the river and the valley, skirting Moel Ddu Fawr, and ascended the heights facing it, whence I might view the whole. The scene was delightful, though I believe it suffered a little from the flat uninteresting black hills above, which rather cast a gloom over its beauty, than added any thing to it. The different rocks that nearly surround the vale, look like so many buttresses to support the vast weight of mountain above them.

The white walls of the little church glittered between the trees, while other numerous objects kept me rivetted to the spot, necessity alone obliging me to quit a scene, than which, the most fertile imagination can scarcely paint a sweeter.

The calls of appetite brought me again to Llangynog. Whilst I was amusing myself in this way, a noisy old man, a wrong-headed mountain politician, frequently interrupted the great progress I was making in the best side of a shoulder of mutton, my hungry stomach not allowing me to reply in any other way than by the monosyllables *yes* and *no*, or a significative nod of the head. When more at leisure, I paid some attention to his rusticated ideas; he lamented the hardships the poor endured, in consequence (he said) of the renewal of the war with France.

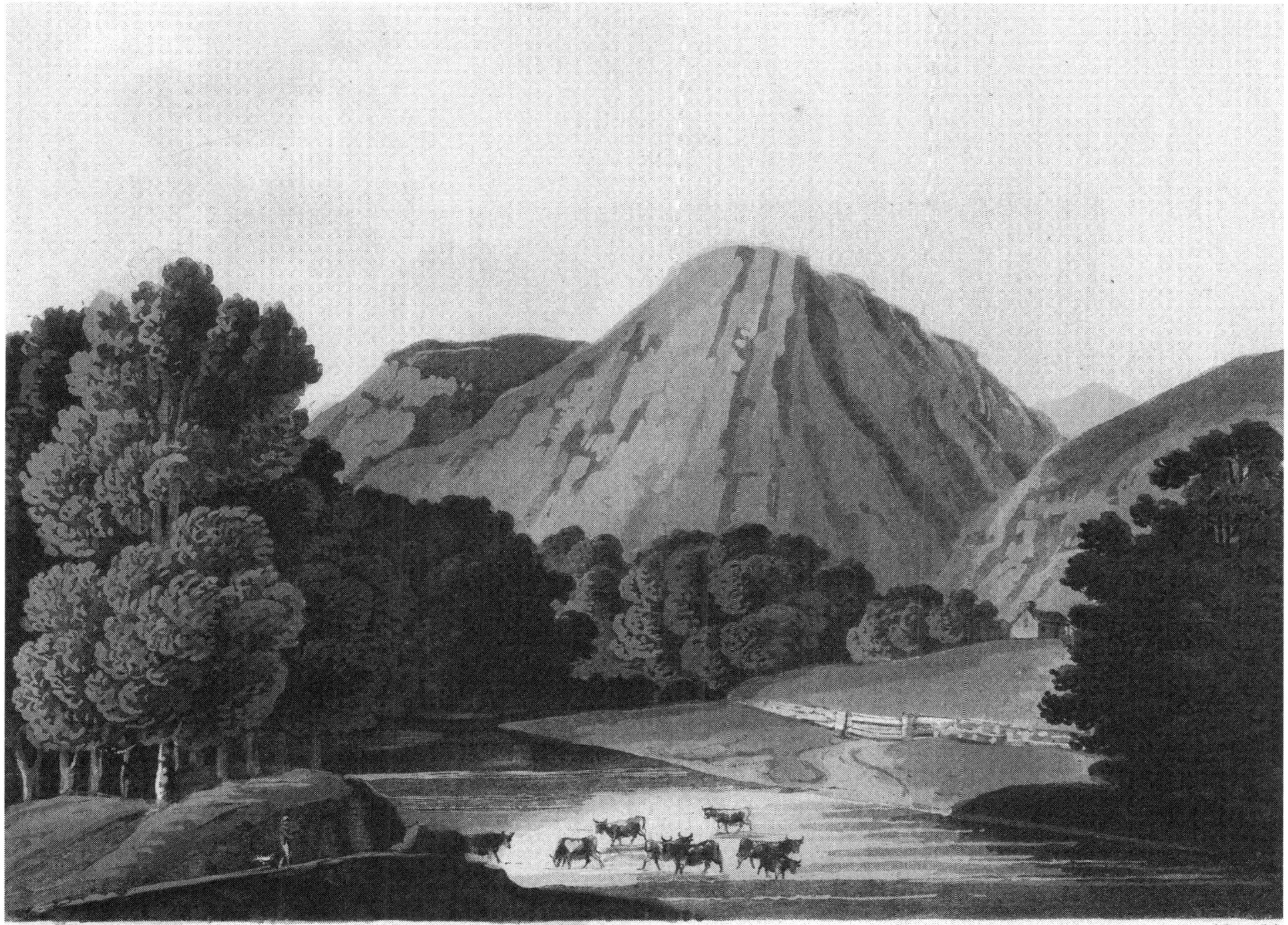

E. Pugh delt. T. Cartwright sculpt.

MOEL DDU FAWR.

Published 15 July, 1813, by E. Williams, Strand.

This being the burden of his complaints, I endeavoured to convince him of the necessity of opposing the Corsican, by stating what it appeared probable would be the case of the country, had we tamely suffered him to mature his schemes of universal empire; all this, on recollection, he was willing to admit, and it seemed to have the desired effect. "You know, my friend," continued I, "that half a loaf is better than no bread." "Certainly, sir," replied he, and added, that "it was better to suffer the little hardships of two meals a-day, for a short time, than be under the government of the *Francod* (the French)." The old man, thus worked into a pitch of loyalty, and getting very warm in reflecting upon the dire consequence of allowing the enemy a footing in his native country, swore "*Myn y Cethrel,*" "By the King of the Infernal Regions," that he, and all his countrymen, would resist to the last, and spill the last drop of Cambrian blood, ere a Frenchman should taste his mutton, ale, or rabbit *; taking off his hat very respectfully, before he applied the pint to his lips, he exclaimed, "Iechid da, a bywyd hîr i Brenin Siors ai Frenhines," *i. e.* "Good health and long life to King George and his Queen:" upon which I immediately rose, doffed my beaver, and giving him my hand (to which, by the bye, he gave though unintended, a very unpleasant gripe), we drank the toast together. The old man bending to his chair, I requested he would stand up a little longer, as I wished also to give a sentiment; we got into the same attitude as before, but by some accident, in taking off his hat, the old boy's wig slipped on the hearth, among the hot cinders; scorning to let such a trifling event take off his attention, he patiently waited for my

* Originally called rare-bit, toasted bread and cheese put into a bowl of ale.

words, which run thus :—"Confusion to Boney, and disappointment to his schemes." It was ridiculous to see with what avidity he dispatched the remainder of his pint of ale; scarcely had I uttered the first words, ending with Boney, when he precipitated the contents, in his hurry, a part to its proper destination, the remainder over his waistcoat, small-clothes, and shoes. On quitting the house, the old boy accompanied me to the door, and as long as he could keep me in view, continually shouted, "Confusion to Boney, confusion to Boney!" which I heard at the distance of some hundreds of yards off.

The numberless instances I have witnessed, of the loyal spirit of my countrymen, fully convince me of their strong attachment to their king and country. This spirit, so universally diffused at present, seems to have been equally prevalent in the days of Elizabeth; we may learn from Churchyard's Dedicatory Epistle to the Queen, what then was the temper of the Welsh: "In trueth," says he, "your highness is no sooner named among them, but such a generall rejoysing doth arise, as maketh glad any good man's hart to behold or heare it: it proceeds of such an affectionate favour, for let the meanest of the court come downe to that countrey, he shall be so saluted, halsed, and made of, as though he were some lord's sonne of that soil." Among them, however, may be found too many whose loyalty, ill understood, may be too prompt to hurry them on to acts of violence. Persons of the unreflecting class, though sometimes of the middling rank, as little acquainted with the science of government, as they are with the system of the universe, are too apt to fall into these improprieties. With such I would persuade strangers to decline all political conversations; lest any expressions, however loyal should be misconstrued by ignorance, and consequently produce maltreatment.

The next morning I left the hospitable house of Garthgylyen Vawr, for Bala. I passed once more the village of Llangynog, on a good road, leaving the infant river Tanad on my left, streaming down a romantic valley; which, though verdant enough, fell far short of its neighbour, the enchanting vale of Pennant. The last mile of this ascent, before we reach the summit, is called Milltir Gerig, or the Stony Mile, from the circumstance of its being peculiarly rocky.

In the beginning of July, 1804, happened an extraordinary instance of the preservation of a child. A boy, five years old, son of one William Richards, of Rhos-y-Gwale, near Bala, with another boy about the same age, went on the hills to gather whinberries. Being very earnest in pursuit of this (to them) delicious fruit, they separated to too great a distance to be within call of each other; and after repeated trials to discover his companion, the latter went home without the other. Richards, the father of the lost child, was out two nights and nearly three days, in an unsuccessful attempt to discover the boy; and the disconsolate parent returned home hopeless of ever seeing him more, and supposing that the little one had fallen into one of the many deep gutters which are on these boggy hills. In the evening of the third day, a man, driving his cart along this road, having a momentary occasion to stop his horses, heard a very pitiful moaning near him; and, on examining the spot carefully, he found the child in a leaning posture, between two large stones, at a distance of eight miles from home. In all probability he would have expired that night, as symptoms of approaching dissolution were very apparent. The reader can better conceive the joys of the parents than I can describe them. After great care and attention the child recovered.

Proceeding on this road, the northern curtain of the sky being lifted up, the beauties of the luxuriant vale of Edyrnion were unfolded. The high peak on the left is called Moelcwn Safnllwyd, upon which is a small house, built by Bell Lloyd, Esq., for the accommodation of a grousing party. Grouse in former seasons were very abundant on the Welsh hills; but of late, since it has become fashionable to invite strangers to shoot, the parties have been so numerous, that they consequently find few birds.

The highest protuberance of the Berwyn mountains, is Cader Fronwen; much to the right of this road, and not seen from it. Cader Ferwyn joins it, but is of less height.

Coming to the edge of the hill, called Drym y Sarn, I was favoured with a prospect, which, if the weather had been clearer, would have been enchanting, but a frowning sky denied me a sight of the remotest craggy prominences of this county (Merioneth). Those mountains called Arteneg, and some others nearer, shewed their craggy points involved in deep shade; the density of the clouds that canopied the hemisphere, occasioning a sable hue over all nature, rendered the whole a scene of awful grandeur which well suited a contemplative mind. The sun seemed to have lost his influence all around, and not a ray escaped to illume any part of the picture. I cannot tell why it happens, that we never (or at least very seldom) see subjects treated on canvass or paper, in this manner, unless it be owing to the difficulty of the performance. To say positively, that this is the reason, would be to wound the feelings of the landscape painters; and I should justly merit the reproaches of those ingenious artists who are at the head of their profession. Rather therefore let it be supposed, that a scene like this is observed only in misty weather; a time very unfavourable to the painter, either for the study of nature with success, or for sketching on the spot; as to colour from nature would be impossible, unless he and his apparatus could be skreened from the wet. To attain so desirable an end, a covering might be made of silk oil-case, that might go over the head, shoulders, paper, *&c.*, with a square aperture to look through, as well as to admit light; and this would, with the lately invented portable stool, afford an opportunity of studying these variations of the heavens with good effect. It is with the greatest deference that I would point out to those of the profession any thing new, or what is not usually practised: but I have often observed these grand variations with the greatest pleasure, and on the more striking appearances of these scenes, have felt a reverential fear for the Author of them. On leaving the hill, I descended quickly into a richly wooded bottom, and followed a beautiful and well cultivated country, till my attention was roused by a romantic little bridge of one arch, called Pont y Cennant, over a mountain-stream which empties itself into the Dee, just below it. I had, for a mile, accompanied a man and his wife, who were going to Bala upon a business of justice. My abrupt manner of leaving them, excited some alarm of my having been seized with a momentary delirium; and they began to be apprehensive that I might plunge over the rocks, and be drowned. On turning my eyes that way, and perceiving great solicitude in the looks of this good couple, I became as anxious to relieve them from their fears, as they were to see me safe; and, accordingly, I brought out my apparatus for sketching the savage wild before me. As soon as they perceived that all was safe, they nodded good afternoon, and went away merrily. This bridge is built from one rock to another, and is well clothed with ivy, which, falling below the lines of the arch, hides it, and makes it assume an odd appearance. The waterfall, right under it, is small: but the water seems to rush through with difficulty to a craggy bottom, where large masses of stone lie scattered about in all directions. These are full of fantastic-looking holes, wrought by the rotary motion of the water in flood times, which add greatly to the picturesque appearance of the scene; and this is still more heightened by rugged rocks on each side, and the adjoining hills above. On the left of the road is Rhiw-Waedog, or the Bloody Brow, an old house belonging to the Dolbens. On the height above the house, was fought a hard battle between Llywarch Hên *, or Llywarch the Aged, and the Saxons: in which, his only surviving son, Cynddelw, was slain. Not far is Llywarch's tent, or Pabell Llywarch Hên, where, it is said, that he finished that affecting elegy, wherein he so feelingly lamented the loss of twenty-three of his twenty-four sons, who fought and fell in the same cause. In this very elegy, he gives directions to Cynddelw to defend the brow of the hill:—

"Cynddelw, cadu dithau y Rhiw;
Arr a ddêl yma heddiw
Cubel am ûn mab nyd gwiw †."

Llywarch was no less celebrated as a poet than a warrior; for the Triads say, that "He was ranked with Llemenig and

* J. D. Rhys's Grammar, 103.

† Llywarch died at the great age of about 150 years: and tradition says he died and was buried in a solitary cell, near Llanfor, Bala.

Heiddyn, as the three free guests of the court of Arthur, in consequence of their eminence as bards."

One of his sons was called Sandde Bryd Angel, or Sandde of Angelic Mien. This British Ganymede, with two others, had a singular escape from the battle of Camlan; owing their safety, as is asserted, to the beautiful symmetry of their persons. Sandde was so extremely handsome, that his enemies opened a passage for him, no one appearing at all hostile, as they all supposed him supernatural.

Pursuing my way over Pen-y-Bont-bridge, at the influx of Pimblemeer into the Dee, I came to Bala, *the Outlet of a Lake.*

CHAPTER VII.

Bala.—Llanycib.—Mr. Lloyd.—Glan-y-Llyn.—Caer Gai.—Castell Condochon.— Fachddeiliog.—Flanfawr.— Bodweni.—Llanderfel. —Crogen.—Llandrillo.—Vale of Edeirnion.—Cynwyd.—Llangar. —Corwen.—Pont y Glynn.—Rûg—Owen Glyndwr.—Moel Forfydd. — Llandysilio-hall. — Crow-castle. —Plas-yn-Pengwern.— Glynnceiriog.—Llangollen.—Llanegwest.—Aqueduct.

BALA, within these twenty years, has been much improved: a circumstance which may have been occasioned partly by the frequent unfavourable notices of those tourists, who, with their judicious and friendly remarks, wished only to remove such objects as, if suffered to remain, would not only be offensive to the eye of strangers, but be perpetual nuisances to the inhabitants. This should ever be the aim and end of all criticism or remark, whether it come in the shape of praise or reprehension; and they whom it may concern, should regard it with no other view. The principal street is *now* kept very clean; and, in consequence of the example of the better sort, the poor people vie with each other in the repair and decorations of their houses. This street presents the stranger with the most grotesque assemblage of houses,—some high, some low; some new, some old; some good, and some bad.

Portland-place falls infinitely short, when put in competition with it, so far as it interests the lovers of art. A thought naturally arises from this comparison. The modern method of building in London, with respect to arrangement, may be justly challenged for want of true taste; as the continuity of parrallel lines, the sameness in the elevation of the houses, in short, the great formality in the whole, makes them ever offensive to the eye. Whoever looks at Grosvenor-square with attention, will soon be persuaded of the striking difference between it and Russel-square, or any other square in the west end of the town: the deviation from uniformity (though even this deviation is too little and imperfect) rendering it the handsomest square in London. Nothing is more evident to the artist and the connoisseur, who are but a little acquainted with the new streets in the vicinity of Cavendish-square, than the tiresomeness of their regularity. It is enough to weary the mind into impatience to quit a scene that cannot indulge it with any variety: the whole street is seen at once, an uninterrupted line of houses, of the same plan on each side. At the north-east entrance into Bala, is an immense tumulus, which, as Mr. Pennant supposes, had upon it a Roman work to defend the pass to the sea. A mile north-west of the town, is Rhiwlas, the seat of Richard Price, Esq. Some alterations which it has lately undergone render its appearance modern, and good: it is situated on the elevated banks of the river Troweryn, commanding a various and extensive view of the country around. The next morning, in the company of a gentleman of the place, we set out on a rambling excursion round the lake. The first object of notice was the little church of Llanycib, in a pretty situation on the north-west shore of the lake. On a tablet in the church is the following epitaph, from the pen of the late celebrated John Wilkes, Esq.

"Sacred to the memory of Evan Lloyd, Clerk of this parish, who died January 26th, 1776, aged 42.

> "Oh, pleasing poet—friend for ever dear!
> Thy memory claims the tribute of a tear;
> In thee were join'd whate'er mankind admire,
> Keen wit, strong sense, the Poet's, Patriot's fire,
> Temper'd with gentleness: such gifts were thine—
> Such gifts with heartfelt anguish we resign."

JOHN WILKES, *Arm. Scrib.*

Mr. Lloyd was of Jesus College, Oxford, where in June, 1757, he took the degree of M. A.: he was much esteemed as an author. His first production was a poem, called "The Powers of the Pen," 4to. in 1765. The second, "The Curate's Address to all of that denomination in England and Wales," 4to. The third, a poem, called "The Methodist," 4to. This being deemed a libel upon a gentleman in this neighbourhood, the issue of a trial was confinement in the King's-Bench; where he became first acquainted with Mr. Wilkes, with whom he continued in strict friendship to the time of his death. The fourth production of his pen was "Conversation," a poem, 4to. The fifth, "An Epistle to David Garrick, Esq." 4to. The sixth, "An Ode, on opening the new Exhibition-room of the Royal Incorporated Society of Artists of Great Britain." Mr. Lloyd's residence, called Fron, may be seen on the side of the hill between this church and Bala.

We proceeded along the road, frequently enjoying a peep at the lake, till we came to the gate of Glan-y-Llyn, a fishing-box belonging to Sir Watkin William Wynn, Bart. Its situation is very agreeable, on an easy slope, near the lake: it is intended to hide the offices by quick growing trees; at present they are as much exposed as the front of the building. The house has two very good parlours, and several smaller apartments on the ground-floor; and above them are the best bed-rooms with small windows, placed immediately under the large projecting eaves. This mode of roofing houses is rather fashionable, but from what corresponding motives they became so it is difficult to learn, as, with the grave and awful air of a mausoleum, they rather command the reverence of the beholder, than tend to excite in him pleasurable sensations. The first time I ever saw a modern projecting roof, it instantly occurred to me that it might serve well as illustrative of a misanthrope, with a slouched hat over his eyes, not wishing to look any one in the face. The melancholy appearance of these jutting eaves but ill accords with the conviviality of the company below them, and are better suited to another description of edifices, as is instanced in that noble building, St. Paul's, Covent-garden; a style which has never failed to give ample satisfaction to all lovers of architecture. The slips of land which dip into the lake, as seen from Glan-y-Llyn, give it an agreeable variety not perceivable from other situations, and, upon the whole, this is an enviable spot. Sir Watkin has upon this water a lugger-rigged boat, and, when under sail, it is a great ornament to the scene. Continuing our walk further on this road, we came to Caer Gai, now a farm-house, though formerly inhabited by one of the first families in the country. On a piece of ground adjoining to the house, are the indisputable remains of a Roman station; tiles, and the delicate small Roman bricks, are continually turned up.

Notwithstanding that the native historians ascribe to Gai Hir ab Cynyr, King Arthur's foster-brother, the building of a castle on this spot, there is better reason to conclude it to have been

Roman, and erected by Caius to defend the passage, as many Roman coins, especially those of the Emperor Domitian, have been found here. Here resided that eminent writer, Mr. Rowland Vaughan, whose translation of Bishop Bayley's "Practice of Piety," and other works, into Welsh, contributed greatly to improve the morals of the people. Two miles from hence is an angle formed by the hills, where, on a very high rock, are the ruins of Castell Condochon, of which no part is entire. Tthere are some small reliques of two rooms, in walls of excellent workmanship, standing a few yards out of the ground, but their use it is not easy to ascertain. One side is marked by a deep fosse. The castle was built with mortar mixed with gravel and sea-shells: the founder, as I understand, is not known.

The approach to this castle is very troublesome, even on the best side, but we ascended by the worst and most difficult road, climbing over very rude and dangerous precipices. About fifty yards from the summit, we were struck with the singularly-threatening appearance of immensely large stones, so oddly stationed, as to alarm us not a little for the safety of the cottagers below. The largest of these stones, which is called Carreg Diddos, or, a Stone giving Shelter (as it gave some years since, to a brace of sheep-stealers), has a remarkable shape. It forms one half of a square, and rests upon its angle; by which position, both ends are thrown up, so as to occasion an appearance which fills the beholder with dread, lest a puff of wind, or any slight accident, should hurl it down this nearly-upright precipice, and shatter to pieces the houses at the bottom. The people have driven wedges of stone under it, to prevent mischief, but this precaution seems insufficient to satisfy the anxious mind of the spectator, who, the more he views

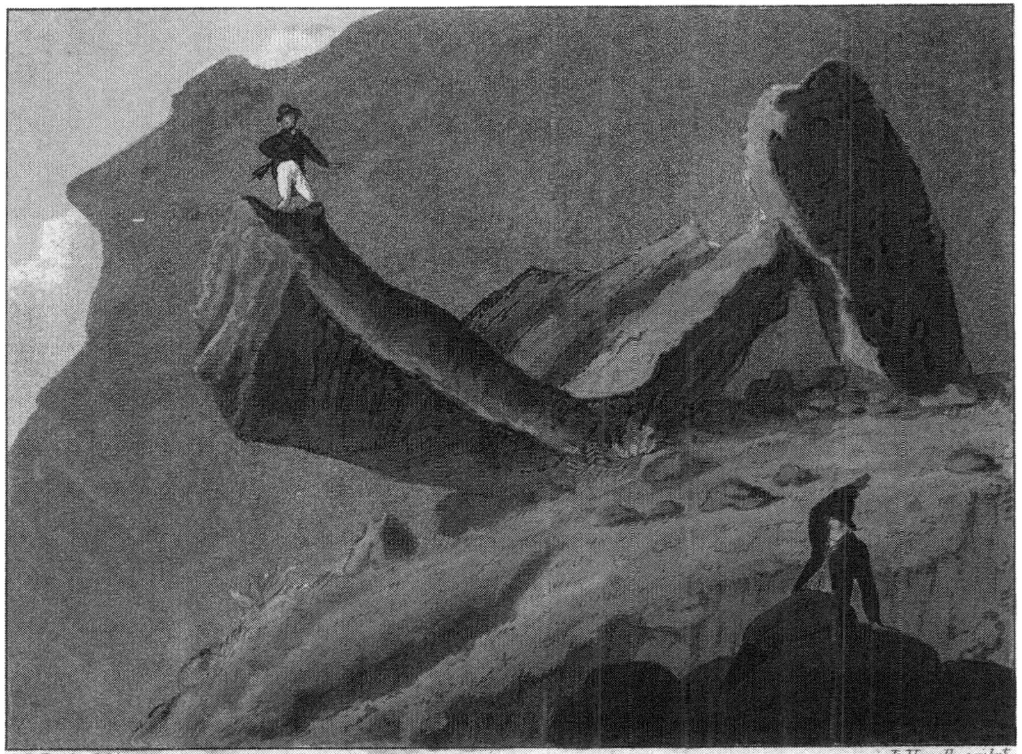

E. Pugh del[t]. I. Havell sculp[t].

CARREG DIDDOS.

Published 15th Nov[r] 1814, by E. Williams, Strand.

it, the more strongly will he imagine that the equilibrium is lost, and that it preponderates over the frightful fall. Whilst I walked on that part,. my companion could not divest himself of fears, lest the stone and I should set off together. Though I ventured upon it, I confess my apprehensions grew upon me, on recollecting (as the reader may suppose from a sight of the print) that a weight much less than my own, might overturn it. It measures round, ninety feet; across the centre, near sixteen feet; and its thickness three feet.

Upon the river, which takes its rise in the mountains, and runs westward of the castle, is a good waterfall, called Rhyadr y Mowy. Our time being circumscribed, we did not go very near to it; but I saw so much of it as to have no doubt, that the artist and the stranger might derive pleasure from a visit to it. The body of water came rushing down with violence over craggy rocks, which seemed dreadfully shattered, and from the height of the fall, and other appearances which it exhibits, I conclude that it must be very picturesque. We now made for the road, and across some beautiful meadows to Llangower church, pleasantly situated on the north-east banks of the lake, the landscape on the other side appearing to great advantage. A little further, on the left of the road, in a field belonging to Pant-yr-Onnen, or Ash-Vale-farm, is a large stone, placed vertically in the ground, and is the remaining supporter of a cromlech, long since demolished. Prosecuting our walk along the road, we were treated with very fine prospects, although, perhaps, not sufficiently diversified. We now approached Fachddeilog, a very neat summer-box, the property of Sir Richard Colt Hoare, and Sir John Leicester, Barts.; at whose joint expense it was erected. These gentlemen visit the place in the summer months;

the spot must be peculiarly well adapted to the inquisitive and exploring mind, situated as it is in the very centre of North Wales, from whence excursions can be made with great ease and convenience. The valuable researches of Sir Richard, as an antiquary, or the sketches of his fine pencil, as a man of taste, may from hence be pursued much more to his satisfaction, than if he had fixed his station in any other place. Fachddeilog is very different from its neighbour, Glan-y-llyn. The rooms are all upon the ground-floor; the centre is occupied by a very handsome one, of thirty feet by twenty-four, with three windows, forming a sextant of a circle; on each side are two smaller rooms, the one a breakfast parlour, the other a bed-chamber. The accommodations for the servants are in a farm-house adjoining, to which there is a vaulted communication. This farm-house, from the judicious contrivance of the architect, has not any appearance of interfering with the new building. A lobby runs the whole length of the house, into which the doors of the several apartments open. The external front is extremely handsome, having a row of columns running along it, except where the dining room projects in the centre. Yet, handsome as this building must be allowed to be, it does not seem to assimilate well with the nature of the country. It may be deemed a degree of presumption in an obscure individual, to criticize on the style of building adopted by gentlemen of acknowledged taste: but, while I may be too much biassed as to the homogeneity of landscape, I am inclined to believe, that when gentlemen are wedded to one particular branch of architecture*, the situation

* This opinion is not peculiar to our author; but it stands on no just principle of taste, and must be regarded as altogether fantastic. During the Roman occupation of this country, it is probable that many classic villas arose on the borders of this lake, and were

is too little consulted, and that hence we see so many modern Roman, and modern Gothic buildings introduced among our hills, instead of the ancient castellated edifice, which is better suited, in my idea, to the wildness of the surrounding scenery. From this house some noble objects are seen at every turn, and among them the high, uplifted, pointed rocks, called the Arrenig, with other charming and diversified scenery, bordering upon the lake of Bala. The little town of Bala is just sufficiently removed, to destroy the bad effect of a nearer view. I have been pretty lavish on the picturesque effect of the internal part of this town, but as I am now speaking of the *tout ènsemble*, I hope I may be understood to speak only of the mere exterior, which has nothing to recommend it, as it lies upon a flat, without even a church-tower to give it a single prominent feature.

We descended into the road, and crossing the bridge, entered the town, after an agreeable ramble of about thirteen miles. To the stranger this must be a pleasant excursion on horse-back, as there is a good road round the lake, and through the village of Llanúchlyn; where, favoured with the weather, he will have an opportunity of seeing the devastation at Pont-y-Pandu; and where, if inclined, he may find a guide to direct him in the ascent of Arran Benllyn, one of the highest of the Welsh mountains.

The lake called Llyn-Tegid, from Teged Voel, or Bald-headed Tegid, a chieftain who lived on its banks, in the fifth century, is sometimes called Pimble Meer. It is a noble expanse of

scattered amid the neighbouring vallies, and who will pretend to assert that they were not as congruous with the surrounding scenery of hill, wood, and water, as the barbarian fortresses, which succeeded to them? What is there in picturesque scenery which peculiarly and naturally associates it with the ideas of gloom, bloodshed, and barbarism? C. S.

water; its length is four miles, its breadth near three fourths of a mile, and its greatest depth forty-six yards, and its boundaries are in general of easy slopes. Great winds from the south-west, even unaccompanied with rain, will make it overflow most of the vallies in the way to Chester. The fish found in it are—perch, pike, trout, eels, and that alpine fish, called gwyniad; the salmo cavaretus of Linnæus is here in great plenty. The fishery of this lake was once the property of the monks of Basingwerk-abbey; Owen Brogyntyn having granted it to God, St. Mary, and the monks of that house; but the whole of it is now claimed by Sir Watkin Williams Wynn. The Dee has long been celebrated by the English bards for its sanctity, and was reputed to foretel events by changing its channel, and, without the intervention of rain, overflowing its banks. From its attributes, the appellation of Duw, *Divine*, has been bestowed upon it; but its generally accepted name, as has been said before, is Dwrdwy, or, "The Waters of Two Springs," anglicised "the Dee."

Bala was formerly dependent on the castle of Harlech. Finian de Stanedon being constable of that castle in Edward II.'s time, this place was committed to his care; and Edward III. rewarded his general, Walter de Mannie, with the fee-farm of Bala and Harlech; and, further, made him sheriff of the county for life*.

Bala boasts of two good inns. At the Bull's Head I found great civility; the servants are attentive, and the business of the house is done with an ease which I have not often seen. Here is a coffee-room, where the gentlemen of the town assemble to read the papers, and where strangers are admitted with much welcome.

Leaving Bala, I went on towards Corwen. The first object which engaged my attention was the pleasant village of Llanfor,

* Dugdale Baron, ii. 149.

one mile off; the church of which is situated upon the acclivity of a hill, from whence the prospect stretches out over Bala lake; where Arran Benllyn darting its serrated head into the clouds, with the noble rocks beyond Pantgwin, and Cader Idris, at the distance of twenty-five miles, covered over with a beautiful air-tint, serve to give the nearer objects a better effect. On ascending the hill, I perceived the scene which I have just described, improve very much, and becoming still more and more bold as I got upon more elevated grounds. One can hardly fancy a more pleasant and agreeable situation than this; the surrounding prospects exhibiting the greatest luxury in vegetable nature. The valley beneath seems profusely rich in pastures, while the slopes and banks are covered with plentiful crops of corn. A few yards above this church is a tumulus, whose head has been reduced, but for what purpose I could not learn: it was originally of much larger dimensions than the one at Bala. The road now led me by the side of the Dee, and I found myself shut up in a beautiful sylvan country, every fifty yards of which presented new features of rich scenery of wood, hill, and water.

By the side of the river that flows gently through the meadows, which are now much confined between the hills, the pictures are very numerous, and they are always decorated with trees well grouped, between which are frequently observable other good secondary objects. Following the river is preferable to ascending the heights on either side, as the more picturesque objects beyond Bala are considerably diminished by so great a removal from the eye, and there is nothing in the intermediate space to remedy the deficiency. It will be necessary for the artist frequently to leave the road, if he wishes for good studies.

I met here with a poor woman, an inhabitant of the neighbourhood, gathering sticks upon the road, with her unfortunate idiotic son, who was confined to his mother's side by means of a string attached to both their waists. Whilst I was exchanging a few words with the mother, the son eyed me for a moment with that vacant stare so common to those in a similar condition: he then bent his eyes to the ground, eagerly watching his mother's motions, and when she set forwards, he studiously placed his feet in the prints made by her's, which I suppose he did with precision, as every step seemed to give him great pleasure. He was eighteen years of age, nearly six feet high, and an extremely handsome figure: walked erect, and with a grace unusual to those of his description.

The scene continued variable and picturesque about the river, which now assumed a bolder aspect, frequently plunging among rocks and dark shady woods, and forming excellent studies for the painter. Bodweni, the residence of Mr. Evans, is in a most enviable spot on the banks of the Dee: the quiet that reigns here amidst wood, water, meadows, and mountains, renders the situation one of the happiest that can be conceived. To none can this neighbourhood be more suitable than to those who are devoted to either of the three sister arts. The tranquillity of its scenes, the moderate price of provisions, the peacefulness of its inhabitants (whose freedom from excesses, and whose apparently innocent, blameless, yet cheerful, conduct through life, render them happy objects of imitation), all combine in recommending this spot as a most desirable retreat.

"To Temperance all our liveliest powers we owe,
She bids the judgment wake, the fancy glow:
For her the artist shuns the fuming feast,
The midnight roar, the Bacchanalian guest;

And seeks those softer opiates of the soul,
The social circle, the diluted bowl—
Abhors the haunts of noisy bustling trade,
And steals serene to solitude and shade:
There calmly seated in his village bower,
He gives to noblest themes the studious hour;
While Genius, Practice, Contemplation, join
To warm his soul with energy divine."

From hence the draftsman might, with great facility, visit the most romantic scenery of North Wales. To Dolgellau is a distance of twenty miles; to Bethgelert and Snowdon, the noble and magnificent scenes of Tan y Bwlch, or Festiniog, twenty-five miles; to the rich scenery of Llangollen, twenty miles; to the woody glens, and the beautiful variety about Mallwyd, seventeen miles; and he may thence easily reach the banks of the Virnwy, at Dolanog-bridge; and the vale of Myfod. On the roads leading to all these places, many good and excellent subjects for the canvass present themselves. Mr. Evans very politely walked with me through the different mazes about the river; which the several tributary torrents and streams, between Pimblemeer and this place, swelled to a very formidable appearance. The bed of the river is very rocky; and the many abrupt turnings in it have, from length of time, not only formed these rocks into most fantastic forms, but, assisted by the incessant action of the water, have worn and excavated its channel to a vast depth; and formed those numerous black pools, which so exquisitely harmonize with the different circumstances, which here in their union, constitute the picturesque. This aspect of the scene is conspicuous for two miles further: but the artist must prepare himself for crossing the river frequently; and he will easily find fords and other conveniencies, which will enable him the better to choose his points. As I approached Llanderfel, the country again began to open, and exhibit scenery very dissimilar to what I had just quitted. I had often heard great things of this spot; but must have yet remained somewhat disappointed, had I not ascended the hills above the village, from whence the various mountains, between it and Bala, came in view, and at once swept away all that prejudice which the first sight of the place had created. The scenery is great, and there is such an extraordinary variety in it, and particularly of such majestic traits as characterize the pictures of Salvator and De Loutherbourg, that no artist will ever think it too troublesome to walk up the heights to behold it. On descending I entered the village; and curiosity not permitting me to leave the church unvisited, I found it as neat within as its external appearance promised. In a small dark room on one side of it, is a wooden figure, I believe of a lion, but the several parts of it that might have distinguished its species, are all in ruins: this is supposed to have been an appendage of the cross that proved fatal to Friar Forrest. Here was also, formerly, a long pole with an inscription upon it, said to have been St. Dorfel's walking-stick, which, some years ago, was removed to Crogen, before the time of the present resident; and has long since been lost: probably, its fate was decided in a sacrifice to an oven, or by some similar means of destruction. It would be well if such sacrilegious pilferings were properly resented and exposed: this would be the means of preserving to the churches their ancient deposits and ornaments, and of saving those ornaments from annihilation. A parishioner might with propriety have put the question, " By what authority do you arrogate to yourself a right of removing from the church, those venerable relics of antiquity, originally intended to dignify and embellish it? or, Sir, were it in your power (which it can never be) to claim a relationship to St. Dorfel himself, how can you justify your conduct, in taking from a church what he and his successors designed should always remain there?" It is remarkable how often these instances occur in Wales.

St. Dorfel Gadarn, or Dorfel the Mighty, a son of Hywel ab Emyr Llydaw, was a saint of the sixth century, and was the patron of this church: the great wooden image of him was, in ancient times, a subject of much idolatrous worship. It is said that the Welsh had a prediction that this statue should set a whole forest on fire; and it was brought to London in 1538, to supply the fuel which consumed poor Friar Forest to ashes, in Smithfield, for denying the king's supremacy. The gallows to which he was suspended by his middle, had upon it this inscription:—

"*David Dorvel Gutheran*,
As sayeth the *Welshman*,
Fetched *outlawes* out of hell.
Now he is come with spere and sheld,
In harms to burn in Smithfeld,
For in Wales he may not dwel.

"And *Forest* the frier,
That obstinate lyer,
That *wylfully* shall be dead:
In his contumacye,
The gospel doeth deny,
The Kyng to be supreme heade*.

And thus the prophecy was completed in the burning of the image, and the Forest consumed, in presence of the Lord-Mayor, Dukes of Norfolk and Suffolk, Lord-Admiral and Lord Privy Seal, and many others of the *nobility*. Bishop Latimer, placed in a pulpit opposite to the fire, endeavoured, but in vain,

* Halle's chr. ccxxxiii.

to bring Forest to a sense of the crime of opposing his religious opinions to those of his royal master, whom he denied to be the head of the church.

In the church-yard is an inscription on the grave-stone of one Gayner Hughes, who died in 1786, aged thirty-five. It is so obliterated, that I could not well transcribe it without the assistance of the clerk. It related something singular of this young woman, though in ambiguous terms. I was therefore under the necessity of making some inquiries; and have consequently found, that she lived eight years without any other sustenance than a spoonful of water per day; having not the least desire for food of any kind, and not feeling the smallest pain. She kept her bed during this time. The people say she was the greatest beauty of Meirion, and the toast of the surrounding country

On quitting the village my eye glanced upon a cottage, in which the parish school was conducted. A gentleman of very respectable appearance, whom I judged from his dress to be a clergyman, was then in the benevolent act of examining the children; and his posture of leaning over a little one, left no doubt of his solicitude for their improvement:—

> "Delightful task! to rear the tender thought,
> To teach the young idea how to shoot!"

It must carry with it its own reward, in the happy reflection that so much good is done to society, by enabling these poor children, in a little time, to know their duty as good servants and good subjects, by which instruction they may escape many evils attendant upon ignorance; the too apparent cause of much of that mischief, ignominy, and unhappiness, to which we are witness in low life.

On the south side of the river is Crogen, *or the Gill,* the seat of Bell Lloyd, Esq. : the situation of which is scarcely to be equalled. The surrounding scenery is bold and sublime; and its approximation to some of the finest points of Nant Nanhwynen, under Snowdon, is very evident. As a whole, it also commands the greatest estimation of the followers of the arts; but by pursuing the course of the Dee, the artist will find many detached pictures of the richest kind. I here crossed a handsome bridge of several arches; and from a cottage at some distance, called Tyn-y-Wern, the country behind looked very fine. A noble rock which nods over the road, and shoots up to a considerable height, is an important object, that is well contrasted with the woody acclivities, and the mountains above Llanderfel. Striking down into the meadows, the whole scene varies its form very agreeably, and becomes a rich picture.

The river side in these meadows afforded pretty woody subjects, which had a variety in them, that nearly betrayed me into the imprudent measure of following the river to Corwen: but being roused by some difficulties in the way, I recovered the road near the romantic village of Llandrillo.

This church is dedicated to St. Trillo, the son of Ithel Hael, a prince of Armorica. On entering it, I heard the authoritative voice of the schoolmaster, whom I found on the point of chastising a pretty curly-headed little boy, for some neglect or other: but on seeing me he approached with a very handsome and ceremonious bow, which would have gone off well, even at a levee, but for the unlucky pawing of his thighs, on bringing his body again to the perpendicular He readily began to dilate upon the various curiosities contained in the church : but, with all his oratory, he was not able to persuade me that it had a single article worthy of notice. The church-yard, indeed, exhibited at one view, a vast exanimate population ; a circumstance, as I should suppose, arising from the extensiveness of the parish, since the neighbourhood does not seem to abound with inhabitants. From the elevated grounds above the village, we look down upon the rich and beautiful vale of Edeirnion, the exuberant appearance of which, naturally reminds one of the Land of Promise, "flowing with milk and honey." It continues its splendour for four or five miles further to Llangar, where it terminates. Though it cannot, in point of the picturesque, pretend to rival the romantic vale of Nanhwynen, nevertheless, the mountains and rocks on each side bear sufficient marks of roughness and boldness of prominences, to arrest the attention of the artist; and the valley also, through which the Dee, with bosom broad and full, winds its course, is diversified with objects which occur in a way with which he must be highly pleased. The sides of the hills are frequently covered with wood, and the flat itself is bespread with a profusion of trees and verdure, which render it extremely beautiful. Those who may have had equal opportunities of weather and situation to view this luxuriant prospect, will not think me too lavish in its praise if I term it another Eden.

It is a matter of some surprise, that in this fertile vale there should be so few gentlemen's summer boxes: four only, I believe, are to be seen in the space of about nine miles, and some of these are stationary residences. Leaving Llandrillo, I passed, on my left, the old house of Hendwr, the occasional residence of —— Passingham, Esq. It lies low, in the woody meadows by the river side. Further on is Cynwyd, or *the Source of Mischief.* This is a pretty little hamlet, situated at the mouth of a dingle which runs up between the hills: several houses in it are concealed in a labyrinth of young wood, of almost impenetrable thickness. Though the circumstance of the wood's being of early growth renders the whole less picturesque, than if it had more age, yet there are allurements about it, which from some points become irresistible to a draftsman. Here I struck up the dingle for half a mile or so, to visit a water-fall on the Trystion. Twelve years ago I saw this subject more advantageously, for since that time some young ash-trees have, very injudiciously, been suffered to grow in front of the fall, thus precluding a sight of it from those points, whence it would best make a picture. The old mill is an object of much consequence, as from its age and figure, it increases the rustic effect of this hollow, and were the obstruction just mentioned removed, it would not only agree well with the fall, but considerably enhance the value of the whole. The water rushes down a precipice of forty or fifty feet, in one uninterrupted sheet, through a prodigious cleft in the rock, which seems to have been the effect of a momentary convulsion of nature. This fall is situated at the very top of the glen, which is shaped like an amphitheatre, and well clothed with wood.

Here is a very pleasant mountain-path to Corwen, from whence the stranger may visit this hollow in an agreeable walk before breakfast.

Returning to Cynwyd, I proceeded along the public road, leaving Gwerclas, a good-looking house, on the left; and I soon reached the village, or rather the church, of Llangar. A stile leads from the road, and over a small enclosure, to the church. A high hedge and a sort of stile of large slate-stones, placed erect, obstructs all view of the church-yard, till the instant you enter it. This seems to have been an ingenious artifice to surprise the unwary stranger. This sacred ground presents to the view a vast assemblage of elegant grave-stones, beyond any thing with which I have hitherto met: it is indeed so well tenanted as scarcely to leave room for another inhabitant. The ground of the church-yard, shaded with tall trees, is a considerable slope, so that the tombs, as well as the church, seem half sunk into the earth. Its site, upon the verge of a hill, at the junction of the Alwen with the Dee, admirably agrees with the melancholy solemnity which pervades the place. In my humble opinion, the beautiful lines of the poet were never better adapted than to this spot:—

"Beneath those rugged elms, that yew-trees shade,
Where heaves the turf in many a mould'ring heap,
Each in his narrow cell, for ever laid,
The rude forefathers of the hamlet sleep."

GRAY.

Another mile brought me to Corwen, or *White Choir*, a small town on the eastern extremity of Merionethshire. The native defenders of their country were then closing the day's exercise: a fine set of young men, expert in the manual part of their duty; their conduct under arms irreproachable; becoming soldiers, in whom attention to discipline can alone secure a fair chance of success against the enemy. The preparation for the accommodation of the volunteer officers, produced, at the inn, an unusual degree of bustle: and I became apprehensive that I should be obliged to seek my conveniencies twelve miles off: but it was soon announced that I might have a bed. I was shewn, literally, into a black hole, which they called the back parlour; a circumstance, however, to which I easily reconciled myself.

The church is of the crucifix form, and spacious: near the altar, in a niche, is a monument of one of its ancient vicars.

On the south external side of the church, is a representation of Owen Glyndwr's sword (or rather dagger), insculptured in a large stone.

It has descended to us by oral tradition, that every attempt to erect a church elsewhere in this neighbourhood, was uniformly baffled by some supernatural power: till one night the founders were directed, in a vision, to a stone, now to be seen in the church walls, called Careg-y-big, and informed, that the spot on which it stood, was to be the site of the building; which was accordingly erected without further molestation. In the church-yard is a singular cross, the shaft of which is sunk into a large stone.

Owen Gwynedd made this place the rendezvous of his forces in 1165, when he stopped the career of Henry II.: and some slight remains of his encampment are still visible above the town.

Above the town stands an immense rock, which aspires to the clouds. But though it is of great height and extent, it has no divisions, no breaks or prominences, but exhibits a continuity of line and surface, which is altogether tame and uninteresting. The church-yard has in it a college for six widows of clergymen of the established church, who die possessed of the cure of souls in this county, built in consequence of a legacy of Wm. Eyton, Esq., of Plaswarren, in 1750.

Quitting this place I made directly west, to the fall at Pont-newydd, alias Pont-y-Glynn, of the river Ceirw. I had seen this magnificent picture some years before, and could not resist the alluring temptation of visiting it once more. The river winds softly and quietly along a mountain-valley, till, meeting with this abrupt and craggy descent, the waters are poured down, under a single-arched bridge, in a volume, which becomes instantly convulsed by the resistance of the massy black crags, over which the bridge is seen pensile from rock to rock: then forcing its way, and foaming over other rude precipices and dislodged rocks, it at last finds temporary ease in a deep, large, circular basin in the bottom, from whence it starts again, over a rough bed of stone, through a deep woody dingle, which, for a quarter of a mile, is almost denied the light of day, from its vast depth, and its confinement between two high woody hills. The river, at a place called Pandy, finally finds repose, and steals along the quiet vales till its union with the Alwen. The great road from London, through Shrewsbury, to Holyhead, is brought to the verge of this scene, and is cut through the solid rock; a work of great labour. From the road this chasm is seen to advantage, but the artist will rather chuse his points from the bottom. There are difficulties that present themselves to him in descending, but, if he has had a little practice in this way in Wales, he will know how to accomplish the task. When here before, I was advised to use a long pole, which I did, and it proved very useful in leaping from one rock to another; by these means I was enabled to follow the river, and to see the noble scenery from the fall to the end of the glen. Quitting this wild and romantic hollow with much reluctance, I kept by the river side, through the beautiful meadow grounds by the old house of Maesmor, the residence of —— Lloyd, Esq., till I came to Rûg*. The old family mansion has been totally erased, and at a small distance from its site, has been erected, by the late Colonel Salisbury, of the Guards, a very handsome house, built

* Pronounced Reeg.

of a stone resembling Portland. It has two fronts; the northern distinguished from its opposite, by a portico of four columns of the Ionic order: the apartments are spacious and convenient. In both fronts the offices are judiciously kept from the eye, by a young plantation, which in a few years will prove a handsome ornament to the house. The grounds are well laid out, and, in process of time, the whole will make a show of much elegance. The colonel's brother and successor, Colonel G. Vaughan, has in his possession the dagger of Brogyntyn, and his drinking-cup *; the drinking-cups of Owen Glyndwr, and several other articles of antiquity. Here it was, that Gruffydd ab Conan, king of Wales, after his victory at Carno in Montgomeryshire, in 1077, was treacherously taken and confined by Murian Goch. Hugh Lupus had him conveyed to Chester, where he remained twelve years in prison: but at length the brave youth Cynric Hîr, of these parts, undertook his release. He went to Chester under pretext of purchasing necessaries, and watching an opportunity when the keepers of the castle were feasting, conveyed his prince away on his back to a secure retreat, notwithstanding that the king was loaden with chains.

Owen Brogyntyn, a chieftain of the twelfth century, was once the possessor of this place. He was lord of Dinmael and Edeirnion; and from this great man are descended the present family.

I soon passed the pretty little domestic chapel on the demesne; and leaving Corwen on my right, and the Dee between, I fol-

* This silver cup is called the Brogyntyn, and will hold a pint of liquor. After dinner, and on a gentleman's first visit to this hospitable house, he is presented with this cup full of ale, and after dispatching the contents at a draught, his name is recorded in a book, in which are the signatures of several thousands of gentlemen, who have had the honour of drinking out of the Brogyntyn.

lowed a bye-road for three miles, without the occurrence of any object of importance, save one general view of the vale of Corwen, which, to say the most of it in this part, with respect to the picturesque, does not come up to mediocrity. I have examined it from the most favourable situation near Llansaintffraid, but on looking down from hence towards Llangollen the difference is striking. The calcareous rocks which seem to support the vast sides of Berwyn, now assume a great boldness of character; the passes of the mountain sometimes occur, and occasion several romantic protuberances of this rocky substance, some of which are half covered with wood, and others loaded with it to the lofty summits. This rich and highly wooded valley winds and shifts its course as the great headlands protrude themselves in the way, making pictures of incomparable value. This little church is dedicated to St. Fraid, or, as the English call her, St. Braide, who lived in the seventh century. The vale (now assuming that name) of Dwrdwy, will be ever distinguished in the British annals, for having produced that intrepid hero, Owen Glyndwr, who, in the commencement of the fifteenth century, made so conspicuous a figure, as a soldier, and a defender of the liberties of his country. His house which Iolo Goch, his bard, compares, with respect to magnificence, to Westminster-abbey, was situated near this village. It was encircled by a moat, and surrounded with every thing that could administer to hospitality, a park, warren, orchard, vineyard, fishpond, *&c. &c.* The bard speaks highly of the good cheer of the house, and bestows much encomium on Glyndwr's lady, in the following strains:—

"His wife, the best of wives!
Happy am I in her wine and metheglin.
Eminent woman, of a knightly family:

Honourable, beneficent, noble.
Her children come in pairs;
A beautiful nest of chieftains."

The lady, whose virtues the bard thus celebrates, was daughter of Sir David Hanmer, of Hanmer in Flintshire, one of the judges of the King's-Bench, who was appointed to that situation by Richard II., in 1383.

Glyndwr was strongly attached to the cause of his master, Richard, with whom he was a personal favourite. He was enraged at the murder of that prince, who was also much beloved by the Welsh. The malevolent spirit of Reginald, Lord Grey of Ruthin, several times represented Owen to Henry the Usurper, as a disloyal man, who wilfully disobeyed his orders: but the fact was, that Lord Grey designedly neglected to deliver the king's commands to Owen, till the time was nearly elapsed, and it became impossible for him to get ready to attend his majesty in his expedition against the Scots. By this act of treachery, Reginald turned the king's frowns on Glyndwr, and he immediately took possession of all his lands, or such parts of his estates as were near to his own. Owen peaceably remonstrated against this violence, but without remedy. This and other acts of oppression compelled Owen to arm, and to throw off the English yoke. He retaliated most amply upon Lord Grey, recovered all his estates, and after many vicissitudes, and an indecisive struggle of fifteen years, the hero died unconquered, but predicting the total subjugation of his country, when its supporter should be no more. He died on the 20th of September, 1415, in the sixty-first year of his age, and is supposed to have been buried at Monnington; but no monument perpetuates the spot of his interment. In the year following his demise, peace was restored to both parties. Owen had been liberally educated, and brought up in one of the inns of court *, and for some time followed the profession of a barrister.

Crossing the handsome bridge of Llansaintffraid to the south side of the river, the view from its steep banks towards Llangollen, becomes excessively rich and grand. The verdant valley, with its vast profundity and its profusion of wood, in which the Dee is frequently buried, and as often seen undulating in one broad sheet, is of itself great and fine, even passing description; and every circumstance in the view seems to hold it out as a paragon of nature. The lofty mountains which flank it on the north and east, on the confines of Denbighshire, some with serrated tops, and others of conic forms, with the continuation of the Berwyn mountains on the south, and Dinas Brân-castle, peeping over a promontory in front which dips his head in the Dee, with Eglwyseg's stratified rocks at its back, make up a composition for a picture of wonderful grandeur. Such is the face of the country for eight miles to Llangollen. Moel Morfydd, a mountain in the county of Denbigh, on the opposite side of the river, is a noble object for many miles round, and Snowdon recognizes him as a rival, at the distance, as the crow flies, of sixty miles. At a place called Coed-Drwg we enter Denbighshire; and a little further on the other side of the river, is Llandisilio-hall, the residence of Thomas Jones, Esq., an amateur, and a friend of the arts. It is situated on a gentle rise, hardly perceptible, on the verge of the Dee, nearly surrounded by a profusion of wood, and by the huge mountains above, which shelter it from the chilling effects of the northern

* The Temple.

and easterly winds. The river now assumes a character very opposite to what it exhibits from its birth-place, and it rushes in torrents over a bed of black laminated rocks, worn by the unceasing and rapid circumvolution of the water, into various fantastic forms.

Near this place is shewn a chasm in the river, called Llam-y-Lleidr, or the Thieves' Leap, deriving its name from a story, for the authenticity of which I dare not vouch. A man, who had been detected in pocketing what was the property of another, perceiving no other means of escaping the punishment due to his dishonesty, took to his heels with a host of pursuers after him. But finding no way to elude the grasp of one of the foremost, who then pressed him hard, he had recourse to a stratagem: springing suddenly out of the road, his antagonist was unwarily thrown out considerably, and then gaining the river's side, as his danger gave wing to his efforts, he at once flew over the gulf, from fifteen to eighteen feet across, landed on the other side, and was never heard of more. His pursuer, nothing dispirited, came furiously to the river, and making an unsuccessful spring, plunged into the abyss, from whence he was with difficulty saved.

Gradually returning to the right for two miles, I arrived at Llangollen, where a friend of mine received me at his own house.

I cannot suppress an anecdote of an artist, who happened to call at an inn, not a thousand miles from hence, for refreshment and a bed. The circumstance would have been more ludicrous had it not happened in church-time, and on a Sunday, which prevented the insolence of the people from being so completely exposed, as it would otherwise have been. Mr. B——, the gentleman to whom I allude, on entering the house, met the waiter, who, as it seems, was lord paramount of the premises, and requested to know what he might have for dinner. The fellow eyeing him from top to toe, and without returning an answer, asked Mr. B. with a most supercilious turn of the eye, if he had brought a horse with him. "No," was the reply:—"Then," returned the other, "we have no time to provide a dinner for you." Proceeding a little further into the house, he met with the sprightly landlady, from whom he expected better and more conciliating language. But, alas! he was now as much mortified as before, as she likewise demanded whether or not he had a horse; and on finding that he was on foot, negatived his request for dinner.

Observing a lean old man in an obscure corner, eagerly devouring the refuse of a blade-bone of mutton, Mr. B. made up to him, saying, "Good appetite to you, Sir." "I am never without one," replied the other. "You are a happy man and seem to fare well. Your having a horse with you entitles you to eat, I suppose: but, pray why not have your dinner at a table, in comfort, and command the waiter to pay you some attention." "Sir," replied the poor old man, "you are mistaken: for me to *command the waiter*, would be to ensure my own rejection. To dare to enjoy my dinner in the way you prescribe, would be the most certain means to deprive me of it in any way; and as to a horse, I possess several now on these premises, yet, Sir, I am obliged to put up with insults from those whose duty it is to obey all my lawful commands. But if you have not a horse, I would advise you to seek your accommodations elsewhere." Mr. B. was greatly astonished at the relation of the old man*; and, wishing him a good day, was going to quit

* The quondam master of the house, supplanted for a reason *to be guessed at.*

the house, but meeting the waiter again in the hall, who a second time peremptorily refused to accommodate him, Mr. B. indignant at such treatment, caught hold of this bantam-cock by the collar and the tail, and sent him into the street; where he left him sprawling in the mud, greatly to the amusement of some butchers and others who were then on the spot.

Early in the morning I set out to enjoy the many grand views in the neighbourhood. The artist and the lover of picturesque scenery will here find himself surrounded with objects of wonderful grandeur, which will allow full scope both for contemplation and admiration; no part of the principality can shew so many pictures concentrated in a circle of three or four miles: one cannot go thirty yards, without observing such alterations in the grounds as form fresh views; and let the painter stroll where he pleases, he is certain of meeting many objects, that must inevitably give him the highest satisfaction. From a high rock called Craig-y-Gath, the scenery is very fine, with the town below and many other objects of much consequence. From the river a few hundreds of yards below the church, that edifice, and a part of the town, with wood and the lofty rocky mountains above, make a fine picture; a few yards below the little bridge over a mountain-stream, looking across the Dee, is a delightful spot, with the castle under a canopy of wood, rising upon the banks of the rivulet. To expatiate upon the numberless picturesque points, would be irksome to the reader, and the artist will not be at a loss, for it is not possible he should go wrong. One situation I must not omit, as strangers, not immediately concerned with the arts, may, as well as the painter, find pleasure in occupying it: I mean Dinas Brân-castle, with its varied views. Though the remains of this castle are poor, and will not form a picture from any point of its area, yet they come in well in a distance. The hill upon which it stands, is in shape of a blunted cone; it is high, but the Eglwyseg rocks, to which its base attaches, are higher. A man five years since, being gulled by a dream, begged leave of Mr. Lloyd, of Trevor-hall, to dig within the walls of the castle for treasure, which his delusive vision told him was to be found there; he toiled hard for some days, but suspecting at length, that it was but the phantasm of a drowsy man, he wisely gave up the pursuit. The vale of Glyndardwy exhibits a prospect from hence, if possible, more delightful, than from it is that of this castle, described a few pages back.

This is called by the Welsh, Castell Dinas Bran, from Brân, a proper name, as Llowarch ab Brân, or it may derive its name from the rivulet that trickles down its side, called Brân. Its founder is not known; but it has been the chief residence of the lords of Yale, one of whom, it is conjectured, gave it being. When Gryffydd ab Madog, the traitor, went over to the English in the reign of Henry III., he was obliged to secure himself against the fury of his countrymen in this air-built fastness. A circumstance is related that most strongly corroborates the repeated accounts of the cruelty of Edward I. On the death of Gryffydd, Edward committed the guardianship of his old partisan's two sons, the eldest to John Earl Warren, and the other to Roger Mortimer, two men well taught in the school of the tyrant, whose nomination to this wardship they well understood:—they accordingly destroyed the innocent children, and afterwards took possession of their estates. Mortimer seized Chirk, and Warren laid hold of Bromfield. The cruel disposition of Edward is now made a subject of doubt: but what is to become of the many historical facts; the piteous lamentations of the sufferers, and the testimony of Sir John Wynn, who wrote from MSS. of undoubted authority? Britons lament the fate of their bards, whom

"Edward's cruel sword consign'd
To slaughter all."

Leland speaks of an eagle that annually built its nest on the opposite rock, and when a person was let down by a rope to take its young, he was obliged to be secured in a basket, with another to protect his head from the gripes of the old bird.

The castle in 1390, contained the celebrated beauty Myfanwy Vechan, descended from the house of Tudor Trevor; her father then held this place, it is thought, under the Earl of Arundel. That elegant bard, Howel ab Einion Llyglieu, who flourished about 1600, fell deeply in love with this lady, to whom he addressed a poem, full of the finest touches of feeling; the concluding lines have been thus agreeably paraphrased by the Rev. R. Williams of Vron, near Mold:

"And cans't thou, without pity, see
The victim of thy cruelty;—
Pale with despair, and robb'd of sleep,
Whose only business is to weep?—
Behold thy Bard, thy Poet, languish,
Oh! ease thy Bard's, thy Poet's, anguish;
And for Heaven's sake, some pity shew,
Ere to the shades of night I go!
O fairer than the flowers adorning
The hawthorn in a summer's morning!
While life remains I still will sing
Thy praise, and make the mountains ring
With fair Myfanwy's tuneful name;
And from Misfortune purchase fame.
Nor e'er to die shall I repine,
So Howel's name may live with thine."

The next morning I went to a beautiful retired valley close to this village, to see Plâs, or Llys Pengwern, the seat of Tudor Trevor, Earl of March and Hereford, about the year 924, whence the Mostyns of Mostyn are lineally descended; and it is still their property Several of the windows of this house are still perfect; some of the rooms also, now occupied as hay-lofts, *&c.* have their original ceilings with arched ribs. In the side of the house is a large stone lately found, when making some alterations, and judiciously inserted there; it has upon it an inscription, and a carved representation of a sword. The inscription is evidently a fragment, it is the name, Gronw ab Jorwerth. The Mostyn family derive themselves from Jorwerth ddu of Pengwern.

From hence I climbed the mountain south of the town, to Llansaintfraid Glyn Ceiriog, frequently arrested in my way by the magnificent scenery round the town. Crossing this uninteresting mountain, I came in sight of Glynn Ceiriog, and descending a very steep hill, passed through this straggling, odd-looking village, at the end of which, on inquiring of a person my way to a place two miles further, he very readily volunteered to accompany me to it. The romantic scenery of this mountain-pass is very excellent, and nearly wears that appearance of nudation, so apparent in Nant Beris in Carnarvonshire; and though unattended with the terrific variety which is to be met with there, yet it has sufficiently connected with it, rocks and mountains, with the river Ceiriog making its way through the vale, to give a faint idea of the above place. Craig * y Velin Deirw is a noble object, very high, and shattered into good

* Craig, a Rock.

forms. At the foot of this rock, five years ago, an immense block of stone, of many tons weight, started from its bed, and came down the mountain with great velocity; a house was exactly in its way, but, happily for the inhabitants, who were all at home, it was prevented doing them mischief, by other stones which lay in the same line. It bounded horribly, attended by a loud crashing noise, that called forth the attention of the people, and the last bound that it made, was into the midst of these stones. We arrived at the extremity of the pass, a visit to which I would recommend to the artists who come to Llangollen. At the extremity of the pass, my companion turned into a farm-house, where he was well known, to light his pipe, which he carried about as a stomachic, and, as he conceived, a remedy against the oppression of the lungs. A young female, dressed in the russet mountain-habit, much attracted our admiration: so much beauty and simplicity appeared through all her guise, as might have beguiled the heart of a prince; her manner of tendering the delicacies the house afforded, was so artless and unaffected, that we could not resist the temptation of accepting something from her hand. A thought arose, which those of my profession are allowed to indulge, to request she would give me leave to draw her likeness; this she no sooner understood, than her beautiful face was become suffused with as much rouge, as would have served half a dozen stage lovers; all my endeavours, seconded by those of my guide, proving unavailing, I tried what could be done by stealth, a scheme that met with no better success: immediately concealing her beauties and her blushes with her apron, she obliged me, with whatever reluctance, to give up the contest.

Parting with my civil companion, I returned by the way I

came, to the summit of the mountain, and then turned to the left, to the extremity of the woody glen, called Nant-y-Bache. At first it is narrow, the semicircular end of it covered with thick wood, through which issues a rippler, that experiences a fall of many feet; from the profusion of young wood about it, it is barely seen: but it would make a show, if a few saplings were cut away. This rivulet pours down its agitated waters through the glen, murmuring as it rolls over its craggy bed, for two miles; till it finds partial repose in the bosom of the Dee. Here is a handsome walk through the wood to Llangollen. The artist would be highly delighted with this spot, looking down from which he will recognize the rocks of Eglwyseg, and Crow-castle, detached from the woods, and the rocky eminences on both sides. The glen, about half way down, opens, and shews some finely cultivated farms, with their houses mounted on high, and often half hid with wood; rendering the whole highly picturesque.

This is altogether so beautiful a retreat, that no strangers making any stay at the village, should leave it unvisited. It is, indeed,—

> " ———— A pleasant grove
> With chaunt of tuneful birds, resounding loud;"

a delightful spot, that cannot fail to produce the most lively sensations in the minds of all, those only excepted who are stupidly lost to the pleasures of rural scenes like this. The best way, for the sake of variety and contrast, would be to ascend the mountain road, and return by the walk through the wood

Llangollen is a large village, but meanly built; nevertheless, it is excellently adapted to the wildness of the scenery that surrounds it; in which respect, any thing else than what it is, would

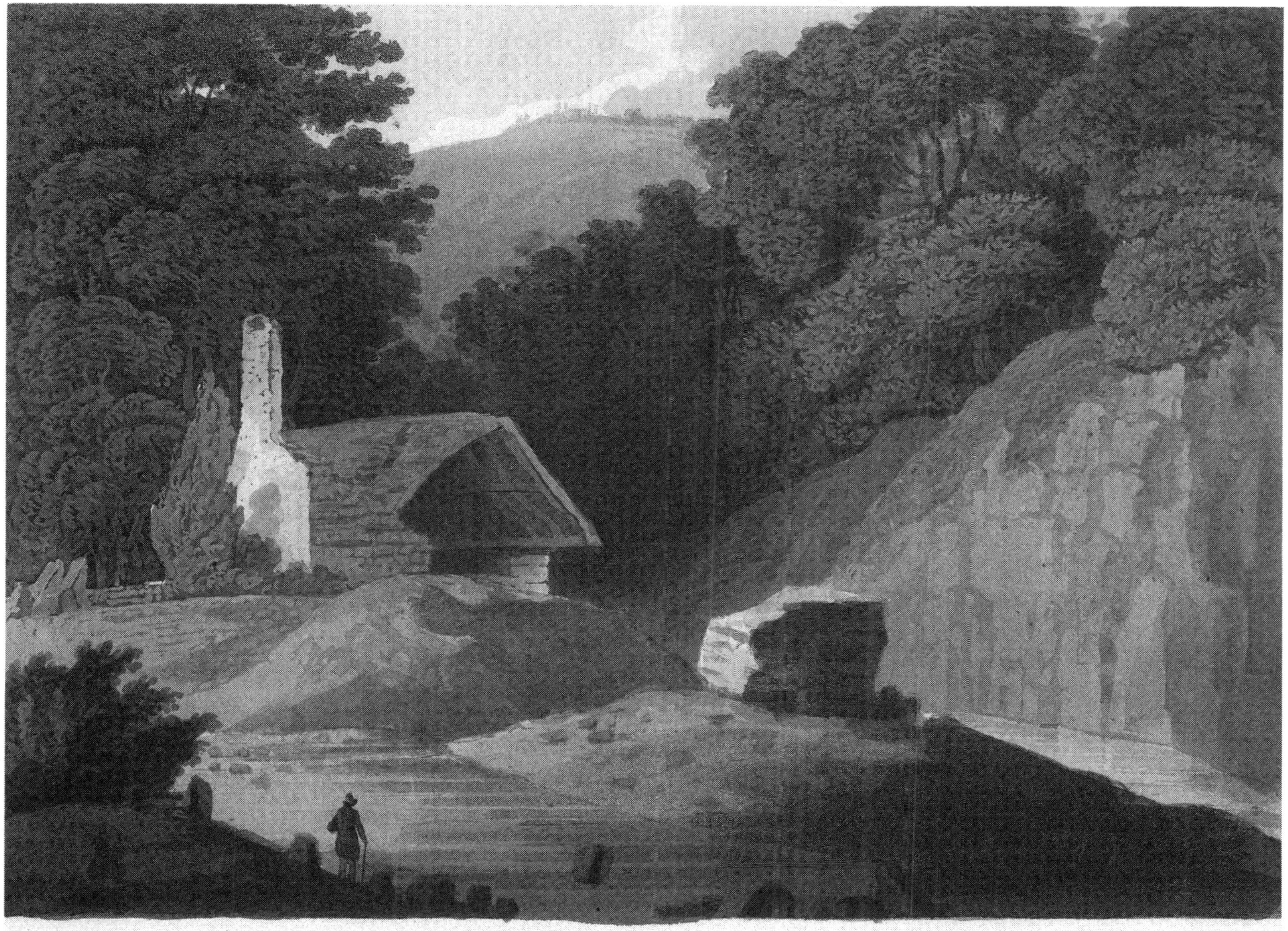

ON THE STREAMLET CROSSING LLANGOLLEN.

Published 15th April, 1813, by E. Williams, Strand.

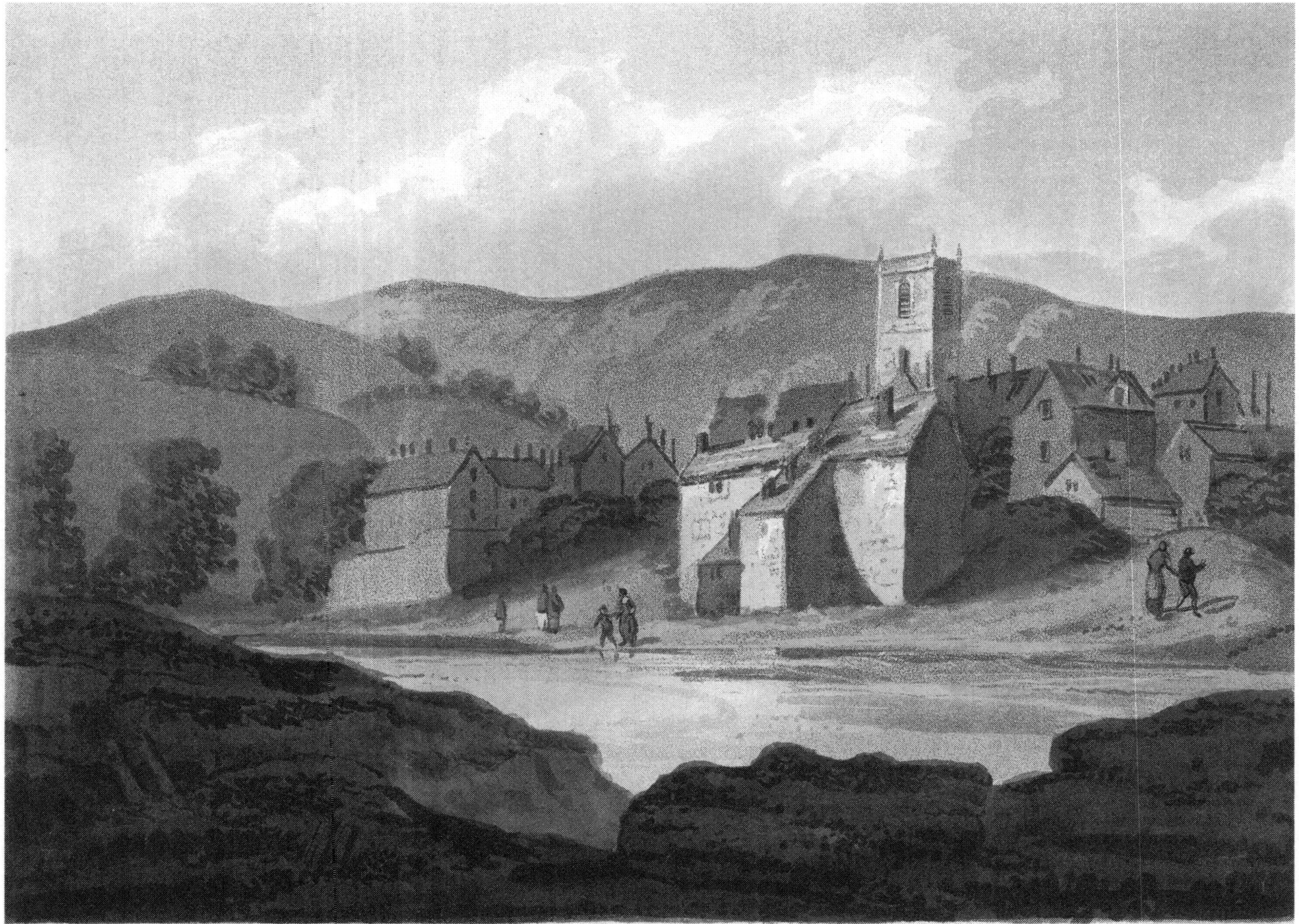

E. Pugh del. T. Cartwright sculp.

LLANGOLLEN.

Published 15 January 1825, by E. Williams, Strand.

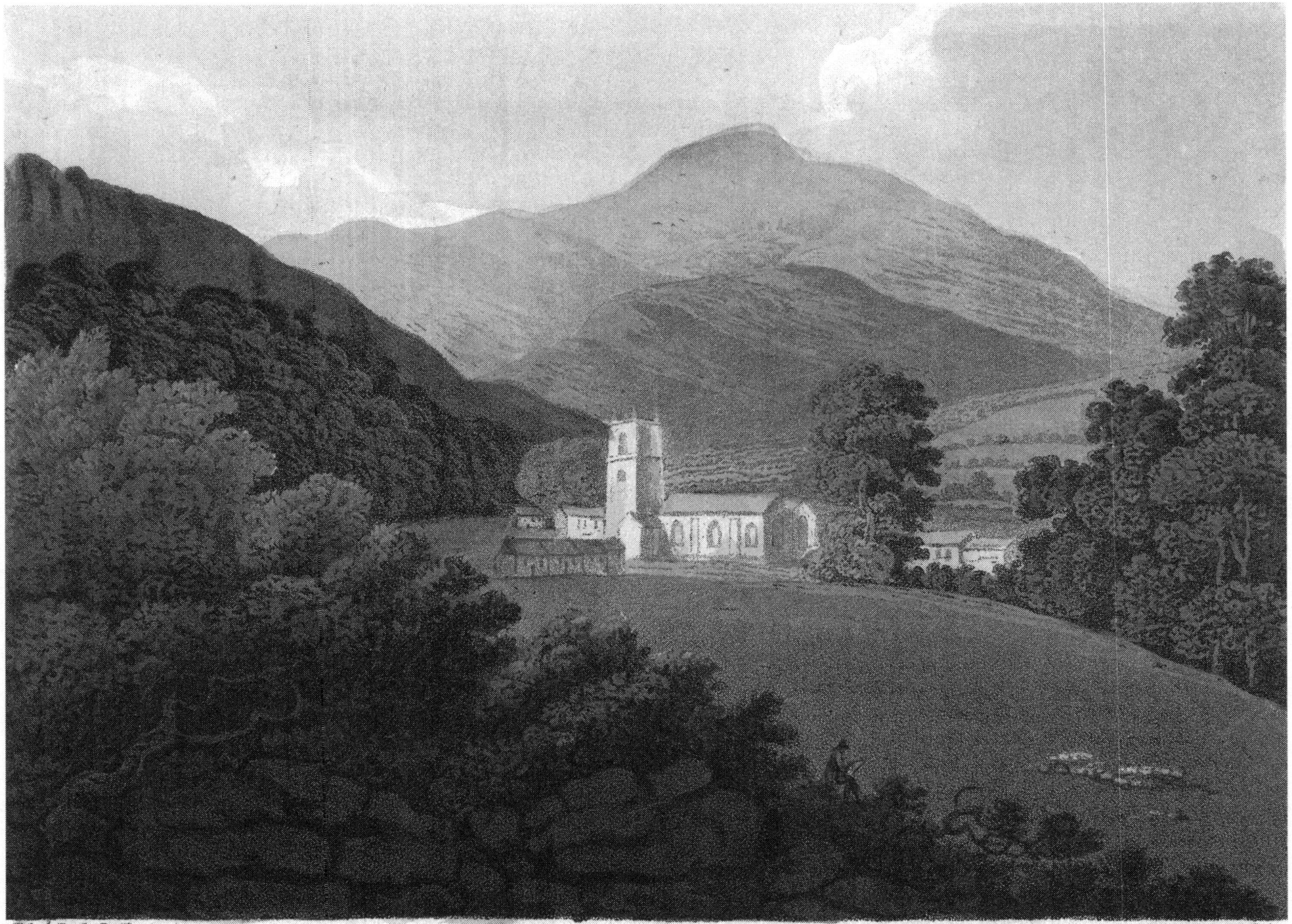

Edwd. Pugh Delt. *Thos. Cartwright sculpt.*

LLANGOLLEN.

Published 15 April 1813, by E. Williams, Strand.

tend to destroy the effect which it now has. The houses are built, very irregularly, of a black grey sort of lime-stone, frequently leaving interstices unfilled with mortar, save on the inside. The interior of the church is neat. In the east window is the subject of Christ in the garden :—" If it be possible, let this cup pass from me," *&c. &c.*; a picture well painted on glass by Eginton of Birmingham. This church is dedicated to Collen, a saint who lived about the middle of the seventh century: he was descended by his mother's side, Matholwch Lord of Cwl in Ireland. A little below the bridge, has been lately erected a factory, belonging to Messrs. Turners of Manchester; which certainly stares one in the face so much, as to be a great offence to the eye of a follower of the arts. A violent opposition was made to its erection by many gentlemen in the neighbourhood, and Messrs. Turners succeeded in purchasing the ground only by a witty stratagem. The consideration of its being an unpleasant object to the eye, ought, however, to give way to the more important circumstance of its becoming the source of employment to a number of children, who, otherwise, would have been a burden to the parish: it must also, in some degree, add to the strength of our trade, and contribute its share in countervailing the efforts making on the continent to supplant us in foreign markets. These things considered, it will, in a great measure, palliate the disagreeable effect of it in a landscape; though, if these gentlemen could have fixed upon a spot lower down, where this building might have been erected more appropriate, it would, perhaps, have been better

The bridge here is a fine old structure, built by the first John Trefor, Bishop of St. Asaph. It has four pointed arches, and is accounted one of the three beauties of Wales. It is erected upon the solid rock, and is of such amazing strength, as to have withstood the immense bodies of water, that have so often, in the course of nearly four centuries, overflowed the banks of this river. Strangers are here sometimes surprised by a phenomenon, for the singularity of which, till explained to them, they are wholly unable to account. The river has been known to rise in a few hours, so as to overflow its banks, and even to the height of the bridge, apparently without any cause, in the finest weather, when there has been neither rain nor thaw. The reader will recollect, that the Dee issues from that fine piece of water, Bala lake; when the wind is south-west, and blows a fresh gale for a few hours, this lake pours such torrents of water into the river, as to have the effect of a strong tide rushing through a narrow confined channel with great fury, often committing ravages in its way. Large trunks of trees, and disjointed fragments of cottages and out-buildings, have been seen to come down with the flood; but the strong and sharp-angled buttresses of the bridge, have turned them through the arches without injury. This bridge adds greatly to the picturesque effect of the scenery from various points. The neighbourhood boasts of no gentlemen's houses, except Mr. Jones's already-mentioned, Dinbren, Rev. Mr. Roberts, and nearer still, Twr or Tower, Mr. Price's, some time the residence of the celebrated Miss Seward: who could not have chosen a more retired spot, in which to compose her beautiful and much-admired poem of the Vale of Llangollen.

The stranger must visit Llanegwest, in the vale of Crucis Abbey, two miles and a half north of this place, with which he will be highly gratified; it stands in a flowery little valley, pent up between the high rocks of Eglwseg, and a ridge of hills that run north and south, parallel to each other; it is well wooded about, and surrounded by some very fertile meadows and corn fields.

The ends of the east and west transepts are nearly entire, and are much admired by travellers. The abbey is of the modern Gothic architecture, somewhat mixed with the Saxon, which is observable in a semicircular entrance to the west transept, and in the round tracings above, extending from one side to the other; under which are three pointed arches, including in each two smaller pointed ones, intended for the transmission of the light. Above these again, is a handsome round window, comprising eight partitions, like some in Westminster-abbey; making up a beautiful whole, which has been the subject of many a fine picture. The east transept * seems of a prior date; and is rather less elegant, but not less picturesque. The view here embraces many objects that unite to render it a subject not to be equalled in its kind in North Wales. This end has three pointed windows, rising from two or three feet of the ground, to half the height of the buildings. Above these are two narrow lancets, traced or bordered with stones which project a little from the surface of the building, and continue between the lower windows to the ground. The top of this end is considerably mutilated, and, but for two or three yards of a perfect line, its shape would have been left to conjecture: it was, like its associate, pointed. The cloister, having been converted into a farm-house, has undergone many alterations within, and, by its diversity of lines, possesses excellencies in the picturesque, that second well the Gothic remains of the abbey. The hills likewise come happily to its assistance. The late Mr. Lloyd of Trevor-hall, a few years be-

* I have lately seen a good picture of this by Mr. Ibbetson.

fore his demise, built a small summer cabin fifty yards from this venerable pile: but instead of a *neat modern* building, had he erected one in the style of the abbey, it would, in my judgement, have shewn a better taste. The stranger must be struck with the inward appearance of the cloister, once the habitation of the abbots. The kitchen, with a strong arched ceiling, is directly under the barn, but the noise of the thresher's flail is not heard when the door is shut.

The whole of this edifice impresses the mind with an awe, and a sort of religious fear, of which, while in view of it, it is not possible to divest oneself. The beautiful ash and other trees which fill the area of the building, add to it an air of solitude and melancholy, strongly denoting it a place wasted and forsaken by man. This was a house of Cistertians, founded by Madoc ab Gruffydd Maelor, Lord of Bromfield, in the year 1200. Reyner Bishop of St. Asaph, bestowed on it half the tithes of Wrexham, and in 1227, his successor, Bishop Abraham, bestowed the other half: the monks also obtained the patronage of several other livings. At its dissolution, the revenue of the house was (to follow Dugdale's account) £188 per annum, and according to Speed, £214 3*s.* 5*d.* The last abbot was John Herne, who, on his surrender, received an annuity of £23; other surviving monks received £10 13*s.* 4*d.* in annuities, which were, with the above £23, all the charges remaining in the year 1553 *.

Guttyn Owain, a bard of the fifteenth century, composed two awdwls or odes, praising Dafydd ab Iefan ab Iorwerth, and Sion or John, both abbots of this house; and, above all, highly

* Willis's Abbeys, II. 312.

commending their hospitality. He mentions their having four courses of meat, bright silver dishes, claret, and other wines. The bard seems particularly happy in the idea of his having been blessed by the abbot John, whose three fingers were covered with a profusion of sparkling rings.

This abbey was the property of the crown, till the ninth of James I.; who made it over to Edward Wooton, afterwards Lord Wooton. Lady Margaret Wooton possessed it in 1654.

In a field adjoining the road, is a round pillar, replaced upon a mount where it formerly stood, and this field is still called Llwyn y Groes, the Grove of the Cross, from the wood that once surrounded it. Its height was originally twelve feet, but it was reduced to six by the fanatics in the civil wars. It is now inserted in a large square pedestal, and a Latin inscription upon it is rendered illegible, but the antiquary, Mr. Edward Llwyd, has preserved the first part, which runs thus:—"*Concenn* filius *Catcli*, *Catcli* filius *Brochmail*, *Brochmail* filius *Eliseg*, *Eliseg* filius *Cnoillaine*, *Concenn* itaque pronopos *Eliseg* edificavit hunc lapidem proavo suo Eliseg." Concenn (or Gyngen) was grandson of Brochmail or Brochmel Yscithrog, who was defeated at the battle of Chester in 607, which fixes nearly the time this pillar was erected.

Before I leave Llangollen, I must bear public testimony to the friendship of a good and truly honest man, whose house has ever afforded me as much comfort, as his conversation and genius have yielded me pleasure. I am aware, that from the unaffected modesty of my excellent friend, I may in some degree incur his reprehension: but I hope that his good-nature will excuse the effects of a grateful remembrance, when I announce, as the subject of my just praise, the name of Mr. Edward Edwards.

For three miles the verdant vale of Llangollen exhibits its beauties in a very agreeable manner; and, inspirited by the presence of Crow-castle, yields much pleasure to the traveller; who will also see on the left, Trevor-hall, the seat of the late Trevor Lloyd, Esq.

The grand aqueduct, just finished on this spot, is built of stone resembling Portland-stone, and the effect which it produces, from whatever point it is viewed, is highly pleasing: it is, indeed, a structure which cannot be seen without admiration. It has the following inscription on one of the central piers:—"The nobility and gentry of the adjacent counties, having united their efforts with the great commercial interest of this county, in creating an intercourse and union between England and North Wales, by a navigable communication of the three rivers, Severn, Dee, and Mersey, for the mutual benefit of agriculture and trade, caused the first stone of this aqueduct of Pont Cussullte to be laid on the 25th day of July, 1795: When Richard Middleton, of Chirk-castle, Esq. M. P., one of the original patrons of the Ellesmere-canal, was lord of this manor, and in the reign of our Sovereign George III. when the equity of the law, and the security of property, promoted the general welfare of the nation, while the arts and sciences flourished by his patronage, and the conduct of civil life was improved by his example."

Pont y Cyssyllte, a bridge of several arches, close to it, is quite eclipsed by its stupendous height and magnitude. In it we recognise the great water conveyances of ancient Rome,

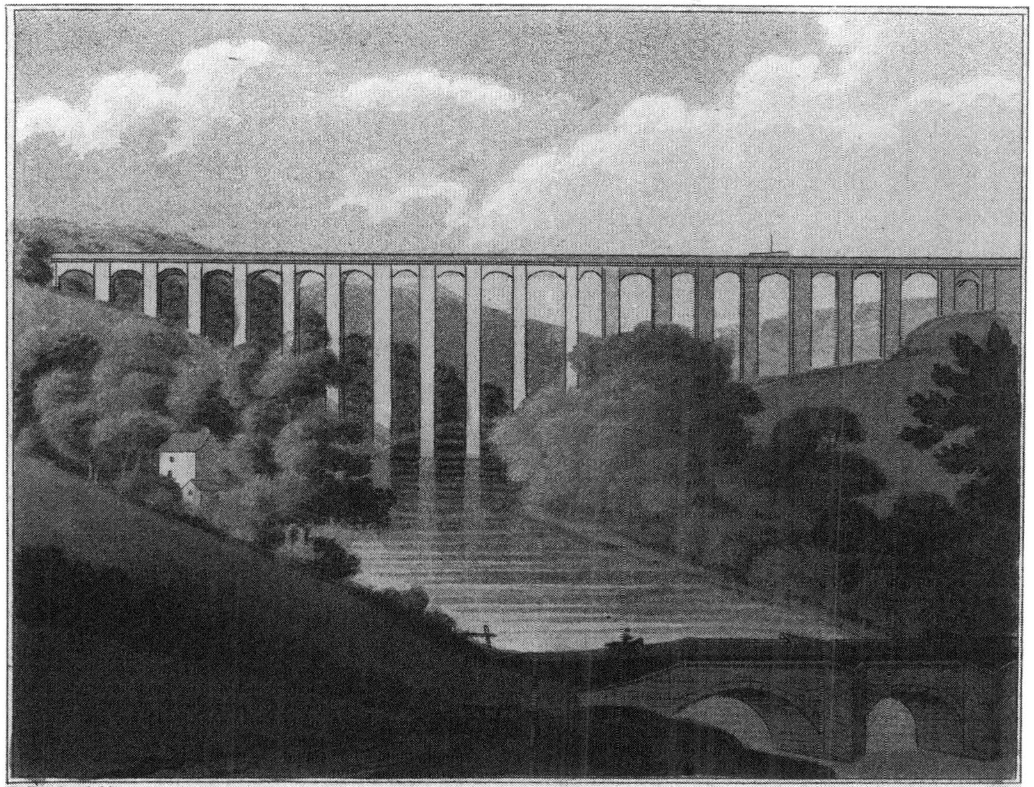

E. Pugh del^{t}. I. Havell sculp^{t}.

PONT CYSYLLTY AQUEDUCT.

Published 16th Novr 1814, by E. Williams, Strand.

which though superior in point of length, were inferior in other respects. Its direction is north and south, crossing the Dee at right angles. It forms, connected as it is with the surrounding fine scenery, a noble and a magnificent picture, but to view it to the best advantage, the stranger must ascend the acclivities on either side of it, from whence he will be highly pleased with a scene, in which there is every concomitant circumstance that can please the lover of nature and of art.

The extent of the aqueduct is nine hundred and eighty-eight feet, and exhibits nineteen arches, each forty-five feet span. The summit has a water-trough of cast iron, one thousand and nine feet in length, and in breadth eleven feet eight inches. The elegant piers lessen upwards gradually, from ten feet width and twenty-one feet depth at the base, to seven feet width and twelve feet depth at the top. These piers are one hundred and sixteen feet high from the river, and from their ending, to the greatest height of the building, twenty feet; making the total elevation, one hundred and twenty-six feet. To each end of the aqueduct are added ten feet six inches of iron-work. From centre to centrc of each arch, are screwed together eleven strong iron plates, as strengtheners.

The lime rocks here are very great, and, by calcination on the spot, are rendered fit for immediate use; and, as the Ellesmere-canal is opened for public traffic, they must yield immense profit to the proprietors, who are now enabled to supply all the neighbouring counties, Chester, Liverpool, *&c.* One mile further, we enterthe road from Rhuabon to Chirk: leaving the latter place to the right, and turning to the left, we come to two or three houses on the road. In the field facing these is a delightful prospect of the vale of Llangollen, with the Dee sweeping majestically between its wood-clothed heights. Passing the New Bridge, on the left appears Plâs-madoc, a handsome house, the residence of Thomas Youde, Esq. I now entered the respectable village of Rhuabon.

CHAPTER VIII.

Rhuabon. — Wynnstay. — Nant y Bele. — Erddig. — Wrexham. — Elihu Yale.—Bersham Iron-works.—Nanl y Ffrydd—Kate of Cymmau.—Brumbo Hall.—Caergwrle-castle.—Hope.—Plas Têg. — The two Leeswoods. — Tower.—Mold.— Mr. Wilson. R. A. — Maes Garmon.—Gwysancy Euloe-castle.—Hawarden.—Flint.

THE church of Rhuabon is dedicated to St. Mary, and is a fine pile of building. Its tower is massy and picturesque: at each angle is a buttress that runs up nearly to the top, which is ornamented with embrasures. In the interior is an elegant monument to the memory of the late Sir Watkin Williams Wynn's first wife, the Right Honourable Lady Henrietta Williams Wynn, third daughter of Noel Duke of Beaufort, who died in the bloom of youth and beauty, aged twenty-one years. The figure of Hope, reclining on, and half-covering with her drapery, an antique urn, was executed by Mr. Nollekens. Near this is another elegant monument by Rysbrack, to the memory of Sir W. W. Wynn, Bart., father to the above, with a long Latin inscription, not more lavish of praise than was justly his due, both as a leader in the senate and a friend of his country. Ever since his demise, he has been properly styled by his countrymen, the *Great Sir Watkin*: nor is his character, in England, held in less estimation. He was lost to his friends, the public, and his countrymen, by a fall from his horse, on the 26th September, 1749. It is related, that an over officious pick-thank, who had very early intelligence of his death, hastened to court, to communicate it to his majesty, George II.; but that the king, contrary to the expectations of this eye-service man, replied, "Then, have I lost an excellent statesman, and a good subject:"—

> "———— A friend to truth! of soul sincere,
> In action faithful, and in honour clear!—
> Who broke no promise, served no private end—
> Who gain'd no title, and who lost no friend!"

Here is also another monument of two recumbent figures, of John ab Ellis Eyton and his lady. The Wynns acquired the estate of Wynnstay, by marrying into this ancient and respectable family.

The late Sir Watkin presented the church with a handsome organ, and a marble font, on a tripod of great elegance; which was used for the first time at his eldest son's christening, in 1772.

Several ancient monumental stones have, at different times, been removed from hence, which, from their mutilated state, were probably thought to be of no value. One, however, has been preserved and inserted in the church-yard wall, by the gate facing the inn: its situation is the most ridiculous and whimsical that can be conceived.

Those instruments of correction, the stocks and whipping-post, are placed close to this stone; and there seems to have been a joke intended, when these different articles were fixed here. This stone was once a recumbent monument of a lady: but here it is placed erect, shewing a delicate figure in the act of earnest supplication, who, with uplifted hands, seems to entreat, and with the greatest humility to implore, remission, or at least a mitigation of punishment for the unfortunate sufferers, whose cries pierce the surrounding air. But executioners, alas! are inexorable; her tears, her tender solicitude and prayers, avail not; and the culprits are left to that punishment which their offences demand.

The entrance into Wynnstay-Park is through a beautiful avenue of lofty trees, among which is one of the largest oaks in the kingdom. The circumference is about thirty-three feet, and though the trunk appears firm, the branches, forming large timber, are in a state of decay. Several of them have, within the last twelve years, dropped off; before which period, it was the boldest specimen of the picturesque oak that could be any where seen: it will yet make a fine picture, and is indeed, of itself, a study. On the right of this, in a woody recess, but exposed on one side, is a very handsome monumental column, to the memory of the late Sir Watkin: its summit has a gallery, and the whole is crowned with a bronzed urn, from a design by Mr. Wyatt. Wynnstay is well situated, on a gentle rise, and commands a very interesting and delightful prospect of a valley, diversified with every thing that can satisfy a rational mind: nor does the colouring, given to it by Lord Lyttleton, exceed reality, though his lordship might be somewhat too hasty when he compared it with the vale of Festiniog, with which it does not so well assimilate as with many other spots which he must have seen. This and Chirk-castle, formerly two rival houses, stand boldly fronting each other; full of animation, as if their masters had not yet forgot their old electioneering contests.

Wynnstay was erected at different times, and, consequently, shews various specimens of architecture: but if these additions give no beauty to the building, they have increased the comfort of the house: its dimensions are now great, and its apartments convenient. Sir Watkin has no collection of pictures here, but his town-house contains some valuable ones. These grounds furnish the artist with many good subjects, two of which, painted lately by Mr. Decorte, were shewn me by that gentleman, executed in his usual admirable style. On the verge of the demesne is Nant-y-Bele, or the Dingle of the Martin; known to few painters. Its character is very dissimilar to any thing with which I had hitherto met. The best situations to view it from are the northern high grounds, which are accessible from Rhiwabon by footpaths, or by a road at the back of Wynnstay. From these rocky heights the stranger will perceive a scene of wonderful richness and grandeur. The nearest space is occupied with a vast and awful profundity, a circumstance which reduces the noble Dee, in appearance, to half its magnitude. This river pursues its tortuous course between woods and rocks, loud murmuring, as if in continual turmoil and disquietude, in consequence of its incessant tumbling over its shelvy bed, till it finds repose and quiet in the milder and more effeminate grounds of Cheshire. Looking westward, the first and nearest objects that obtrude themselves on the sight are, magnificent woody prominences, shooting up into various and alluring forms; beyond these is that great rocky mountain, called Fron-fawr, and facing this are the great lime-rocks, the smoke issuing from the kilns of which adds to the general effect. The aqueduct, though partially seen, is yet of great importance in the view, and renders it more an Italian than a British scene. The rich and verdant vale of Llangollen comes in happily, as a contrast to the bolder parts, and Castell Dinas Bran, though, as I have observed before, it will not make a picture near its walls, is from hence an object which

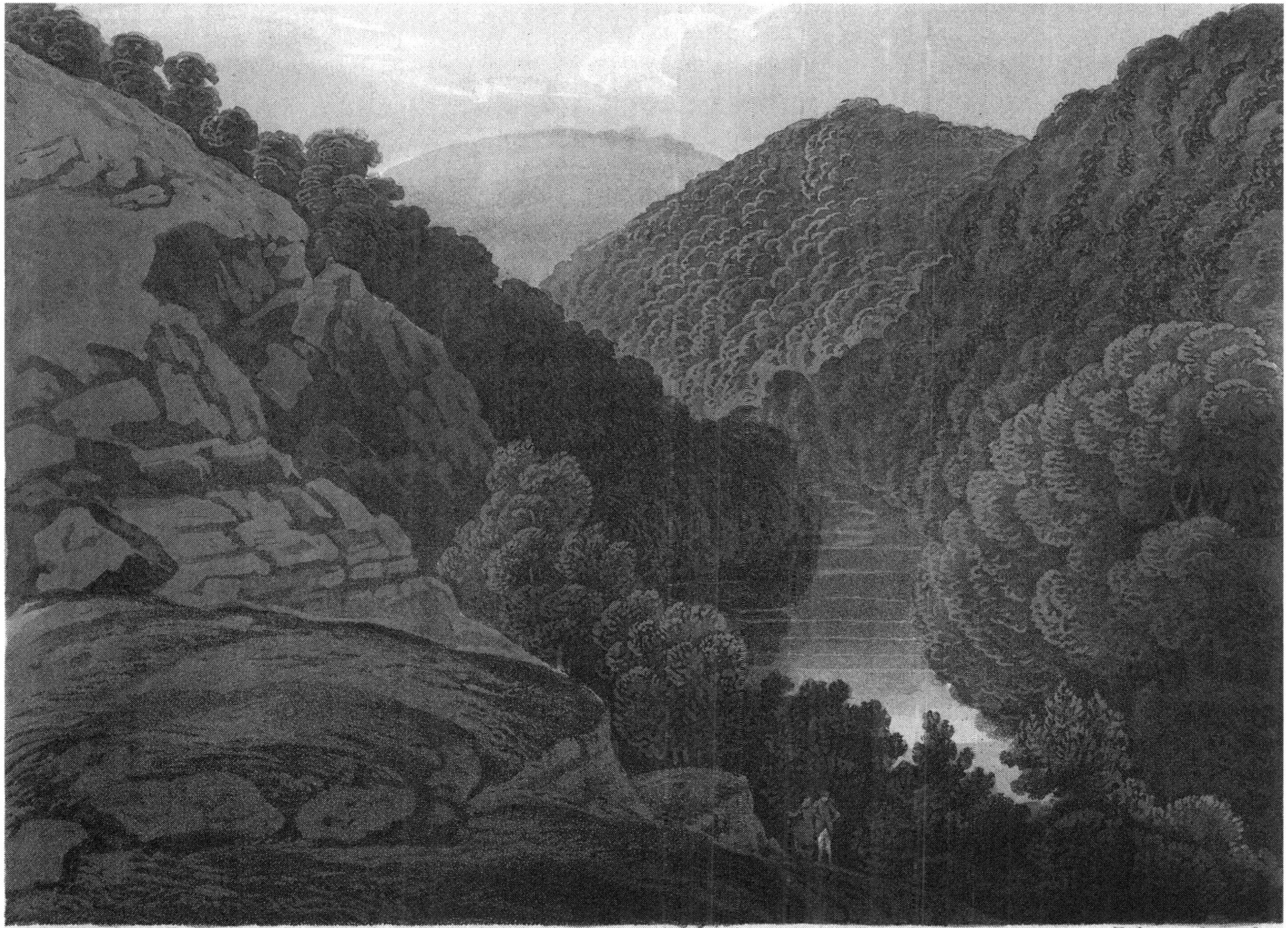

E. Pugh del. T. Cartwright sculp.

NANT-Y BELA.

Published 15 May 1813, by E. Williams, Strand.

commands the enthusiastic admiration of the man of taste, and the involuntary respect of the man devoid of it. The whole of this picturesque scenery finishes with a variety of mountains in the distance, several miles beyond the village of Llangollen. Sir Watkin has now in his possession an enchanting picture, painted by the inimitable Wilson, from this spot. Looking down the river, the scenery continues very majestic, and its character approximates to that of the picturesque Wye. The high banks, which, from the hills above, approach the water in beautiful curvilinear lines, are most profusely covered with rich old wood. From Pont-Newydd, or New-Bridge, to a little beyond Oreton, the extent of this scenery is about seven miles, but that part of it which is now more immediately under notice, is, without doubt, the most interesting. Sir Watkin has begun some beautiful walks through these woods; a circumstance which must give pleasure to those who may hereafter visit this wild spot, as they will thus be enabled to get to situations which are now inaccessible.

The day after my arrival at Rhiwabon, a wedding was solemnized, after which a good deal of mirth and good humour were displayed. It is very observable among the Welsh, that, upon every occasion of public meeting and festivity, their conversation and their songs perfectly accord with the occasion; whether it be matrimony, burial, feats of activity, favourable news, *&c.*; and the old bards have furnished them with such a variety upon all subjects, as to enable them to follow their minstrel in their turns, without hesitation.

From hence to Wrexham is a pleasant road of four miles, diversified with some handsome houses, one of which, well worthy of notice, is Erddig, the seat of Philip Yorke, Esq., son of the author of the "Five Royal Tribes of Wales." This is a fine spacious house, situated on a gentle rise with a beautiful little river flowing at its feet. The grounds are extensive, as are the gardens, all of which are richly decorated with a variety of wood and walks, accessible to strangers on certain days, and the Sunday promenade of the inhabitants of Wrexham and its neighbourhood.

Wrexham is the best, and much the largest town in North Wales, and is to that part of the principality, what Carmarthen is to South Wales. It carries on a great tanning trade, and is conspicuous for the shoe, skin, glove, and other trades of less consequence. This is the grand mart of North Wales, where the Welsh hold an old established annual fair on the 23d of March; when the inhabitants, for the space of nine days, exhibit for sale horses, horned cattle, pigs, *&c.*; and the various manufactures of the country, as well as those of England, Ireland, and Scotland, find their way also to this fair. The cottons of Manchester, the hardware and brilliant trinkets of Birmingham, the ribbons of Coventry, and even the silks of Spital-fields, have here displayed their splendour—have darted their variegated rays, and have flashed their irresistible temptations, amidst groups of beautiful females of the town and neighbourhood. The beaux, no less than the belles, are bewitched into purchases at this time, to embellish and set off their persons in a vicinity, where the majority of both sexes are votaries of fashion and gaiety. Here are three squares, called by the names Manchester, Birmingham, and Yorkshire, where goods from those places are sold; besides two squares for the sale of Irish linen and other goods.

The church has been frequently noticed; and as long as it

shall remain, it must be a subject of admiration. The interior is handsome; and the walls, floor, and pews, are kept in a perfect state of cleanliness and repair; a circumstance which adds much to the effect of this Gothic building. It has a few monuments, of which, that which is most deserving of notice, was executed by Roubiliac, in memory of Mary, daughter of Sir Richard Middleton, of Chirk-castle, who died April 8th, 1749, aged fifty-nine. In this production, the sculptor seems to have excelled all his other works. The lady is represented, as if all restraint was at an end, bursting from the shattered tomb, and taking her flight to the abode of the "just made perfect." The attitude is very beautiful and flexile; agreeably harmonizing with the countenance, in which are artfully expressed the several emotions of surprise, hope, and admiration. A little cherubic figure, sounding a trumpet, appositely announces her emancipation from the grave, or, to carry the notion further, proclaims her welcome to the joy of angels above. A pyramid, in the distance, is seen tumbling to pieces; a happy emblem, typical of the last and universal crash of nature, which, strong as those mighty structures appear, will prove them to be but ill calculated to withstand the awful and conclusive shock. Over the altar is placed a small, but finely-painted picture, by De Heere, of Christ instituting the sacrament of the Lord's-Supper: this was a present to the church by Elihu Yale, Esq., of Plâs Grono, who brought it from Rome. This gentleman, if we may guess from his epitaph and history, was an odd compound of good and bad. He had once been a governor of Madras, and, from what follows, must have been a severe one. His groom, having been unwell, rode his master's horse two or three days to take the air, without his leave, a liberty which so enraged him, that he ordered the poor man for execution, and he was accordingly hanged! for which enormity Elihu was severely called to account in England*. Thus the worst side of the picture is upon record; and we must give his friends credit for the best side, which his epitaph, placed in the church-yard, thus describes:—

"Born in America, in Europe bred,
In Afric travelled, and in *Asia* wed,
Where long he liv'd and thrived; at *London* dead.
Much good, some ill he did: so hope all's even,
And that his soul through mercy's gone to Heaven.
You that survive, and read, take care
For this most certain exit to prepare;
For only the actions of the just,
Smell sweet and blossom in the dust.
"*Interred*, 22*d July*, 1721."

The church is a vicarage in the diocese of St. Asaph, and, the parish being very large and populous, it has under it two chapels of ease, one at Bersham, and the other at Minera or Mwyn-Glawdd, the Mine on the Dyke, so called from Offa's-Dyke, which is contiguous to it. The steeple was blown down on St.-Catherine's day, 1331. The church also was destroyed by fire, about 1457; and was rebuilt a little before the year 1472: on which occasion the religious of the day had recourse to their usual stratagem. They granted indulgences during forty days, for five years to each subscriber to so pious a work; and that the present church should be so extremely handsome, and enriched with so many ornaments, is a matter of little or no wonder, for when people were licensed to give full scope to their inclinations, let their bent be what it might, and the noble monitor *Conscience*, the faithful regulator of our actions, was allowed to be superseded

* Harris's Coll. Voy. i. 917.

by papal authority, it is not surprising that, for such an unwarrantable permission, they should be willing to contribute with liberality.

The next object of our admiration was the church-tower. This is the most elegant specimen of the light modern Gothic of the florid style, perhaps, in the kingdom. Its height is one hundred and thirty feet; it tapers a little towards the top, which ends in four turrets, each finishing with a pinnacle, between which, on each side of the tower, are three smaller ones.

The sides of the tower have been richly ornamented, particularly with a number of statues of saints, fixed in pointed niches: but few have been preserved from the destructive efforts of the ruthless hand of Time. The outside of the nave, and the aisles of the church, have been ornamented with embrasures, and, between the windows, with pinnacles.

Many prints of this elegant edifice have, at various times, been published, but the one most deserving of notice, and the most correct, is that in aquatinta, from a drawing by Mr. Allen, engraved by Mr. Cartwright*. The church-yard, lately railed round with iron, is a spacious spot of ground, and pretty well covered with tomb-stones, among which are several with eccentric inscriptions: the following is mentioned in the Spectator:—

"Here lies interr'd beneath these stones
The beard, the flesh, and eke the bones } 1668.
Of *Wrexham* clerk, old *Daniel* Jones."

But the facetious biographer of Shore might as well have

* There is a print, etched by Mr. J. Boydell, wherein the minutiæ have been laboriously attended to.

favoured us with a little of his history, as content himself with saying,

> "Here lies *John Shore*,
> I say no more—
> Who was alive
> In sixty-five. *October 9th.*"

Wrexham is supposed to be of Saxon origin, as the ancient name, *Wrightesham*, very plainly intimates. Earl Warren, as Dugdale informs us, had a grant of it *. Here were formerly a few merchants, and buckler or shield makers: but since the disuse of these weapons of defence, the neighbourhood exhibits manufactories that give birth to more decisive instruments,—instruments which have often (since those times) proved the best logic against the pride and boast of our enemies: I allude to the great cannon-foundery belonging to Mr. Wilkinson.

The town-hall, an old edifice, stands in the principal street; and, since the assizes have been held at Ruthin, is used as a market-house. The circumjacent country is so fertile, and so beautifully varied with gentle hills and dales, that it has enticed a great number of the better sort of families to reside in it: the neighbourhood, consequently, is very populous. The Eagles and the Lion are the two best inns; though two or three smaller ones afford equal entertainment to the pedestrian tourist. A mile from the town is Acton, the handsome seat of Sir Foster Cunliffe, Bart. This place was once the residence of the ancient family of Jefferies; of uncontaminated credit and consequence, until it had the misfortune of producing, in the seventeenth century, that remarkable character in history,

* Dugdale Baron. i. 12.

George Jefferies, Chancellor of England, a person of well-known abilities, but of a cruel and unrelenting heart. Acton stands upon an easy elevation, commanding fine prospects of the country : it is well wooded, and has been greatly improved and beautified by Sir Foster. Leaving Wrexham, I went west of it to Bersham iron-works, belonging to John Wilkinson, Esq. These works are immense, displaying such a profusion and tumultuous medley of machinery, as to leave the mind not a little astonished at the sight of it. As a concern of great magnitude I have never beheld a work of this kind half so wild, half so picturesque. I was sorry that I had so badly contrived this day's walk, as not to be on the spot early in the morning, in which case, I might have employed a few hours to advantage. The evening appeared lurid, and the sun receding towards the horizon in cold blue clouds, left no doubt of their intention ; this spurred me on to a quick pace, and taking a passing view of the princely house of Plâs-power, the residence of —— Lloyd, Esq., delightfully situated in a fine woody spot, I was soon after enveloped in profound darkness and a lasting shower of rain, through which with much difficulty I reached Brymbo-hall, the residence of Thomas Jones, Esq.

The next morning wearing a different aspect from that of the preceding night, my first business was to visit the extraordinary and wild dingle, called Nant-y-Ffrid. A mile on my way to it I met with some noble lime rocks : at the time I saw them, they were cut into very fantastic and humorous forms, but from the great trade in this article I am afraid this effect will soon be spoiled.

The romantic character of Nant-y-Ffrid is not surpassed by

the wildest scenery of Merionethshire, and, in some respects, it assimilates well with the boldest pictures of Carnarvonshire; its several parts consist of water, wood, rock, and mountain, and the whole untouched, and consequently uninjured, by the destructive hand of art. The right side of it for near a mile is coated by a fine hazel wood, in which are imbosomed several cottages, raised on gentle elevations. The nuts produced here are of the finest sort, and very little, if at all, inferior to the filbert; they are conveyed to the Chester and Liverpool markets, which yield to the farmer a produce equal to culture without the labour. The stranger may soon be lost in the labyrinths of this extensive wood; the trees are grown to a height and strength almost incredible; the trunks and even branches of the greater part would make excellent timber.

The fine and ripened fruit retarded my steps for some time.

At the extremity of this wood, a scene bursts suddenly on the sight, the very adverse of, and roughly opposite to, the one just mentioned. It seems disposed to compeer the savage appearance of the finest parts of Nant Ffrancon, near Bangor. For three-fourths of a mile the artist will perceive a noble rocky scenery, in a state of complete denudation: but the part most calculated to give the highest pleasure, is the end of the dingle, where the fine cliffs dart up in the first style of the picturesque, shewing their rugged fronts in rude disorder; devoid of that tame and mural appearance, so offensive to true taste, they are broken into a variety of forms that render them almost unrivalled pictures. The Cegidog, a mountain-river that rushes down between the rocks, was at that time small, from the great drought that distinguished the summer: but, after much rain, a

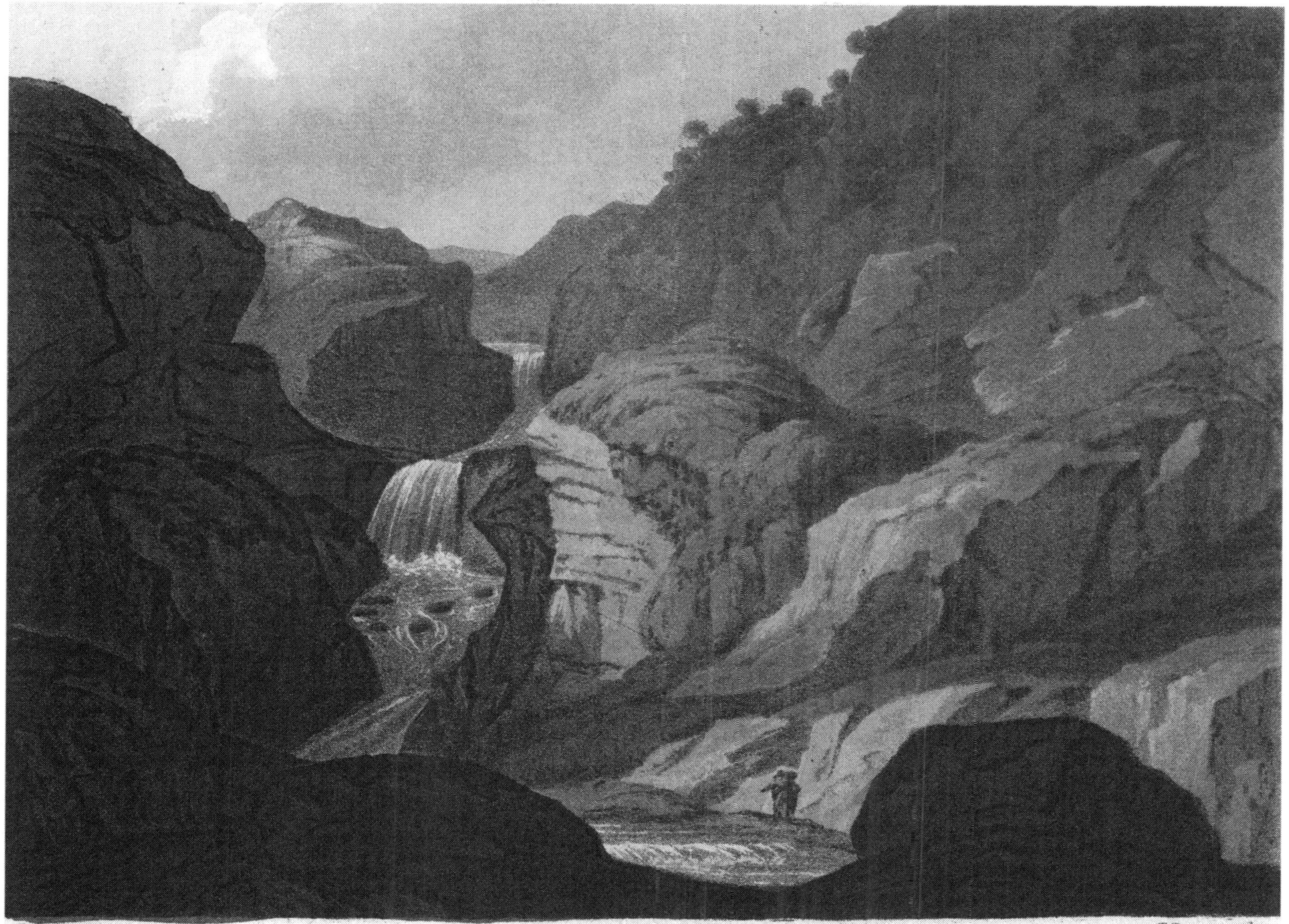

E. Pugh del. T. Bonnor sculpt.

NANT-Y FFRIDD FALL.

Published 15, July, 1813 by E. Williams, Strand.

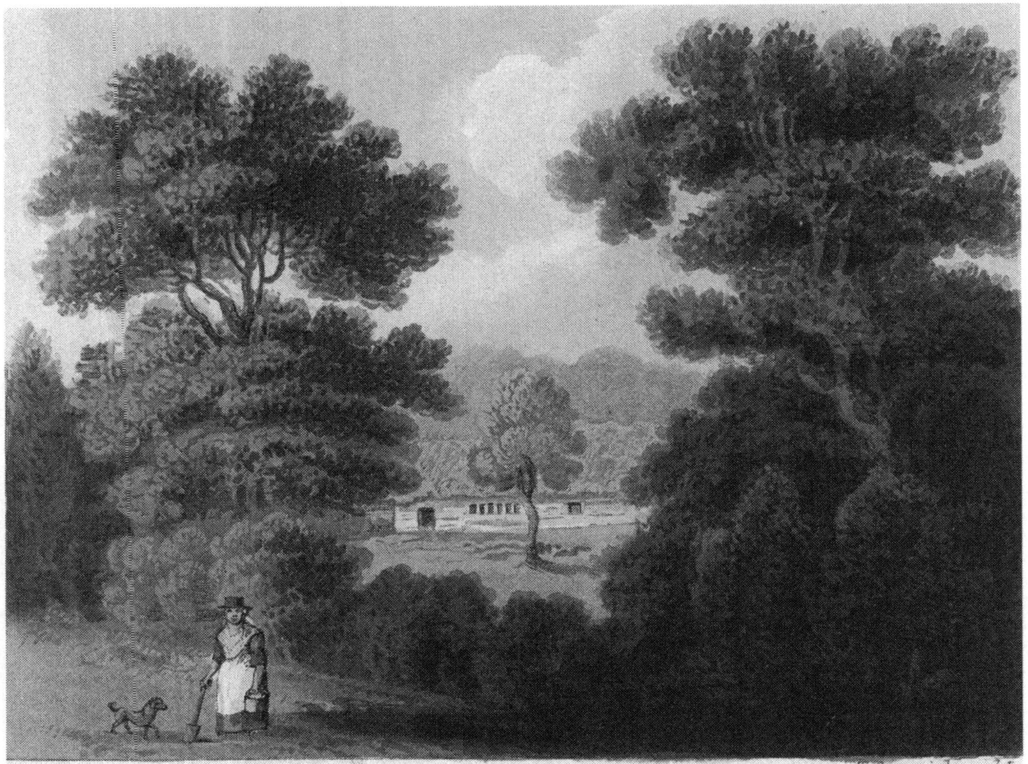

E. Pugh del.^t T. Cartwright sculp.^t

KATE OF CYMMAU'S COTTAGE.

Published 25, Septr 1814, by E. Williams, Strand.

vast body of water comes thundering down, increasing the effect of the scenery to a height of the utmost magnificence ; it then appears one continued torrent from the hills, though at other times, it shews three successive falls.

A sort of melancholy sullen gloom, seems to reign here, enough to prevent the approach of the timid and superstitious.

Some trials for lead have been made here, but without success ; the several shafts are never entered but by the poor people of the neighbourhood, when unemployed in their regular course of labour, and they procure as much ore, perhaps, as will just requite them for their trouble.

Allured by a beautiful descriptive poem, entitled, "Kate of Cymmau *," I digressed a little from my regular way back, to visit a cottage that appeared, from the description, to be the favourite abode, and its inmate the personification, of rural seclusion. As it is imbosomed in the deep shades of a woody glen, the stranger, though well instructed, might easily go astray in the mazes of this sylvan region, ere he fall in with the humble cot. I found the worthy and venerable Kate, at eighty-four, possessing all her faculties unimpaired, and earning her daily bread by industrious labour; she has always been remarkable in the neighbourhood for her innocency and unrivalled good name: she also possesses every distinctive trait of national character, and though so long a resident on the confines of England, is (which is extraordinary) without a word of English. The scenery on this spot is so rich with wood, and other circumstances, that I am persuaded a description

* In Llwyd's Collection of Poems.

of it in the poem just alluded to will be well received by the reader:—

"Where rolls the Cegidog*, highly born,
With hasty steps to meet
The Allyn, Ferrig, sister waves,
It washes Cummau's † feet.

Astonished by a world of charms,
By every rural grace;
The Naiads twist and curl its course,
As loth to leave the place.

The stubborn oak—the forest's pride,
In love with scenes like this,
Leans from the rocky cliff, and bends,
The playful streams to kiss.

The alders wave, the willows twine,
The ash ambitious towers:
While laughing Satyrs bend the boughs,
And braid them into bowers.

And he who with poetic eye,
Explores this blest retreat,
Will, unforeseen, a cottage find,
And in it—good old Kate."

I have contrived, without hurting the feelings of this worthy creature, to give a portrait of her and her cottage, which upon examination with Kate herself, will be found to be a faithful likeness. I have preserved both her character and dress, nor have I forgotten her faithful Toby; she is represented turning

* A mountain-stream, already mentioned, passes Cummau and ultimately falls into the Dee near Eaton, in Cheshire.

† "Pronounced Cumma, the plural of Cwm, a Dingle, the name of a house and township in the parish and manor of Hope (or Estyn) in Flintshire."

up the fruits of her industry, for she undertakes the task of cultivating her own garden. On bidding adieu to poor Kate, though a stranger to her, she bestowed upon me many heartfelt blessings: and if the wishes of the good have any influence above, how rich the benediction!

Getting into a narrow lane, and employing myself in sketching an object that pleased me, I heard frequent snuffling, but supposing it to be my dog after something in the hedge, paid no attention to it, till roused by a loud snort that obliged me instantly to "right about face:" when lo! a horrible-looking bull stood with his horns close at my heels; my wits deserted me at the moment, so we kept staring at each other for some time, myself bending over his head, which he held in a manner ready to toss me up in the air, should I dare to affront him. In such a dilemma I knew not how to contrive my escape. I ventured, however, to withdraw one foot backwards; as this seemed not to offend him, I did so with the other with equal success, and getting a little bolder, I moved off very gradually towards a gate in the road, in adagio movements, not very unlike those of a French dancing-master in a minuet; Dafydd Bull, all the time, turning his curly front, and keeping his eye on my motions: feeling myself, in some measure, out of danger, I attempted to drive him away, for which imprudence I was now put into greater terror than before, for the animal danced upon the spot, and tore up the hedge; but seemingly tired of this frolic, he made towards me gently a few paces, and after a good stare, a few swaggerings and tossings of the head, and a hollow roar, as if complimenting me on his departure, he proceeded down the lane, bellowing like *a bull*, the woods and rocks re-echoing the thundering sounds. In a few minutes I saw him enter a meadow, where his females received him with that indifference, which his roving disposition, and want of gallantry, seemed to deserve.

It may not be improper to notice, that this neighbourhood is often infested with these animals: and but two days after this, I was in a moment ushered into a situation, where every instant I expected to be gored to death by one, cried down by the country as being unfit to live. Some years ago, I saw, a few miles from hence a bull, in a paroxism of madness, attempting a furious attack upon a troop of horse, then on their march from Mold to Wrexham, who were drawn up in the road to receive him; but the thick hedge proving too stubborn, he was not able to get either through or over it. I understood that some lives had been lost from the imprudence of the farmers, in not securing their cattle at that season of the year when they become ungovernable. The prevalence of this vicious temper in them is attributed to the echoes, common to hilly and woody situations, which teaze them into jealousy and rage.

The great collieries and iron-works, so numerous in this neighbourhood, chiefly belong to Mr. Wilkinson, and employ a great many hands. The salubrious air of Nant-y-Ffrid having given an edge to my appetite, I returned by a different road to the hospitality of Brymbo-hall, where I soon received every gratification a hungry man could wish for.

Mr. Jones enjoys from hence one of the most luxuriant and delightful prospects in Great Britain; the beautiful objects, if all enumerated, would fill a volume, some of the principal are the following:—southward, the Montgomeryshire and the Breddyn-hills, and Rodney's-pillar; the isolated Wrekin, with great part of Shropshire; Wynnstay and Chirk-castle; the Clay and

Abberley hills; the towns of Shrewsbury and Ellesmere; Hawkstone-park, the seat of the late Sir Richard Hill, Bart.; and a line of Staffordshire-hills; eastward, the peak in Derbyshire; the range of Blackstone-edge; nearly the whole of Cheshire, and the lower part of Lancashire; Chester; a reach of the Dee; all the wide part of the Mersey, to Runcorn; Liverpool and Prescot; Gredington, the seat of Lord Kenyon; Wrexham; Peckforton-hills; Beestow and Caergwrle castles. This great expanse of country, seen from north to south, is about one hundred and fifty miles in a straight line; eastward, sixty: embracing such a variety of interesting objects, natural and artificial, as is scarcely credible. The house having an easterly aspect, is a happy circumstance: as when the sun is in its meridian, there can be no obstruction to a clear view of the whole, except when rain or mist obscures the scene.

It is said that this very respectable old mansion was erected by Inigo Jones; a small addition has since been made by another architect, but that part built by Inigo has so much of his style that it would be unreasonable to start an objection, and his manner is even observable through some modern alterations: but an extremely handsome little building, adjoining the house, intended originally for a domestic chapel, seems decidedly to settle the point.

To Mr. and Mrs. Jones, for their politeness and very hospitable attention, are due my most grateful remembrances. Their friendly disposition towards those artists who have the pleasure of their acquaintance, is a proof of their taste and esteem for the liberal arts; a trait of character, which it is much to be lamented, is not more common.

Two miles from hence is Gwersyllt, and two miles further still, is Gresford; all this neighbourhood is highly enriched with wood, hills, and dales, watered by the beautiful river Allyn, which, from its winding course, gives the artist frequent opportunities of including it in his sketches; it is a spot very likely to detain him for some days. The remains of Caergwrle-castle, on an isolated rock of considerable height, must be considered as an important object; especially when seen shooting up at the extremity of several woody glens, whose uplifted rocky sides, presenting some fine old wood, are not without diversity of lines, mutually crossing each other, so as to render them interesting in a picture.

From the summit of these wood-capped hills, is exposed to general notice, a most fertile and verdant country, chequered by beautiful seats, farm-houses, and cottages—

> " A sylvan scene, which, rising by degrees,
> Leads up the eye below, nor gluts the sight
> With one full prospect; but invites by many
> To view at last the whole."

DRYDEN's *State of Innocence.*

Caergwrle-castle has been so battered by time and rebellion, that no traces are left of its elevation or original plan; it stands high, and, like Dinas Brân, the fragments are too poor to tempt the pencil; on the north-west it is open to the Vale of Hope, but on all other sides it is shut up, save when it salutes the different little vallies, which seem proud to acknowledge it as their master.

This fort was formerly protected on the accessible sides by

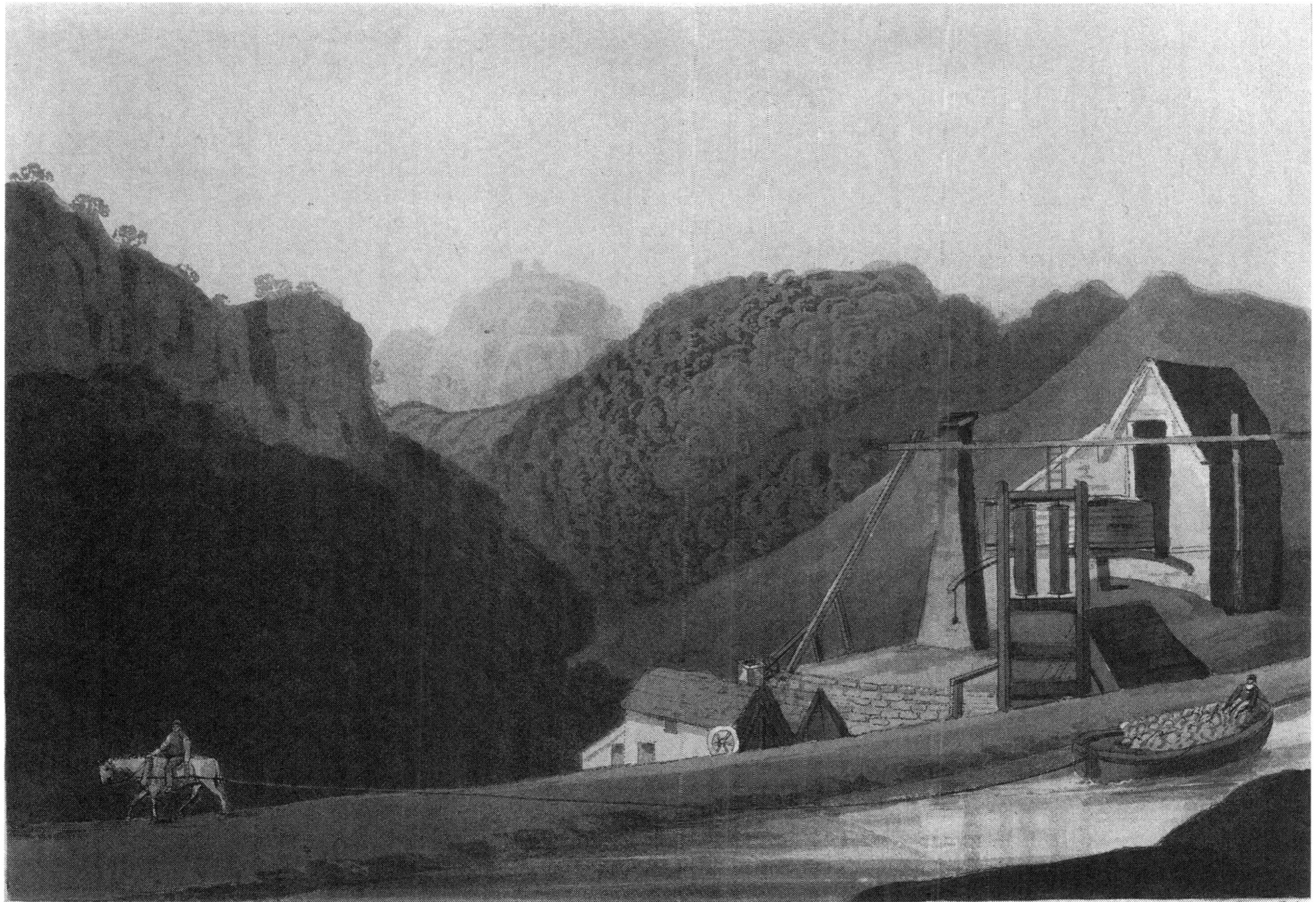

E. Pugh del.t T. Cartwright sculp.t

CAERGWRLE CASTLE.

Published 15 May 1814, by E. Williams, Strand.

deep fosses, cut into the rock. On the north-east is a rampart of earth and stones, with a fosse enclosing a large area; and as this is characteristic of British works, it is conjectured to have been, in early times, a British post, for the protection of this pass into Wales. David, the brother of Llywelyn ab Gryffydd, held it and its dependencies from Edward I.: but meeting with very injurious treatment from Roger de Clifford, Justiciary of Chester, who endeavoured to dispossess him of his rights*, he made complaints against him. David, after this, highly incensed by these wrongs, sided with his brother, and left a small garrison here, which surrendered in 1282 to the king, who bestowed the castle on his beloved Eleanor, from whom it acquired the name of Queen Hope. Her majesty lodged here on her way to Carnarvon, to give Wales an English prince.

The town of Caergwrle, or Caer-Gawr-Lle, or the Camp of the Giant-Legion (for so the Britons called the twelfth legion, *Lleon-gawr)*, was a Roman station. The place still retains the rectangular form.

Camden † says, that in his time a hypocaust was found near this place by a gardener, in digging the ground: it had a brick floor, and brick pillars, supporting a roof of polished tiles. It was found at some depth in the ground, and appeared in every respect complete. On the tiles was this inscription, Legio XX., or the twentieth legion, the same that was stationed at Chester. There are also traces of Roman roads in this neighbourhood.

Caergwrle is at present small and insignificant, consisting of a few straggling houses, and of that appearance which indicates

* Powel, 350.

† Camden, ii. 828.

their being inhabited by labourers only. Passing the river, I soon entered the better hamlet of Hope. The church here, dedicated to St. Cynfar, has two Gothic windows, with painted glass : but from their great ramifications, and the frequent misplacing of broken panes, the subject is not describable. It contains a few old monuments of the Trevors of Plas-Têg : one is mural, to the memory of Sir John Trevor, Knt., Secretary to the Earl of Nottingham, victor over the Spanish Armada, and comptroller of the navy in the time of Elizabeth and King James I. He died at Plas-Têg in 1629, aged sixty-seven.

The church-yard is large, and contains a vast collection of tomb-stones. Curiosity leading me to read some of the inscriptions, I was not a little surprised to find that, with very few exceptions, the ages recorded by them were from sixty to a hundred years. On mentioning this circumstance to a gentleman in the neighbourhood, he assured me the spot was deemed the most healthy in North Wales, and that the memorials of the dead for ages, and the experience of the living fully proved it. Fevers and other dangerous maladies, he said, scarcely ever here subdue the young, or the middle-aged ; and that those whom length of years have rendered less vigorous, and less capable of resisting the inroads of chronic disorders, fall, generally, full of years to the grave.

"Their name, their years, spelt by th' unletter'd Muse,
The place of fame and elegy supply ;
And many a holy text around she strews,
That teach the rustic moralist to die."

GRAY's *Elegy.*

The Red-Lion public-house is an old building, the exterior

of which would scarcely entice the notice of a stranger, but on entering it, he will readily allow that first impressions are fallible, and that he must not always trust to them. The parlours are made agreeable rooms, by the ingenuity of the two sister landladies, who have executed the painting and embellishing parts with so much taste and neatness, as not to be excelled by any of the brethren of the pound-brush.

After pursuing the road for a short space, I left it, and, crossing some beautiful savannas, soon reached Plas Têg, sometimes the temporary summer residence of Lady Dacre, and said to have been built by Inigo Jones; but for this I have not been able to gain any decisive authority. The house is of a castellated appearance, of a quadrangular form, with a square tower at each angle, terminating with a dome. It has five floors, a hall, forty-three feet by twenty-three, and a spacious staircase leading to a dining-room of the same dimensions. The rooms in the towers are also spacious. The architecture of the house exhibits nothing of Inigo's manner, it is graced by no ornaments, either Grecian or Roman, such as we perceive in his works, and if he had projected any part of the mansion, or works about it, it must have been the gateway to the court-yard, which, indeed, from its elegance of design and execution, might have been the production of the immortal Inigo. From its small size, however, and its partial concealment by high trees, it may easily escape the notice of strangers. The house was built by Sir John Trevor, in 1610, and stands at the foot of a hill, the grounds behind which are well wooded; but a few large trees only, in front, prevent its entire exposure to the vale.

On the right of the road, on a high headland that shoots forward into the valley, is the beautiful house of Heartsheath, the property of Colonel Wardle, which commands these meadowy grounds, the picturesque church of Hope, and the proud and elevated castle of Caergwrle. Further on is a house called Fferm: having the appearance of age I took it for another place. Addressing myself to the farmer in Welsh, he replied, "I conna toak Welsh, measter." "Well, sir, you can talk English:" "Oi, oi, zur, I con toak English very wool." "So it appears," said I.

Still further on a little is the very respectable old mansion of Pentrehobin. On the left are the two Leeswoods; the first, the residence of the Rev. Hope Wynne Eyton, the other, now occupied by its owner, Mr. Garnon, was once the residence of Sir George Wynne, who, in his golden days, spared no expense in its erection and decorations, and in the profusion of costly ornaments of gardens and grounds, many of which yet remain in a perfect state. Exquisitely beautiful iron gates are distributed in different parts of the grounds: but those which have the greatest power of attraction, are at the entrance of the lawn, in front of the house. In none of my perambulations in different parts of England, have I ever seen any thing of this kind half so handsome in design, or so rich in composition, and neither the metropolis, nor its neighbourhood, offers a specimen of the kind, fit to compare with it. The family arms, crests, *&c.*, are happily blended and interwoven with the pointed summits of each compartment, and the whole is guarded by two noble piers, one at each end, supporting an admirably-carved sphinx.

The house is of brick, and, viewed at a distance, makes a figure that commands notice; but it is all a trick, common in the days of its erection, to deceive the eye, for, of itself, it is small, and receives its consequence from the circumstance of all

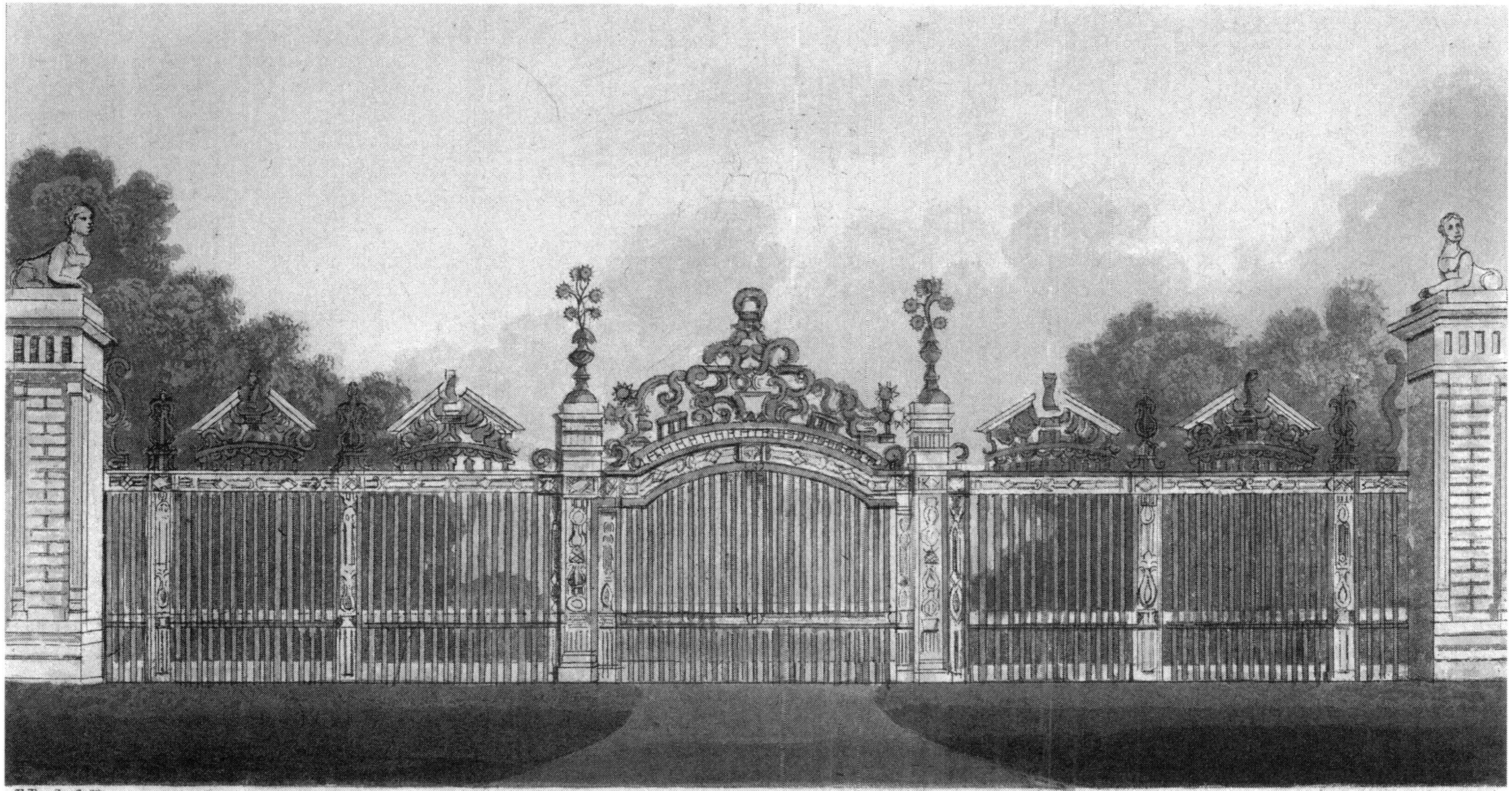

E. Pugh del^t. T. Cartwright sculp^t.

THE GATES OF LEESWOOD.

Published 15 August 1814, by E. Williams, Strand.

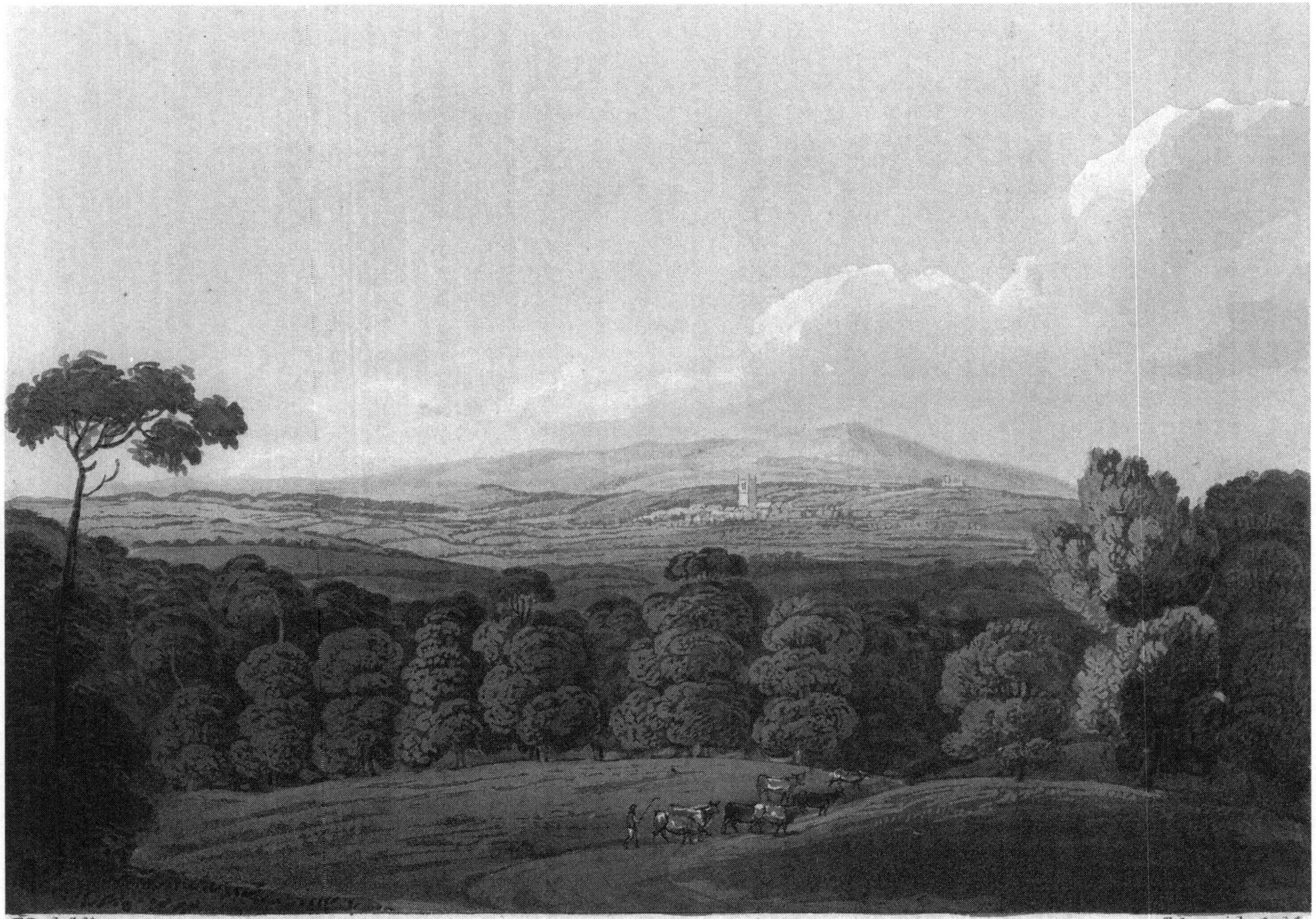

E. Pugh del.t T. Cartwright Sculp.t

THE VALE OF MOLD.

Published 15 October, 1813 by E. Williams, Strand.

the offices, stables, *&c.*, being brought to the front. The rooms being small, bear no proportion to its general appearance of grandeur, nevertheless it well accords with the sentiments of the times, when the pleasure of society consisted more in meeting in small parties, and spending the day in temperance and social conversation: a mode of living infinitely more happy in its effects, than that which distinguishes the fashionable taste of the present day. The family bath is in a rustic cot, close to the principal gates, which, by what I could learn, is not distinguished by any ornaments.

From the high grounds above the house, is a charming view of Mold and its vale; and the reader, should he ever visit the spot, will thank me for recommending to his notice, what must yield him pleasure—a magnificent landscape of nature, richly embellished by art.

Half a mile from Llceswood is the ancient house, called Tower, the residence of the dowager Mrs. Wardle: it is situated on the side of the hills, in a recluse well-wooded spot, with which it happily agrees. To the old and picturesque part of the house are some modern additions, which, producing a glaring contrast, fail to raise those emotions which it would have done, if the latter had corresponded with the former. When the wind is from the north, this otherwise comfortable mansion must be annoyed by the smoke and vapours of the adjacent collieries.

During the wars of York and Lancaster, a singular affair happened here, when the house was the property of Reinallt ab Gryffydd, ab Bleddyn, one of the six noble and gallant British captains, who defended Harlech-castle against Edward IV.

Reinallt and his people frequently quarrelled with the citizens of Chester; a considerable number of the latter visited Mold-fair, in the year 1465, when a fight was the consequence, and many lost their lives on both sides. Reinallt, however, had the advantage, and having Robert Bryne, linen-draper, Mayor of Chester, among his prisoners, he led him to the tower; where, in the hall, he hung him with his own halter; and in a concave ceiling of the same hall, now converted into a parlour, the very self-same iron staple is yet to be seen, having been suffered to remain there as a memento.

Mold, a neat little town of Flintshire, is, with respect to its local situation, in a handsome valley of some extent, nearly surrounded by gentle acclivities; most of which are in fine tillage, while some are covered with wood. The Allyn, passing the town and through the vale, falls into the Dee, near Farnden, in Cheshire.

The assizes for the county are held here. Though the least in North Wales, this county is esteemed the richest, and deserving therefore, as one would imagine, a more accommodating public-hall: the present barn-like crazy old building appearing better calculated to receive, on an emergency, a set of strolling players, than for the solemnity of a court of justice.

The next object that offers itself to view is the church dedicated to St. Cluned, a lady of the fifth century *: a structure of so much exterior elegance, as to tempt the stranger to visit the interior, which consists of a handsome nave and two aisles. The roof, beautifully carved in wood, is supported by two rows

* Cambrian Biography.

of light Gothic pillars; over the capitals are figures of angels bearing shields. The pointed arches are elegant, as are also the beautiful broad obtuse-arched windows, which are ranged in regular order on each side. The walls are ornamented with sculptured figures of animals, much in the *outre* style of some of our cathedrals. The church was built in the time of Henry VIII. and the Gothic style is evidently the same, though perhaps not so light as that encouraged by his father Henry VII. There is an air of lightness pervading the whole of this edifice: like Wrexham-church, it is very neatly kept, and, in some respects, in its interior, I think I may venture to say, that it is superior to it.

Here are several monuments, of which the most deserving of attention is that in memory of the great antiquary Robert Davies, Esq. of Llanerch * in Denbighshire. It is a whole length, leaning upon an urn, dressed in a Roman habit, with the toga thrown over the shoulders, and hanging in grand folds down to the feet. The contour of the figure is graceful, yet bold; and the whole is executed in a style which, exclusively of his other works, will do honour to the memory of Cheere the sculptor.

The following epitaph, on Dr. Wynne, composed by himself, being somewhat singular, I thought it worth transcribing.

* Mr. Mutton Davies, father of this gentleman, was a man of much excentricity. The gardens of Llannerch, within the memory of man, were made by him in the foreign taste, with statues, obelisks, and water tricks. Strangers were led towards a sun dial, and curiosity seldom failed to make them approach it, when it instantly spouted water into their faces. On the dial was written;—

Alas! my friend, time soon will overtake you;
And if you do not cry, by G—d I'll make you.

William Wynne of *Tower*, D. D.
Some time Fellow of All Souls College in Oxford,
and Rector of *Llanvechan* in this diocese,
departed this life, March 3, 1776,
aged 77.
In conformity to an ancient usage,
from a proper regard to decency,
and a concern for the health of his
fellow-creatures, he was moved to give
particular directions for being buried
in the adjoining church-yard,
and not in the church:
And as he scorned flattering others
while living, he has taken care to prevent
being flattered himself when dead,
by causing this small memorial to be
set up in his life-time.

God be merciful to me, a sinner!
Heb Dduw, *Heb* ddim *.

The tower is a modern erection, but in perfect unison with the church: it is extravagantly covered with carvings of chimerical animals of different descriptions.

On the north side of the church is a common table monument, to the memory of the father of modern landscape-painting, with the following plain inscription, " Richard Wilson, Esq. Member of the Royal Academy of Artists, interred May 15th, 1782, aged 69." He lies by the side of his reverend father, mother, and brother. His father was the rector of Penegos in Montgomeryshire; and his brother was the collector of excise for this district, the duties of which office he discharged with fidelity and honour; but it was reserved by nature for Mr. Richard Wilson to

* Without the favour of God we are destitute.

be most distinguished. This gentleman rose to such a height of perfection in the arts, as to eclipse the (till then) unrivalled abilities of Claude himself, and to him must be attributed that spirit of execution, that chaste mode of colouring, which has of late years so successfully introduced the water-colour painters to the notice of the lovers of art. Mr. Wilson's manner was original, and strictly his own; nor would his judgment suffer him to be seduced to adopt a mode which was prevalent in his day, and was as foreign to nature, as it was offensive to true taste. Mr. Wilson, in short, has, by his wonderful productions, left a legacy to the arts, of inestimable value; and would the younger artists but study it, it might lead them on to pre-eminence and celebrity. Mr. Wilson is universally acknowledged to be, among artists, what a diamond is amongst gems, *a brilliant of the first water.* His works, so long as the threads of the canvass remain, will speak more eloquently for him, than the pens of the most able writers.

While Mr. Wilson was in the zenith of his art, his country seemed to have forgotten him; and it is remarkable, in a nation pretending to encourage and honour the polite arts, that his remains, for upwards of thirty years, should be so much disregarded, as to have no national memorial, no monument of respect to distinguish them from the ashes of the vulgar.—No! he lies under a plain stone, within the reach of a plebeian's purse. To the great man of whom we have now been speaking, may be added the names of his great contemporaries, Sir Joshua Reynolds, Romney, Gainsborough, Wright, *&c.*, as instances of this ungrateful disregard to departed genius.

The handsome and stupendous cotton factory, close to the town, is the property of some merchants in Manchester. It is lighted by about two hundred and twenty windows; and is a useful neighbour to Mold, as it employs a great number of the poor. The machinery in it is great:—

> " As when young striplings whip the top for sport,
> On the smooth pavement of an empty court
> The wooden engine whirls." DRYDEN.

At the north end of the town stands a mount, partly artificial, the British name for which is Wyddgrug, and by the Latins it is called Monsaltus, the *Lofty* or *Conspicuous Mount*. The ancient British, and after them the Saxons and Normans, made use of this defensible height, cut it into a convenient form, and erected upon it a castle. It seems to have been strongly fortified by deep fosses and other works: the keep was on a place much elevated by art. This mount is now called the Bailey-hill, from the word Ballium, or Castle-yard: from it is a fine prospect of the surrounding country.

In the reign of Henry I. and the beginning of that of King Stephen, Robert, surnamed (from his residence here) de Montalto, high steward of Chester, became the possessor of this castle. At this time it was very strong, and many attempts upon it failed; till the Britons, unable any longer to bear the ravages committed by the garrison, laid siege to it in 1144, under the command of Owen Gwynedd, Prince of North Wales, and after an obstinate defence, took it by storm. The garrison were all slain or made prisoners; and the fortress was razed to the ground *.

It must have been restored after this: for we find that it was again taken by Llywelyn ab Jorwerth, in the winter of 1198;

* Powell 196.

and, about 1267, it was besieged a third time, and demolished by Gryffydd ab Gwenwynwyn, Lord of Powys. In 1322, Gryffyd Llwyd, who first brought the news to Edward I. that a son was born to him in Carnarvon-castle, and who, after our conquest had sided with the English, till, by experience, he found their yoke intolerable, took up arms, overran North Wales, and the Marches, and attempted the reduction of this fortress; but failed and was taken prisoner. From this time it was no longer known as a place of defence.

A little before the conquest of Wales by Edward, this part of the country was so covered with wood, as to be a great annoyance to his soldiers. He therefore summoned, from the forest of Dean and the county of Hereford, a great number of cutters, to make a passage through, in a line between Mold and a place at that time called Swerdewood; and insisted that the owners should not be allowed to claim any thing for the damage done to their property: another instance of the *benevolent* disposition of this monarch.

Near a mile north-west of the town is Maes Garmon, where was fought that celebrated battle the *Victoria Alleluiatica*, in which the Britons, under the command of the two bishops *Germanus* and *Lupus*, confounded and destroyed the pagan Picts and Saxons; who, in 420, were carrying desolation through the country. This eventful battle took place in Easter week. Their chief, *Germanus*, instructed his soldiers to attend to the word he should give, and to repeat it with vigour. Accordingly, at the proper time, he pronounced *Alleluja!* the whole army caught the sacred sound, which they repeated with such energy, that the mountains echoed the religious exultation; and both combined to strike such terror into the invading foe, that he fled in the utmost consternation. Numbers fell by the sword, and as many perished in the adjacent river. The late Nehemiah Griffith, Esq. of Rhual, erected on the spot an obelisk, of which a plate is given, with Rhual, the residence of Mr. Griffith, in the distance. On the obelisk is the following inscription :—

Ad Annum
ccccxx.
Saxones Picti bellum adversus
Britones junctis viribus susceperunt
In hac regione Hodiec. Maesgarmon
appellata; cum in prælium descenditur,
Apostolcis *Britonum* Ducibus Germano
et Lupo, Christus militabat in Castris;
Alleluia, tertio repetitum exclamabant:
Hostile agmen terrore prosternitur;
Triumphant
Hostibus fusis, sine sanguine
palma Fide, non Viribus obtenta.
M. P.
in Victoriæ Alleluiaticæ memoriam
N. G.
1736.

Mold has in it two small inns. I left the place for Gwysaney, a fine old stone edifice a mile off. It has a spacious hall: the domestic chapel, within the walls of the house, remains as in its pristine state, with the pews up, and the desk with the prayer-books upon it: but in a state of total neglect. The best apartments are small; but exhibit the remains of the style of old and social times. Gwysaney stands upon a high hill commanding a noble prospect; and, from the dingles and woods below, becomes a fine object for the easel, as from these points it has the air and appearance of some noble fortress. This house, in the civil wars, was thought to have sufficient strength to be garrisoned: but suffering the fate of all the rest of the king's defensive stations, it

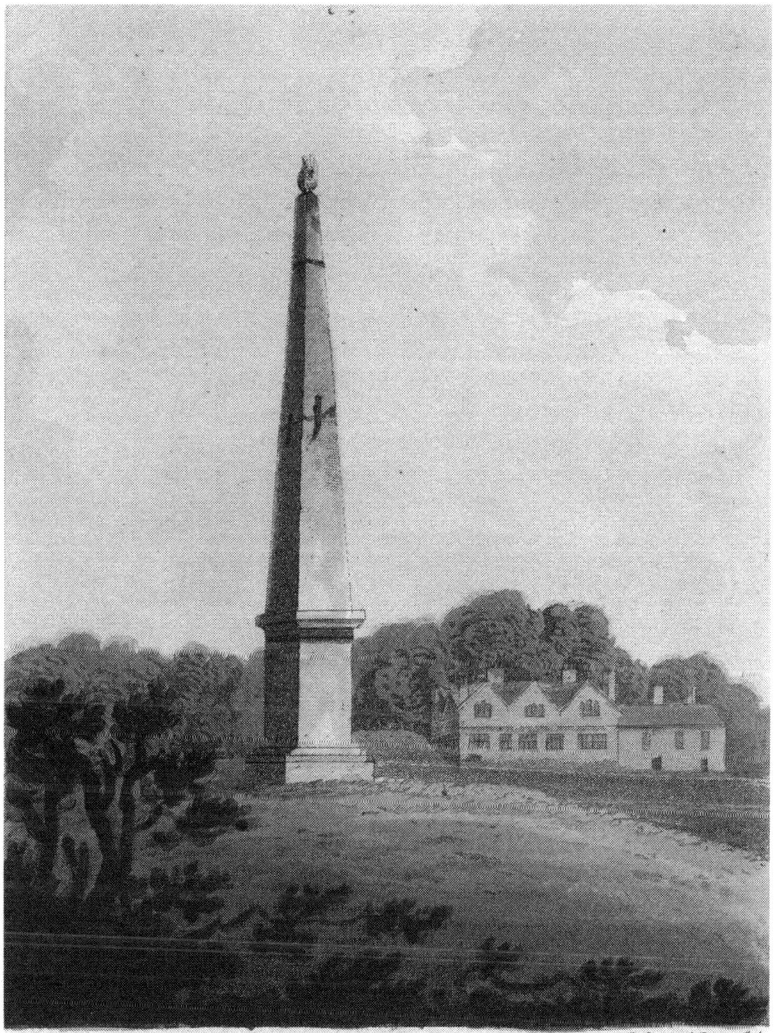

E. Pugh del.t T. Cartwright sculp.t

HALLELUJAH MONUMENT.

Published 26 May 1814 by E. Williams Strand.

surrendered to Sir William Brereton, on the 12th of April, 1645. Crossing the country, unassisted by a path, I met with nothing of interest, till Euloe-castle made its appearance. This is situated near the public road, two miles north-west of Hawarden, and buried in a deep glen of thick wood; which strongly opposes the traveller's approach to the building. It seems not to have been of any great extent: this, however, from the difficulty of access, it is not easy precisely to ascertain.

This fortress seems to have consisted of two parts: a tower, guarded on the sides most accessible by a strong wall, makes up one part; and the remains of a round tower, attached to an oblong yard, the other. This is overgrown with ivy; and the whole would be an interesting picture if so much of the surrounding wood were cleared away, as would shew it to the opposite banks. In the year 1157, a great battle was fought in the woods near this place, yet called Coed Eulo, or Eulo Woods. A large detachment of the flower of the army of Henry II., sent by him from his camp on Sultney (a great flat between this place and Chester), was surprised, and defeated, by David and Conon, enterprising men, sons of Owen Gwynedd, whom their father had dispatched with a strong party, from his camp at Basingwerk. The English were suffered to march along the plains, but when entangled amidst the woods and steeps of these confined glens, the Welsh fell upon them unexpectedly. The attack was fierce and dreadful; and, consequently, the slaughter great: and the victors pursued the flying enemy even to Henry's encampment. The king, immediately after this, with a view to repair the disgrace, brought his whole army to the attack at Coleshill near Flint; but from thence he eventually retreated with additional disgrace.

The founder of this fortress is unknown: but it is probable that

Henry erected it to prevent similar misfortunes. It has been in ruins for centuries; and Leland calls it "a ruinous castle or pile" in his time.

The manor of Euloe was vested in the crown in the twenty-sixth of Henry VIII. who granted it to Peter Stanley, Esq., a gentleman of his household In the reign of Elizabeth, Edward Stanley held it for £20 10*s*. per annum.

Hawarden is a neat village, well inhabited, and commands a view of Chester, the hundred of Wirral, and the estuary of the Dee. The church is a handsome and a venerable pile, and contains a pretty allegorical monument, by Mr. Banks, to the memory of Thomas Boydell, Esq., of Trefalyn-hall in Denbighshire; consisting of a female figure in a leaning posture over an urn. This gentleman was brother to the alderman, the foster-father of the arts.

This living is more than two thousand a year in value; and is in the gift of Sir Stephen Glynn, Bart. The rector performs all episcopal acts, those of ordination and confirmation excepted, grants licences, registers and proves wills, and has his court, proctors, and other officers.

The castle stands upon an eminence, a little out of the public road, south of the village. Though it consists of fragments only, they are of such a bold description, particularly the circular keep, as to form, from several points, rich subjects for the pencil: but the whole comes in best from the head of the beautiful well-wooded valley, west of it; where the artist may vary his points at pleasure; and he will know how to leave out some unappropriate ornaments in the grounds.

This castle, in old time, has alternately been in the possession of the Welsh and the Saxons. It was, on the conquest, comprehended in the extensive grant, made to Hugh Lupus; and afterwards it came to the Barons of Montalto, or Mold, who made it their residence. In 1264, Llywelyn ab Gryffydd, Prince of Wales, and Simon de Montfort, the rebellious Earl of Leicester, established a peace between Cheshire and Wales; the latter obliging Henry III., then his captive, to make absolute cession to Llywelyn of this fortress, the sovereignty of Wales, and the homage of its barons. As soon as Leicester's rebellion was suppressed, Hawarden relapsed to the crown. The year 1280 was distinguished by a general insurrection of the Welsh, under the command of Prince Llywelyn, and Dafydd his brother; who, after great variance, had just then been reconciled. This was to have been an attempt, embracing things of no less magnitude than the preservation of their liberties and their ancient mode of government. Dafydd, on the night of Palm-Sunday, 22d March, it being very stormy and favourable to his design, attacked the fortress, put the garrison to the sword, and took prisoner Roger de Clifford, Justiciary of Chester. Dafydd (or David) though a man of courage, was not an honourable character: having been equally deceitful to his brother, his country, and to Edward I.; and to the latter, he, at length, forfeited his life. After Llywelyn's decease, he was taken, imprisoned, and suffered a distinguished but a cruel death, at that time not in use in England: by order of a parliament, held at Shrewsbury, in 1283, he was drawn to the place of execution by a horse, there hung, quartered, and the several parts of his body exposed in different places of the kingdom. From this time, this castle passed through various hands. Sometimes it belonged to the crown, and at others it was possessed by the royal favourites, till the civil war: when again it experienced its usual vicissitudes of fortune. In 1643, it was garrisoned, for the parliament, by one hundred and fifty men, of Sir Thos. Middleton's regiment: when, in November, a number of the king's forces, drawn from Ireland, and landing at Mostyn, in this county, made their appearance before the castle; a verbal summons by a trumpet was followed by several letters, between Lieutenant-Colonel Marrow, and John Warren, and Alexander Elliot, the commanders of the garrison. Several letters are here omitted; but the rejoinder from the besieged will shew the fanaticism of the parliament party.—

"Sir,

"We have cause to suspect your disaffection to preaching, in regard we find you thus employed. If there be innocent souls here, God will require their blood of them that shed it. We can keep our *allegiance*, and the castle too; and, therefore, you may take your answer, as it was in English plain enough before: we can say no more, but, God's will be done *."

These letters passed without effect, nor would the following cavalier-like summons, of Captain Sandford, have had better success, but for an accumulation of forces on his side, and the want of provisions on that of the garrison.

"Gentlemen,

"I presume you very well know, or have heard of my condition and disposition, and that I neither give nor take quarter. I am now with my firelocks (who never yet neglected opportunity to correct rebels) ready to use you as I have done the Irish: but loth I am to spill my countrymen's blood; wherefore,

* Rushworth, part iii. 300.

by these I advise you to your fidelity and obedience towards his majesty, and shew yourselves faithful subjects, by delivering the castle into my hands for his majesty's use; in so doing, you shall be received into mercy, *&c.*: otherwise, if you put me to the least trouble, or loss of blood, to force you, expect no quarter for man, woman, or child. I hear you have some of our late Irish army in your company: they very well know me, and that my firelocks use not to parley. Be not unadvised; but think of your liberty: for I vow all hopes of relief are taken from you; and our intents are not to starve you, but to batter and storm you; and then hang you all, and follow the rest of that rebellious crew. I am no bread-and-cheese rogue, but, as ever, a loyalist, and will ever be, while I can write or namc

THOMAS SANDFORD,

November 28, 1643. *Captain of the Firelocks.*

I expect your speedy answer this Tuesday-night, at Broad-lane-hall, where I am now your near neighbour."

The garrison suffered a fortnight's siege: but surrendered on honourable terms to Sir Michael Earnley.

After this, the king's garrison, in its turn, surrendered to Major-General Mytton, on the 17th of March, 1645, after a month's siege; and was then dismantled by order of parliament, and about 1670, reduced to its present state by William Glynn, the owner.

The most entire part is a broad, circular tower, which was originally the keep to this fortress; upon the whole, these fragments are still equally important to the antiquarian traveller, and the artist.

The castle is the property of Sir Stephen Glynn, Bart., whose handsome residence is but a few hundreds of yards from it.

This is a great coal country: the coals are conveyed by means of a rail-road to the Dee, two miles distance, whence they are shipped to different parts of the kingdom.

On leaving Hawarden, I followed the Dee to Flint, by Connah's-quay, where vessels take in their cargoes of coals; it is also an out-port to Chester: this proved a very uninteresting walk of eight miles.

Flint, which gives name to the county, is a small, dull town; without trade, and with few inhabitants: though situated upon the broad estuary of the Dee, it derives no advantage from the tide, owing to the great sand-banks before it; it has no other concern with the watery element, than as it affords a daily ferry to Parkgate and Chester.

The county jail is a good plain structure, and as far as wretched man, who is become an object of the displeasure of the law, can derive any comfort from a prison, this certainly must afford it to him, in a measure denied to many in similar situations. It stands upon a small rise, nearly adjoining the castle-walls: its site is airy and open: the rooms are dry, clean, and consequently healthy; it was erected in the year 1785, and, as a tablet over the front door relates, in the sheriffalty of Sir Thomas Hanmer, Bart., and at the expense of the county,

"Aided by the subscription of several of the gentry,
who,
in the midst of most distressful days,
voluntarily took upon themselves part of the burden
in compassion to such of their countrymen,
on whom
Fortune had been less bounteous of her favours.
JOSEPH TURNER, *Architect.*"

The castle, which is a square, seems to have been a fortress of great strength, but not of much extent. Of the four circular towers, one at each angle, that which was originally the keep, or master-tower, is called the double-tower, and is by much the largest: its circumference is about one hundred and twenty feet. The gallery, formed by the inner and outward walls, had a communication with the inner tower by four arched doors; these outward walls have the same centre, that falls in the area of the inward tower, which area is nineteen feet in diameter. The walls of this venerable pile have suffered great annoyance from the people; who, in spite of the adjoining prison, have undermined them for the ignoble purpose of erecting pig-sties, and other mean buildings; the free-stone square window-frames are also objects of plunder. If, from the careless indifference of the magistracy, such acts are in future suffered to go unnoticed, these remains will fall a sacrifice to depredation and ruin. Flint-castle is washed by the tide; but its very dull, heavy appearance, its want of elevation, and its being void of turrets and other light ornaments, together with the great extension of dead wall, renders its aspect spiritless, and I would almost say unfit for near views: nor has it much interest at a distance; but, having to back it good rising woody grounds, an artist, from a boat on the water, may find a few favourable points.

Camden says that the castle was erected by Henry II., and finished by Edward I.: it is not dissimilar in style to that of Beaumaris, built by the latter; and might principally owe its erection to the same architect; but if we compare it with the castles of Conway and Carnarvon, it will not redound much to Edward's taste.

The first event worthy of notice that happened to this fortress was, when Llywelyn ab Gryffydd surprised and took it, in 1280, at the time when his brother David overpowered the garrison of Hawarden. The insurrection of the Welsh at this time was the natural effect of reiterated and sanguinary oppression. After this it became possessed by the crown.

To this place was Richard II. inveigled by Percy, Earl of Northumberland, who assured him, that Bolingbroke wished only the restoration of his own property, and to give a parliament to the kingdom. Northumberland, with a small train, first met the king at Conway, on his return from Ireland : and, though he had at mass taken the oath of fidelity to his majesty, he treacherously seized him at Pen-maen Rhôs, near Abergeley, and conveyed him that night to the castle. The next morning the king beheld a large army, commanded by his rival, marching along the sands, which soon surrounded the fortress. Bolingbroke respectfully approached the king as he was descending the keep *: he even fell upon his knees, but as in mockery, for he immediately assumed a different deportment, and with a sharp high voice " badde bring forth the king's horses : and then two little nagges, not worth forty franks, were brought forth : the king was set on the one, and the earl of Shrewsbury on the other, and thus the duke brought the king from Flint to Chester, where he was delivered to the Dukc of Glocester's sonne, and to the Earl of Arundel's sonne, that loved him but a little, for he had put their fathers to death : who led him straight to the castle †."

Froissart relates, that Richard did not meet with ingratitude from man alone, for his favourite greyhound, *Mathe*, totally

* Or dongeon, as then called.

† Stowe's Annals, 322.

deserted him, and ever after followed his rival: the king, in a conversation with the Duke of Lancaster, says, "The grayhounde maketh you chere this daye as kinge of England, as ye shall be, and I shall be deposed: the grayhounde hath this knowledge naturallye, therefore take him to you; he wyll folowe you and forsake mee." Richard, at the time of his capture, had no more than twenty attendants with him; from hence he was conducted to London, where, upon a formal charge of oppression and bad conduct, he was deposed in full parliament, and is said to have been starved to death in 1399, in the thirty-fourth year of his age, and the twenty-third of his reign.

In the civil war, in 1643, Sir Roger Mostyn, Knt., as governor, nobly defended the place against the joint forces of Sir William Brereton, and Sir Thomas Middleton, and did not surrender till all provisions, and even horse-flesh, failed.

It is worthy of remark, that the said Sir Roger (predecessor of the present Sir Thomas Mostyn, Bart.) was so excessively attached to the interests of Charles I., as to have spent no less than sixty thousand pounds in his service, which obliged him to desert his family-seat in this neighbourhood, and put up with the ordinary accommodations of a farm-house. In 1646, this place fell again into the hands of the loyalists: and again, on the 29th of August, surrendered to Major-General Mytton; and the next year was dismantled by order of the parliament.

On the restoration, it was claimed by the crown, under which it is still governed by a constable, who is also the mayor of the town.

Flint, united with Rhyddlan, Caerwys, Caergwrle, and Overton, sends a member to Parliament. At present William Shipley,

Esq. fills that situation; and Sir Thomas Mostyn is the representative for the county.

It would be advisable for the artist to keep the turnpike-road from Hawarden, through Northop and Halken to Holywell; he may frequently have opportunities for sketching on, and sometimes out of, the road, in openings that run up into the mountains. Here are two inns; though I did not put up at the Royal Oak, I understand that is a very comfortable house, and that the landlady is obliging to her customers, and is not wanting in civility even to the pedestrian.

I proceeded the next day to Holywell, meeting no variety worth recording.

CHAPTER IX.

Holywell.—Legend of St. Winefred.—Basingwerk Abbey.—Downing.—Roman Pharos.—Maen Achwynfan.—Captain Morgan.—Newmarket.—Funnon Asaff.—Diserth.—Bodryddan.—Rhyddlan.—St. Asaph.—Kinmel.—Bodlewyddan.—Denbigh.—Bella.—Sir Hugh Middleton.—Lleweny.—Bryn-y-Bella.—Bodfari.—Moel Famma.

HOLYWELL is a handsome and populous town, having many good houses: the principal street is spacious, and kept in good order: and the people seem busy in their different avocations. In the situation of the town, nature has done more for it than art could ever have devised: it has an adjunct of uncommon usefulness in that surprising phenomenon, St. Winefred's well; the body of water issuing from it in one minute, is twenty-one tons, or eighty-four hogsheads, and in the coldest winters it is never known to freeze: the quantity thrown up in summer is a little less than in winter; and, what is extremely singular, this amazing force occasions not the least bubbling on the surface, nor could I, when immersed in it, perceive any agitation in the body of the water; notwithstanding the strength of the spring, I found not the least inclination to be buoyant; the smallest pebble will gravitate to the bottom, as soon as it would in standing water.

This stream commences its first operations upon the wheels

of a corn-mill, a few yards from its source; after performing its duty here, it falls rapidly, and produces very beneficial effects upon the machinery of several grand and extensive cotton-mills; these have huge reservoirs of water, as agents to act upon various engines of the buildings, without which a mere narrow stream would be incapable of executing the work. Further down, the stream gives motion to several copper, brass, and lead mills, the produce of which, are both for home and foreign consumption. The copper is for sheathing ships' bottoms, and forming a variety of articles for our domestic use: brass and copper wires, and various toys, *&c.*, for the African trade, on the ivory, gold, and slave coasts of Guinea; where human creatures (possessing faculties, if but allowed to improve, that might shine as much in arts and sciences, as the most civilized people on earth) were, till the late prohibition, purchased with these, and such-like baubles of Birmingham, Manchester, and London, at the profit of one thousand per cent. Disgraceful commerce!—The merchant and dealer in human woe

"Did not feel for man; the natural band
Of brotherhood was sever'd, as the flax
That falls asunder at the touch of fire.
He found his fellow guilty of a skin
Not colour'd as his own; and having power
T' enforce the wrong,—for such a *worthy* cause,
Doom'd and devoted him, as his lawful prey."

COWPER'S *Task.*

Recurring again to the well, the spring is enshrined in a beautiful specimen of the light, or commonly speaking, modern Gothic architecture, introduced into England at the latter end of the reign of Henry II.; and afterwards revived and encouraged by Henry VII. This building is but small, the outside front has three tall, pointed, open arches, between which, and at each angle, are very light buttresses; above these are three windows, each enclosed in a square frame, having three pointed compartments; above these again is the entablature, the frieze of which is decorated with the grotesque figures of monkies, rats, and other animals. From this circumstance, Mr. Grose supposes, this building was erected prior to the time of Margaret, mother to Henry VII., to whom its erection is attributed; but this, I presume, can be no criterion: as there are yet to be seen numbers of buildings, so ornamented, in the days of Henry VII. and Henry VIII.: such as the church of Mold, in the time of the latter monarch. The interior is superlatively beautiful; the well, whence issues this vast body of water, is polygonal, the columns about it rise up, and branching various ways, produce a canopy of several elliptical arches, which converge to a point in the centre; the legend of St. Winefred, on the springstone, bears a shield with the arms of England, nearly defaced; above is the chapel, now a school: the two sides are also thus arched. The roof still exhibits some remains of crutches, *&c.* testimonies of the many and effectual cures produced by immersions in the outer bath; these cures were well and advantageously handled by the bigoted Catholics of the times, in which they are said to have been effected, who attributed them all to the miraculous efficacy of the blood of the vestal Winefred. These superstitious fooleries, invented to gull the ignorant, having been long since buried with those who devised them, have given place to the more rational opinion, that those cures, as well as others in our days, have been effected by the sanative healing quality of the water—a quality infused by the God of

Nature. Mr. Addison seems to be of this opinion: "Why may not the cold-bath," says he, "into which they plunged themselves, have had some share in the cure?" The ancients held cold-baths in great esteem, frequently dashing into these reservoirs of health; and, in England, where nervous affections are so common, it were well if the inhabitants used them more frequently.

The story of St. Winefred has often been related; but for the amusement of those who may not have fallen in with it, I give it epitomized.

St. Winefred is said to have been a beautiful virgin of the seventh century; daughter of Thewith, a potent lord of this place; her mother's name was Wenlo. Her uncle, St. Beuno, under whose care his niece resided for religious instruction, had built a church here for the edification of the pious. As Winefred was one day walking on this eminence, Cradocus, son of King Alen, a youth of profligate and impetuous character, met her, and passionately struck with so much beauty, made urgent dishonourable advances. Struck with horror, the virgin had recourse to flight. The prince, pursuing her, in the phrensy of disappointment, drew his sword, and severed her head from the body. The punishment of his atrocity was instant; he fell dead on the earth, which immediately opened and ingulfed his impious corpse. The head of Winefred, when cut off, rolled down the hill, and on the spot below the church, where it rested, burst forth, instantly, this perennial spring. Until this extraordinary occurrence, the valley, it seems, was called Sychnant, or Dry Valley, having no water in it.

St. Beuno, offering up his prayers, re-united the head to the body; and a small line, lighter than the colour of the neck, ever

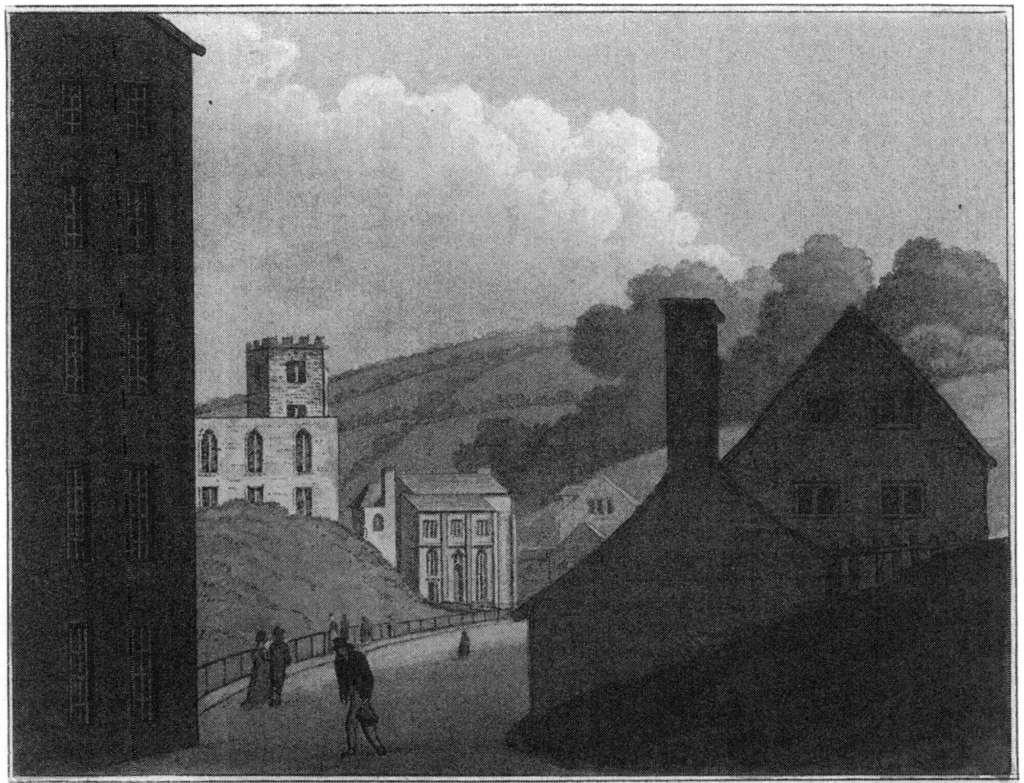

E. Pugh delt. I. Havell sculpt.

ST WINEFRID'S WELL.

Published 15th Novr 1814, by E. Williams, Strand.

encircled it, to commemorate the miracle. Winefred, however, fifteen years afterwards, died in earnest: and was buried at Gwrtherin, in Denbighshire, where she had become abbess of the monastery. After her remains had quietly rested about five hundred years, on a contest among the monks for the possession of such precious relics, they were removed, in the reign of Stephen, to the abbey of Shrewsbury. Her decollation is celebrated by Roman Catholics, on the 22d of June, and her translation, on the third of November; but no longer with such pomp as in former times.

Such was the credulous blindness of those days, that a bell, belonging to the church, was christened in honour of her; the gossips, on the occasion, laid hold of the rope, and gave it a name, the priest at the same time sprinkling it with holy-water, baptised it in the name of the Father, the Son, *&c.* After the ceremony, the gossips gave a grand feast, and made handsome presents, which the *priest* received *in behalf of the bell;* which, on being rung, had the miraculous power of diverting thunderbolts, allaying storms, and driving away evil demons! What became of this marvellous bell, it rests with the Catholics to shew. In the Protestant church it is not to be found.

On the same authority it was said, that the pebbles in the well, having red spots upon them, were marked with the blood of the virgin; a story well refuted by Mr. Bingley, whose researches have ascertained these supposed pebbles to be a vegetable production, *byssus jolithus,* the violet-smelling byssus.

The church, dedicated to St. Winefred, is upon the acclivity of a hill, close to the well; it is handsome, supplied with galleries, *&c.*, making the appearance of some of our best modern English churches: the tower is old and of different architecture.

From the very low situation of the church, the bells cannot be heard through the town; to remedy a defect so inconvenient to the inhabitants, a man is employed to ring a small bell about the parish, to give them notice of the approach of the time of service. The man is thus accoutred: a long leather strap thrown over his shoulders, and coming down in front nearly to the knee; to this strap is suspended a bell, which the person guides by its handle; and he is furnished with a cushion, fastened to his knee, to secure it from harm from the frequent repercussions of the instrument. I have introduced him in the view of the well, *&c.*

From hence is a pleasant walk of one mile through the wood to Basingwerk-abbey. This building is so demolished, as to leave no part standing that can interest the painter in any great degree. It falls far short of the vale of Crucis-abbey, nor does it seem that it ever, even in its pristine state, possessed any beauties equal to that. The architecture is of the Gothic mixed with the Saxon, as discovered in round arches and short columns; it is well wooded about with some fine sycamores, elms, ash, *&c.* These grounds being open, strangers will find agreeable views over the great bog-sands on the Dee, Parkgate, Neston, and Gayton*; and beyond these, part of Lancashire.

The refectory of this abbey is tolerably entire, and has a large recess on the side; above it were the dormitories of the monks. The chapel of the Knights Templers was a good

* The wake at this beautiful village is the subject of a little humorous poem, by Richard Llwyd, of Beaumares.

building, and still exhibits some remains of its beauty, in the elegant pilasters between the pointed windows. These knights were a military order, introduced, and this house established, by Henry II., to protect the devotees to the well

Henry III. granted it a charter with many benefits, confirming the donations of Ranulph, Earl of Chester, and those of other barons, *viz.* Holywell, Fulbrook, and the chapel of Basingwerst, Holes, and a moiety of Leeche, Five pounds of the revenues of Chester, Calders, with its inhabitants, *&c. &c.*; several other grants were added in different times.

Pope Martin V. furnished the abbey with many indulgences and pardons, to sell to the deluded devotees, which the fanatic Mary renewed by the influence which Goldwell, Bishop of St. Asaph, had with the Pope, to whom he went for protection on the accession of Queen Elizabeth. The last abbot, Sir Thomas Pennant, embraced the Protestant faith; and renouncing his former scruples, married Angared, daughter of Gwillim ab Gryffydd, ab Gwillim.

At this time the revenue of the abbey was, according to Dugdale, £150 7*s.* 3*d.*; and, by Speed's account, £157 15*s.* 2*d.*

Here was a castle, said, by Lord Lyttleton, to have been built by an Earl of Chester, but no remains of it are to be seen.

Henry II., in 1157, after escaping the snare laid for him at Eulo, restored, fortified, and manned this castle, and made it a place of retreat and security in case of any future disaster; experience had taught him to act with more precaution; and, to avoid penetrating into the forests, that time abounding in this country, he marched along the plains. The castle, however, was not long in existence, for the gallant Prince Owen Gwynedd, after repeated attacks, took it by storm, in 1165, and laid it level with the ground; nor was it ever after known as a fortress.

The great population of Holywell and its vicinity, has created the best market in the north of the principality; the town on the market-day is exceedingly crowded with people from all parts, twenty miles round. Provisions and articles of apparel, brought from Chester, Mold, Ruthin, Denbigh, and other places equally remote, find a ready sale among the men belonging to the different great lead-mines* in the neighbourhood, as well as the several factories and other works in the town. Holywell was without either fair or market till 1703, when both were granted by letters patent to Sir John Egerton, Bart.

The man of taste, the philosopher, and the antiquary, will here find ample scope for researches and contemplation in the different works of art and nature. The woods, between the town and the river Dee, offer to the artist some beautiful views, with agreeable vistos of the sea, *&c.*; the town itself, situated between the hills, is no despicable object. The high grounds above the town, in hollows that run up the hills, also present some fine scenery: the fore and middle grounds, supplied with rocks, woods, cottages, *&c.*; the estuaries of the Dee and Mersey, forming the promontory of Wirral, in Cheshire; with the distant land of Lancashire, and the still more distant county of York, make up a scene of great value. As the sun travels towards the west, these distant lineal objects die away very harmoniously into the horizon: which, if well represented, and happily combined with the nearer objects, could not fail to give a high degree of satisfaction to the proper judges of landscape.

* These mines are very ancient, and Giraldus speaks of them in his time.

The hollows and hills surrounding Holywell, afford a variety of fine subjects; and though it cannot be said that they are of the bold and terrific sort, such as are recognized in the western counties of North Wales, yet they are very picturesque, and possess the proper requisites, and sufficient interest, to detain the painter for a while, to observe and copy their beauties.

To —— Camden, Esq., a gentleman of consummate taste and talents in painting, I am obliged for much politeness, and for an advantageous view of the variegated beauties in the neighbourhood. Mr. Camden's fine pictures shew him to be indefatigable in the pursuit of the arts, in which he has attained to great eminence. In the processes for the discovery of permanent colours, and the mode of incorporating them with such unctuous matter as may, when transferred from the pallet to the canvass, approach the nearest to the colouring of the old masters, it is to be hoped that this gentleman will meet with success adequate to his perseverance. It would, in my opinion, highly gratify the public, if they had the pleasure of annually seeing Mr. Camden's pictures in the Royal Exhibition.

At the King's Arms I found much civility and comfortable accommodations.

Quitting Holywell, I ascended by the upper road to Downing, the seat of the late celebrated Thomas Pennant, now the residence of his son. On the way were discovered a few excellent spots for sketching, but on nearing Downing, the country appeared much more favourable for that purpose; looking over some thick woods to the sea, and through beautiful avenues between the hills, the eye will often meet with subjects calculated to give it exquisite pleasure.

Downing is a respectable-looking old mansion, and its truly sylvan situation, in a lawn surrounded and adorned by noble woods on easy elevations, renders it an enviable spot. The late Mr. Pennant, who knew well the value of woods free from noxious weeds and useless shrubs, would never suffer such crowded superfluities to entwine round the trunks of the trees: and, from this management, they now appear very healthy, and grow to an amazing height, beauty, bulk, and perfection. The careless indifference in this repect, observable in many parts of England, as well as of Wales, is very reprehensible.

The artist will find a feast in the rich woody glen, through which runs a rippling stream, forming small cascades, and hastening to meet the briny tide below: here, particularly, he will have excellent opportunity of studying trees of various and numerous species; and the different openings and windings will give him the advantage of well-disposed light, happily contrasting with the accidental shadows falling on other parts. This is, certainly, a luxuriant spot.

> "No tree in all the grove, but has its charms,
> Though each its hue peculiar; paler some,
> And of a wannish grey:—the willow such,
> And poplar, that with silver lines its leaf,
> And ash far stretching his umbrageous arm;
> Of deeper green the elm; and deeper still—
> Lord of the woods, the long-surviving oak."
>
> COWPER.

On the opposite banks of this rivulet, is Upper Downing, the residence of Thomas Thomas, Esq., in an excellent situation. The traveller would find it a pleasant excursion to Downing through Whitford; and, two miles further to Mostyn-hall, the ancient seat of the Mostyns, and still the residence of a baronet of that name; and then to return by the lower road, near the Dee, to Holywell.

Near Whitford is a Roman Pharos on a hill, called Garreg, or the Rock, which overlooks the sea. It is a very strong single round tower, and has square windows with frames of free-stone. From the base the building tapers a little, by three regular gradations, lessening as they advance to the summit: there are also two large entrances into it. Had not the edges of these been demolished, they would, probably have pointed out to the antiquary the time of its erection. The country people call it an old windmill; but it bears incontestable proofs of its having been a Roman light-house, to guide the navigators along the hazardous channel of the Seteiæ æstuarium, or the estuary of the Dee. The inside diameter is about thirteen feet, and the walls are four feet six inches thick: over each door is a square passage similar to a chimney, which opens on the outside, about half its height. It is not improbable that these funnels gave the lights, which appeared in the manner that our iron forges emit their flames at night: if so, it well agrees with the genius of the Romans, in works of art; for by this mode, the mariners could with greater certainty discover their bearings as they sailed along: because in nearing, passing, or leaving the shore, these lights would be seen sometimes singly, and sometimes together. This mode has advantages over the single lights, which are now used. This is merely offered as a conjecture; but Mr. Pennant says that the lights were exhibited in eight small square openings at the top; which, however, do not appear calculated to be sufficiently luminous.

At the foot of this hill, in a small enclosure near the road, is a remarkable stone, carved over with various ornaments in bass relief. It stands erect, tapering from its base till it meets its circular end, which includes a Greek cross. Beneath this, after some pretty lace-work, is the diagonal cross of St. Andrew; and underneath this stands a naked figure, in a dancing attitude, bearing a spear in his hand. This must have belonged to some religious house or church in this neighbourhood, probably to an ancient chapel, called Gelli, near the spot; now converted, as I believe, into a farm-house.

This stone is twelve feet high, two feet four inches broad at the base, and ten inches in thickness. It is called Maen Achwynfan, or the Stone of Lamentation: before such pillars, penances were completed, which concluded with weeping and the usual marks of contrition, for offences worthy of the punishment inflicted.

Whilst I was sketching this pillar, a number of people who were going to see the local militia exercise, collected about me. They soon entered into criticisms, in Welsh, upon my dress, person, *&c.*; and it was with the greatest difficulty that I kept my countenance. During this time, many observations were made, which might have alarmed a Frenchman, had he been on the spot, and could have understood them. Some would have it that I was an Englishman, or, pretending to be one, might be a spy: others, more sagaciously, made me out to be a Frenchman, who was approaching the sea-coast for the purpose of taking soundings. One little fellow, on observing my trowsers, became fully of this opinion; remarking, that a Frenchman, who had passed that way a few days before, had on just such another pair. As none seemed to oppose this observation, he grew very warm, and proposed to stop my progress through the country. One man, however, who stood right before me, not satisfied that this was the case, very calmly observed, that really he could not perceive the least indication of any thing French, either in my features or person; and, therefore, proposed moderation in their proceedings. The little hero, not pleased to have his sentiments thwarted, replied in the most animated manner, that it must be as he had said, as there were a hundred to one against an opposite opinion; and proposed the enormous bet of sixpence, that the stranger was one of the *Ffrancod* (French). Upon this, I tipt my partizan an oblique hint, which he instantly understood, and closed the mighty bet; when I turned to the little man, and, with a countenance which I could scarcely keep quiet, asked him, in his vernacular language, how he could be so imprudent as to lose his money at such a rate? He looked extremely abashed, and without another word, quitted the ground amidst the laughter and shouts of all that crowd, which the moment before were as sagacious as himself.

On the side of the road, near a large pool, is Plâs Captain, so called from Captain Morgan, who lived there in the troublesome time of Charles I.; and, taking an active part, was killed, and buried by this sheet of water: his grave is yet to be seen. A few years ago, an old man of the neighbourhood, flushed with the hopes of finding treasure in the captain's coffin (which is of oak and very entire), dug into the grave till he came to it: but greatly to his disappointment, found only the skeleton, and two night-caps covering the cranium of the poor Captain. The under one was of silk, and is now preserved by the family: the other was of very strong cotton, so altered in colour, as to partake of that of rotten wood; but which, since, by bleaching and repeated washings, has been brought to its original whiteness, and seems as strong and fresh as when first woven. This cap is in the possession of Fanny, who keeps the Cross-keys inn at Newmarket, two miles from Plâs Captain.

From the hills above Newmarket are some fine scenes. Those high mountains which form the eastern flank of the vale of Clwyd, come in very finely, while the varied flats between them and the foreground, receiving interest from their situation, add, in their turn, to the picturesque effect of the mountains, and other circumstances which abound on the spot.

Newmarket is but a small village and of little note, since the celebrated races and hunts have been discontinued.

The tumulose grounds, about this place, must be a treat for the traveller; and in no part of Wales is to be seen such an assemblage of them: they are covered with turf, and seem smaller than those which I saw in the western counties. The urns found in them prove them to be sepulchral. Near this place, as is supposed, was the great slaughter of the Ordovices, or the ancient inhabitants of Powisland and Gwynedd (now North Wales), by Julius Agricola, the Roman general, under the Emperor Domitian. The Ordovices were a fierce and warlike people, inhabiting a mountainous country; who, acquainted with the advantages of their situation, continued free amidst the subjugation of their neighbours, and were the last people in Britain unsubdued by the Romans.

The church has no claim to notice: there is, in it, however, a very singular stone, upon which are carved some ornaments, and a hand unsheathing a dagger, with an inscription, which is, as I believe, beyond the power of any one to decipher.

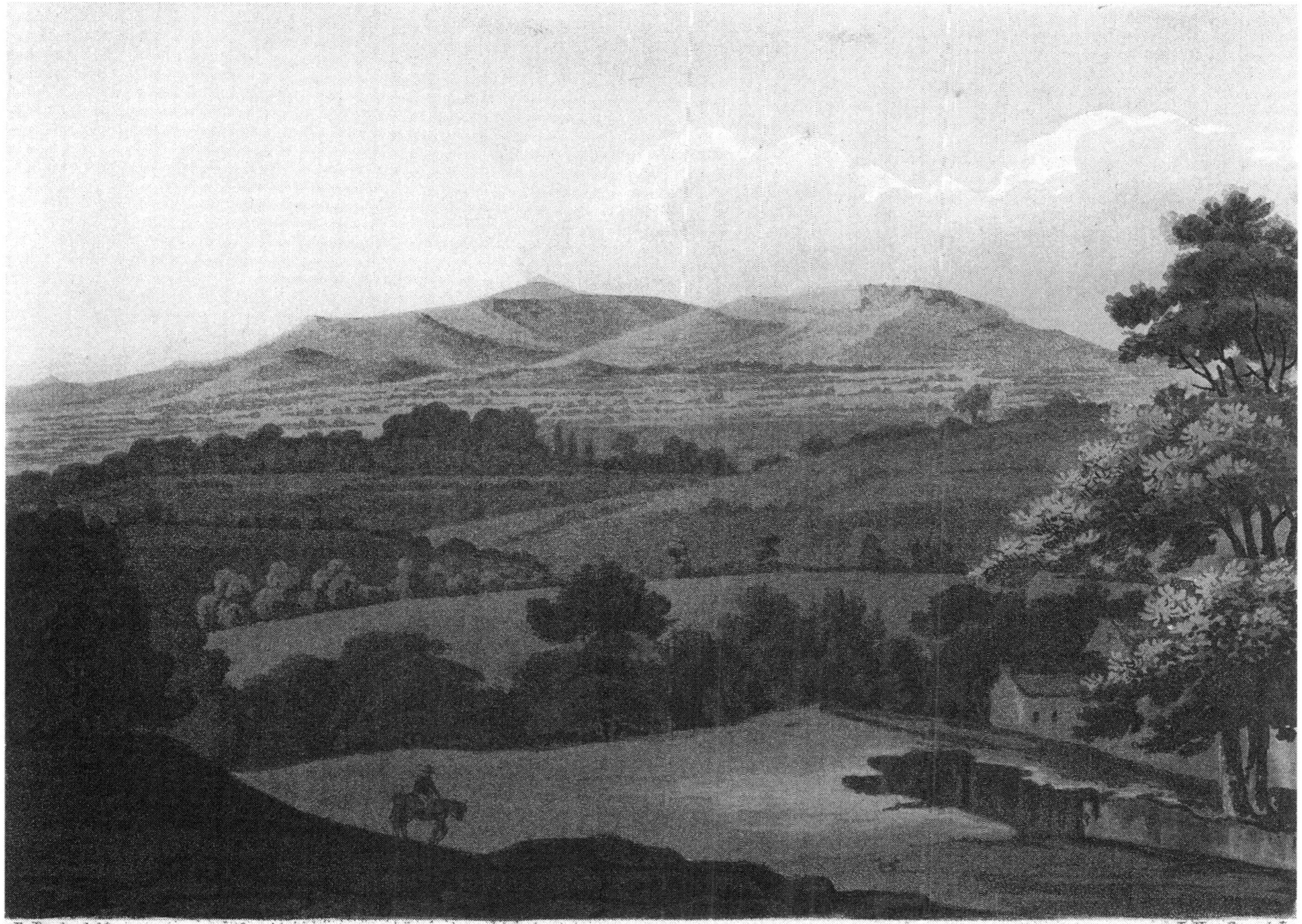

E. Pugh delᵗ. I. Havell sculpᵗ.

CLWYDDIAN HILLS FROM NEWMARKET.

Published 15 January 1814 by E. Williams, Strand.

Before I quit Newmarket, it is but fair that I should recommend Fanny's house to the stranger's notice; her Christian name is better known than the sign on the wall.

Westward of the village one mile, and a little out of the road, is Ffunnon Asaf, or St. Asaph's-well; where the stranger will be much surprised to see the quantity of water that issues; which is of such force as to turn a mill scarcely sixty yards from it; its greatest flow is supposed to be nearly equal to that of St. Winefred's-well; and, like that, its water is as clear and transparent as crystal.

The polygonal stone-work about it, shews the respect in which it was once held; and, formerly, it had its votaries as well as St. Winefred's. Its situation is at the foot of an easy ascent.

Some years ago, the miller was surprised to find all the movements of the mill suddenly suspended; he instantly sprang out to learn the cause of so uncommon a circumstance. Finding nothing near him which could impede the passage of the water, he hastened to the source, when, to his astonishment, he found it perfectly dry. As he sat by the side of the well, musing on so strange a phenomenon, he perceived a bubbling in the interstices of the wall and the flooring, the water making efforts to disengage itself; and in a few minutes, the miller (who all this time began to be fearful that he should see no more grist in his mill) was highly pleased to find that the spring had regained its usual vigour and power of acting. The water, from the commencement of its return, was as pellucid as ever; from which fact, it may be supposed, that, whether this obstruction was caused by the falling in of rocks, or of any other matter which choaked the subterraneous passage, the obstructing substance was free from clay or earth, or otherwise it must have discoloured the stream.

The artist will perceive some good scenery upon the river, between Newmarket and this well, and indeed for a mile on to Diserth. On the public road, and on each side of it, he will find very fine denuded rocky pictures, which must please him highly; and if he will frequently quit the road, he will find most exquisite scenery, connected with impending craggy eminences, between which he will have very agreeable peeps at the great Ormshead in Carnarvonshire, with the intermediate space occupied by the Irish sea, and the marshes of Rhyddlan. I would recommend the artist to try the road to Melidon from Diserth. Though I did not go far that way, I am led to believe, from the nature of the high grounds about, that he would be repaid for his trouble. The fine rock just above the village, must not be overlooked. The stream which used to fill the rocky basin above, has been diverted into another course; but it flowed through the crannies of the rock, and formed a curious circuitous cascade on the abrupt side of it facing the village. Diserth is a small hamlet, consisting of a few scattered houses, situated in a bottom among rocks: near it is a neat box belonging to the Rev. Mr. Strong.

The church has in it very little to amuse the stranger, if we except the old painted window; the pictures on which are better executed than what is common to old country churches. A window in the chancel has this inscription:—" Sir John Conway, 1636;" the time probably when the windows were painted. The cemetery exhibits very singular tombs.

The castle here, situated on the brow of a very lofty rock, supposed to be of British origin, exhibits very poor and shattered remains, which from no point whatever will make a subject for a picture. It was fortified by Henry III. in 1241: but in 1261 it was brought to this ruinous state by Llywelyn ab Gryffydd. There

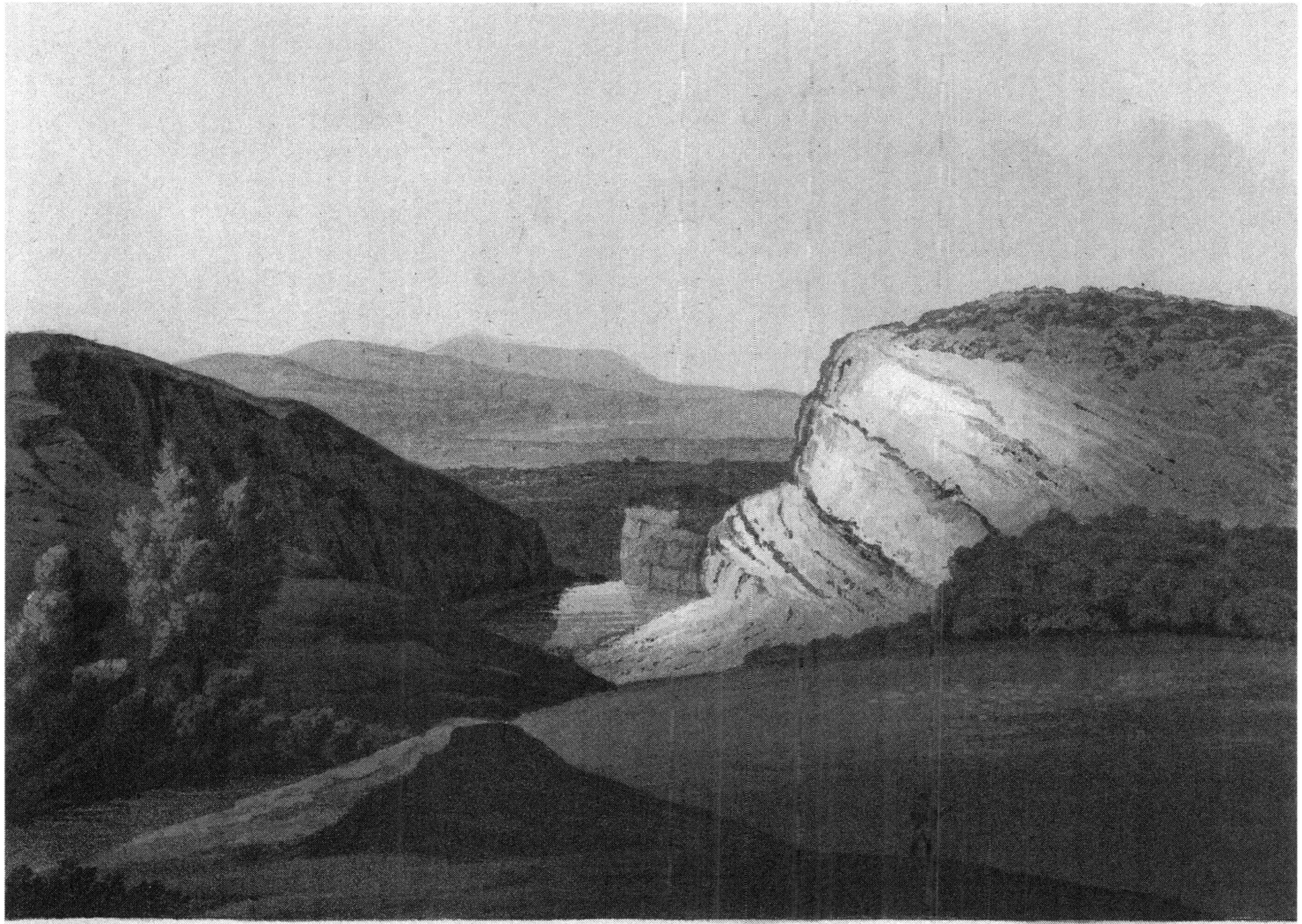

E. Pugh Del.ᵗ *T. Cartwright Sculp.ᵗ*

VIEW NEAR DYSERTH.

Published 15 July 1813, by E. Williams, Strand.

are some outworks, and some fosses cut through the solid rock. This fortress was overthrown by mining, a process of attack which was practised before the use of gunpowder.

Siamber Wen, a little south of the castle, is a ruin, once the residence of Sir Robert Pounderling, constable of the castle; " a valiant knight and prudent," who had one eye knocked out of its socket by a gentleman of Wales, when sporting at a tournament. On his being requested to challenge him a second time to " feates of armes," on meeting our gallant countryman at the English court, he declined a combat which he well guessed might prove fatal to the remaining organ of vision; saying, it was not his wish that the Welshman should knock out the other eye.

I now passed through the wood at Bodryddan, an old house patched up at much expense: it is in a good situation, looking towards the sea, and at present the residence of the Dean of St. Asaph. A little beyond it is Rhyddlan Marsh, celebrated for a most obstinate battle between the Welsh and the Saxons, about the year 795; when the former, under the command of our monarch Caradog, who fell in the conflict, lost the glory of the day, though our enemies had to lament the fall of their king Offa. After the battle, the conquerors committed a most horrible massacre on the inhabitants, nor did they spare the children. That beautiful, but plaintive Welsh air, called Morfa Rhyddlan, well known to professors of music, was composed on this occasion. It is very observable, that through most of the British music, there is an air of melancholy that distinguishes it from the Irish, the Scotch, or English. This may possibly be ascribed to the frequent wars in which they were engaged with their numerous foreign invaders, and the continual broils among themselves, under their own princes: in both which the never-ceasing loss of a number of friends and favourites must be perpetually calling forth the wailings and plaintive sorrows of the bard.

Rhyddlan, in Flintshire, is a poor town, and has for centuries lost its celebrity. It stands upon an easy eminence above the Clwyd; and is one of the outlets of the country for exporting corn, timber, *&c.* in small coasting vessels: several houses in the town retain an air of importance, expressive of former and better times; and are now occupied by labouring people. Its nearness and exposure to the sea, gives to it and its vicinity a cold chilly appearance; and there is no other motive to induce a stranger to visit it, than the castle. This is a massy structure, the whole of which, on a near inspection, is of a favourable aspect for the painter, and some parts of it may be selected for grand pictures; nor will its interest to the painter be diminished, if viewed at a distance. If the artist will follow the river above the bridge, or towards sea, he will from thence be gratified with an excellent view of Rhyddlan-castle, though there is very little to second it, and from the want of wood, it makes but a naked appearance.

This castle is a square building, with a round double tower at two opposite angles; the other angles are supplied with single ones. The declivity towards the river has been defended by walls and square towers; the one still entire is called Twr y Silod, or the Tower of Spawns, or young fishes, from its nearness to the water. In early times it often changed masters, the Welsh and the Saxons alternately commanding it. It was, by the orders of William the Conqueror, fortified with new works; and those probably were the square towers, being precisely characteristic of Norman architecture. Henry II. in 1157, strengthened the castle and the garrison; but ten years after, Owen Gwynedd took and dismantled it. Henry, after this, refortified and bestowed it with Emma his natural sister, and two other castles on David, son of Gwynedd.

In 1255, Edward I. possessed this fortress; he found it useful in the conquest of Wales: it was the rendezvous of his forces on the occasion, from whence he could with ease supply his armies.

Edward, knowing that the Welsh were averse to him in so near a neighbour, determined to make this fortress impregnable to any future attempts: he therefore rebuilt it at a considerable expense; the ruins of this last-mentioned erection are those now remaining, save the square towers noticed before. It is said that Edward held a parliament here, to give salutary laws to his new subjects, and to divide their country into counties. This was probably a council, convened by him, for the purpose of forming such laws, as might secure peace and safety among a people not yet reconciled to their new master.

In the civil war, when garrisoned for the king, it surrendered to General Mytton in July, 1646, and was dismantled in the same year by order of parliament.

From hence is a pleasant walk of two miles to St. Asaph, leaving Pengwern, the handsome seat of Sir Edward Pryce Lloyd, Bart. on the right.

St. Asaph, a bishop's see, is but a small place; the most prominent object here is the cathedral, in which the stranger will find little worthy his notice.

The choir has been lately decorated by the gentlemen of the county, with a most superb painted window, executed by Mr. Eginton of Birmingham. The three centre compartments describe, by allegory, the last tortures of our Saviour; this allusive picture is represented by several naked boys, in the act of preparing the different instruments of cruelty, which the Jews employed in these most atrocious inflictions. The design may do some credit to the first inventor, but it is not new; the idea of children, whose immature judgment preclude them from knowing the difference of right from wrong, may, perhaps, not unaptly represent the extreme ignorance of the Jews, in not discerning by the writings of their fathers, and, by all the signs of the times, that Jesus was their Messiah.

Other compartments contain Alpha and Omega, *&c.* The remainder of this handsome window is occupied with the coats of arms of the subscribers. This introduction of armorial bearings into subjects of such a sacred nature, is surely a great impropriety, though an old custom, established in ages of superstition, may sanction it: their admission, upon another ground, is rather improper; for the eye of the beholder is continually teazed by so much glare, that it cannot repose upon the picture any length of time without interruption.

The prodigiously heavy tower of this edifice, is raised upon four lofty Gothic arches, as usual in the centre.

The stranger will be agreeably treated with a superb view of the vale of Clwyd from the summit of this tower, to which there is a very safe and easy access by a broad Helix stairs. Six miles to the north is the Irish sea, which frequently displays scenes of much interest, from the circumstance of a vast number of ships going to and from Liverpool. The country from hence towards the shore appears rather bare, and the contrast is very observable on looking towards the opposite point; where this noble luxuriant vale fixes the eye upon its many attractions. Though it must be admitted that the prospect from hence is very fine, yet it is to be hoped the reader will accompany me to a point, from which may be seen, to yet greater advantage, the various beauties of this enchanting spot.

In the south aisle, attached to one of the pillars, is a monument of David ab Owen, in his episcopal dress, who died in 1512. Some rude hand has mutilated the face. St. Kentigern, Bishop of Glasgow, being driven from his see in 543, retired to this place; where he established a monastery for nine hundred and sixty-five monks: those who were not learned, in number six hundred, were for labour and procuring provisions; and the literate, to perform divine service daily without intermission. He also built a church here; but, being ordered back to Scotland, he named for his successor, Asaph, a pious Briton, and a man of good family; grandson of Pabo Post-Prydain, or Pabo the Pillar of Britain; a saint to whom is dedicated a church in Anglesey, where his effigy, yet perfect, is to be seen. About this period, belonged to this bishoprick, though esteemed poor, not less than five mansion-houses, which were made away with by Bishop Parfew in Edward VI.'s time. St. Asaph was the patron of this church, and in 596 was buried in it. This edifice was burnt down in 1282; in consideration of which, Edward I. granted to the see four hundred and nine acres in its vicinity, then valued at sixpence per acre. In 1402, it was again burnt by Owen Glyndwr; who, at the same time, did not spare either the palace or the canons' houses. After remaining eighty years in ruins, it was rebuilt by the worthy Bishop Redman. The chapter consists of a dean, archdeacon (who is the bishop), six prebendaries, and seven canons; besides which, belong to the cathedral, four vicars choral, four singing men, four choristers, and an organist. The arms of this see are thus blazoned, sable, two keys in saltier argent.

St. Asaph stands well upon a rising ground above the river Elwy, from which the town is called in British, Llan Elwy. Over the Elwy is a handsome bridge of several arches, and the Clwyd runs a little to the eastward of it.

St. Asaph is a very picturesque object from various points. It has been the subject of small engravings, but deserves a more respectable notice. The cathedral being a heavy building, will not entice the artist to draw near its walls, but at a distance it shews itself to advantage, and the scene altogether has a beautiful combination and variety.

The palace, built by the late prelate Dr. Bagot, on the site of the old one erected by David ap Owen in 1503, though small, is handsome; but it is nearly secluded from observation on all sides, except from the cathedral tower, which is the only clear object it has in view.

The parish church standing near the bridge, is a neat building, in which the people of the town and country hear divine service in Welsh; the higher orders go to the choir.

Though the White-Lion Inn here has no competitor, Mr. Howes, the landlord, pays every attention to the comforts of travellers. When a pedestrian enters the house, the question is not "Have you a horse with you?" but, after enumerating the various eatables contained in the larder, "Pray, sir, what shall I have the pleasure to send you?" The dainty article is no sooner mentioned, than the highly bleached cloth with its different appendages, the deep shadowy silver, and the shining steel, with other necessary *et ceteras*, like magic are displayed before him;

these forerunners of comfort to the hungry traveller, are immediately followed by the smoking feast, arranged in proper order; all this, and the celebrated national beverage cwrw gorau*, the best ale, cannot fail to produce the most agreeable sensations.

I repassed the bridge, leaving the deanery on my right, and entered immediately into the Denbigh and Conway roads; the one branching to the left, the other to the right; the latter is very pleasant, lying for the greater part on the sea-side; passed the new house of Kinmel†, the extremely handsome residence of the Reverend Edward Hughes, a proprietor of the Paris mines of Anglesey. The site of this house‡ is good, backed by a fine wood and open to the sea, which is bordered by the shores of Lancashire, Westmoreland, Cumberland, and Scotland. A mile on this side is Bodlewyddan, the seat of Sir John Williams, Bart. this house has nearly the same prospects as those commanded from Kinmel. It is truly laughable to see the numberless whimsical mistakes in the Welsh names of places, *&c.*, that occur in the writings of English tourists: here is an instance of the ingenuity of the author of a "Month's Tour;" who, when speaking of the latter house, and, from its pronunciation only, calls it *Bottle-within*. This appellation would have well accorded with an inn on the road, but would be too ludicrous to be the name of the mansion of a gentleman of respectability and fortune; al-

---

* Pronounced coroo gorey.

† In the old house of Kinmael, a few hundreds of yards from the new house, is a room called Cromwell's Parlour. At that time, Colonel Carter, an officer in favour with Cromwell, lived here, but it was not known that the Protector ever visited this part of the country.

‡ Rebecca has for a few years been employed in painting classic decorations here.

though the reader may be well assured that the vaults contain many a good *bottle within*, and that they are, upon all proper occasions, dealt out with that honourable and munificent liberality so characteristic of the ancient manners of the country.

Returning by the side of the mountain, where I frequently met with good pictures, I came to Pont Newydd on the river Elwy. Though this place was familiar to me, I could not resist the pleasure of visiting it again, especially as it gave me an opportunity of better ascertaining its worth to the arts. In the first place let me advise the painter and the traveller (for in this case both are concerned) before they descend into the glen, to turn up the gentle rise into the fields, from whence they will have a sight of this romantic spot, the beauty of which is made up of a delightful variety that contribute to enrich the scene. The projecting perforated rock on the left, thrusting its bald forehead to the water, is a good feature; opposed to it are the several woods, hills, and mountains, rising up in good style, and watered by the noisy Elwy; which, taking its rise in the mountains, travels through a channel rendered picturesque by the rapid movements of great bodies of water, collected in a course of many miles.

From hence it is expedient to descend to the bridge and mill below, and follow the river towards the hills, under a beautiful wood, from and beyond which, there are scenes that would tempt a Salvator. Returning from hence by the river-side, I came to the caves, one of which has a walk through it, lately made by —— Lloyd, Esq., of Cefn, whose house stands in a good situation, but is not seen from this side. From the high grounds of Galltvaenan, and different other elevated spots, the artist will find some good woody scenery, much to his purpose;

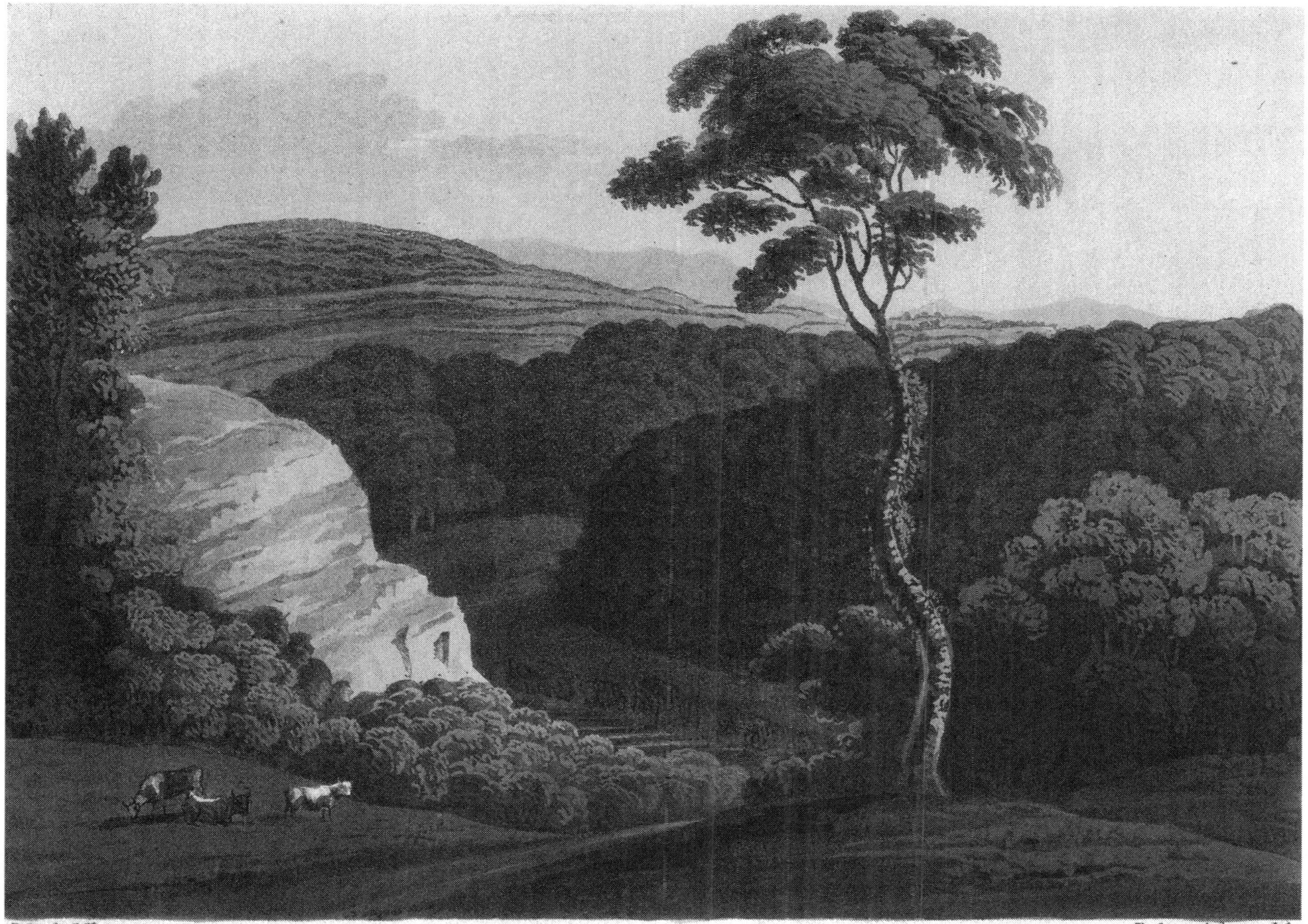

E. Pugh del.^t T. Cartwright sculp.^t

VIEW ON THE ELWY.

Published 15 October 1813 by E. Williams, Strand.

the bridge will also come in well, with a variety of objects that surround it.

The character of this place is very dissimilar to any thing that has yet fallen in my way; though it partakes not of the nature of the wilds of Snowdon, yet it has its points, which, if well treated, would be as delightful as many there; and though it may not parallel the most picturesque glens of Merionethshire, it excels the most splendid appearances of the kind, that came under my notice in Montgomeryshire. As this place is not three miles, either from St. Asaph or Denbigh, the artist to whom it is very little known, by carrying his dinner and flask in his pocket, may spend the day on the spot.

From hence to Denbigh, leaving the road now and then, the pedestrian will not be a little pleased to see some agreeable peeps at the vale of Clwyd. This is a good neighbourhood, where gentlemen's seats are as numerous as the owners are respectable; though they are not remarkable for splendid wealth, or sumptuous appearances, yet they are distinguished for much cordial sincerity and friendship in their social intercourse, and no less, on every emergency, for sound loyalty and patriotism.

The old house of Foxhall is now a fine picturesque ruin, and is of that species of architecture that prevailed in the time of Elizabeth, the windows being square shaped, with stone munnions, and heavy; this mansion was consigned to the hammer some years ago, and it may be feared, that it will soon be knocked down by a still more destructive weapon.

On entering Denbigh from this road, the stranger will be sensibly affected by the grand and noble ruins of the fortress, standing upon a high craggy rock, above the town, with several detached surrounding parts. The aspect of the town from this side is truly picturesque; the mass of houses towering up to the castle, and built of the same materials, has the singular appearance of ruins: partaking of the nature of that structure, the stranger can hardly divest himself of the idea that the whole town and castle, from the wild and confused heaps which they appear to form, are the remains of some magnificent and romantic bulwark.

Night now coming on, I entered an inn. Here I was shewn a little, but full-grown dog, which after a hearty supper, weighed only three pounds, and might easily be put into a quart pot; such was his courage in defending his portion of supper, that he resisted the galling bites of very large dogs with scorn, indignation, and successful perseverance.

The morning breaking out very fine, I got to different situations in the town, and had several fine views of the castle; the one from the back lane, north-west of the town, is incomparable. With regard to the situations out of the town, that from the wood-covered rock, called Park Pierce, is grand, in which the composition is a very happy one, taking in the hills and wood-lands beyond the castle.

The artist, from several parts of the castle, will form a good guess of the points, most eligible to sketch from.

The destruction of this fortress was not so complete as to render it of no consideration to the arts; the grand entrance is a fine Gothic arch, of immense thickness, over which is the statue of its founder, Henry Lacy, Earl of Lincoln; it is an excellent fragment, and several towers, half ruined and dispersed about, are also objects calculated to amuse the draftsman; and the stranger, let his profession be what it may, will find much amusement about these mutilated walls. Churchyard has drawn a fair description, in the following lines:—

"This castle stands on top of rocke most hye,
  A mightie cragge, as hard as flint or steele;
A massie mount, whose stones so deepe doth lye,
  That no device, may well the bottome feele.
The rocke discends, beneath the auncient towne,
About the which, a stately wall goes downe,
With buildings great, and posternes to the same,
That goes through rocke, to give it greater fame."

"If cannon rorde, or barkt against the wall,
Friends there may say, a figge for enemies all:
Five men within, may keep out numbers greate,
(In furious sort) that shall approach that seate."

The view of the vale of Clwyd from this castle is a little confined, and does not embrace all those beautiful objects, the sea, *&c.*, as when seen from Ruthin or St. Asaph; nor are these places within its command. Nevertheless, this curtailed view of it drew this observation from the venerable Lord Thurlow, who spoke of it in most rapturous terms, and declared, "That in all the countries on the continent, or in the British isles, through which he had travelled, he never beheld any thing half so beautiful and luxuriant." King Edward I., after the execution of David, brother to Llywelyn, gave the lordship of Denbigh to Henry Lacy, Earl of Lincoln, according to his accustomed policy, which secured his new acquisitions, by bestowing on his followers the great lordships of Wales. On the death of Lacy, this place came into the possession of Thomas, Earl of Lancaster, his son-in-law. After Thomas's disgrace, Edward II. bestowed it on Hugh De Spencer, who proved an oppressor, and abridged the privileges of the inhabitants, granted them by the Earl of Lincoln. This feudality thus passed through various families till the time of Elizabeth, who, in 1563, bestowed it on her favourite Robert Dudley, Earl of Leicester. On his entrance into the lordship, the tenants made him a present of two thousand pounds: notwithstanding which, he became dissatisfied and compelled the freeholders to raise the old rents, of two hundred and fifty pounds per annum, to eight or nine hundred pounds; and, at his pleasure, enclosed the waste lands, to the great injury of the tenants. They, however, had the spirit to resist and level his encroachments. This was construed into a rebellion; and two hopeful young men, of the house of Lleweny were, for the pretended offence, executed at Shrewsbury. Elizabeth, aware of the still more serious evils that might arise from these irregular proceedings, interposed, and allayed the discontents by confirming, by charter, the quiet possession of the tenants*. At present this manor remains in the hands of the crown.

The castle covers a large space of ground. It is built much in the style of that of Carnarvon, having the remains of several polygonal towers. Here is shewn the spot where had been a well, in which, as Holland, Camden's translator, tells us, a promising boy of Lacy's, having been drowned, "the most sorrowful father conceived such griefe, that he gave over the worke, and left it unfinished." When Edward IV. was besieged here,

* Baron Pryce's Speech.

without hopes of relief, he was allowed to retire, on condition of his quitting the kingdom for ever; which he did, in 1470, (though not in consequence of this capitulation) by taking shipping at Lynn.

In November, 1645, was fought a battle between the royalists, commanded by Sir William Vaughan, and the parliament army, under Major-General Mytton, who completely routed them, taking five hundred horse, and four hundred foot, and leaving many dead in the field of battle * In the following year, however, we find the castle again in the possession of the loyalists, and governed by Colonel William Salisbury, of Bachymbyd, in the neighbourhood, surnamed Salisbury with the Blue Stockings. Mytton again besieged it about the 16th July: but so stout was the resistance of Salisbury and his garrison, that they did not surrender the place till the 3d of November, and then on the most honourable terms.

The chapel close to the castle, dedicated to St. Hilary, is a very poor building, and unworthy the borough of Denbigh. Situated on a bare rock, it has no burying-ground, and when any of the inhabitants leave this world for another, their remains are deposited at Whitchurch, the parish church of Denbigh, a mile from the town. Near this chapel are the walls of a large unfinished church, one hundred and seventy feet by seventy-one, which was begun in 1579, under the auspices of the Earl of Leicester: but which, with some other buildings, he left incomplete on account of the people's hatred to him in consequence of his detestable tyranny. The Earl of Essex passing through this

* Whittock, 179.

place on his Irish expedition, and hearing that a large sum of money was collected for the purpose of finishing the church, very civilly borrowed it, without ever returning either the principal or interest. The building, thus deserted, and afterwards defrauded, has remained ever since in the same state; though it may seem extraordinary that no fresh contributions should have been made to complete it.

The town-hall, comprising the assembly rooms, is situated in the market-place. The town is populous, and carries on a good trade in gloves, leather, and shoes, with the West Indies. It is not well built; the upper part is old, and scarcely a good house is to be seen in it. A few years ago, the lower parts had many vacuities in the principal street, which, however, are now filled up, in general, with neat and agreeable houses.

I should merit reprehension, were I here to omit the mention of a man, whose extraordinary talents, unassisted by education, have acquired a high degree of admiration among his countrymen, and given him the flattering appellation of the Cambrian Shakespeare. Mr. Thomas Edwards was born in 1739, at Penporchell Isaf, a tenement in the parish of Llan Nefydd, and county of Denbigh, formerly the property of Iolo Goch, the celebrated bard of Owen Glyndwr, and near Llechryd, his residence. He was paternally descended from Cawryd ap Cadfan, Lord of Dyffryn Clwyd; and maternally, from the Rev. Edmund Prys, Archdeacon of Merioneth, to whom his countrymen are indebted for their version of the psalms.

In his infancy his parents removed from his birth-place, and settled at Nant Isaf, in the adjoining parish of Henllan, a circumstance from which he derived the appellation by which he was so generally known of Twm o'r Nant, or Tom of the Dale, and from him, Nant in return will probably acquire a celebrity which will endure as long as its acres.

Mr. Edwards, after a various and eventful life, died in his 72d year, and left a widow and three daughters, residing in the town of Denbigh. He procured his "daily bread" by the occupation of mason and bricklayer. Like his archetype, the Avonian Swan, tutored by Nature, he owed nothing to art or education. His dramatic compositions are a lively picture of the manners of his countrymen; for in the provinces of wit and humour, he is without a rival; and though a layman (like the great moralist, Dr. Johnson) he has written sermons in the language of energy, and in a manner peculiarly his own.

I shall conclude this short account of this original genius, with a copy of verses addressed to him in 1790, by the late Mr. David Samwell, Surgeon to the ship Discovery:—

To Mr. Thomas Edwards, of Nant, the Welsh Shakespeare, on his having been adjudged CADAIRFARDD, *or the* FIRST BARD, *at a meeting of the Welsh Poets, held at St. Asaph, the 25th and 26th of May,* 1790.

"O thou, to whom (St. Asaph's mitred town)
Judgment and Taste decreed the laurel crown!
Distinguish'd friend, whom Wales with triumph owns
Among the first of her poetic sons;
Thou to whom Nature's liberal hand has given
The power 'to scale Invention's brightest heaven!'
O! were the Muse but partial to my vows,
Wreaths of immortal green should deck thy brows:
And thy fair fame should future poets fire,
To gain the proud distinction of the lyre.
But though with weak acclaim thy worth I hail,
Yet shall not Friendship's warmest wishes fail;
Since thy own works to future times consign'd,
Shall prove the matchless vigour of thy mind,

And to thy name a monument shall stand,
Till Gomer's ancient language leaves the land.
Like that great Bard, who sung on Avon's shore,
Thy mind ne'er drank of Greek or Roman lore;
Yet Nature well the want of these supplied,
To shame the poor attempts of letter'd pride:
To thee, in early youth, the Goddess brought
Enraptur'd visions of poetic thought;
Creative fancy, various, unconfin'd,
The glance sublime, and energy of mind!
Since first the Muse, sweet native of the sky,
With grace attractive fix'd thy infant eye,
As o'er thy rugged mountains thou hast stray'd,
Oft hast thou woo'd the visionary maid,
Oft caught her whispers in the vernal gale,
Of Nantglyn's wild and deep romantic vale;
Where the fair Alwen *, list'ning on her way,
Would linger long, enamour'd of thy lay.
Thou heir to Cambrian bards of elder days,
When warriors toil'd to win the poet's praise:
Whose bold, impassion'd, and heroic strains
Inspired new valour o'er the tented plains:
And bade the British youth to battle fly,
With firm resolve to conquer or to die!
Those bards, whom Edward's † cruel soul consign'd
To slaughter all:—but the immortal mind;
Which, after ages have revolved, we see
With renovated lustre shine in thee;
Whose energetic, bold, and glowing song
Displays the force and spirit of our tongue.
Should pert Malignity, with Dullness, come,
And strive to blast thy laurels in their bloom,
Let cold Contempt alone thy breast inspire,
'Know thy own words, and reverence the lyre!'

DAFYDD DDU FEDDYG."
AI CANT.

Llundain, Mai, 1790.

* A river. † Edward I.

Here lived, a few years ago, a fortune-teller, of the name of Sionett Gorn. On her death, it was not likely that so lucrative an office should be suffered to lie dormant; and it has, ever since, been filled up by two *wonderful* women; of whom it is reported that they can see into futurity with *half an eye,* and that many of their remarkable predictions have been eventually verified. Among their devotees I had the curiosity to pay a visit to the one most in repute. I was requested to take a seat in the passage, the lady being then deeply engaged in her calculations on the fate of a man, who was weak enough, as I understood, to come from Barmouth, a distance of sixty miles, to consult this old woman. I could plainly hear their conversation. It seems that this person had a complaint upon him, similar to a consumption; which was not understood by the faculty of the neighbourhood; but which he fancied to have been the effect of a curse, on a visit to Llanelian well, by some secret enemy. She managed this man's case with a good deal of art, and, it may be added, with excellent advice. She told him that he might easily prevent any mischief to himself, by frequent petitions to the Almighty; and that he might rest assured if he did not succeed, that the fault was his own, in not praying with that degree of fervency which his case required: but that if he should prove sincere, he would get the better of his complaint in a short time. After paying the fee, he was dismissed, and I was ushered into the presence of this awful divineress. I was requested to take a chair opposite to hers, when she wished I would tell her the business I came upon, and be free and communicative. I took out my sketch-book: but being dilatory in my reply, "Come, come," said she, "I know your concerns, you are bashful, a thing very common to those who apply to me: but, as there are only you and I in the room, you need not be under the least apprehension of being heard. But," continued she, " I know your business and employment: you are a merchant, and are travelling among your correspondents in this country: but you have been somewhat unhappy for some time, and (with a smile and a bending of the head) you are in love with a pretty lady, whom at present you cannot obtain; but be not too much cast down, the lady is yours." Upon this I replied, that she had well predicted my case:—that I had, accordingly, partly secured the lady already; but wished to know if she liked her, at the same time shewing er her own portrait, in sketching which I had been tolerably successful. She appeared very angry; and whatever use I intended to make of it, she said, she cared very little; she was conscious of having done no harm to any one. The proferred fee, however, appeased her resentment, and we parted very good friends.

The money this woman gets in this way, enables her and her sprightly daughter to live and dress well; and her respectable appearance only increases her consequence among the deluded, who are eager to listen to her jargon nonsense. As since the union of Wales with England, our laws are one and the same, it is pity that these impostors should be allowed thus to cheat the deluded poor! Our magistrates, no doubt, are just as capable of preventing their depredations on the hard earnings of the labourer, as those of London were, in putting an end to the imposture of Mrs. Williams.

Denbigh has three inns, the Bull, the Crown, and the Swan. This borough, in conjunction with those of Ruthin and Holt, sends a member to parliament.

From hence I made towards Bodfary, directly crossing the

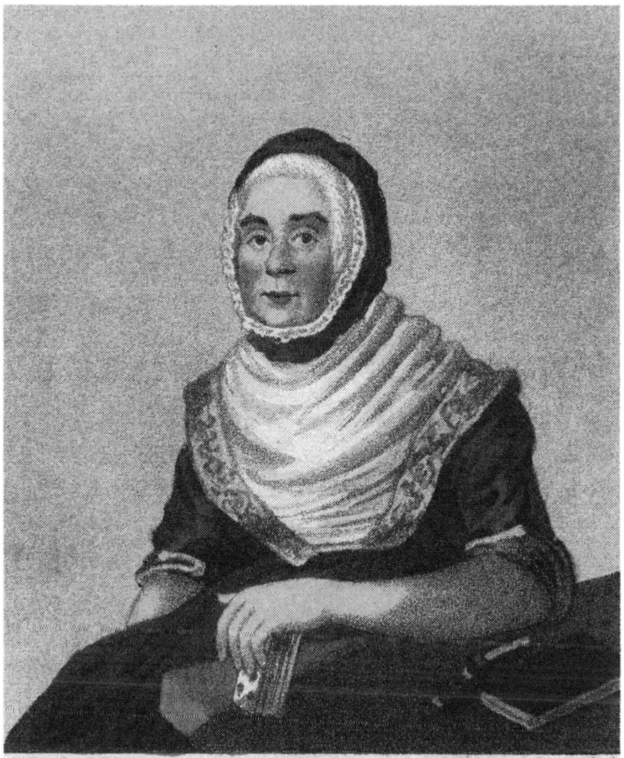

E. Pugh del.t T. Cartwright sculp.t

BELLA, THE FORTUNE TELLER.

Published 15 Feb.y 1815, by E. Williams, Strand.

vale from east to West, distant five miles. The first object in the way is Whitchurch, the parish church of Denbigh, and dedicated to St. Marcellus. The interior is worthy the stranger's notice, as it contains several antique monuments and mementos of the dead; one is to the memory of Richard Middleton, governor of Denbigh-castle, in the times of Edward VI., Queens Mary and Elizabeth. This gentleman had nine sons and seven daughters, several of the former were men of eminent abilities, and celebrated characters; the third son, William, was a marine captain, and a considerable poet; he received his education at Oxford, but preferring a military life, he signalized himself abroad equally as a soldier and a sailor; he was also excellent as an author, and what would be deemed a peculiarity in our days, he translated the psalms into Welsh, an elegant work, composed at sea, and finished 24th July, 1595: this and other productions were published in London about 1600. It is related of him, that he, Captain Pryce, of Plas-Jolin, and one Captain Koet, were the first that smoked tobacco publicly in the metropolis, when the Londoners from all parts flocked to see the novel practice of smoking segars. Sir Walter Raleigh, indeed, is said to be the first smoker of tobacco, privately. King James I. wrote a book against the practice, entitled "The Counter-blast to Tobacco:" but even royalty did not succeed in blasting it, for the amusement has continued ever since. Thomas, the fourth son, was Lord-Mayor of London; he married a young and handsome wife in his old age, which gave rise to a whimsical song, called "Room for Cuckolds, here comes my Lord Mayor." This gentleman was the origin of the family of Chirk-castle. The fifth son, Charles, succeeded his father as governor of Denbigh-castle: but Hugh, the sixth son, was a man of transcendent abilities, the benefit of which, to the remotest ages, will be felt by the city of London, and other places. He began his career with making researches for coals in his own neighbourhood: and, his ill success in this attempt did not deter him from acting in a wider sphere, for which his genius was so well adapted. This gentleman, afterwards Sir Hugh Middleton, Bart., was the dauntless and enterprising adventurer, who had the courage to undertake what great skill and perseverance could alone accomplish: to bid the waters flow to supply the thirsty Londoners, who for years had in vain been in quest of this relief. The plan was formed in the time of Queen Elizabeth. Sir Hugh expended two thousand pounds per month (the produce of Cwmsumlog mines in Cardiganshire) on this work, which he executed in spite of hills, dales, and many other difficulties in his way; now erecting aqueducts, and now giving the water a subterraneous course: and on Michaelmas day, in 1613, he turned the water of the New River through numberless concealed ducts, to all parts of the metropolis, when he was surrounded with an immense concourse of people: King James I., his court, all the corporation of London, and amongst them, his brother Thomas (Lord-Mayor elect) attended. In the procession were sixty labourers, handsomely dressed, and wearing green caps, each carrying upon his shoulders the common instruments of labour, the spade, pickaxe, *&c.*

This river now brings to the company an immense revenue. To the shame of the inhabitants of that age be it spoken, the worthy and magnanimous projector was suffered to spend a handsome fortune without any remuneration; and was so reduced, (heart-rending fact!) as to become a hireling surveyor in different parts of the kingdom, where his genius produced the most beneficial effects. He died in 1631.

A mile from hence is Lleweny-hall, the seat of Lord Kirkwall *. It is situated on the rich and flowery level of the vale, watered by the silent Clwyd. Though several additions, at various times, give the building an irregular appearance, yet it is handsome, and of considerable size. In the ancient hall are a small collection of antique arms, a handsome organ, and a few pictures; among which is a whole-length portrait of that celebrated warrior, Charles XII. of Sweden, by an artist of the northern school. A portrait of Sir John Salusbury, is remarkable for having two thumbs on one hand. There are three more portraits of the Salusbury family, one of whom is Thomas Salusbury, Esq (son to the beautiful Catherine of Beren) predecessors of Sir Robert Salusbury, Bart., M. P. Lanwern-hall, Monmouthshire, a gentleman whose virtues are as well known as that he is descended from one of the most illustrious families in North Wales.

At a short distance off are the bleaching-works, erected by his lordship's father, the late honourable Thomas Fitzmaurice, a gentleman well known for his patriotic zeal for the prosperity of the arts, manufactures, *&c.*, of his country. These works were raised from a design by the late Mr. Thomas Sandby; they are of brick ornamented with stone, and are in the form of a crescent; in the centre is a handsome turret with a clock, the whole front is occupied by a piazza, with square pillars and semicircular arches. In front, in different basins of water, and about the buildings, are the statues of Sobrina, Thames, *&c.*,

* This estate was lately disposed of to the Rev. Edward Hughes, of Kinmel-Park.

from Coade and Sealy's manufactory A few years ago, this was the subject of a print, from a drawing by Mr. Walmsley.

A mile from hence is Bryn Bella, the beautiful residence of Mrs. Piozzi, the literary friend of Dr. Johnson; it is situated on the rise of the hills that limit the valley on the eastern side, and commands an extensive prospect, with the town and castle of Denbigh, as prominent features in front.

Half a mile from Lleweny bleach-works is the village of Bodfari, the church of which is on a charming elevation, commanding, and commanded by, all the vale; it has within but little to notice: the pulpit, indeed, is worthy the stranger's inspection; it is of oak; on the different pannels are well carved several subjects of morality and religion; by whom, and in what time, no mention is made, but it appears to have age.

From the road from Holywell, between the hills, above the church, is a delightful view of Denbigh-castle and town.

Antonine the emperor speaks of a city built by the Romans, which they called Varis, nineteen miles from Conovium. This village shews no remains of such a place, though its name, Bodfari, or the Residence of Fari, accords well with the appellation Varis; but the mountain adjoining, called Moel y Gaer, Fortified Summit, has upon it some fine remains of a military work; it is possible this might be the place alluded to; though one strong objection to it is, that the Romans built their fortifications frequently on flats, and never on lofty mountains. This probably was a British work; as it was common for the ancient Britons to erect their bulwarks on the greatest heights. I am ashamed to say I forgot to visit this mountain, or I could easily have ascertained the fact.

From hence to Ruthin would be a pleasant ride, were the

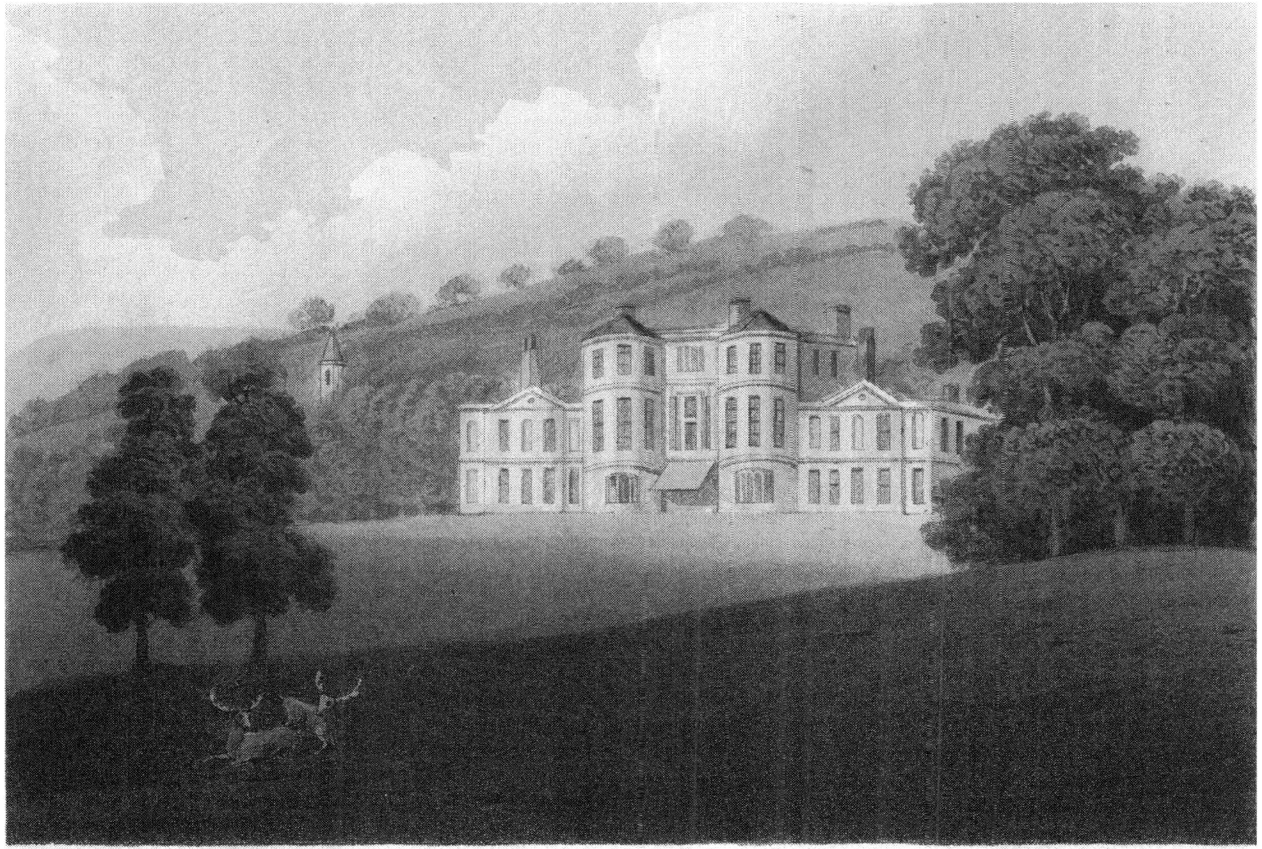

E. Pugh delt. T. Cartwright sculpt.

BRYN BELLA, OR MRS PIOZZI'S HOUSE.

Published 15 June 1814, by E. Williams, Strand.

roads in better condition; at present they are hardly passable for carriages.

On the left is Fronyw, a handsome house with a colonnade-front, the property of Mr. Maddocks, and lately the temporary residence of the Bishop of Killala.

On the summit of a lofty mountain on the left, has just been erected a small cottage, as well for the accommodation of grousing parties, as for the summer-day visits of Lord Grosvenor and his friends; a more enchanting spot for the purpose of surveying the aggregated beauties of the vale of Clwyd, with the mountain-scenery above, and the distant shores of Cheshire and Lancashire, could not be chosen. Further on is Plas-Draw, the residence of Mr. Davies, prettily situated on a gentle rise above the vale. Near this place, I met very unexpectedly with a peep at the mountain Moel y Famma, which is, from its simplicity, a treasure as a picture; two limbs of it running down into the valley, between which the land seems fertile and well wooded. The hill exhibit son this side a fine amphitheatre, but destitute of the terrific and melancholy, observable in the hollows of Snowdon and Cader Idris. The foreground of this view is a delightful site for a house; it is raised just high enough to catch many beauties in the vale, and has this mountain to protect it from the chilling east.

Quitting this sweet spot, and striking through the meadows, I soon reached my native place.

CHAPTER X.

Pool-Park. — A Storm. — Llanfihangel. — Cerrig y Druidion.— Caractacus.— Voelas.—Ysputty Ievan. — Lyn Conwy. — Beddu Gwir Ardydwy. — Helen's-Path. — Bwlch Garreg y Fran. — Penmachno Cataracts. — Pont y Pandy. — Robert Roberts. — Hywell Dda. — Dolwyddelan-Castle.— Pont y Pair.— Vale of Conway.—Gwydir.—Taliesin.—Elfin.—Llanrwst.—Llansanan.— Dyffryn Alet.—Catherine of Beren.—Gwaenynog.—Nantglyn.— Mr. Samuel.—Mrs. Jordan and Mrs. Siddons.—Hunts. —Pont Ychel.—Fine Scenery.

THIS, perhaps, was one of the most beautiful summers ever seen. During a walk of many hundreds of miles, I suffered but two interruptions in my pursuits from rain, and but once only had I eventually cause to lament the unfavourableness of the weather. Intending to rest two days at Ruthin, scarcely had one passed before I perceived the sky altering its aspect. It was but reasonable to suppose, after so long a summer, that a change of weather would now take place. " The same day were all the fountains of the great deep broken up, and the windows of heaven were opened." The rain came down most copiously, and the sky wore a mantle of uniform black. This scene I contemplated with pleasure, because I knew that it would, if continued for two or three days, afford me a good opportunity of seeing the falls of Penmachno to perfection; I therefore sat out early the next morning in a heavy shower, over a hill called Colledfa, a large common one mile south west of Ruthin, which Lord Bagot and others have divided in different allotments for cultivation. On the left is Pool-park, his lordship's summer retreat, in a pleasant bottom well wooded, and commanding a pretty look-out across the vale. From the remotest parts of the grounds towards Clogcainog, the scenery improves among some fine aged wood, catching those celebrated mountains Moelenlly, and Moel-y-Famma, *&c.* Clogcainog is a poor unfrequented village, though the church is better than these mountain-edifices are in general; it once boasted of a fine painted window: but this has been so often damaged, and is so distracted by misplacing the broken glass, that no story or connexion can be easily made out. Here, in a beautiful sylvan valley, running due north, about the centre of it, is a pretty little cottage built by Lord Bagot. On the mountain, near a farm called Maes-y-Tyddin-Ucha, are two stones mentioned by Camden; on one of which is this inscription yet perfect, "Amillin Tavisatoc." Lately a farmer's son, a block-head, in the neighbourhood, to prove the mettle of his horses, attached a chain to this stone, dislodged it, and it now remains at its length. It was reported he intended to break it up for building, perhaps a pig-stye.

The rain now poured down, and the thunder and lightning roared and flashed hideously; on my return down this mountain, my guide, the parish schoolmaster, a civil man, found little difficulty in prevailing upon me to take shelter at Mr. Price's of Maes-y-Tyddin-Ucha, who with great cordiality pressed us to a second breakfast, succeeded by several jugs of fine home-brewed ale, the powerful effect of which warned me to pursue my walk, ere I was incapable of seeing my way over the mountains. The rain, though somewhat abated, in spite of the shelter my umbrella afforded, soon soaked me completely; from hence to Llanfihangel over dreary hills and wastes, a distance of seven miles, is excessively dull and uninteresting. Near this village is a handsome one-arched bridge of a large span that crosses the Alwen; it was built under the inspection of Mr. Penson of Wrexham.

Llanfihangel is a small village; the church singularly narrow, not exceeding twelve feet across. In the year 1781 a great flood happened, which threatened annihilation to the whole village, when this turbulent mountain-river swept away two houses, and a smithery. The height of the water in the church at this time, was nine feet, and a painted line on the wall commemorates the awful event. Two miles further is Cerrig y Druidion (Drudical Remains). I took refuge at the White Lion, kept by Robert Jones;—being a man of retentive memory, he recites with the greatest readiness and perspicuity, and in the most animated manner, some of the finest passages of the ancient bards. The name of this village arose from a number of druidical stones; which, until of late years, were seen here, but which have been since used to make walls. It is a straggling place, situated in a cold damp country, producing very few of the comforts of life; barley, oats, potatoes, turnips, and two or three other garden vegetables, are the only esculents which the soil produces; small black cattle alone being rather numerous. Long after the time of the Druids, indeed, until these few last centuries, this country was well wooded.

On a mountain track of great extent, called Hiraethog, one mile south of the village, are the remains of the citadel of Caractacus, or Caradog, son of Bran ap Llyr; he was a most illustrious character; and, as a warrior, not excelled by any in British history. In the Triads he is ranked with Cynvelyn and Arthur, under the appellation of the three brave sovereigns of Britain *; and with Caswallon and Gweirydd, as the three leaders of battles: by another Triad, he is styled one of the three conventional princes, on account of the war, sovereignty of Britain being conferred upon him, to act against the Romans in their progress through the country. The history of Caractacus is so well known, that it needs not be enlarged upon here. Aregwedd Voeddig, daughter of Ararwy, an intrepid British Amazon, basely betrayed him into the hands of the Romans; and this act of perfidy was denominated one of the three secret treasons of Britain †. Caractacus, in the year 52, was carried prisoner to Rome, conducted himself before the Emperor Claudius, with such manly and magnanimous deportment, as struck his enemies with admiration; and they granted him his liberty.

The rain during the night fell abundantly, nor did it abate till the afternoon, when I contrived (passing Cyrniogeu inn) to reach the comfortable little house at Pentre Voelas. Voelas-hall, half a mile from this house, is a very old mansion of the Wynns; but by a late alliance with the Finches, now belongs to that family; it was once a place of note, but has lost its original splendour, and now exhibits a state of neglect. One of the pillars mentioned by Camden, which he says were supposed to be Roman, still keeps its situation, with the remains of an inscription, now become unintelligible, though Richard Llwyd was

* Cambrian Biography.

† She was "a chip of the old block:" for Avarwy is distinguished for treachery, and is styled in the Triads one of the three most disgraceful men of Britain.

able to ascertain that it was partly Latin and partly Welsh; to the memory of Llewelyn a prince of Wales; and as the places of interment of the other two Llewelyns are known, it is supposed this must have been Llewelyn ap Sytsyllt*, whose burial-place his countrymen are ignorant of; though it is known that he was killed through the treachery of Madog, Bishop of Bangor, in the year 1021.

Leaving this place in the morning, I crossed the river Eletwr, that runs through a very rough dingle, where are some fine bits of rocks and cascades; though neither large nor formidable in appearance, yet they are picturesque and interesting.

Ysputty Ievan, a small village on the Conway (which parts Denbigh and Carnarvonshires), has one tolerable house of public accommodation, near the bridge. The church has in it several mutilated monumental figures recumbent; the valiant Rhys Vawr ab Meredith, of Plâs Jolin, near this place, to whom Henry VII. on the fall of the bearer, Sir William Brandon, intrusted the standard of England at the battle of Bosworth, is here represented in armour, with a chain round his neck; near him is his son Robert, chaplain, *&c.* to Cardinal Wolsey, and the wife of Rhys Vawr.

Ysputty Ievan, or the Hospital of St. John of Jerusalem, was so styled from having formed in those times, in this dreary country, an asylum as well as guard for strangers, under the protection of the Knights. After this order was abolished, this privilege became the plague of the neighbourhood; for the place having no ruling authority, became a nest of thieves and murderers, ravaging the country to a great extent with impunity;

* He was married at the age of fourteen.

till, in the reign of Henry VII., the brave and prudent Meredith ab Evan extirpated them.

I proceeded from hence, along a disagreeable road, by the side of the infant Conwy, for five miles, and followed this brook to a large lake four miles in circumference, called Llyn Conwy, the source of that fine river that empties itself in the Irish sea near Conway. Mr. Baker, a few years ago, built a fishing-box on its side, but it is now in ruins. This place has a black and gloomy aspect, and seems unfriendly both to man and beast, as I could not perceive a single sheep, or an animal of any description, brousing upon the surrounding hills. This lake is much frequented by black-backed gulls: in the breeding season, in one of the rocky little isles they deposit and sit upon their eggs. Some years ago, as a young man attempted to swim across to take the young, he was so terribly wounded by the fierce old birds, scarifying his head and back, that he but barely escaped with his life.

Between the road and this lake, a distance of about a mile and a half, is a dangerous morass; but having lately been much used to this sort of ground, I was less fearful, as I knew by experience where to tread: for a stranger, however, it would be very advisable to engage a guide well acquainted with the nature of the ground; otherwise, they may, by the gay and luxuriant appearance of certain spots, be decoyed into deceitful bogs, and be overwhelmed in an instant. These quagmires exhibit a surface of beautiful green, of various descriptions of water-plants, and by this specious display, often lure the unwary within their smothering grasp.

How true a representation is this of those hollow hypocritical friends, who, while you appear independent of them, can, with ease and seeming liberality, allow you merit, even more perhaps, than usually falls to the lot of human nature to possess : but if the Fates have devoted you to any reverse of fortune, and should place you in the heart-rending situation, of being under the necessity of requiring assistance from those, whose smooth and specious appearance may have beguiled you into a dependence on the sincerity of their attachment, their behaviour will induce you to exclaim with Goldsmith :—

> " And what is friendship, but a name,
> A charm that lulls to sleep,
> A shade that follows wealth and fame,
> But leaves the wretch to weep."

Descending towards Festiniog, I got again into the road, followed it two miles, and passed a beautiful and most romantic lake on the right, called (from the deep shade of the surrounding rocks on the water) Llyn du Bach, or Little Black Pool. Rather lower down I entered a shed on the edge of the road, the most miserable dwelling the mind can conceive : something in the shape of beds occupied the ends of the room ; in the centre, about two yards square, was a fire of turf on the ground, and three little naked children running about. It would be difficult to find out a better school for the rich, than this wretched hut. Night coming on, I hired a guide at Pont yr Avon Gam, to Llyn y Morwynion, half a mile from the road ; this lake is probably two miles round, and contains some fine fish ; the scenery about it is rocky and fine.

It being fair-time, Ffestiniog was in confusion ; and though my walk this day had somewhat fatigued me, the great bustle and noise made by the farmers of the neighbourhood, rendered it advisable to push on three miles further, in a dark and rainy night to Maentwrog, where I found every comfort my situation required.

Autumn being the time of the year for transporting horned cattle from the principality to England, it is customary at a convenient place to shoe the animals, to enable them the better to perform so long a journey : here I had the pleasure of ascertaining with greater precision the mode of performing this annual task. A man takes hold of the animal's nostrils with his left hand, and with his other grasps the right horn ; at the same time placing his right heel tight round the animal's right fore-leg; thus, being ready for the throw, he summons up all his strength, and while he presses the horn downwards, forces the muzzle upwards ; and, keeping his heel close, with one great and sudden effort, brings down the animal on his right side; in the fall, the horn generally enters the ground, in which situation the beast is kept, by the man lying upon his neck. The blacksmith is now engaged in tying all his legs together ; after this, a pole six or seven feet long is placed between his feet and belly ; one end fixed in the ground, the other resting on the animal's side, and held tight by a third person ; the operation of shoeing is then began, which is done by affixing two small plates of iron to each hoof.

Throwing an ox is reckoned among the rustics of Wales, as a feat that requires courage, strength, and activity ; those who are expert at this business are not a little proud of their abilities ; and the man who can best, or, as they term it, *cleanest* throw his beast, assumes no little consequence on the occasion. Those men who undertake to overturn oxen, are mostly low in stature, stout, well made, and active.

In the afternoon I returned to Ffestiniog ; from whence, the next morning, I sallied out in the midst of very fine heavy rain, which in ten minutes completely drenched me. One mile and a half on the road to Penmachno, are to be seen, the Bedde Gwîr Ardudwy, or the Graves of the Men of Ardudwy Some years ago, there was an attempt made to discover the remains of the bodies, but nothing was found that could throw a light upon the following story of them, which is not much unlike that of the Sabine women. In very early times (but which no historian has fixed) the men of Ardydwy, hearing of the beautiful maids of the vale of Clwyd, repaired thither; and, by force, brought off, each of them, a lady: but near this place they were overtaken by the heroes of the vale; a dreadful conflict ensued, and the ravishers were slain to a man; but by some strange infatuation in the fair ones, these men of Ardydwy had already secured their hearts; and rather than return home with their friends, they rushed into an adjoining lake, and there perished; from this event the lake was called Llyn y Morwynion, or the Maiden's Lake. The stones (supposed to have been placed on these men's graves, and insisted on by my ignorant guide to be shewn as such) are yet to be seen on each side of the road, and have a degree of regularity in the arrangement, evidently shewing the original to have been a bardic circle: so the depository of the dead, if such an event ever happened, may yet be found in the neighbourhood.

Near this spot may be traced, Sarn Helen, the Causeway, or the Path of Helen, or more properly Ellen, daughter of Eudaf or Octavius, wife of Maximus the Emperor. This Ellen is frequently confounded by authors, with Ellen the wife of Constantius, who is celebrated by many ecclesiastical writers of antiquity, for cleansing Jerusalem of idols, for finding the cross upon which Christ suffered, and for erecting a church on the spot where he was born.

A little further on is Bwlch Garreg y Frân, from whence, looking down the vale, the stranger will perceive a wildness of prospect, worthy of the pencil of a Wilson. Here Nature exhibits herself in her most grotesque and romantic dress; and in a manner that rivets the attention of the artist. Further, on the height on the right of the road, is a noble rock of a castellated appearance: this presents an object of great whimsicality; some detached stones, so well grouped, and approaching so much to the human shape, that the imagination finds no difficulty in tracing the resemblance to a monstrous giant in armour, guarding his citadel; his posture is that of standing, shewing a sturdy front to the pass below; with a determination which seems to denote, that he is resolved to stand or fall with his charge. The black condensed clouds, together with the torrents that fell from them, added greatly to the singularity of the scene. On leaving this pass, the giant appeared equally terrific; and strangers, approaching him in the dusk, have been frequently alarmed by this man of stone.

I now descended into a swampy road of three miles, between dull uninteresting hills; where the little mountain streamlets had swelled into rivers; which, converging at last into one point, occasioned a prodigious current; so deep and rapid, as for some time to make me hesitate to pass it. Reflecting, however, that if I forded it, my condition could not possibly be worse than it was, being then completely wet, I entered the torrent without ceremony up to my elbows, across a bottom of rough stones, on which I was scarcely able to keep myself steady; my dog, at the same instant, plunging in, was by the stream carried down many yards ere she landed.

The vale of Penmachno, gradually making its appearance, I anticipated the pleasure I was shortly to enjoy in passing through it. On approaching the steep and tedious descent into the cwm, my ears were saluted with a thundering noise, the cause of which I easily understood, though it was as yet unseen. While plodding my way down this shocking road, the sides of the mountains shewed by degrees their watery treasure, which rolled down in numberless cascades of the greatest beauty and splendour; the whole to me, though a native, was perfectly new; it yielded me infinite pleasure: and though it was the only gratification that I had yet enjoyed in this little excursion, it amply compensated for my toil, rendered more severe as it was, by the unpleasantness of the weather.

On gaining the bottom of this vale, the noble cascade on the right, which caused the noise I heard on descending from the hills, appeared in all its unequalled grandeur. Its form is an inclined plane from its commencement on the hill, in one continued unbroken sheet, over a rocky bed to the vale below. This fall, as near as conjecture will enable me to say, is more than a quarter of a mile in depth, and about twenty yards wide. It nevertheless does not possess those requisites that would recommend it to the notice of the painter for imitation; the grounds about it are tame, spiritless, and without a feature of what can be justly called the picturesque. From this description, however, it ought not to suffer the least dimunition of character; for it has so much sublimity, as to render it a most interesting subject of contemplation; it is seen for several miles down the valley: but in my opinion, a visit to it from the Llanrwst side, cannot be so agreeable as from Ffestiniog: for, from Llanrwst it is approached gradually, and of course does not produce that impression on the mind, which arises from the sudden access to it from the latter place. This fall is called Rhyadr y Rhiw Fachno. The other falls, though numerous, are of less consequence. These, however, receive much importance from their nearly perpendicular direction. One on the left, called Rhyadr Dyfnant, is perhaps the highest in North Wales; its fall being, as I should suppose, not less than one hundred yards. The great body of water which tumbles down this black rocky fissure, and is interrupted twice in its descent, renders it exceedingly picturesque, though not adorned with much wood. But the cleft runs up the mountain-side in a wild shattered shape, so that when the waters are accumulated, as they were when I had the pleasure of viewing the scene, it must, notwithstanding some local defects, delight every lover of the picturesque.

When I had reached about the middle of the valley, the sight was very singular. Those little mountain riplers, which in dry summers, are with difficulty seen trickling down the precipitous sides, were now so swoln, as to divide themselves on the summit, before they gained the edge of the rocks, and prepared to hurl them to the bottom; and this accounted for the numerous cataracts which nearly surrounded me.

The vale is so bare of wood, that scarcely a tree is to be seen in it. It is liable to great and dangerous inundations; which, however, fortunately for the inhabitants and those of the vale of Conway, do not often happen; and, when they do, they quickly subside, in consequence of the unrestrained progress of the waters to the sea. The soil appears better adapted to the rearing of cattle, than for the cultivation of corn.

A few hundred yards across the river Machno, a little before we come to Penmachno-village, is a waterfall called Rhyadr Oerant; which, if it were not deficient in height, I should not hesitate to pronounce equal to some of the falls near Festiniog.

A mile from the village is another cwm, in which is a fall called Rhyadr y Glascum. This rushes from a hill, through a narrow sluice, and under a plat that crosses the road *, into a woody dingle below. The fall is about sixty feet, of one unbroken sheet, and upon the whole, very grand.

As there was not the least hope of a cessation of rain, I determined to halt for the night at Penmachno, or the head of the Machno, a small village just within the boundary of Carnarvonshire.

Robert Roberts, the landlord of the public-house, is a very civil man, and has a number of anecdotes in his way, at the service of his guests. His manner of relating a story in English is amusing. One of several I shall give verbatim; but the reader must be first informed, that it is common in the mountainous parts of Wales, among the uneducated, who attempt to converse in English, to mix English and Welsh together, in such a way as scarcely to be intelligible. He began, " I was once, Sir, live un (*a*) America un an inn ; was trydydd osler (*b*) ; ypen osler (*c*) was Irishman ; ael osler (*d*) was Dutchman. I was saw some

---

* A road that leads to a grousing-box belonging to Sir Edward Lloyd, Bart. called Plasynglas cwm.

(*a*) in. (*b*) The third ostler. (*c*) First, or head ostler. (*d*) The second ostler.

trick go to play on the Welshman; but was not take notice, but let um go on with his trick. There was in stable caseg brapor, (*e*) belong to some gentleman, but was a tam bitch for brather (*f*). I was call, by the Irishman, to rub down this mar; the Dutchman was hold her head; and her was kick and bite terrible: the Dutchman was often want to put her head to my back, for to bite me, but I was took pretty good car. The Irishman was slily tell him, to put pen y gaseg (*g*) more to me: I was now directly put my hand under the mar's bally, and pinch her hard on that side where Dutchman stand; the mar now make great noise, and bite the Dutchman's nose quite off: he did run about roaring, like any thing, with his nose in his hand, yn gwaedu (*h*) most terrible. I did go up to him and the Irishman, and say, Aha! the biter is bited, is he? I was then look hard at Paddy, and was tell him, to his teeth, he better no more play tricks with a Welshman; for if you did, I was always sure to be up to you: but," continued he, "when I did see poor Dutchman's face, I was very *very sorry undeed*, er y gwnae efs hyn i mi (*i*).

The wildness and grandeur of the surrounding scenery having lately induced many artists to visit this spot, Roberts has recently added to the scanty accommodation which his house afforded. He acts frequently as a guide, is extremely anxious to give satisfaction, and is well acquainted with every local object, of consequence to the stranger.

The night, on which I slept at this village, was very stormy, and the rain poured down in unceasing torrents; a circumstance

(*e*) A handsome mare. (*f*) For biting. (*g*) The mare's head. (*h*) Bleeding.
(*i*) Though he would have done the like, but unmerited injury, to me.

which afforded me two subjects of contemplation, one of pain, in the apprehension of another ducking, and the other of pleasure; in the expectation of the delight with which I should behold the noble and incomparable falls near Pont-y-Pandu bridge at the Fulling-mill, two miles from hence. After the common preventive against cold, an excellent breakfast, I committed myself again to the watery elements, in company with Roberts and another, who were going in pursuit of some live stock on the mountains. We touched at a farm-house on the road, where I had the gratific tion of tasting that ancient beverage of the ancient Britons, called Medd, in English, Metheglin. It is made of honey, of the flavour of which it strongly partakes, and is a warm invigorating liquor. The scenery about Pont-y-Pandu mill is most magnificent. A little lower down is the junction of the Machno and the Conwy, where the former loses its name in that of the latter. Still lower down is Rhyadr-y-Graiglwyd fall at the Grey Rock, the most awful and majestic fall I had yet seen in all my rambles through the north of the principality. To view this vast profundity from the precipices above, is sufficient to unnerve any one who advances to their brinks. The stupendous beetling rocks, on each side of this foaming cataract, are excessively rich, and their massy jutting fronts press forward in a bold and most sublime manner. The most active powers of the imagination would fail to pourtray a scene of so much interest and grandeur. To feel the force of this assertion, the landscape-painter need only partially glance his eye upon the spot; and he will feel the most lively pleasure in spending a few days in this neighbourhood. These aqueous excavations are of great breadth: their sides are finely marked with fissures and hollows, formed by the constant agitation of the waters, which render them admirably picturesque. The scenery

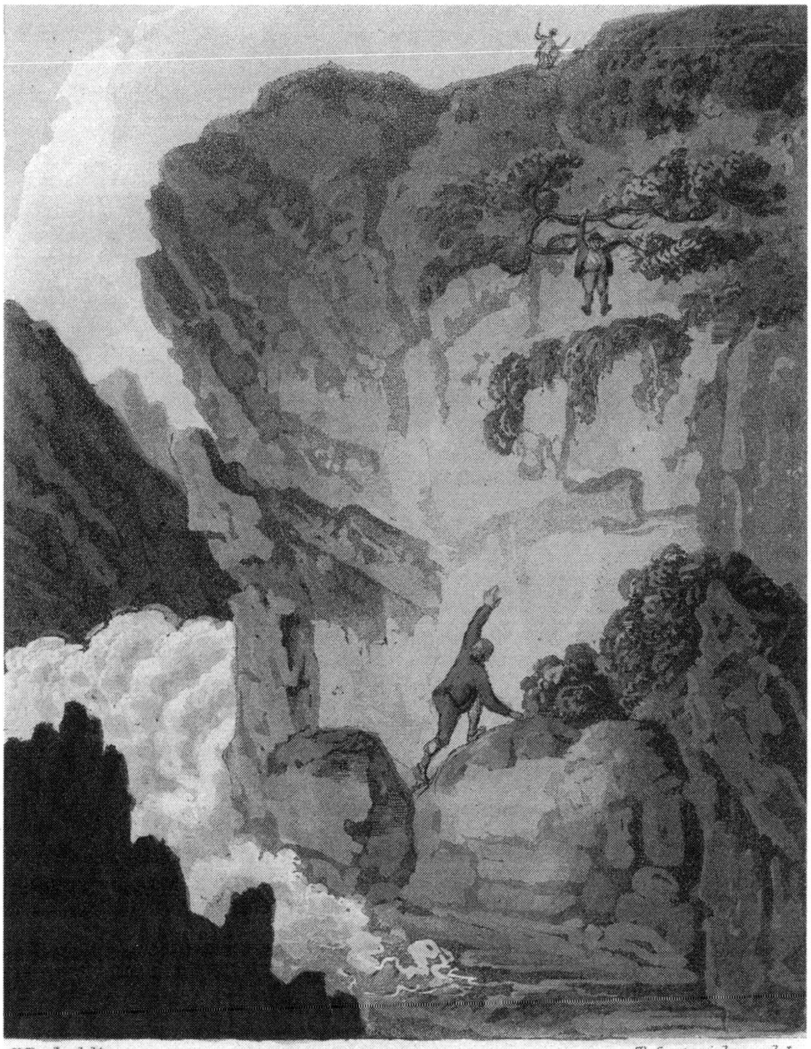

E. Pugh del.[t] T. Cartwright sculp.[t]

THE PERILOUS SITUATION OF ROBERT ROBERTS.

Published 15 August 1814, by E. Williams Strand.

is so, in different degrees, for a mile, following the river as it tumbles over rocks and stones, and, roaring with the utmost rage and violence, threatens destruction even to the rocky masses which stand in its way : nor does it assume a more placid appearance, till it expands in the bosom of the meadowy vale of Conway. The man who can pass this mile without admiration of its various beauties, and without feeling those emotions, which the sublimity of the scenes are so highly calculated to produce, must surely be lost to all susceptibility of attraction from some of the noblest features in the works of nature.

The principal reason which induced Robert Roberts, the guide, to accompany me to this place, though considerably out of his way, was to shew me the spot, where, a few summers before, he was miraculously saved from a death, the most horrid which can be conceived, by the intrepidity of a young man who was then with us, unworthily nick-named Dick Sion Dafydd.

The circumstances attending this extraordinary case shall be related—A gentleman calling at Penmachno for a guide, Roberts was hired, and Dick accompanied them. After shewing the stranger several places, they conducted him to this fall. Roberts, whose assiduity is well known, wishing to find out a way on the verge of this awful precipice, to bring the gentleman right above the falling torrent, that he might be the better able to observe its fury, unfortunately trod upon some soft or rotten turf, which giving way, he was precipitated headlong over this monstrous cliff, and instantly given up for lost by his companions. But, to their astonishment, he was presently heard to call for help ; when Dick, springing to a situation whence he might see his friend, observed him suspended by his arms in a dwarf oak which had grown from the rock. This good fellow hesitated not a moment, but acted upon the first impulse of his feelings; and with a resolute determination, which belongs only to generous minds, either to save Roberts, or to perish in the attempt, crossed the river in two places, at the imminent hazard of his own life, combating the turbulence of the torrent, and surmounting the dangerous pointed rocks which darted up frightfully out of the water. These difficulties overcome, he had yet, before he could get at Roberts, to encounter an opposition which would have appalled any less generous or enterprising spirit. After taking a momentary view of the perpendicular rock, which he had to climb, he sprang up, and vigorously pursued his way through the different crannies and clefts, the nice and narrow ridges, the dangerous edges of the rock, and at last triumphantly reached the old man; and, with one effort of his nervous arm, placed him comfortably in the tree. Roberts declared, that if Dick had not arrived at the moment, he must, from his exhausted strength and great weight of body, in the next instant have been consigned, from shelf to shelf, to the pointed fragments below. From the tree to the summit was nearly a mural front, of many feet: the old man crept up very cautiously, and Dick followed, protecting him in the rear, till happily, at last, both reached the top: where they met the stranger, who all this time had been in the most anxious suspense. His joy on seeing them out of danger, may easily be imagined: it spoke in tears only, the power of speech being, for the moment, suspended *.

The scenery lower down, although the altitude of the rocks is less, is still exceedingly grand, flanked on each side by

* Does not this act of Richard's deserve a gratuitous remembrance of the modern Druidical Society of North Wales?

woods which are grouped in the true style of the picturesque, and which were worthy of the happy pencil of Wilson.

Before I quit this spot, I feel that I am obliged to refute a statement made by a gentleman, upon his entrance into the Vale of Conway from the north end, as that statement involves in it a charge of inaccuracy against one of our finest poets. The words are these:—"On considering the character of this stream*, which has nothing 'foaming' in it, we were immediately struck with the impropriety of Mr. Gray's epithet for it. The poet, indeed, might have been led into the error, by supposing that the Conway resembled the other mountain-torrents of Wales, whose courses are marked by rage and impetuosity; but had he written from actual observation, he would have known its features are of the opposite kind, and that it meanders in peace and silence through the vale."

Now the inaccuracy, after all, rests not with the poet, but with the remarker. Had Mr. Warner written from actual observation, *he* would have known "that the features" of the river Conway, for more than half its length, from its source to its union with the tide at high water, "are of the opposite kind" to a meandering stream. "The poet" was, no doubt, much better acquainted with this river than the tourist, who had seen but a small part of it; for it is a fact, that from Llyn Conwy, far up the mountains, where it rises, this is, literally, a "mountain-torrent, whose course *is* marked with rage and impetuosity," rushing between, and tumbling over, the roughest rocks for fourteen miles, save in one or two places, where it gently flows, for a little distance, "in peace and silence," through the flats. Mr.

* Conway river.

Mr. W. "indeed, might have been led into this error, by supposing that the river Conway, from its appearance near the town of that name, resembled the Thames, and other gently-flowing rivers, in the tame and unpicturesque plains of England.

Mr. Gray, in his admirable poem, "The Bard," without doubt, meant no other rock than some one of those near Pont-y-Pandy, and probably that from which Roberts fell, as there are no others from Llyn Conwy to the Irish sea, that are so consistent with his description. Mr. De Loutherbourg, in his design for the frontispiece to Mr. Jones's beautiful collection of Welsh music, seems to be of the same opinion: for the rock upon which he has placed the bard, very much resembles Craig-Llwyd; and this precipice is truly pourtrayed in the words of Gray—

> "On a rock, whose haughty brow
> Frowns o'er old Conway's foaming flood,
> Robed in the sable garb of woe,
> With haggard eyes the poet stood," *&c. &c.*

I now descended into the Vale of Conwy, anglicised Conway, following the banks of the river to its junction with the Ledr. The scenery all this way is, beyond every thing, fine: the prominent sides of the great and majestic rocks are thickly coated with noble woods, and so diversified in form, as to leave the whole almost unrivalled by any scenery which I had yet seen.

Near this spot is a very deep, broad sheet of water, called Llyn-yr-Afange, or the Beavers'-Pool, having been, in times of old, frequented by those animals. They were also called, by the Welsh, llôst-lydan, or the broad-tailed animals. So highly were their skins valued, that they were sold for one hundred and twenty pence each; whilst the price of those of the martin was only twenty-four pence each; and of the ermine, the fox, the wolf, and the otter, not more than twelve. These were luxuries in the days of the British Solon, Hywel Dda, or Hywel the Good. This celebrated and wise legislator, king of all Wales, in the year 926, accompanied by three bishops, took a journey to Rome, for the purpose of consulting the wise men there upon the measures to be pursued for improving the laws of his realm; which laws were afterwards established with the concurrence, and to the satisfaction of all his subjects. He is ranked, in the Triads, with Prydain and Dyoneval, under the title of the three good princes of Britain.

From hence, that noble split rock which soars to the clouds, called Craig garreg y Gwalch, the Hawk's Rock, from its height, assumes a grand and mighty part; and, from its protuberant shape and roughness, is robed with the picturesque, while on either side the flood, the high uplifted hills—

> "———— Barren some and bare,
> Rock piled on rock, amazing! up to heaven,
> Of horrid grandeur: some with sounding ash,
> Or oak broad-shadowing, or the spiry growth
> Of waving pine, high-plumed."

I know not whether Dolwyddelan-castle, about three miles distant, was ever an object for the pencil. One of its towers, deemed in tolerable condition, lately, in the dead of the night, came tumbling down with a crash which roused every creature in the neighbourhood. I am sorry my time would not allow me to go to this spot: but I believe that I may rely so far upon the information which I received, as to advise the artist to walk to the village. The precipitous and bending sides of Moel Siabod, as I know, are close to it; and they of themselves, would be sufficient to induce me to visit the spot, at any other more favourable time.

This castle was the residence of Jorwerth Drwndwn, and here was born his son, Llywelyn the Great.

Near Bettws-y-Coed is Pont-y-Pair *; a bridge of several arches, over the Lligwy, curiously built on a very singular fall of rocks. This impetuous river, pouring through it a tremendous volume of water, combined with the great aperture or pass between the rocky eminences on each side the road, renders it a wild and romantic picture. One mile and a half up this pass is the fall of Rhyadr-y-Wenol, spoken of before, which at this time, must have foamed in high perfection.

I was by this time, as may well be supposed, become a subject of pity to the people on the road, who compassionated my half-drowned condition; to which, however, the thought of being surrounded by so many noble and wonderful works of nature, rendered me perfectly insensible.

The Conway now assumed an appearance of somewhat less perturbation: yet still it was not free from great agitation, for the immense body of water, which swelled it nearly to a level with its banks, swept down with great velocity in terrific undulations, menacing destruction to every thing in its way: it is here, from its great wideness, a noble sheet of water. The valley now opening into grand breadth, looks exceedingly luxuriant, ornamented with some handsome boxes, farm-houses, *&c.*, and the large village of Llanrwst shews itself to great advantage.

---

* See Index.

The road now leads through the fine woods of Gwydir *, which descend from the amazing heights of the cloud-capt rocks above, to the river's brink. Gwydir-house and estate is now the property of Lord Gwydir. The entrance is through an antique gate, into a square court, the sides of which are formed by the house and offices. The house is pleasantly situated, with beautiful meadows between it and the river; the rooms are not only few, but small, and ill adapted for a gentleman's country residence, in the taste of the present day.

Strangers, who may have leisure and opportunity, would do well to walk to the heights above the house, as from thence they will be highly gratified with fine prospects of Snowdon, and other high mountains, with some fine lakes. In their way they will find the little family chapel, pleasantly situated in the wood. It is wainscotted, and *ornamented with paintings* by some very *unhappy genius* indeed, whom the Muse never blessed. A clergyman performs service in it four times a year.

One of the lakes upon these hills, called Llyn Geirionydd, is noted for having had on its banks the residence of the celebrated poet, Taliesin, justly styled by his countrymen, Pen Beirdd, or the Chief of the Bards. He flourished about the year 560, and in the time of that petty prince, Gwyddno Goron-hir.

The history of Taliesin bears some resemblance to that of Moses. Elfin, a young prince, the son of Gwyddno, had, by his own folly and extravagance, been considerably reduced in his circumstances; and his father had assigned to him a weir for his support. On visiting this wear one night, a leather bag

* Compounded of Gwy, Water, and Tir, Land; *i. e.* Land subject to be flooded, as it occasionally is, by the river Conway, originally Cynwy, the First or the Greatest River.

was discovered tied to the pole of the weir, in which an infant was found, alive, and unhurt. The sight of the child, supposing this an unfavourable omen, aided by the recollection of his former excesses, so affected Elfin, that he burst into tears. He dealt very tenderly with the infant, and caused the utmost care to be taken of him, and ever after, as if to reward the excellence of his subsequent conduct, Elfin prospered. Taliesin, when grown up, addressed a most beautiful moral ode to his guardian and patron, supposed to have been presented to the prince by the infant bard, on the night on which he was discovered. The poem is called " Elfin's Consolation," and has been translated from the Welsh by a lady. Its length will apologize for my inserting only the first part of it.—

" Elfin deg taw ath wylo
Na chabled, *&c. &c.*

" Elfin, fair as roseate morn,
Cease, O lovely youth! to mourn;
Mortals never should presume
To dispute their Maker's doom.
Feeble race, too blind to scan
What the Almighty deigns for man;
Humble Hope be still thy guide,
Steady Faith thy only pride;
Then Despair will fade away,
Like demons at th' approach of day.
Cynllo's prayers acceptance gain,
Goodness never sues in vain;
He who form'd the sky is just,
In him alone, O Elfin! trust;
See glistening spoils in shoals appear,
Fate smiles this hour on Elfin's weir!"

Lower down, on the side of these heights, and near the road, is a water-fall, called Rhyad y Park Mawr, or the Fall near the

E. Pugh del. *T. Cartwright sculp.*

LEOLINUS MAGNUS'S COFFIN.

Published 26 Nov. 1814 by E. Williams Strand.

Great Park. It is, probably, fifty feet high: but the water coming down in two unbroken sheets, renders it less picturesque than if they had been brought to one point, which might in this instance be easily effected. The surrounding scenery is good, tempting the artist to follow the hollows higher up; but my chilly comfortless condition preventing my doing so, I passed the bridge, and entered the little inn at Llanrwst.

The church stands pleasantly on the banks of the Conwy. It is dedicated to St. Rystyd, or Restitutus, who, in 361, was archbishop of London. The little annexed chapel contains some relics of antiquity, highly to be prized; and some others of later date. The first object, with which the stranger is struck, is the stone coffin of Llywelyn the Great, Prince of North Wales. A copper-plate, fixed on the inside, has this inscription:—"The coffin of Leolinus Magnus, Prince of Wales, who was buried in the abbey of Conway; and, upon the dissolution, removed thence." It measures in length on the inside, seven feet one inch; in breadth at the head, three feet three inches; at the feet, one foot ten inches; in depth, eleven inches; and in general thickness about three inches and a half. It is handsomely ornamented with raised quatrefoils all round. The lid has as yet eluded the vigilance of some people earnest in its discovery. The magnanimous Llywelyn reigned from A. D. 1194 to 1240. He was the pride and the glory of his countrymen; and upon all occasions where their liberty was threatened, he never feared to present a front to his enemies, the very appearance of which was, to them, more formidable than the points of the Britons' weapons. But his destiny did not permit him to bestow upon his countrymen that happiness, which his courage and talents foreboded, and which their merits deserved. The despotic and restless ambition of King John, his father-in-law, called out all the energies of Llywelyn: but his troops, from their paucity of number, sometimes proved inadequate to the task of conquering the great superiority of forces brought against them. He was therefore under the necessity of sending his princess to make up the breach between them; and more than once did her embassy prove successful, especially at that, almost hopeless, crisis, when her husband was encamped on the mountain, called by his name, Carnedd Llywelyn: and King John, with a vast army, was making great havock in the plains below, and Bangor blazing at the same time.

In this chapel, likewise, is a tablet to the memory of Margaret, daughter of Rowland Vaughan, of Caergai, near Bala, who died aged eighty-nine. This lady was a Welsh poetess of considerable merit. There are also several fine engravings on copper-plates, one of which, to the memory of Dame Sarah Wynne, wife of Sir Richard Wynne, of Gwydir, who died in 1671, is of matchless execution. The beautiful contour of a female kneeling at prayer, is most graceful: the drawing rivals that of Cipriani, and the engraving excels that of Bartolozzi, as being bolder, and possessing more free and unembarrassed touches of the burine. This plate, while it commemorates the well-born dame, is, also, an honourable monument of the skill of the ingenious artist, and bids fair to hand down his merits to future ages: and as long as the elegant touches and lines shall remain, the name of Gwillim Vaughan, though as yet not on the records of the fine arts, must be held in high estimation. The ground upon wnich this church stands, was given by a son of Nefydd Hardd, in expiation of the foul murder of Idwal*.

* See Cwm Idwal.

The elegant bridge of three arches, is well known to have been erected by Inigo Jones; whom the people of this place claim as a native of Dolwyddelan: but though there is reason to believe that his father was a native Welshman, Wales had, certainly, not the honour of producing his more celebrated son; for he was born in the city of London. The shape of the bridge is the most airy and delicate; and yet it has withstood the attacks of floods, and the pressure of heavy loads of timber, since the year 1636, the date of its erection.

The village is large and populous, and approximates to the size of some of the best Welsh towns. In the centre of it is the market-hall, a decent and convenient building. The houses in general, though small, are good and comfortable.

After enjoying a cheering dinner, and a quantum of cwrw da, I clambered up a steep and tedious road to the hills, on my way to Denbigh; and, looking back frequently as I ascended, I beheld the summits of Snowdon, the cone-shaped Moel Siabod, and the other British alps, rising, as I advanced, in the most magnificent style imaginable. The sublimity of the scene, and the clearness of the atmosphere, which rendered every object lying between me and Snowdonia visible, were temptations too potent to be withstood; especially from one point, near the top of these high grounds, from whence the prospect was so increased in grandeur, that I did not leave it without the strongest reluctance.

Passing over a track of ten miles of uninteresting mountains, without a single object that could amuse either the eye or imagination, I came to the village of Llansanan, where I passed the night. Near this place is a lead-mine, newly opened, likely to be very productive of valuable ore.

The church, dedicated to St. Sanan, is destitute of every thing that can amuse the stranger.

This vast track of country, in circuit not less than seventy miles, stretching from Abergeley north to Eglwys Fach, to the hills above Llanrwst, straight to Capel Voelas, to Gweddelwern, to Cyffylliog, to the hills above Denbigh, and thence back to the heights above Abergeley, is without interest; consisting of soft, flat, and headless mountains, and an extent of boggy ground, feeding only a few sheep and black cattle.

Dyffryn Alet, close to this place, an elegant house in a confined valley of that name, surrounded by black, naked hills, and much too good for the situation, was built by Mrs. Meyrick, afterwards Mrs. York, of Erthig, near Wrexham; who has lately much improved the surrounding grounds. It is at present the residence of Robert York, Esq.

From hence, after a walk of several miles across some black and barren hills, through Llanfydd, I reached the abode of the beautiful Catherine, called Beren-house; a building of great solidity, but little elegance; assuming more the appearance of a cell, than of a family residence. This celebrated lady was daughter and heiress of Tudor ap Robert Fychan, of this house. Being very handsome, she was first courted by John Salusbury, Esq., heir of Lleweny; on whose death, it is said, she promised her hand to Sir Richard Clough, who led her to church at the burial. She was handed from church by Morris Wynne, of Gwydir, Esq., who, enamoured of her personal charms, softly whispered to her his wish of being her second husband. She very readily replied, that she had already accepted the proposals of Sir Richard, in her walk to church: but assured him, that should Sir Richard leave her a widow, he might depend upon her word, that he should be her third. Sir Richard also died, and Catherine married Mr. Wynne, whom also she buried, and married a fourth husband, Edward Thelwell, Esq., of Plasward. But alas! after all this succession of vows, poor Catherine herself met the common fate of mortals; and was interred at Llanyfydd, but without a monument. Her picture, supposed by Lucas de Heere, is now at Llewesog-lodge, Mrs. Wynne's mother's. Four miles brought me, for the third time, to Denbigh.

Early the next morning I set off for Nantglynn, by Gwaenynog, an excellent house, the residence of the Rev. Mr. Middleton, rector of Rotherhithe. The grounds here are well wooded; and from various points may be had some fine peeps into the Vale of Clwyd, as well as good views of Denbigh-castle.

In a sylvan bottom in these grounds, by the side of a river and wood, is a small neat monument, erected by the late proprietor, Mr. Middleton, to the memory of the great moralist, with the following inscription:—

Samuel Johnson, L.L.D.
Obiit XIII die Decembris,
Anno Domini
MDCCLXXXIV.
Ætatis suæ LXXV.
This spot
Was often dignified by the presence of
Samuel Johnson,
L.L.D.
Whose moral Writings, exactly conformable to the
Precepts of Christianity, gave Ardour to Virtue,
and Confidence to Truth.

Following rather a good road for two miles, I came to the village of Nantglynn, the native place of Mr. David Samwell; less known, perhaps, from his having sailed round the world with that celebrated circumnavigator, Captain Cook, as Surgeon to the ship Discovery, than from some specimens of metrical compositions, which cannot fail to hand down his fame to posterity, as an English poet of considerable elegance. He was an eye-witness of the catastrophe which deprived the world of the useful life of that officer; and he wrote a detailed account of the unhappy affair, which has since been inserted in the Biographia Britannica His father was a respectable clergyman, for many years resident in this parish. Mr. Samwell died in 1799, and was buried in St. Dunstan's West. Most if not all of his MSS. are now in the possession of a gentleman in London, Mr. Jones; who, it is to be hoped, will favour the world with their publication.

My journey to this place was to gain, if possible, either an affirmative or a negative to a report in circulation in this country, that the celebrated Thalia* of our day, was born in a respectable ancient house, half a mile from the village called Plas yn Nantglynn, but I met with no satisfactory, or decisive account; though several old people assert, positively, that Miss Bland (the proper name) was the daughter of a Mr. Jordan Bland, one of three brothers, Irishmen, many years ago residing here. Could this have been duly ascertained, we should then have to boast, that Wales had given birth to two of the most admired actresses whom the world ever saw; the modern Melpomene having been born at Brecknock, in South Wales.

Leaving this place, I soon gained the heights above it, where I met a large coursing party, at the head of which was a

* Mrs. Jordan is the daughter of a Mr. Bland, an Irishman, by a lady of Pembrokeshire, of the family and the name, as I believe, of *Philipps;* remotely related to Lord Milford, and to the writer of this note.

clergyman, near eighty years of age, and, wonderful to say, possessing all his faculties in full vigour. It is very common in Wales, annually to invite the better sort of people in a neighbourhood, to a hunting dinner: the profits of which are intended for the tenant of the public-house where the party dine, and is generally tantamount to the rent of the premises for the year. The owner of the public-house, or some gentleman of respectability, patronizes the hunt, and is called, for that day, the comptroller. The publican takes care to have in reserve, a quantity of excellent ale, brewed some months before, for the occasion. The most wealthy of the company spend from three to four shillings each; and others, from eighteen pence to two shillings. Most of the company depart at about eight or nine o'clock, in good order: but the few who stay till a late hour, degrade themselves into a state of intoxication, when their warm disputes, on the merits of certain dogs in the chase, sometimes end in a battle. It is observable, however, that fracas of this kind are lessening, year after year, and that some of these entertainments pass off in good order and decorum.

I now descended rapidly into a rich woody glen, in which is immured the little village of Cuffylliog. Although this narrow confined valley is well stocked with wood, it does not bear the character of the picturesque; till it begins to open at a place called Pontuchel, or the High Bridge: where, indeed, the scenery is grand. Its value is much enhanced, by the union of another woody dell, belonging to Lord Bagot, where the wood, noble and lofty, is extremely fine. The river passes under a bridge of one arch, and over a rocky bed for two miles, till it loses its impetuosity on its introduction into the vale of Clwyd. The rocks here are not of that wild cast, which we see in Carnarvonshire; nor do they possess the character of some of less note. They, nevertheless, serve as an agreeable contrast to the wood-covered height on the opposite side of the river. The artist may find amusement here, and it is but a little out of his way from Ruthin to Denbigh; and he will meet with some pretty little peeps in following the rocky bed of the river from the mill to the public road. But if he ever go from Ruthin to Denbigh, by this road, I would advise him to mount the hills from hence, and, keeping the vale of Clwyd in sight, he will pass over some fine dingles to Denbigh.

A pleasant walk of two miles across the fields brought me once more to Ruthin.

CHAPTER XI.

Llanferres Mines. — Llanarmon. —Tumuli. — Plas-y-Nant. —Dr. Carter.—Fairies.—Llanrhydd.—Court Beans.—Parish Conflicts. —Craig Eyarth.— Coedmarchan Marble. —Ruthin.—Dwy Goes Gawr. —Dr. Gabriel Goodman. — Plasnewydd. — Llandegla. — Bodidris.— Bwlch-y-Rhiw Felen. — Llywarch Hên. — The Blue Shaver.—Chirk-Castle.—Chirk Aqueduct.—Shrewsbury.

THE weather continuing favourable, it now became a matter of some moment to embrace the opportunity offered to make two or three small excursions about this neighbourhood. The next morning, therefore, I ascended the hills on the road to Chester; and, passing the Loggerheads a little, turned to the right, across the stratified rocks of Llanferres. Here are seen, the once great lead-mines belonging to Lord Grosvenor, and others: at present there are but a few men at work, and the ore is hardly worth the expense of getting it up.

In this rocky neighbourhood I expected to find some favourable circumstances, that might lure the artist to quit the high road. But I cannot hold out any temptation of this nature; for these rocks, bearing no formidable character, appear peeping out of the ground, here and there, in small scattered masses; and the nudity of the whole is not at all likely to give pleasure. But should the tourist, in any former visit to the vale of Clwyd, have ascended Moel y Famma, in that case, it would be highly recommendable to go this way to Llanarmon *, where he will find, in that church, some singular and curious monuments. One inserted in the wall of the church on the outside, when rebuilt a few years ago, is to its patron saint, the noted Garmon or Germanus, Bishop of Auxerre, who contributed, with St. Lupus, to defeat the Saxons and Picts, near Mold. He was sent over to Britain, by a council of the church of Gaul, under the pretext of preaching against the Palagian heresy ; but, in fact, to bring the Christian inhabitants under the discipline of the church of Rome. He arrived in this country in 429.

In a niche in the church, is the tomb of the grandson of Unyr ab Moriddig, ab Sandde Hardd, with his figure recumbent, bearing on his shield the arms of that warrior. The tradition is, that being engaged in a crusade, he was killed by a wound in the abdomen ; when his bowels, falling out, they were seized by a dog :—an incident carved upon the lid of the tomb, merely a stone chest, in which his body was sent home.

Near this stands another very rich gypsum monument, most profusely ornamented with coats of arms. The front has three semicircular arches ; the middle one is occupied by a tablet, on which is a long Welsh inscription ; the others, being open, discover a figure in armour, in the ancient recumbent posture at meals; the head reclining upon one hand, while the other grasps a dagger. Four pilasters support an entabla-

* The Rev. Mr. Lloyd, of Caerwis, the gentleman who accompanied Mr. Pennant in his Welsh tour, *&c.*, was born and partly bred in this parish. Mr. Lloyd, by way of distinction, for his virtues and his genius, was called Blodeu, or the Flower of Llanarmon.

ture, at each end of which is a female figure, chaunting a requiem to the spirit of the departed. On the centre is a circular ornament, with armorial ensigns: the base has thirteen compartments, with arms, below which is an expanded embellishment, with a winged seraph.

By the inscription, I learn, that this monument is to the memory of Evan Llwyd, of Bôd Idris, Esq., one of the deputy lieutenants, custos rotulorum, and a justice of the peace for the county of Denbigh; a captain in the service of Charles I. He was son and heir of Sir John Llwyd, and nephew of Sir Evan Llwyd; twelfth in regular descent from the famous Ynyr of Iâl, a hero rewarded for his valour by Prince Owen Gwynedd; and the tenth in inheritance of the name of Llwyd. He had ten sons and four daughters. He died in Anglesey, on the 17th April, 1637, from whence his widow had his remains conveyed to be interred with his ancestors.

Tumuli are rather numerous here. Some years ago in one were found, on its being opened, several urns made of clay, red on the outside, but stained black within by the ashes which they contained: parts of the bones of thighs and arms, and even a scull, were found, which had escaped the fire of the funeral pile. This custom was of very high antiquity, even among the most polished nations of Greece and Rome, as well as the most barbarous. The northern nations and the Druids practised it: but with the persuasion that whatever mechanical instruments or implements the deceased employed during this life, would be wanted in the next, all such effects were carefully deposited with the sacred dust. This fact is ascertained, by the evidence of many singular articles, of now unknown use, which are found in these tumuli in the present day. The construction of the tumuli is not always the same, sometimes the urns are found with their mouths downwards, resting upon a flat stone, covered over with earth and loose stones, then a layer of soil, and the whole covered with turf. Others have the urns enclosed in a square chest, composed of four stones, and finished with earth and turf; and others are still differing from these. Those interred in these sepulchres are supposed to have been heroes who died in battle.

Near the village is a sycamore of a very extraordinary kind; its foliage, through the season, is of a most beautiful bright gold colour.

From hence over the hills to Ruthin, is one of the pleasantest walks in the united kingdom. If it be thought tiresome to ascend the mountain on this side, there are some objects in this Vale of Llanarmon, which appear to recede as one advances, which will attract attention, and will highly recompense the labour of the walk The summit once gained, the stranger will be rivetted to the spot, by the enchanting beauty of the prospect. On the left the eye looks down over a noble profundity of mountain and wood, to the amazing richness and abundant luxuriancy of the unrivalled Vale of Clwyd; the contrast between which, and the rocky, unproductive appearance of the Vale of Llanarmon, is obvious and striking.

If the weather should be propitious, the traveller will be reluctant to leave the hill; and, when he does quit it, each moment will teem with expectation. Nor will this expectation be disappointed: for, at every hundred yards, he will be presented with a new, and most delightful picture. On leaving the summit, the foot-path (for this is no carriage-road) leads close to the edge of a precipice, not of rock, but of solid turf, of very great depth. Some of the Ruthin school-boys on their way over this mountain to Llanarmon wake, have been known to roll down to the bottom, for their amusement, at least a quarter of a mile; a sight of it will convince the stranger, this feat cannot be accomplished by every one. Still descending along the concave side of this hollow, and through a small farm-yard, the stranger suddenly comes to a sylvan scene, the most quiet and rural that can be conceived; where peace seems ever to reign, unruffled by ambition; and where the solitary cottager, protected on all sides by the towering mountains above him, feels secure from the asperity of the winter's storm, and enjoys happiness through the medium of his own industry. At the lower extremity of the beautiful lawn adjoining the farm-yard, is a railed fence and a gate, that leads to a thick wood; embosomed in which is the picturesque moss-covered cottage,

> "—— —— close
> Environed with a ring of branching elms
> That overhang the thatch, itself unseen
> Peeps at the vale below, so thick beset
> With foliage of dark redundant growth."

A few yards further, an effect like enchantment is produced, by the prompt appearance of the handsome Gothic villa, Plas y Nant, in a small verdant opening, surrounded by an almost impenetrable wood, of such a variety of species as it would be endless to enumerate. It is watered by an ever-babbling stream; which, impelled by every successive fall, rushes with a murmuring noise through the deep glen to the meadows below. On the south side of the house, on the acclivity of the hill, the artist will find some excellent studies of the willow and birch of various sorts, with some fine ash and elms.

This handsome box, with the tall trees about it and the conic hill above, is a sweet picture; and it may be considered as such from other points of view; the artist will be able to sketch to advantage from the sides of the mountains, looking down the glen, to obtain a peep of the vale. This little Elysium owes its first cultivation, and the house its existence, to Thelwall Price, of Bathafarn Park, Esq., who erected it about fifty years ago. When the estate came into the possession of the late Rev. Doctor Carter Thelwall, of Redburn in Lincolnshire, this spot was improved, the house repaired, and made convenient, annually to entertain his friends of the vale. They first dined at the mansion, and the ladies and gentlemen as they felt inclined, walked or rode the mile, to tea and the lightsome dance.

The great stillness of the woods was excellently calculated to give effect to the soft and melifluous sounds of the flute; which always upon these occasions, was touched by the fingers of skilful performers; the doctor himself was an excellent player upon this instrument: always happy to contribute to the amusement of his friends, he would conceal himself in the dark and silent recesses of the wood, and delight them with the melody of a Florio, the execution of a Nicholson, or the still more bewitching performance of an Humphreys.

Such was the benevolence of this gentleman's heart, that, no wonder the poorer unprovided clergy of the neighbourhood, often felt his friendship and acknowledged his munificence; but such was also the manner in which he bestowed his favours, that "his left hand knew not what his right hand did;" a third person was never present on these occasions; and his gifts were always made easy to the receiver; accompanied with expressions, synonimous with, "My dear Sir, 'tis only a bit of waste paper, good morning; to- orrow I expect the pleasure of your company to dinner."

On disengaging hands, the befriended found his own full of sweetest *notes*, that banished thence the discords of indigence and chased away the sounds of melancholy. When this benevolent man died, every class of society in this neighbourhood felt the severity of their loss; nor indeed was his loss less felt in other places. The Chester Infirmary found twice every year the sum of £50 deposited in the letter-box by an unknown hand, which discontinued only on the demise of this good man.

> " No more the soft Eolian flute
> Breathes thro' the heart the melting strain,
> The powers of harmony are mute,
> And leave the once-delighted plain."

This estate came into the possession of Lord William Beauclerk, on his marriage with Miss Carter, the only daughter and heiress to Dr. Carter. She was a lady of most amiable manners, and well taught in the school of honour and humanity; she trod in the steps of her good father and mother, but died a few years after her marriage. The estate is now the property of the Rev. Butler Clough by a late purchase.

The existence of Fairies in former times was very little doubted in Wales, as well as in England. Some degree of credit is still given to these stories by elderly people, upon whose minds they had made an early impression.

The following anecdote I had from an inhabitant: who, whatever credit it received from others at the time, did not profess seriously to believe it. Many years since, thirty or forty perhaps, two young men from Llanarmon agreed to walk over the hills to Ruthin fair, to meet their sweethearts. Having presented the fairing, enjoyed the dance, and the cheering, but harmless conversation of the fair ones, with the envied addition of the luxurious, lingering, parting kiss, they set out homeward; having entered some way in this wood, at the time when "the iron tongue of midnight had told twelve," the awful blackness of the sky, worse than Cimmerian darkness, conspiring against them, by some unlucky chance they lost each other. The foremost, who had suffered much entanglements in the thorny thickets, after repeated hallooings without a return from his companion, was deluded into a belief that he had regained the mountain, and was out of hearing. That shrewd and knavish spright, called Robin Goodfellow, who "misleads night's wanderers, laughing at their harm," had thus separated the two friends: one of whom reached his home safe that night; the other did not arrive at his till day-light: but in such a plight, as rendered both his features and person doubtful to his nearest relations; his face much swelled and covered with wounds, his countenance wan, and his clothes torn to tatters; he took to his bed immediately; but when a little recovered, he thus stated his situation in the wood.—A few minutes after losing his companion, he was surrounded by a bright illumination, and numerous fairies appeared dancing about to very melodious music, as if they were in the zenith of merriment and exultation; whenever he attempted to escape, he was left in total darkness; and filled with such fear, that he preferred following them whithersoever they went. to the apprehension of being left behind; they seemed to glide along beautiful undulatory walks; without the least molestation from the prickly and thorny bushes, which annoyed him in every step he took. Thus was he compelled to follow, and be led about a round, "through bog, through bush, through brake, through brier," till the harbinger of day,—

> "The cheerful Chanticleer, with his note shrill,
> Had warned once, that Phœbus's fiery car
> In haste was climbing up the eastern hill,"

and had admonished thence the fairy tribe: leaving the poor wretch in a state which scarcely allowed him strength to crawl to his home.

Below the woods is a large field, and other patches of forty or fifty acres, that fifty years ago were covered with some of the finest oak in Great Britain; which were felled, at a blow, by the fatal arm of necessity. Lower still is Bathafern: the house is small and old, and the situation low and unfavourable as to prospect. Half a mile further is Plâs Llanrhydd, lately the snug and comfortable residence of the Reverend Mr. Roberts, deceased; nothing can surpass the neatness of the gardens and the grounds.

The little church here is dedicated to St. Meugan, an astrologer, and also physician to King Vortigern; it contains a curious old mural monument of John Thelwall, of Bathafern, and his wife, kneeling before an altar: behind each, respectively, are also kneeling, ten sons and four daughters.

This respectable old family came from Thelwall, in Cheshire, from which they took their name. Of the sons we are informed that John, the eldest, died at the good old age of 97: and left a posterity behind, amounting to upwards of two hundred and forty. Bevis, being accoutred in armour, must have been a warrior; Sir Eubule was master of Jesus-College, Oxford; Ambrose, the ninth son, began his life as clerk, under the great Sir Francis Bacon, with whom he was so much a favourite, that Sir Francis contrived a singular mode of rewarding him; he succeeded in persuading the king to knight all the masters in chancery, by which Ambrose received a gratuity from each of one hundred pounds, but as his brother, Sir Eubule, was one of the masters, he remitted to him his fees.

Here is also a beautiful bust of Ambrose, with short hair and a peaked beard, and ruff. It is not a little remarkable, that at present only two remain of this numerous family, bearing the name, *i. e.* the Rev. Edward Thelwall, of Bath, whose family is as likely to keep up the respectability of the race, as it is probable they will perpetuate the name of the Thelwalls of Bathafern. One of the sons, like his namesake, Bevis, on the monument, follows the same profession of a warrior, and though young, has already achieved honourable deeds, and acquired laurels in the sacred cause of his country.

Half a mile further is a deep and narrow sandy entrance into Ruthin. On an elevation in this road is a rock, where, at the wake, is sometimes held a court by the merry people of the town, called Court Beans: so named after one Richard Beans, the founder, a man of great whim and drollery. It seems to have been formed upon the plans of the court of King's Bench, and the court of Piepowder; it is as complete a burlesque, perhaps, as was ever witnessed. The penal code is the invention of Beans, and is replete with ludicrous punishments, for a variety of suppositious crimes. Two judges are appointed annually: they are equipped in the habits of their different trades, shoemakers, tailors, *&c.*, but with the appendages of the long, musty white wigs, tattered gowns, and soiled bands, which had seen better days, when dignifying the heads and backs of some more venerable judges. The decisions of this jocular court, are as whimsical as the appearance of its several members. As is usual upon the circuits, the court in imitation go in a body towards the church: but decency forbids a nearer approach than to the church-gates; from whence they proceed to the court, and then to business. One of its laws enacts, that when it is proved that a man has been beaten by his wife, he shall be carried about the town in a chair fixed to two poles, on the shoulders of four men; and exposed to all the ridicule of both sexes.

A wake originally was the eve feast of the dedication of the church of the parish, in which the wake was held; and religiously observed by the Roman Catholics of those early times, by watching and praying all night: but it seems, for ages past, to have lost every trait of religion; and is now kept for several days by feasting, and by rural diversions. Formerly, horse-races formed a part of the amusements, but these are nearly put out of countenance by a law, that forbids any horse-race for a plate of less value than fifty pounds, under the penalty of five hundred pounds, and the forfeiture of the horse. This is a wise law for discouraging a species of idleness and gambling, that would impoverish the lower orders.

Wakes now in North Wales are very much on the decline, nor are they carried on with one-fourth the spirit which influenced those who attended them thirty years ago; when I can just recollect such scenes of barbarity and disgrace, as the better instructed inhabitants would now be ashamed of. The young men of the surrounding parishes would assemble all their force, and visit the wake; and, towards the evening, when the liquor had begun to operate upon their senses, the men of one parish would easily be provoked to quarrel with those of another; and both would turn out, and the rencounter would commence with clubs, sticks, and stones, in a most furious manner; the parties would break each other's lines, and then would ensue a desperate confusion. I have even seen females enter the list in defence of their brothers: and even in the middle of rivers, scuffle and contend with robust men; and sometimes, by superior adroitness, gaining some advantages over them, contributing to turning the scale of victory. Had certain tourists travelled in those days, and accidentally witnessed such a scene, they would, probably, have represented the Welsh as a set of savages, barbarous as the Caffres of Africa, and entire strangers to the laws of civil society: forgetful of those more disgraceful mobs and riots, which now and then infest other parts of the kingdom, and of the mutinies and lawless excesses which sometimes break out even in the first seminaries in the nation; to the latter of which, I was once myself on the point of falling an unoffending victim. These outrages in North Wales, however, are now heard of no more, having dwindled away into an occasional single battle or two, now and then, between individuals, and even these, we hope, ere long, to hear to have ceased; and that such discord and brawlings have no longer existence.

The artist, taking a boy as a guide from Ruthin, will be pleasingly amused by a delightful walk through the meadows, to Craig Eyarth, or Eyarth Rocks, two miles from hence, following the river to the deep chasms upon it. Though the pictures are not very numerous, yet they are good; the artist should go as far as the mill, and even further, to take in the mountains on the east side of the vale, that run obliquely to the base of the drawing; these are kept at a proper distance by the fine hanging wood on the right, and the craggs opposite, which

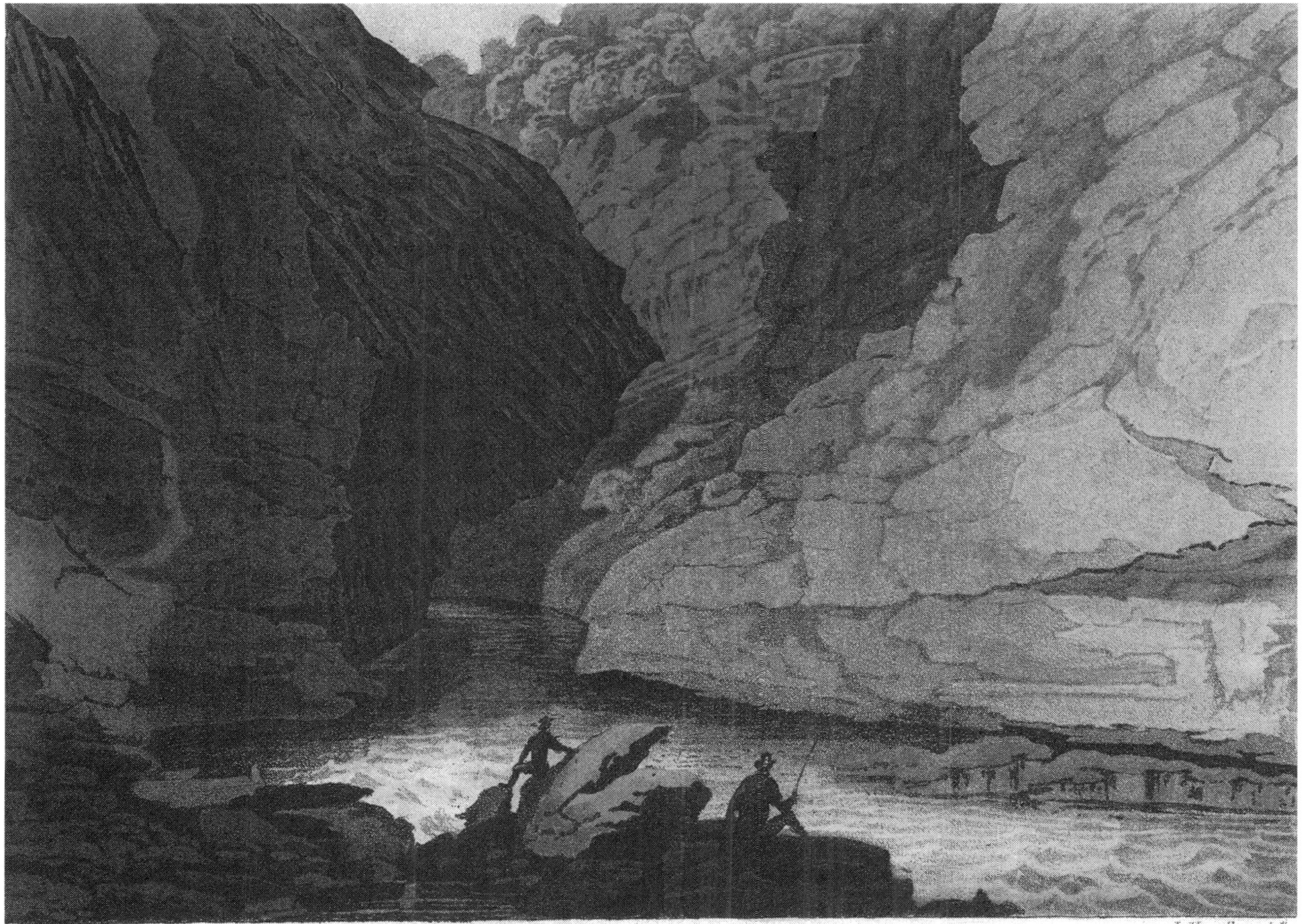

E. Pugh del.t

I. Havell sculp.t

EYARTH ROCKS.

Published 15 April 1814 by E. Williams Strand.

cut them very agreeably. Reverting to the chasms on the river, the rocks are very singular as well as picturesque. In one place on each side the stream, they incline downwards very abruptly, and come nearly in contact with each other; thus forming a narrow dark channel, which, at its entrance, has a very grotesque and gloomy appearance. In great floods, this spot exhibits a dismal aspect: the great quantity of water, nearly filling this rocky amphitheatre, and labouring to make its way through the channel, seems to groan in the struggle to get free, and presents a very tumultuous scene. The spacious and curious horizontal fissures at the base of the rocks were formed, no doubt, by the force of the water in high floods; and they are now the daily receptacles of foxes, whither these crafty animals retire after their nightly marauding in the neighbourhood. These cavities run many yards underneath immense bodies of marble rocks, and the stranger will feel greatly surprised, that so much weight does not press itself into the river: it is, indeed, reasonable to suppose, that, one day or other, this will be the case. The wood above the river may afford some amusement to the artist; and when he is inclined to return to Ruthin, and wishes to vary the prospects, it will be advisable for him to direct his course towards the road, and turn up through the wood called Coed y Gawen, to the top of Cocd Marchan; a barren rocky mountain, from whence there is a delightful view of the vale.

The rocks of calcareous marble on this mountain are rather remarkable, from the circumstance of their having horizontal planes, without any other protuberances than what arise from a curious incrustation on the surface, with sometimes deep perpendicular gaps. This marble is really handsome, of a purple hue, with variegated marks or vestiges of marine productions; and many of the old houses in the vale have chimney-pieces made of it: but the country stone-cutters either have not the skill or the patience to prepare this stone for more general use. I take the opportunity of thus intimating the want of a spirit of adventure in the vale, and its vicinage. There is now, however, a company from Liverpool making a trial, and very ardent hopes are entertained of its ultimate success.

The late Hon. Mr. Fitzmaurice, with a zeal which did him the greatest credit, had several meetings with the merchants of Liverpool, thirty years ago, on the subject of forming a navigable canal* from the hills in the south end of the vale, to the sea; by which the hidden treasures of the country, as well as what is known to exist there, might be exported, to the enriching of the proprietors, as well as to the benefit of the poor labourers. That there is coal in the vale is demonstrable: iron, its never-failing attendant, is visible: that there may be lead, is probable: that there is slate is likely to be true; and lime rocks are common. The marble also on this mountain, would form a considerable part of the traffic, as a useful article in the decoration of fire-places, tombs, *&c. &c.*

Why Mr. Fitzmaurice failed to bring his scheme to a favourable conclusion, I know not.

It is very observable in most parts of North Wales, that the miners and manufacturers are strangers; and it may be confidently predicted, that this will be the case, sooner or later, in the Vale of Clwyd, as the inhabitants seem to wish to hug them-

* This may easily be done, at little expense, the land being free from rock, and level with the tide.

selves in the security of five per cent., rather than to speculate by an easy subscription, at the hazard of losing, comparatively, a small sum of money ; but which, eventually, may return one hundred per cent. yearly. These gentlemen seem to leave to others a probable chance of amassing large fortunes ; which, from the locality of their situation, more properly belongs to themselves.

The stranger now enters Ruthin close to the castle walls. This fortress was built by Edward I. ; who, in the year 1281, gave it, with the hundred of Dyffryn Clwyd, to Reginald de Grey, who did homage for it at Chester, to Edward's son, the first Prince of Wales of the English line. From the family of the Greys it devolved to Richard, Earl of Kent; who sold it to Henry VII. It was granted to Dudley, Earl of Warwick, by Queen Elizabeth. It is now in the possession of the Middletons, of Chirk-castle ; and, on the demise of their brother, became the property of his sisters and coheiresses.

The British and ancient name of this castle, according to Llwyd, is Castell Côch yn Gwernvor, or Red Castle, contiguous to a swampy ground.

In the civil war between Charles I. and his parliament, while the castle was garrisoned by the royalists, it was besieged for two months by the parliament forces under General Mytton, to whom it surrendered; and, soon after, by an order of the house of commons, it was destroyed *. The fortress, in its present state, makes but a poor figure: for time, assisting the ravages of war, has reduced it to an object scarcely worthy of the artist's notice.

* Drake's Parliament. Hist. 14.—355.

"This castle stands, on rocke much like red bricke,
The dykes are cut, with toole through stonie cragge:
The towers are hye, the walles are large and thicke,
The worke it selfe, would shake a subject's bagge,
If he were bent, to buyld the like agayne:
It rests on mount, and lookes ore wood and playne:
It had great store, of chambers finely wrought,
That time alone to great decaye hath brought."

CHURCHYARD.

There is a drawing of this castle now in the British Museum, which agrees well with Churchyard's description.

There is not, about this town, or, I may add, scarcely any where, a better situation for a modern good house than the site of this castle; for it would have in view the whole of the valley; and the surrounding grounds belonging to the same family are beautiful, and capable of great improvement if suggested by taste. The ground might soon be cleared of its ponderous load, by giving the refuse stones for the improvement of the public roads.

The summit of this castle is not raised much above the town, yet there are a few good peeps from it.

The town, it is observable, is built upon a lofty bank in the centre of the vale; and nothing can give the reader a better idea of it than a church, wherein the pulpit, raised high in the nave, represents this town situated about three-fourths in the valley, and the galleries the mountains on each side.

The market-place being at the highest point, the artist from thence will perceive a few good pictures on looking down the steep streets into the vale. Strangers, who are fond of viewing the varied beauties of nature, will be pleased to follow me to a spot, to which I have long ago promised to bring them, to behold the Vale of Clwyd in its highest splendour of dress.

The clerk of the church is an intelligent and obliging man, who will conduct strangers to the top of the church tower, by an easy spiral staircase, from whence the valley is seen to greater advantage than from any other spot. I am aware of my inability to do justice to it in description, and probably were it left to the simple, though correct delineation of old Churchyard the poet, it might be enough, who says,—

"Now to the vale, of worthie Dyffrin Cloyd,
My Muse must passe, a soyle most ritch and gay:
This noble seate, that never none anoy'd
That sawe the same, and rode or went that way:
The vewe thereof, so much contents the mynd,
The ayre therein, so wholesome and so kynd:
The beauty such, the breadth and length likewise,
Makes glad the heart, and pleaseth each man's eyes.

This vale doth reach, so farre in vewe of man,
As he farre of, may see the seas indeede:
And who a while, for pleasure travalye can
Throughout this vale, and thereof take good heede,
He shall delight, to see a soyle so fine,
For ground and grasse, a passing plot divine.
And if the troth thereof a man may tell,
This vale alone doth all the rest excell."

And so it does most evidently: Churchyard must have viewed it with the eye of taste, and with a judgment matured by much travelling and observation:—A later author, Lord Lyttleton, also characterizes it under these words:—" The next morning we went to the top of the hill, from whence we had a view of the whole Vale of Clwyd, from one end to the other, which is equalled by none in England for fertility and beauty *."

* Lord Lyttleton's Letters to Mr. Bower.

The stranger, now supposed on the tower, is so much elevated, as to see the whole of the town, and at the same time to command all the surrounding country, the scene is diversified by such a multiplicity of objects, that it requires great steadiness to contemplate them all, with that degree of pleasure, which they are calculated to produce in the mind of strangers, who might be induced to repeat the lines of Cowper, and say,—

" ——————— we have borne
The ruffling wind, scarce conscious that it blew;
While admiration, feeding at the eye,
And still unsated, dwelt upon the scene.
Thence with what pleasure have we just discern'd
The distant plow slow moving, and beside
His lab'ring team, that swerv'd not from the track,
The sturdy swain diminish'd to a boy!"

In a direct line towards the north, the valley appears as level as a bowling-green, but divided into beautiful meadows as far as Rhyddlan, seventeen miles off. The mountains on the east side are very high near the town, but lessen gradually towards the sea, whence the handsome, undulating lines terminate. The mountains over-looking the vale on the western side, are neither so high nor so interesting as those on the east; yet their sides in parts have a rich covering of wood, which, on a near approach, are pleasing to the sight. The level of the valley has the greatest profusion of trees and wood, which renders its appearance extremely rich and beautiful. The river Clwyd is seen meandering centrically in silence, but it is soon lost among the woods. In great floods, if the human mind could for a few minutes overlook the distress which such a calamity causes, one must be presented with a grand sight indeed, as the waters are accumulated to such a height, as to cover some thousand acres of fine land: but one happiness is, that they do not often hap-

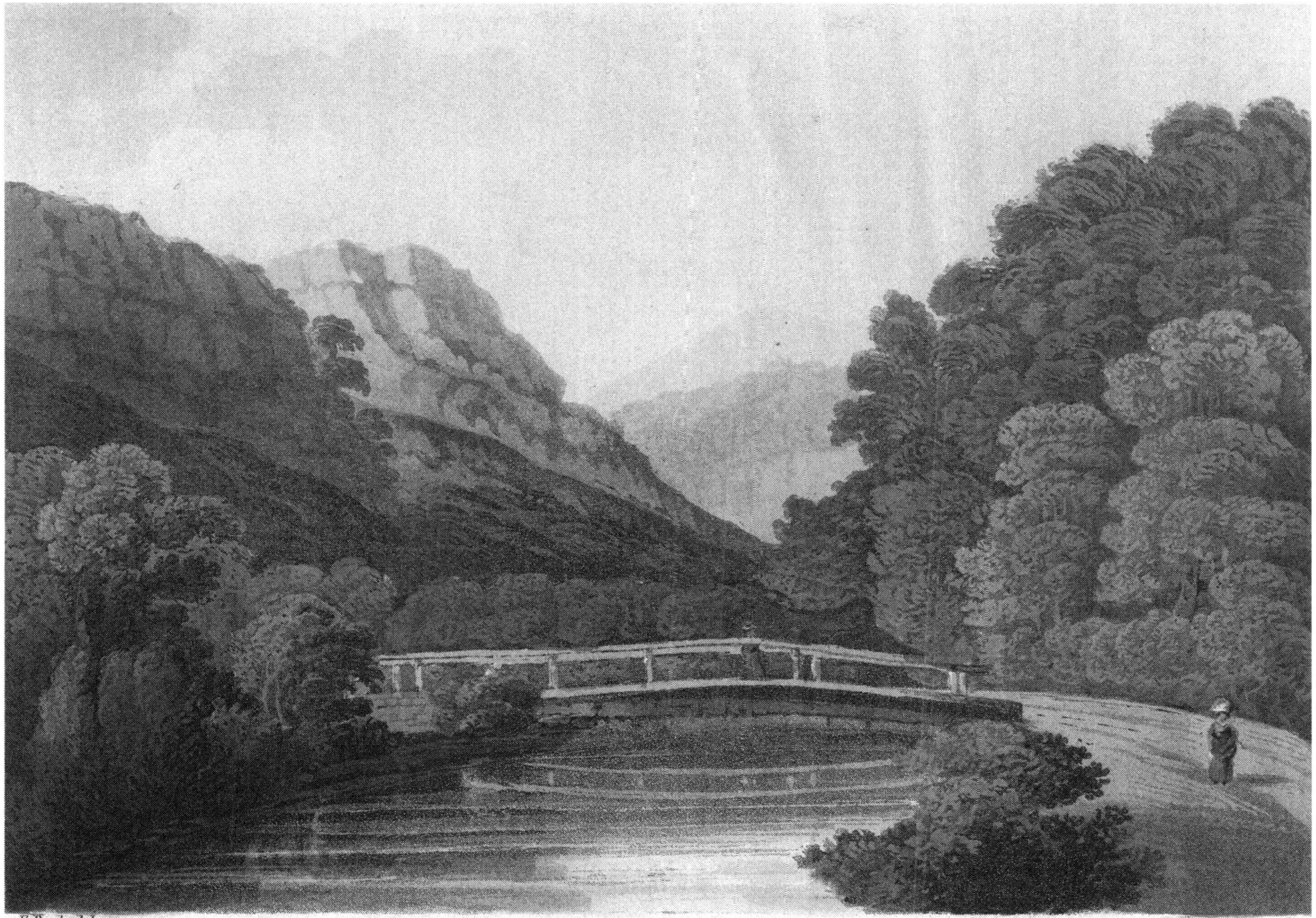

E. Pugh del.　　T. Cartwright sculp.

VIEW ON THE CLWYD NEAR EYARTH.

Published 15 June, 1813 by E. Williams, Strand.

pen: if they should, however, occur after housing the corn, they rather tend to fertilize the ground.

This vale yields plenty of every description of the finest vegetables, and animal food. The sheep on these mountains are very numerous: they are also as small as any in North Wales; and are, consequently, deemed the sweetest mutton; a considerable quantity of which is sent in presents to London and other places. The price of every article of living, in all parts of Wales, has experienced, of late years, a great advance; and much out of proportion to the earnings of the poorer inhabitants: but to the English, who have been accustomed to higher charges, every article appears moderate. I have taken pains to ascertain the difference of expense in living between London and this part of the country. A young man, who can spend two hundred pounds per annum in town, if equally moderate in his expenses, may live here for a hundred and fifty, including the maintenance of a horse, which it is not to be supposed that he can keep in town. All ranks in society may live in this country at the same rate: *i. e.* for about two-fifths less than in London. From this tower are discerned innumerable houses; some gentlemen's seats make a figure on the acclivities of the hills; while those in the bottom are but partially seen through the woods. The handsome farm-houses, the cottages of the peasantry, scattered wide over hill and dale, the many towns and villages in the view, and the sea crossing the end of the vale at right angles, are circumstances which complete a scene of incomparable beauty.

The prospect southward differs from that in the opposite point, inasmuch as it is bounded by some noble mountains at the distance of five miles, in a semicircular sweep. The country this way rises in frequent mounts, swelling in a beautiful manner; and as often covered with wood, with rich and productive arable and meadow lands between, and ornamented with a few gentlemen's houses, *&c. &c.* Upon one of the mountains eastward, is a natural but singular curiosity, called Dwy goes Gawr, or the Giant's Legs: they are well shaped, lie close to each other, and the feet are turned the same way. I have been upon the spot, and found this strange appearance to be occasioned by two small springs taking the same direction for about one hundred and fifty yards, and then disappearing. The space over which the water flows is occupied by a soft bog of very short light-coloured grass, surrounded by a dark furze, which generally covers these mountains; and which makes these odd forms visible from the sea. The fertile brains of my countrymen, of former times, never failing to account for any singularity, have attached a legend to these shapes which is seldom told. It is said that a mighty giant once descending these mountains, on an errand of love, being rather in a hurry, and not taking much heed to his steps, stumbled, and for a few minutes remained senseless at his length. His feet, having made a deep incision in the ground, opened these springs, and caused the water to flow as far as his knees; the coolness of which, at that moment, refreshed and made him sensible of his situation. Upon this he sprang up, and continued his journey, without suffering from the accident, or experiencing the least diminution of the ardour with which he set out.

The stranger will recognize the hills of Llainwen, from whence this beautiful and elegant valley, from a happy point of view, forms an agreeable and interesting contrast to the wild and picturesque vale of Llangollen, from the celebrated Nant y Bela;

and both are subjects highly worthy of being published as large prints; a way in which neither of them has as yet been noticed, but which the public may, ere long, I hope, expect to see.

After descending the tower, the stranger will be pleased with the sight of a handsome church, which originally was of Gothic architecture: but, having been, many years since, partly rebuilt, its outward appearance was converted into Grecian, and it was finished with Attic or Athenian balustrades.

One half of the ceiling is extremely curious; it is strongly ribbed with large ornamented timbers, interwoven with others at right angles, forming a vast number of small square compartments; each of which is distinguished by some singular and beautiful carved device, or representation of fishes, fowls, quadrupeds, and wreathed initials of persons' names, *&c.*

Near the west window of the northern aisle, which at one time was the nave, it seems a part of the ceiling was unfinished, and it is said, that one Davies, an excellent sign-painter of the town, now several years ago, was employed to paint those squares in imitation of the carved ones; and (with due respect to his memory be it noticed) he has succeeded so well, as to deceive ninety-nine out of a hundred who view them.

This church was once a monastery belonging to a house of the Bonhommes*, a species of Augustines who came into England in 1283. But they continued in this monastery only a short time, as John, son of Reginald de Grey, made it collegiate in 1310; when the building was large, and extended very much eastward. The cloister, attached to the north side of the church, is the official residence of the warden. The parlours have very

* Leland Itin. iii. 135.

beautiful ceilings, which from the key-stone fly off in handsome eliptic arches; and the whole shews, through some modern alterations, what it originally was, when inhabited by the priests of other times.

The church contains a bust to the memory of that excellent character, Dr. Gabriel Goodman, who was forty years Dean of Westminster; a native of this town, and a favourite of Queen Elizabeth. He is represented in his canonicals, wearing a peaked beard. He was a useful friend of Camden the historian, whom he much assisted in his travels through the kingdom, and who acknowledged his friendship in these words:—" A right good man indeed, and of singular integrity, an especial patron of my studies." The doctor had also a monument to his memory in the chapel of St. Benedict, Westminster-abbey, where he was buried. He left this world for a better, on the 17th of July, 1601, at the age of seventy-three years. The dean, as a theologist, and an assistant in the translation of the Bible into English, distinguished himself greatly by his version of the Epistles to the Corinthians. He founded a school and an hospital in this town; the school being for the free education of the poor children of Llanelidan and this town. This school has produced some great men of very splendid talents in the law, church, and state; and the names of Archbishop Williams, Lord Kenyon, Baron Perrin, Dr. Parry (once master of the school), Bishop of St. Asaph, Dr. John Davies, an eminent author, Dr. Tucker, late Dean of Gloucester (who received the greatest part of his education here), Archdeacon Edwards, Dr. Hugh Owen, Counsellor Maddocks, Dr. Thomas Hughes, son of a former master, at present residentiary Canon of St. Paul's, the late John Lloyd, Esq., judge of a circuit of South

Wales, and the present Mr. Baron Richards, with many other men of note, will remain as testimonies of its excellence. This school, of late years, has been considered as lamentably on the decline; but now, from the abilities and exertions of the masters, on whom devolves the care of this seminary, its friends hope to see it yet revive, and rise once more to that fame and celebrity to which it had arrived in the time of those illustrious and learned tutors, the Rev. Messrs. Hughes and Parry; when it was emulously resorted to by respectable pupils from all parts of the kingdom. The situation, for a public seminary, for health, accommodation, and cheapness of provisions, is certainly not excelled by any in Great Britain. The guardians of this seminary are the Bishop of Bangor, in his character of President of Christ's Hospital in this town, and the Warden of the same, who jointly form a corporate body. The head master is appointed by the said president, or in case of his omission, to appoint one within a month after a vacancy, by the said warden. The head master appoints his assistant or second master, as he is denominated; and it is required that both should be graduates of either of the universities. A moiety of the rectorial tithes of the parish of Llanelidan, are granted by letters patent of Queen Elizabeth to the president and warden for the support of the two masters, of which the head master has two-thirds, and the under master the remainder. The statutes of the school, for the due execution of which the masters are made responsible to the warden, are said to be nearly transcribed from those of the King's-school of Westminster. Lately was found, under some rubbish in the church, a headless recumbent monument of a lady, with an inscription so imperfect, that nothing could be learned from it: but the arms certainly denote her to have belonged to an English and not a British family, as they are not borne by the Welsh. This lady must have been the daughter of some Englishman in the garrison of Ruthin, prior to Henry VII.'s reign.

The hospital, called Christ's, is for twelve poor people, who are clothed, and in other respects maintained, by the produce of the yearly tithes of Ruthin and Llanrhydd, purchased by Dr. Goodman, and since aided by other donations. Great complaints were made of some former wardens, against whom a petition was presented to the Dean and Chapter of Westminster, who are trustees to the charity, and appoint the warden to enforce the full payment of the weekly allowance of the poor recipients. This affair, however, is still buried in a considerable degree of mystery, which, I believe, those now on the spot are not generally able to resolve; and charity forbids us to suppose, that men of such affluence could attempt to divert from its proper channel so humane a charity. Since the induction of the present warden (the Reverend Mr. Newcome), however, the weekly payment has, by that gentleman's judicious management, been increased; and to this generous attention is to be ascribed much of the additional comfort which the poor now enjoy. The warden of Christ's-hospital is the principal clergyman of the parishes of Ruthin and Llanrydd, and according to his statutes, keeps two chaplains or curates under him to do the duty of these parishes. His own duty, in addition to the superintending the school and hospital, being only to preach and catechise occasionally in the said parish churches.

The county jail is a neat and convenient edifice, built in 1775, by the late Mr. Turner of Chester, at the expense of the county; the magistrates of which were sensible of the miserable state of the old prison, and determined to erect a building which should in some measure alleviate the wretched state of its inmates.

Mr. Turner has very judiciously formed the strong cells of criminals on the ground-floor, where they are free from damp and every other annoyance so common to the dungeons of old prisons ; the cold damp air and filthiness of which, in a confinement of one week, becomes often a sufficient punishment for the guilty, much more for one who is only suspected of guilt. The debtors live above stairs. The courts are spacious and contain baths and other conveniencies; and the whole is kept very clean and neat, reflecting no little credit upon the jailer.

The house of correction adjoins, and is also kept in good order.

The Town-hall, a very neat building, and internally handsome, has been lately erected, under the direction of Mr. Penson, the ingenious architect of Wrexham; and it occasionally serves as an assembly-room.

This building includes the archive, or Record-office, in which are deposited the judicial papers of the county.

Lord Grey, being a great oppressor of Owen Glyndwr, the latter directed his vengeance against him, and recovered the estates of which Grey had robbed him. Owen causing himself to be proclaimed Prince of Wales on the 20th of September, 1400, surprised, sacked, and burnt Ruthin to the ground, at the time when a fair was held, and caused the utmost consternation. When he had completely punished Lord Grey, he returned to the fastnesses of the mountains near Corwen.

Dean Goodman presented to the wardenship a handsome silver goblet and his portrait, which are held in great estimation. He likewise presented the corporation with a goblet. The corporation also received two smaller ones from the hands of Sir Hugh Middleton, the projector of the New-river. On discovering that the name of one of the aldermen had been erased from these, and inquiring the reason, I was told, that many years since, he was hanged near the town for having poisoned a relation, because he would not dispose of a small estate, which enabled him to rear a numerous infant family. This miscreant, before he was suspended, poisoned himself, and, as it is said, the jailer also.

Before I quit my native place, I wish to enter my protest against certain nuisances permitted to prevail there, offensive to the inhabitant, and still more disgusting to the stranger; and earnestly to recommend to those who have the direction of its police, their speedy removal.

While pigs are allowed to wander about the town, and in droves to perambulate the streets, by night and by day, at their pleasure; a lover of order cannot but suggest that this liberty seems to border a little upon licentiousness; and, that if the grunting tribe are thus permitted to cross your path, and to crowd your way without control, they will next extend their privileges, and enter your house *sans ceremonie*. Without wishing, therefore, any infringement on their proper and inalienable rights, I would humbly submit, that the *swinish multitude* be restrained within legitimate bounds; and be taught, that they are not to encroach with impunity on the decencies and conveniencies of civil society.

Another suggestion which I would offer, is to those who have the direction of the scavengers; that in sweeping the streets, instead of heaping up the refuse into what they call tommenydd (dunghills), there to stand several days in rank and file, to the annoyance of our eyes and noses by day, and to the peril of the passengers by night, they would at once remove it altogether from the street, and wheel it off to its proper receptacle.

Here are three inns, the White-Lion, the Cross-Foxes, and the Cross-Keys.

After having stayed here a short time, I quitted Ruthin with that reluctance which every son must feel on leaving a good and an anxious mother in tears.

A mile from the town, southward, is Plasnewydd, the handsome and comfortable mansion of David Shuckforth, Esq.; a gentleman, who, from his constant residence in the country, and from the unceasing practice of those good deeds which flow from a benevolent heart, makes himself respected by all: and the lovers of agriculture will be much gratified by the exemplary cultivation of his farm.

I proceeded over the hills to Llandegla; where this church is dedicated to the virgin St. Tecla, who, after being converted by St. Paul, suffered martyrdom, under the tyrant Nero, at Iconium. Bodidris, near to it, is an old mansion, the property of Sir Thomas Mostyn, Bart., who is maternally descended from the ancient family of the Lloyds of this house. It takes its name from Idris, a son of Llgwelyn Aurdorchog, or of the Golden Torques, the then Lord of Yale.

Sir Evan Lloyd, Bart., was the last male of the family, and descended from Ynyr ab Howel, ab Moriddog, ab Sandde Hardd. Ynyr, for his courage at the battle of Corwen, in the year 1165, was rewarded by his Prince Owen Gwynedd, with the township of Gellygan: at the same time, he received from the prince the very honourable addition to his arms, of four bloody strokes, or, paly of eight, *or* and *gules;* a distinction obtained by this circumstance—Ynyr, after the battle, while talking with his prince, accidentally drew his left hand, which was smeared with blood, across his sword, on which he left the traces of his four fingers.

This house is situated in two counties, and a large dining-table, which a little while ago was placed in the kitchen for the use of the servants, stood on the boundary; so that those on one side dined in Denbighshire, and those on the other, in Flintshire.

The house contains a canopied state-bed, called Gwely Cant-Punt, or the Hundred-pound Bed, from its original price; which was presented by Queen Elizabeth to the family. The hangings are of white satin, lined with yellow silk, richly ornamented with flowers by the queen's maids of honour. The furniture of the room, with a curious cradle, is coeval with the bed. Here is shewn a large building, erected in the civil war as a stable, which contained a regiment of horse; the family of that day being indefatigable in the cause of royalty.

The afternoon turning out very wet and stormy, I was soon prevailed upon by the obliging tenant, Mr. Parry, to stay the night, and sleep in the superb bed; and I thus secured to myself the honour while living (aware of the impossibility of it when dead) of *lying in state.*

The morning proving fine, I bade adieu to this pleasant family, and bent my steps towards Llangollen. The pass of Bwlch y Rhiw Felen, in my way, is noted for having been the place where, in the sixth century, Gwell and Sawyl, two sons of the bard and Prince, Llywarch Hên, lost their lives in a battle, fought to expel the Saxons and Irish out of this part of the island.

From the summit of this road is a curious and picturesque view of Crow-castle, or Castell Dinas Brân. The hollow, on the side of which this road winds down, is truly awful and grand. On the left of it begins the Eglwyseg rocks, with hills protruding across the pass in excellent outlines: the castle rising above them, and bounded by the semicircular hill beyond Llangollen, finishes an august and noble picture. Artists may amuse themselves on the sides of these hills, but need not go to their tops, for I found them healthy, tame, extensive, and of no interest; except from the summit of a conic mountain, sometimes denominated the Sugar-Loaf; from whence is a grand, full, and noble sight of the Vale of Clwyd. This steep, unpleasant road, is avoided by horses and carriages, a new one being opened for their better accommodation on the west of it.

On the side of this fine hollow is a house where lived Edward Davies, better known here by the significant title of Cneifor Glâs, or the Blue Shaver, from his rapacious temper and the colour of his clothes. He was a low factious man, and a partisan on the side of Cromwell; for his seeming zeal for the cause, he was recommended by Colonel George Twissleton, in 1654, to the office of Steward of the Court Leet, in the manor of Vale Crucis. The following anecdote, however, proves that he would not scruple to abandon his party's interest for his own.—At the time when a great reward was offered by the usurper, for the apprehension of Sir Evan Lloyd, of Bodidris, Davies accepting a greater from the royalist, concealed him in a cellar, under the parlour; whenever a party called at the house for his assistance, or to know if he had heard any thing respecting Sir Evan, he would seem in a violent rage, stamping the floor with his feet, swearing, that if Sir Evan was any where *above ground*, he would soon have him in safe custody; but this stamping the floor, was, it seems, a contrivance settled between them, for Sir Evan to remain quiet, while his enemies were in the house.

Having in another place described the country from hence to the Aqueduct, I shall now merely say, that I passed Vale

Crucis Abbey, and Llangollen, and reached Chirk-Castle, the seat of the late Mr. Middleton, at present the occasional residence of Robert Middleton Biddulph, and Frederick West, Esquires, who married the two elder Miss Middletons.

The form of this castle is a quadrangle, with a handsome court-yard of large area within. It has a round tower at each angle, and one in front. The best apartments are a saloon, fifty-six feet by twenty-seven ; a drawing room ; and, on the first floor an elegant gallery, one hundred feet by twenty-two. This is well stocked with old portraits, many of which are from the pencil of Sir Peter Lely, and represent most of the family, as well as some gentlemen, who, I believe, were not connected with it. A head of Rubens, by himself, stands a conspicuous specimen of excellence, and is the clearest picture of that eminent painter that I have ever seen. The view from hence is very fine, and it is said by the inhabitants that they can see seventeen counties from the house. The stranger is shewn into one room to view a picture painted by a foreigner, who was requested to represent the cataract of Pistill Rhyadr. The gentleman who ordered it observing to the artist that he had forgot to ornament it with sheep, he replied, "O Sere, you vant som sheeps, I vil then put som sheeps :" he, accordingly, altered the right side of the picture, and painted a number of *ships* at anchor, and the sea for a distance.

Before the erection of the present castle, and on the same spot, stood a fortress, called Crogen; this, with the territory attached, called Tref y Waen, was the property of the Lords of Dinas, and continued in their possession till the time of Gryffyd ab Madoc. The present castle was founded by Mortimer, but it continued in his family but a short time; and was sold by his grandson John, to Richard Fitz Allan, Earl of Arundell, in which family it remained three generations. It was afterwards resumed by the crown, and granted to Wm. Beauchamp, Earl of Abergavenny. Subsequently we find that Elizabeth granted it to her favourite, Dudley, Earl of Leicester, on whose death it went to Saint John of Bletso, whose son, in 1595, sold it to Sir Thomas Middleton, Knt., Lord-Mayor of London. To the honour of this family be it remarked, the whole of the princely estate is always under increasing improvements in agriculture; nor is there less regard paid to the wants and comforts of the tenantry, who experience every indulgence in repairs to their farms, that necessity can require, under the upright stewardship and able superintendency of Mr. J. Roberts.

On leaving this place I immediately came in sight of a fine aqueduct, which, from its situation, is not so pleasing as the one at Pont Cysyllty, but which, however, is a stupendous work. It crosses a small valley, through which runs the little river Ceiriog, under a very handsome one-arched bridge. Directly above this river, and close to the new canal, is a coal-mine, which is very productive, and promises to be a fortune to the proprietor.

After crossing this river I quitted my native country, and entered the county of Salop; where my ears were soon assailed by

"The savage din of the swift pack
And clamours of the field:—detested sport,
That owes its pleasure to another's pain;
That feeds upon the sobs and dying shrieks
Of harmless nature—dumb, but yet endued
With eloquence that agonies inspire,

Of silent tears, and heart-distending sighs!
Vain tears, alas! and sighs that never find
A corresponding tone in jovial souls." COWPER.

This music ceased only with the sounding of the mort, when I entered the little town of Oswestry, where, taking chaise, I soon arrived at Shrewsbury; which place being an avenue to the southern parts of North Wales, as Chester is to the northern parts of the same country, it will, for that and other reasons, claim a right to some description.

This town stands upon a peninsula, formed by the noble river Severn, and connected, near the extremity, with the main land, by two very handsome stone bridges. It is a large and handsome town, the streets are built without regard to order, running in all directions; those that occupy the southern part of the peninsula, are fresh and handsome, but rather narrow. The walk in the quarry, extending from one end to the other, about 500 yards, between rows of lime-trees, is a delightful promenade by the side of the river, which here forms a crescent. On the summit of a lofty bank opposite, is the Orphan-house, erected at the expense of £13,000, and originally designed to receive a number of children from the Foundling Hospital, in London, but subsequently converted to a House of Industry. On the lawn above this walk is the church of St. Chad, a rotunda with a handsome tower attached to it, lately erected.

It has been said that St. Chad's, from its splendid appearance, and rotund figure, is better adapted for a place of entertainment, than for the purpose of religious exercises. Though it is somewhat gay outwardly, yet it deserves not this severity of remark; for it is universally allowed that, comparatively, the modern Gothic architecture, common to our English churches and cathedrals, is a superb manner of building; and if we refer to the account given of the Temple of Jerusalem, erected by Solomon expressly "for the name of the Lord God of Israel," we shall find that the splendour of that most magnificent edifice, with all its ornaments, which were of the most costly kind, was an offering and a dedication that he accepted, when "the burnt offerings and the sacrifices were consumed." The acceptable worship of the Deity, indeed, does not depend on the exterior decoration of the building:—is not confined to this place, or that; to a splendid church, or to an humble chapel. The insinuations, therefore, thrown out in some itineraries against the architect, fail of their end; and instead of being a reproach to him, are really an impeachment of their own judgment.

St. Alcmund and St. Mary are fine churches, each having a handsome stone spire. The former has a painted window, by Mr. Egginton; the subject of which is Faith kneeling. The abbey church, dedicated to St. Giles, will attract the attention of the artist. The county-hall, the new jail, and Millington's Hospital, are handsome modern buildings. The castle stands near the jail. Mr. Pennant supposes it to be either of Saxon or British origin, from the circumstance of the keep, or barbacan, having been on a large artificial mount, yet entire; though the foundation is ascribed to Roger de Montgomery, the great Earl of Shrewsbury. This building looks castle-like only when viewed with the town, when the contrast is observable; and, combined with the river, they make an agreeable picture.

Shrewsbury-castle was the principal seat of Roger de Montgomery, who, by the bounty of the conqueror, possessed nearly the whole of this county; after him it devolved to his sons, Hugh and Robert, the latter of whom was obliged to surrender it, with his other great possessions, to Henry I. It was dismantled in the civil wars, and presented, by Charles II., to Francis, Lord Viscount Newport, afterwards Earl of Bradford. In more recent times, it became the property of Pulteney, Earl of Bath, in whose family it still remains.

Shrewsbury, from the evidence of history, is a place of great antiquity. It was for some ages the seat of the princes, and the capital of Powys land. By the Welsh it is called Mwithig, or the Delight; conjectured to have been so named from the pleasure which the princes derived from the beauty of its situation, among groves of alders, *&c.*

In the time of Edward the Confessor, it was a place of note, called, by the Saxons, Scrobbes Byrig, and contained two hundred and fifty-two houses. The burgesses paid annually in excise, £7 16*s.* 8*d.* When his majesty lay in the town, twelve of the most respectable inhabitants guarded his person; and when he went out to hunt, the better sort of burgesses rode as his guard, properly accoutred.

Henry I., Richard I., and other succeeding princes, granted charters to the inhabitants, till Queen Elizabeth made it a body corporate, and Charles I. afterwards confirmed and enlarged her royal grant. At present it is governed by a mayor, twenty-four aldermen, and forty-eight common-council men, a recorder, a steward, sword-bearer, and three serjeants-at-mace.

In the year 1219 this place was defended by strong walls, recommended for the security of the town by Henry III., who likewise assisted the inhabitants with money for their erection; on the south-east side of the town, parts of them are still in repair, and, like those of Chester, fit to walk upon.

Here is a free school, founded in the year 1552, by Edward IV.

Queen Elizabeth added much to the original endowments. It was originally built of wood. In 1595 this building gave place to an elegant one of stone, containing the school-room, the master's houses, and a fine library with some valuable antique curiosities.

Shrewsbury, the woolstaple of North Wales, derives much trade from the sale of Welsh flannels, webbs, stockings, *&c.*, and has a large starch manufactory. In the best part of the town are some handsome shops; and those of jewellers exhibit a profusion of plate, precious stones, and trinkets, emitting so attractive a radiance, as may render it requisite for many to be on their guard, and to follow the example of the late facetious John Wilkes; who, on entering the shop of Messrs. Jefferys and Jones, in Cockspur-street, took off his hat; and lifting up his eyes, with folded hands, gravely ejaculated,—"Lead us not into temptation."

Shrewsbury has a theatre royal, conducted by the managers of the Chester and Manchester houses; and, besides the season, in which the dramatic performances continue for several months, it opens again for the race-week, which takes place in September.

Considering my tour as now completed, I returned to London by the same sort of conveyance as that which brought me into the country eight months before, having endeavoured in the course of that time to procure as correct information as I could of this portion of the ancient Britons: a people, whose manners, habits, and propensities, have not as yet been faithfully delineated by the pen of any traveller, Mr. Pennant excepted.

FINIS.

London: Printed by W. Clowes, Northumberland-court, Strand.

INDEX.

D

E

F

G

M

THE END.

London: Printed by W. CLOWES,
Northumberland-court, Strand.

ROBERTS S CHRONICLE OF THE KINGS OF BRITAIN, 4to. in boards, *2l. 2s.*

Ditto, large paper, in boards, *3l. 3s.*

ROBERTS'S SKETCH OF THE EARLY HISTORY OF THE ANCIENT BRITONS, *5s.*

ROBERTS'S REVIEW OF THE POLICY AND PECULIAR DOCTRINES OF THE MODERN CHURCH OF ROME, 8vo. boards, *6s.*

THE POETICAL WORKS OF DAFYDD AP GWILYM, in Welsh, with his Life in English, by William Owen, 8vo. in boards, *12s.*

GORCHESTION BEIRDD CYMRU, being a Select Collection of Welsh Poetry, in Welsh, 4to. sewed, *10s. 6d.*

WILLIAMS'S (Edward, the Welsh Bard) POEMS, Lyric and Pastoral, 9 vols. 12mo. in boards, *10s. 6d.*

Ditto, elegantly bound, 2 vols. *18s.*

WELSH ATLAS COMPLETE, being New and Accurate Maps of all the Counties of North and South Wales, beautifully coloured, and neatly half bound, in 4to. *1l. 1s.*

YORK'S ROYAL TRIBES OF WALES, with 12 beautiful Portraits, in 4to. boards, *1l. 7s.*

THE MARRIAGE CEREMONIES OF ALL NATIONS, scarce and curious book, *12s.*

PENNANT'S TOURS IN WALES, with 44 beautiful Plates, 3 vols. royal 8vo. in boards, *3l. 13s. 6d.*

PENNANT'S HISTORY OF THE PARISHES OF WHITEFORD AND HOLYWELL, 4to. fine Plates, elegantly bound, *1l. 7s.*

PENNANT'S LITERARY LIFE, Plates, 4to. in boards, scarce, *15s.*

LLOYD'S HISTORY OF CAMBRIA, now called Wales, 4to. in boards, Plates, *2l. 2s.*

ROWLAND'S MONA; or, the Antiquities of the Island of Anglesey, 4to. very neat and scarce, *1l. 10s.*

STRUTT'S CHRONICLE OF ENGLAND, 4to. many Plates, neat and scarce, *1l. 10s.*

DR. JOHN DAVIES'S WELSH AND LATIN, AND LATIN AND WELSH DICTIONARY, folio, very neat and fair Copy, very scarce, *3l. 3s.* 1632.

JONES'S HISTORY OF BRECKNOCKSHIRE, 2 vols. royal 4to. many Plates, in boards, *6l. 10s.* 1805.

FENTON'S HISTORICAL TOUR THROUGH PEMBROKESHIRE, many fine Plates, 4to. large paper, in boards, *5l. 15s. 6d.* 1811.

FENTON'S HISTORICAL TOUR THROUGH PEMBROKESHIRE, small Paper, 4to. boards, *3l. 10s.* boards, 1811.

WYNDHAM'S TOUR THROUGH MONMOUTHSHIRE AND WALES, with many very fine Plates, royal 4to. very elegantly bound, and very scarce, *3l. 13s. 6d.* 1781.

JONES'S MUSICAL AND POETICAL RELICS OF THE WELSH BARDS, folio, very scarce, and neatly bound, *2l. 10s.*

CANWYLL Y CYMRY; or, the Welshman's Candle, 8vo. in boards, *5s.*

Ditto, neatly bound, *8s. 6d.*

POWELL'S HISTORY OF WALES, 8vo. very scarce, and elegantly bound in Russia, *2l. 2s.*

LLEWELYN'S HISTORICAL ACCOUNT OF THE WELSH VERSION OF THE BIBLE, sewed, very scarce, 1768.

THE POETICAL WORKS OF EDWARD RICHARDS IN WELSH, and his Life in English, 8vo. sewed, *3s. 6d.*

DAVIES'S WELSH BOTANOLOGY, in Latin, English, and Welsh, 8vo. in boards, *12s.*

THE LIFE OF THE AUTHOR OF THE LETTERS OF JUNIUS, the Rev. Dr. James Wilmot, with Portrait, fac-similies, &c. 8vo. in boards, *16s.*

WILLIAMS'S HISTORY OF MONMOUTHSHIRE, with Map and many Plates, 4to. boards, *1l. 11s. 6d.*

WILLIAMS'S OBSERVATIONS ON THE SNOWDON MOUNTAINS, scarce, 8vo. boards. *8s.*

PRITCHARD'S DIVINE POEMS, 8vo. scarce, *10s. 6d.*

Ditto Ditto, in Welsh, *7s. 6d.*

THE LIFE OF MERLIN, SURNAMED AMBROSIUS, with his Prophecies and Predictions interpreted, 8vo. neatly bound, *10s. 6d.*

Ditto Ditto, in boards, *8s.*

BINGLEY'S COLLECTION OF FAVOURITE WELSH AIRS, folio, sewed, *10s. 6d.*

A NEW MAP OF CARDIGANSHIRE, from actual Survey, 4 large Sheets, coloured, and on Canvass and Rollers, *2l. 12s. 6d.*

GIRALDUS CAMBRENSIS, translated by Sir Richard Hoare, Bart. with 60 beautiful Engravings, 2 vols. royal 4to. in boards, *7l. 17s. 6d.*

LLWYD'S ARCHÆOLOGIA BRITANNICA, very neat and scarce, *1l. 10s.*

WELSH COMMON PRAYER, large letter, folio, well bound in rough calf and lettered, *2l. 10s. Oxford,* 1801.

WILLIAMS'S DISSERTATION ON THE PELAGIAN HERESY, 8vo. in boards, scarce, *4s. 6d.*

MANBY'S HISTORY AND ANTIQUITIES OF THE PARISH OF ST. DAVID'S, in SOUTH WALES, many Plates, royal 8vo. in boards, *15s.*

Lightning Source UK Ltd.
Milton Keynes UK
UKOC01f1932101113

220742UK00008B/122/P

9 781108 061483